# Modern Office Procedures

# Modern Office Procedures

**Charles Francis Barrett**
Automated Office Occupations Instructor
Regional Occupational Program (ROP)
Daly City, California

**Grady Kimbrell**
Educational Consultant
Santa Barbara, California

**Pattie Odgers**
Associate Dean of Instruction
Coconino County Community College
Flagstaff, Arizona

**West Publishing Company**
Minneapolis/St. Paul   New York   Los Angeles   San Francisco

**Copy Editor:** Allen Gooch
**Composition:** Parkwood Composition
**Illustrations:** Rolin Graphics
**Index:** Teresa Casey

**West's Commitment to the Environment**

In 1906, West Publishing Company began recycling materials left over from the production of books. This began a tradition of efficient and responsible use of resources. Today, up to 95 percent of our legal books and 70 percent of our college and school texts are printed on recycled, acid-free stock. West also recycles nearly 22 million pounds of scrap paper annually—the equivalent of 181,717 trees. Since the 1960s, West has devised ways to capture and recycle waste inks, solvents, oils, and vapors created in the printing process. We also recycle plastics of all kinds, wood, glass, corrugated cardboard, and batteries, and have eliminated the use of styrofoam book packaging. We at West are proud of the longevity and the scope of our commitment to the environment.

Production, Prepress, Printing and Binding by West Publishing Company.

Library of Congress Cataloging-in-Publication Data

Barrett, Charles Francis.
    Modern office procedures / Charles Francis Barrett, Grady Kimbrell, Pattie Odgers.
        p.    cm.
    Includes index.
    ISBN 0-314-01899-9 (soft)
    1. Office practice. 2. Office practice—Automation.
I. Kimbrell, Grady. II. Odgers, Pattie. III. Title.
HF5547.B316   1993                                                          93-9868
651—dc20                                                                    CIP

# Contents in Brief

Preface    xiii

About the Authors    xv

Chapter  1    The Office Environment    2
Chapter  2    Computer Systems in the Office    34
Chapter  3    Processing Information with Computers    76
Chapter  4    More Automation for Information
              Processing    128
Chapter  5    Telephone Procedures    168
Chapter  6    Filing and Managing Records    206
Chapter  7    Processing Business Documents    246
Chapter  8    Accounting and Record Keeping    286
Chapter  9    Sending and Receiving Mail    326
Chapter 10    Managing Office Activities    362

Reference Manual    409

Glossary    431

Index    437

Credits    441

# Contents

Preface   xiii

About the Authors   xv

■ Chapter 1   The Office Environment   2

Office Design   5
Workstations   6
Work Flow   11
Organizational Makeup   12
Office Safety   14
Summary   15

Review & Application   16
Quiz   19

Activity 1–1: Application Form and Employment Test   21
Activity 1–2: Word Processing Applications   27
Activity 1–3: Word Processing   32
Activity 1–4: Word Processing   32
Activity 1–5: Word Processing   33

■ Chapter 2   Computer Systems in the Office   34

Computer System Classifications   37
Software   41

The Information Processing Cycle  43
Summary  55

Review and Application  56
Quiz  59

Activity 2–1: Computer System Classifications  61
Activity 2–2: Types of Computer Storage  63
Activity 2–3: Word Processing  65
Activity 2–4: Word Processing  65
Activity 2–5: Word Processing  66
Activity 2–6: The Information Processing Cycle  67
Activity 2–7: Computer Hardware Devices  71
Activity 2–8: Computer vs. Electronic Typewriter  73
Activity 2–9: Word Processing  75


■ Chapter 3   Processing Information with Computers  76

Word Processing  79
Information Processing Software  94
Summary  107

Review and Application  109
Quiz  113

Activity 3–1: Word Processing  115
Activity 3–2: Word Processing Cycle  117
Activity 3–3: Word Processing Careers  119
Activity 3–4: Word Processing  121
Activity 3–5: Word Processing  121
Activity 3–6: Word Processing  122
Activity 3–7: Word Processing  122
Activity 3–8: Word Processing vs. Desktop Publishing
   Software  123
Activity 3–9: Computer Software  125


■ Chapter 4   More Automation for Information
             Processing  128

Other Automated Office Equipment  130
Telecommunications  137
Integrated Office Systems  143
Summary  146

Review and Application  147
Quiz  149

Activity 4–1: Electronic Typewriters and Calculators  151
Activity 4–2: Dictation Procedures and Techniques  153
Activity 4–3: Word Processing  155
Activity 4–4: Reprographics  157
Activity 4–5: Word Processing  159
Activity 4–6: Telecommunications  161
Activity 4–7: Word Processing  163
Activity 4–8: Integrated Office Systems  165
Activity 4–9: Word Processing  167

# Chapter 5   Telephone Procedures   168

Proper Procedures  171
Other Important Procedures  179
Types of Telephone Calls  181
Reference Materials  183
Telephone Equipment  184
Summary  188

Review and Application  189
Quiz  191

Activity 5–1: Word Processing  193
Activity 5–2: Word Processing  193
Activity 5–3: Telephone Messages  195
Activity 5–4: Word Processing  199
Activity 5–5: Word Processing  199
Activity 5–6: Word Processing Applications  200
Activity 5–7: Time Sheet  203

# Chapter 6   Filing and Managing Records   206

Filing Systems  209
Preparation of Records for Filing  212
Classification and Retention  214
Location of Permanent Records  216
Filing Equipment  217
Basic Indexing Rules  218
Basic Alphabetizing Rules  219
Preparation of Filing Supplies  221
Where's the Folder?  223
Electronic Storage  224
Advantages and Disadvantages of Electronic Files  227
Summary  227

Review and Application  229
Quiz  233

Activity 6–1: Word Processing   235
Activity 6–2: Word Processing   236
Activity 6–3: Word Processing Applications   237
Activity 6–4: Word Processing Applications   243


■ Chapter 7   Processing Business Documents   246

Business Letters   248
Memorandums   253
Legal-Size Envelopes   254
Business Reports—Manuscript Typing   256
Travel Arrangement Documents   258
Meeting Documents   261
Rough Drafts and Proofreaders Marks   262
Legal Documents   264
Tickler Files   266
Summary   267

Review and Application   269
Quiz   273

Activity 7–1: Word Processing   275
Activity 7–2: Word Processing   276
Activity 7–3: Word Processing Applications   277
Activity 7–4: Time Sheet   283


■ Chapter 8   Accounting and Record Keeping   286

Accounting Activities   288
Record-Keeping Activities   302
Summary   307

Review and Application   309
Quiz   313

Activity 8–1: Financial Statements   315
Activity 8–2: Word Processing   317
Activity 8–3: Word Processing   318
Activity 8–4: Word Processing   318
Activity 8–5: Advantages and Disadvantages of Credit   319
Activity 8–6: Inventory   321
Activity 8–7: Record-keeping Activities   323
Activity 8–8: Word Processing   325


■ Chapter 9   Sending and Receiving Mail   326

Incoming Mail   329
Outgoing Mail   334

Reference Materials   343
Unauthorized Use of Postage and Supplies   345
Summary   345

Review and Application   347
Quiz   349

Activity 9–1: Word Processing   351
Activity 9–2: Word Processing   352
Activity 9–3: Word Processing   353
Activity 9–4: Word Processing   355
Activity 9–5: Zip Codes   359
Activity 9–6: Word Processing   360

■ Chapter 10   Managing Office Activities   362

Organizing Yourself   364
Managing Your Time   367
Keeping a Calendar   371
Planning and Scheduling Business Meetings   376
Handling Travel Arrangements   382
Summary   387

Review and Application   390
Quiz   393

Activity 10–1: Word Processing   395
Activity 10–2: Word Processing   396
Activity 10–3: Keeping an Appointment Calendar   397
Activity 10–4: Word Processing   401
Activity 10–5: Word Processing   402
Activity 10–6: Getting Organized   403
Activity 10–7: Managing Time   405
Activity 10–8: Word Processing   407

Reference Manual   409

Glossary   431

Index   437

Credits   441

# *Preface*

The inspiration for **Modern Office Procedures** resulted from the experiences of one of the authors, who spent several summers doing temporary work in a wide variety of offices. These experiences, combined with consultations with many of the most knowledgeable people in office employment, showed clearly that changes in the business office curriculum were needed to prepare students for the office of the 1990's.

**Modern Office Procedures** provides practical, up-to-date information that will prepare students for working in offices in the 1990's and into the 21st century. The emphasis is on practical applications—everyday skills and knowledge needed to be successful—rather than on theoretical office concepts and methodology. This includes extensive information on effective use of computers and software programs, new telephone equipment, and other new office technology. **Modern Office Procedures** also focuses on attitudes and human relations emphasizing the fact that office success depends on "people skills" as much as on functional skills. This includes understanding the importance of team work and the value of self-confidence. Because many office workers in the 1990's will work for more than one boss, students are also provided information on how to prioritize their work and satisfy their bosses.

In response to comments that many office skills texts are dull and lifeless, the authors have attempted to make **Modern Office Procedures** interesting, as well as informative. In addition to using an easy to understand, lively, conversational writing style, they have developed an abundance of high-interest features to capture and hold the students' attention.

■ Each chapter of **Modern Office Procedures** opens with "Before You Begin" questions to help spark student interest. These questions are repeated as "In Conclusion" questions at the end of the chapters so that students can see how their knowledge and opinions have changed as a result of studying the chapter.

■ Special features within each chapter such as "Making Office Decisions," "What's Your Attitude," and "Human Relations" emphasize the importance of these topics to the use of real life scenarios.

■ Perspectives of managers from major corporations are provided in the feature "Industry Focus."

■ Practical suggestions are provided in the marginal "Office Tips."

■ "Large Office/Small Office" compares the tasks and environments in large and small offices thus giving students help in evaluating their personal career interests and objectives.

■ A comprehensive section of end-of-chapter study aids are found at the end of each chapter.

■ A quiz and activities close each chapter. The activities allow the students to apply what they learned from the textbook, therefore, bridging the gap between school and their office careers. Many of the activities will help the students prepare for word processing applications.

The authors have also developed an Instructor's Manual to accompany **Modern Office Procedures.** Features of the Instructor's Manual include lesson planning materials, answer keys, suggested solutions for activities in the text workbook, and computer application activities that require the use of word processing, data base, and spreadsheet software. In addition, each chapter includes an activity designed to practice the material presented in the Reference Manual section of text. Two transparency masters are included for each chapter. There are tests and answer keys, a pretest, and final exam.

**Modern Office Procedures** contains an abundance of practical information, high-interest features, and activities. The authors believe that this approach will insure content comprehension and thoroughly prepare students as office professionals to move successfully toward their ultimate career goals.

# *About the Authors*

**Charles Francis Barrett** received his Bachelor of Science degree from Stonehill College and his Master of Arts degree from San Francisco State University. For over 20 years he has been a business education instructor for the San Mateo County Office of Education's Regional Occupational Program (ROP). In addition, he has been a Supervisor of the ROP's Evening and Saturday Division. He is also a Teacher/Trainer for the California State Department of Education's Designated Subjects Credential Program. He is the author of various articles for state and national publications. His accomplishments include San Mateo County ROP Teacher of the Year, and his program was recognized as one of the most outstanding vocational programs in the country by the U.S. Department of Education. For many years Charles has been an active member of the California Business Education Association of which he has been a section officer and held statewide committee chairs. He has kept current in his teaching by working as a word processor/secretary for private industries.

**Grady Kimbrell** has been involved in business and career education for more than twenty years. He began as a business education teacher in Kansas and California, supervising his students on the job who were part of a school-sponsored work-experience program. Later he served as District Coordinator for Work-Experience Education in Santa Barbara, California.

An interest in research and computers led to Kimbrell serving as Director of Research in Santa Barbara Schools. This experience, in turn, led to a variety of consultancy opportunities both in schools and private businesses.

Kimbrell's first business and career publications were motivated by the apparent lack of realistic goals voiced by students in California schools. Those early efforts were well received and provided encouragement for developing new programs and more than a dozen books dealing with business and career education.

Kimbrell holds degrees in business administration, educational psychology, and business education.

**Pattie Odgers** completed her Ed.D. in Curriculum and Instruction at Northern Arizona University in Flagstaff, Arizona in 1989. She has taught over 50 different courses in computer awareness and applications, office and personnel management, and office skills to high school and community college students in Arizona and overseas in West Berlin and Stuttgart, Germany for fifteen years. Dr. Odgers worked for IBM Corporation as an advanced marketing support representative and marketing representative in Los Angeles and Monterey, California and Worcester, Massachusetts for six years. In addition, she operated a successful home secretarial service in Phoenix while her children were young.

Dr. Odgers has written ten complete office and business curriculum guides for the state of Arizona, Flagstaff School District, and as an educational consultant for ITT Educational Services. Active in numerous professional associations for over 20 years, Pattie has recently served as president of Arizona Business Education Association (ABEA) and on the editorial board of the *ABEA Journal*. She is currently Associate Dean of Instruction overseeing all occupational areas at Coconino County Community College in Flagstaff, Arizona.

# The Office Environment

# Objectives

After completing this chapter, you will be able to do the following:

1. Describe an office environment.
2. Describe how partitions divide work areas in an office.
3. Describe an office employee's workstation.
4. List adjustments that can be made to a workstation to make it more comfortable for an employee's size.
5. List adjustments that can be made to eliminate glare on a microcomputer screen.
6. List suggestions to compensate for sitting too long at a microcomputer.
7. Explain the flow of work in an office environment.
8. List two examples of the organizational makeup of an office environment.
9. List hazards to office safety and preventive measures for each.

# New Office Terms

ergonomics
modular design
office work flow
organizational makeup

partitions
safety hazard
workstations

## Before You Begin . . .

*Using an electronic typewriter or microcomputer, answer the following questions to the best of your ability:*

1. *How does an office environment, including an employee's workstation, look?*
2. *What are four office safety hazards? Give examples of ways to prevent them.*

Anne is a student in an automated office occupations program in the Midwest. Someday she wants to work as a clerical employee for a large company. Anne understands the clerical tasks that are done in an office, but she has no knowledge of what an office looks like. Does it look like her classroom? Does it look like the school office? Does it look like the local copy center?

Anne's instructor gave her the name and phone number of three former students who are currently office workers for different companies. Anne made appointments to visit each person at his or her office.

Anne visited Ivan, who works for a food processing company. Ivan gathers sales figures for the marketing department. Anne also visited Sylvia, who works in the office of a bank. Sylvia processes time sheets for the payroll department. Finally, Anne visited Darrell, who works part-time for a computer parts manufacturer. Darrell uses a microcomputer to merge and save letters for the word processing department.

At each company, Anne was able to tour the complete office facilities. She realized that although the companies handled different products, the offices were similar.

*Many of today's large offices are divided into individual work areas. This provides a quiet work area for concentration as well as for more privacy.*

## ■ OFFICE DESIGN

The three offices Anne visited were all cheerfully decorated with lively painted walls and matching carpeted floors. They used soft colors and texture (wood and fabric) to enhance their tasteful quality. The office spaces appeared to be comfortable yet efficiently planned to be productive.

Many executives had their own private office rooms. However, the clerical employees' work areas were divided by carpeted partitions that averaged approximately five to six feet tall.

**Partitions** are panels used to separate or divide a large area into smaller work areas. Research by the National Office Products Association has shown that in some offices, the height of the partitions depends on the type of work being done. For example, an accounting department may use three-foot-high partitions, a recreation area may use four-foot-high partitions, work areas of lower-level managers may use five- to six-foot-high partitions, and work areas of executives may use floor-to-ceiling partitions (walls).

In some work areas, employees share space so that they may work as part of a team and share job functions. In these situations, partitions are low and serve merely as connections for furniture additions, not as walls separating employees. This type of design provides a more open environment for employee interaction. It also accommodates the computer systems that have become an important part of a contemporary office. The employees in this type of work area frequently share records, equipment, and information.

## ■ WORKSTATIONS

Years ago, office employees worked at desks. Today, most office employees work at workstations. **Workstations** are areas that are similar to desks except that they are larger and contain more electronic equipment. In many offices, partitions separate the workstations, providing for more privacy.

Many of the workstations in the offices Anne visited contained a microcomputer and a multifunction telephone. They also contained shelves and storage space for paper, binders, manuals, pens, pencils, books, printouts, and computer disks. Near the workstations were computer printers that were shared by two or more employees. Anne was told that in some offices, employees also shared electronic typewriters.

The workstation in figure 1–1 is a **modular design.** This means that it is made of pieces that can easily be taken apart, rearranged, and put back together. The design is simple yet functional. It allows equipment

Ramon is a support staff person in the corporate office of a large bank. He works for Mr. Martin, a senior vice president.

Mr. Martin came out of his office one afternoon and gave Ramon back some letters he had typed. Mr. Martin said, "Please redo these letters. You should not have indented the paragraphs."

Ramon looked at the letters and said, "You told me to do it that way."

Mr. Martin simply returned to his office without saying a word, and Ramon corrected the letters.

About an hour later Mr. Martin called Ramon into his office and said, "Never again talk to me the way you did when I gave you the letters to correct. If any boss in this company asks you to redo some work, you will do it without comment. That is your job."

1. Was Ramon right in what he said when he got the letters back? Why or why not?
2. Did Mr. Martin handle the situation the correct way? Why or why not?
3. If you were Ramon, what would you do now?

to be moved anywhere on the desk with easy access to power sources. It provides storage to keep frequently used reference manuals within arm's reach, but not on the desk itself.

## Ergonomics

Have you read or heard the word *ergonomics?* It became popular in the late 1980s. **Ergonomics** is the study of the relationship between people and their work environment. It includes the study of ways to change working conditions to make work easier and more natural. Studying ergonomics can also lead to increased productivity.

Ergonomics includes the design of the workstation because the design is critical to the physical well-being of the worker. A workstation that is designed for the employee's size helps the employee to be more productive and to feel less fatigue.

Figure 1–2 is an example of a well-designed workstation containing a microcomputer. This workstation was designed by the National Safety Council with the following guidelines (Reprinted with permission from the National Safety Council booklet *Video Display Terminals . . . The Human Factor* [Chicago: National Safety Council, 1982.]):

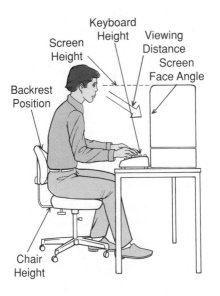

■ FIGURE 1–2
*Workstation with a Microcomputer*

- *keyboard height.* The keyboard height should be comfortable—about 2½ inches from the top of the table to the top surface of the space bar and bottom row of keys. At that height, the desk top can give the needed support to the operator's wrists. If the desk top is the right height, approximately twenty-four to twenty-eight inches, this will make the worker's upper arms form a comfortable angle of approximately ninety degrees. The upper arms will then hang comfortably at the sides, taking the strain off the upper back and shoulders.
- *screen height.* The top of the screen should be no higher than eye level to minimize eye movement.

| PROBLEM | SOLUTION |
|---|---|
| **Keyboard Height** | |
| The keyboard is too high and not adjustable. | Place pads under the wrists to elevate them to a more comfortable position. |
| The keyboard is too low and not adjustable. | Set a pad of paper or a flat piece of wood under the keyboard. |
| **Screen Face Angle** | |
| The screen is too vertical and not adjustable. | Place a small wedge under the front of the monitor to tilt it back. |
| **Chair Height** | |
| You do not know what the proper height of the chair should be. | Complete the following steps: 1. Sit with the soles of the shoes flat on the floor. Keep the shins perpendicular to the floor and relax the thigh muscles. 2. Measure the distance from the hollow of the knees to the floor. 3. Subtract one to three inches. The resulting measurement is the correct height for the top of the chair seat. |
| **Desk Height** | |
| The desk top is too high. | Raise the chair seat beyond the recommended height. Now the legs are dangling, so use a footrest to minimize pressure from the seat front on the legs. |

- *screen face angle.* The face of the screen should be tilted back about ten to twenty degrees for easier viewing—provided this does not increase the glare on the screen.
- *viewing distance.* For comfortable viewing, the screen should be about eighteen inches from the eyes.
- *chair height.* The chair is at a comfortable working height when the worker does not feel excessive pressure on the legs from the edge of the seat. Pressure from the seat front could make the legs go to sleep.
- *backrest position.* The backrest of the chair should fit comfortably at the small of the worker's back to give the back good support.

## Adjustments

Some employees may find their workstation is not ideal and does not meet the above guidelines. If so, the National Safety Council recommends making the adjustments listed in table 1–1.

# R ecall Time

*Answer the following questions:*

1. According to research done by the National Office Products Association, would accounting departments or lower-level managers use higher panels to divide their work area? What height panels do executives prefer?
2. What five items may you find in the storage area of an office workstation?
3. If the workstation desk top is the right height, describe the positioning of the worker's arms while she or he types into a computer.
4. How far should a computer screen be from the operator's eyes?
5. How does the National Safety Council recommend correcting the following situations?
   a. A keyboard is too high and not adjustable.
   b. A keyboard is too low and not adjustable.

## Other Ergonomic Concerns

Employees encounter other ergonomic concerns in the office work environment. Being aware of these concerns can also lead to a more productive workplace.

**Lighting and Glare** Sometimes glare and poor lighting make it difficult to read a computer screen or copy that an employee is working

*This work area contains an electronic typewriter as well as access to a microcomputer. Many offices still have need for electronic typewriters.*

**Susan Schenck**
*Coordinator, Professional Office Careers*
*National Aeronautics and Space Administration/Ames*

Q: Mrs. Schenck, what is a real office environment like for a secretary?

A: Some secretaries have private offices and the newest in computer hardware and software. Others plead for secondhand furniture and equipment. Some secretaries can decorate their own space, putting up posters and choosing paint colors. Others work in conservative areas where the company or manager designs identical anonymous spaces.

Q: What are some of the excitements or pleasures gained from being an office worker?

A: Satisfactions include:

- Tangible completion of projects such as reports and correspondence.
- Seeing one's work makes a difference in the function of an office.
- Learning new software and implementing new techniques.
- Ability to get a job in any industry or any geographic location.
- Seeing how a company works from the inside, and being able to take advantage of promotion opportunities.

---

from. To help solve these situations, the National Safety Council suggests the following:

- Adjust the screen's brightness and contrast controls to compensate for reflections on the screen.
- Close blinds or pull shades to block daylight coming through a window from behind the terminal.
- Try to eliminate or adjust any intense light source shining directly into the eyes.
- Adjust the angle of the screen to minimize the glare.
- Place a glare filter over the monitor to cut down on the glare.

**Sitting Too Long** No matter how comfortable the workstation, sitting still for long periods of time can be tiring and stressful. The following solutions are recommended:

- Stretch occasionally and look away from your work.
- If possible, get up from your terminal and do other tasks.

- If possible, alternate different tasks throughout the workday to vary the work rhythms. Take time out to collate papers or deliver completed work.

**Posture** Shoulder or neck pain may be caused by poor posture while working at a computer terminal. The following solutions are recommended:

- If a person must lean backward to read the screen, new eyeglasses may be necessary.
- If a person cannot read source copy that is lying flat on the table, an upright copy stand may be the solution.
- If a worker leans back too far on the chair or leans away from the chair, the chair may need adjustment.

## ■ WORK FLOW

All the office workers Anne spoke with talked with excitement about the jobs performed in the office section of the companies. The workers explained that their jobs were part of the **office work flow,** which is the activity that revolves around the processing of information. In the business world, information is input (gathered), processed, stored, and output (distributed) in a cycle, referred to as the information processing cycle (see figure 1–3).

Examples of the information processing cycle from the companies Anne visited are as follows:

- Ivan receives input of sales figures from the marketing representatives in different states. He puts these figures into his computer, where they are processed into percentages for each district. Then they are stored on disk. Finally they are sent by electronic mail to the regional manager. (Electronic mail means the information was sent from Ivan's computer to the regional manager's computer via telephone lines.)
- Sylvia receives time sheets from all the employees in the bank. She verifies the time sheets and then puts the total hours into the com-

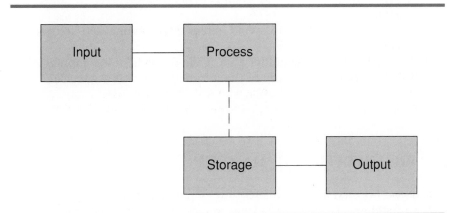

■ FIGURE 1–3
*Information Processing Cycle*

Your boss has a client's meeting scheduled in a conference room that is located on the same floor as your office. The meeting is scheduled for 3 p.m.

Another supervisor began a meeting in the same conference room at 1 p.m. At 2:45 p.m., that meeting is still going on.

It is your responsibility to set up the meeting room. What will you do?

puter. The computer processes the hours and prints paychecks. The information remains stored in the computer. The checks are given to the personnel department to be distributed to the employees.

■ Darrell receives an inventory of parts from the warehouses every three months. This information is put into his computer. The computer processes the information and prints a report that shows which parts must be reordered. The information is stored on magnetic tape. The printed report is sent to the accounting department.

The information processing cycle performed by office workers makes you realize the importance of the office operations to a whole business. Without office operations, companies would not survive. Manufacturing companies depend on office workers to keep inventory and budget figures. Law firms depend on office workers to process and store accurate legal documents. Retail stores depend on office workers to provide sales figures on a daily basis. All companies need office workers to edit and distribute correspondence. All companies depend on office workers to process their payroll and keep accounting records for tax purposes.

Chapter 2 explains more about the information processing cycle and the electronic equipment that does the processing.

# R ecall Time

*Answer the following questions:*

1. What are two ways to eliminate lighting glare on a computer screen?
2. What is one way to avoid stress from sitting too long at a computer?
3. What may cause shoulder pain while working at a computer?
4. What are the four parts of the information processing cycle?

# ORGANIZATIONAL MAKEUP

When you become an employee of a company, you will be responsible for producing accurate work within an allotted time. Someone will as-

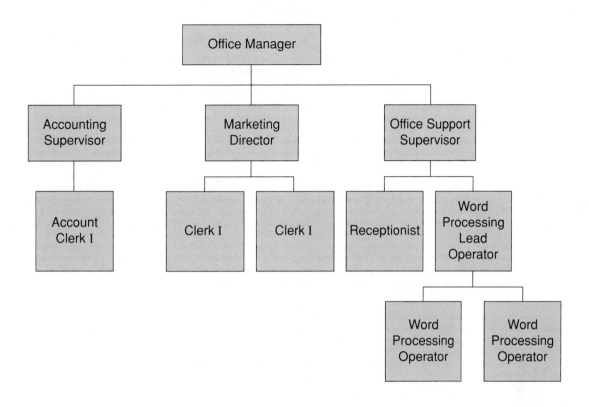

sign you the work and see that it is completed. Depending on the company and the department, the title of this person can vary. Organizational charts illustrate companies' **organizational makeup,** or the way in which employees in positions of authority are determined.

If you were a word processing operator in Company 1, who would you report to? (See figure 1–4.) Yes, the word processing lead operator. This person would report to the office support supervisor.

Company 2 is a small company (see figure 1–5). The secretary is responsible to the senior secretary, who is directly responsible to the owner.

■ FIGURE 1–4
*Organizational Chart for Company 1*

■ FIGURE 1–5
*Organizational Chart for Company 2*

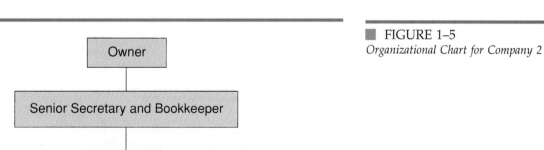

# OFFICE SAFETY

Have you ever tripped over an electrical cord at home? Have you ever had the power go off because too much equipment was plugged into one outlet? Have you ever banged your leg on a drawer that was left open? If not, you are extremely cautious or have been very lucky.

Many people think of work accidents as happening only in factories or at construction sites. However, some accidents also happen in an office environment. These occur when workers are careless or are impatient and try to take shortcuts. Start now to build good safety habits and carry these habits over to your office job.

Office workers have listed the items in table 1–2 as safety hazards on the job. A **safety hazard** is a danger or a chance of being injured.

## R ecall Time

*Answer the following questions:*

1. Refer to figure 1–4.
   a. Who is the account clerk I responsible to?
   b. Who is the marketing director responsible to?
   c. Who is the word processing lead operator responsible to?
2. What safety hazard can cause a file cabinet to fall over and how can it be prevented?

■ TABLE 1–2
*Office Safety Hazards*

| HAZARD | PREVENTION |
| --- | --- |
| Opening more than one file drawer at a time may cause the cabinet to fall over. | Before you open a file drawer, check to see that all other file drawers are closed. |
| Leaving a file drawer open may cause someone to trip over it. | Keep file drawers closed when not in use or when you leave for even a short time. |
| Leaving a handbag or briefcase on the floor in a walking path may cause someone to trip. | Put purses and briefcases into a desk drawer, completely under the desk, or in a cabinet. |
| Not having enough voltage in the electrical outlet for all the equipment may cause a power shortage or a fire. | Before plugging in new equipment, check with your supervisor to be certain enough voltage is available. Have the company upgrade the electrical system when necessary. |
| Standing on a chair that moves may cause you to fall. | Use a step stool or a ladder to reach high places. |
| Stooping and lifting improperly may cause back injuries. | Learn the proper lifting procedures. |
| Leaving electrical cords in the walkway may cause someone to trip. | Keep electrical cords out of walkways or use rubber covers to keep people from tripping. |

14

3. What safety hazard could cause an employee to trip in an office and how can it be avoided?
4. What may cause a back injury on a job and how can it be avoided?

*Accidents like this can be avoided if you think ahead.*

## ■ SUMMARY

We have manufacturing firms, agricultural firms, service firms, government firms, and a variety of other firms. Although their products and services differ, their office environments are often similar. Many companies use the same type of workstations and the employees perform the same type of office functions.

All companies should have similar interests in ergonomics and similar concerns about the safety of their employees. The type of work may differ, but the work flow and the organizational makeup are similar in most companies.

The following questions may help you decide what office environment you want to work in:

- Is the office environment cheerfully decorated?
- Are the employee work areas divided to provide privacy and to allow employees to concentrate on work?
- Are work areas provided for employees to work as a team and to share job functions?
- Do the workstations allow for the storing of materials and manuals as well as hold the necessary office equipment?
- Are the workstations adjustable for the size of the employee?
- Does the lighting appear to be adequate for the total work environment?
- Is there an organizational makeup defining the duties of the employees?
- Is office safety a constant concern of the company administrators?

### In Conclusion . . .

*When you have completed this chapter, use an electronic typewriter or a microcomputer to answer the following questions:*

1. *How does an office environment, including an employee's workstation, look?*
2. *What are four office safety hazards? Give examples of ways to prevent them.*

# Review and Application

## REVIEW YOUR VOCABULARY

Supply the missing words by choosing from the new office terms listed below.

1. The study of the relationship between people and their work environment is called _____ .
2. Workstations that are made of parts that can easily be taken apart, rearranged, and put back together are made by _____ _____ .
3. Some workstations are divided by _____ for privacy.
4. The _____ is the area where an employee works that holds equipment and other work-related materials.
5. The _____ _____ _____ in an office revolves around the processing of information.
6. Employees in positions of authority are determined by the _____ _____ of an office.
7. A chance of being injured on the job is a _____ _____ .

a. ergonomics
b. modular design
c. organizational makeup
d. partitions
e. safety hazard
f. office work flow
g. workstation

## DISCUSS AND ANALYZE AN OFFICE SITUATION

Denise is an office worker for a law firm. One of her duties is directing clients to attorneys' offices.

Denise is going to a party directly after work tomorrow. This is an important party for her, and she plans to wear nice evening clothes. She is thinking of saving time by wearing her evening clothes to work and then going directly to the party.

Should Denise dress this way at her job? Does it make a difference? Why or why not?

## PRACTICE BASIC SKILLS

### Math

1. For each item in the following purchase orders, multiply the number purchased by the price listed in the computer supply catalog below. Then add the prices for all the items in the purchase order.

a. Purchase order 1
   8  printer stands _____
   6  storage trays _____
   3  computer dustcovers _____
   4  glare filters _____
      Total _____

b. Purchase order 2
   4  printer mufflers _____
   12 antistatic sprays _____
   4  deluxe computer printers _____
   4  modular tables _____
      Total _____

c. Purchase order 3
   14 storage trays _____
   3  printer stands _____
   1  deluxe computer printer _____
   1  modular table _____
   5  computer dustcovers _____
      Total _____

### Computer Supply Catalog

| ITEM | PRICE PER ITEM | |
| --- | --- | --- |
| | If you buy 1–5: | If you buy more than 5: |
| Printer stand | $ 32.50 | $ 30.00 |
| Printer muffler | 74.00 | 70.00 |
| Storage trays | 17.75 | 14.00 |
| Antistatic spray | 8.25 | 7.00 |
| Computer dustcover | 28.50 | 25.00 |
| Deluxe computer printer | 390.00 | 370.00 |
| Glare filter | 95.50 | 90.00 |
| Modular table | 580.00 | 540.00 |

2. Garrison Contractors does not have the time to do its payroll this month. It hires a computer service company to do the payroll. The computer service company charges $95 per hour. The work will take twelve hours. What is the total cost?

3. Doss Brothers Dairy needs to purchase new draperies for its office because the sun is causing problems with the computer monitors. The draperies cost $62.75 per yard. The company needs eighteen yards. What is the total cost?

4. The supervisor of office services suggests to management that the company pay for eye exams for all the computer operators. The eye exams cost $45 each and the company has eight operators. What will be the total cost to the company?

## English

1. *Rule:* Most nouns form their plurals by adding *s*.
   *Example:* One pencil, two pencils
   *Practice Exercise:* Form the plurals for the following:

   | | |
   |---|---|
   | accountant | desk |
   | calculator | manager |
   | computer | typewriter |

2. *Rule:* Nouns that end in *y* with a vowel before the *y* form plurals by adding *s*.
   *Example:* One key, two keys
   *Practice Exercise:* Form the plurals for the following:

   | | |
   |---|---|
   | attorney | day |
   | boy | delay |
   | buy | valley |

3. *Rule:* Nouns that end in *y* with a consonant before the *y* form plurals by changing the *y* to *i* and adding *es*.
   *Example:* One deputy, two deputies
   *Practice Exercise:* Form the plurals for the following:

   | | |
   |---|---|
   | agency | lady |
   | baby | laundry |
   | city | party |

4. *Rule:* Nouns that end in *o* with a vowel before the *o* form the plural by adding *s*.
   *Example:* One trio, two trios
   *Practice Exercise:* Form the plurals for the following:

   | | |
   |---|---|
   | cameo | radio |
   | igloo | stereo |
   | patio | tattoo |

5. *Rule:* Nouns that end in *o* with a consonant before the *o* form the plural by adding *es*.

*Example:* One cargo, four cargoes
*Practice Exercise:* Form the plurals for the following:

| | |
|---|---|
| echo | potato |
| hero | tomato |

6. *Rule:* Some nouns form their plurals in different ways.
   *Example:* Foot, feet; man, men; child, children; mouse, mice; deer, deer
   *Practice Exercise:* Form the plurals for the following:

   | | |
   |---|---|
   | goose | sheep |
   | moose | tooth |
   | ox | trout |

## Proofreading

1. Retype the following report, correcting all errors:

   CREATING LOW-STRESS RELATIONSHIPS

   Krames Communications suggests the following for creating low-stress relationships on the job.

   Listen Actively When you listen with sencitivity toward the speakers feelings, you are better able to understnad the speaker and can then respond by honestly expressing your own thoughs and feelings.

   Give Compliments Complimenting people lets them know you have noticed them. Give out at least one complement a day for a job well done, a suggestion at a meeting, or even a neu suit or hairstyle.

   Smile at People Smiles and courtecy keep communication open, even when you bring critisism or bad news. But while you are courteous, do not gloss over what needs to be said—express your feelings honestly.

   Admit if You are Wrong If you honestly admit when you are wrong, co-workers will trust you more. They will know you are being honest and fare, be more willing to share information with you, and admit when they are wrong.

2. After printing out the report in proofreading exercise 1, make the following changes and print a new copy:

   - Use uppercase for the underlined words.
   - Delete all the underlines.
   - In the paragraph titled "Listen Actively," change the word *honestly* to *truly*.
   - In the paragraph titled "Give Compliments," delete "a suggestion at a meeting."
   - Add this paragraph to the bottom:

   SHOW APPRECIATION

   Whether you give a co-worker a gift for a job well done, write a letter of commendation, or just say thank you, showing appreciation lets others know you recognize their contributions.

## APPLY YOUR KNOWLEDGE

1. Arrange the following words into alphabetical order. Using a microcomputer or an electronic typewriter, tabulate the words into three columns.

| | |
|---|---|
| time sheets | design |
| panel | workspace |
| privacy | functional |
| environment | keyboard |
| glare | guideline |
| elevate | height |
| stressful | posture |
| process | cycle |
| responsible | chart |
| safety | outlet |
| hazard | electrical |
| compliment | communication |

# QUIZ

*Write a **T** if the statement is true or an **F** if the statement is false.*

____ 1. Partitions are panels used to separate or divide a large area into smaller work areas.

____ 2. Executives no longer use private offices; partitions are used instead.

____ 3. Workstations are only used by managers and executives.

____ 4. Workstations are permanent fixtures. They can never be taken apart or rearranged.

____ 5. Ergonomics is the study of the relationship between people and their work environment.

____ 6. A workstation that is designed for the employee's size helps the employee to be more productive and to feel less fatigue.

____ 7. Never adjust the height of a typing chair.

____ 8. Never adjust the computer screen's brightness and contrast.

____ 9. The computer screen should never be more than six inches from the operator's eyes.

____ 10. Shoulder or neck pain can be caused by poor posture while working at a computer terminal.

____ 11. No matter how comfortable the workstation, sitting still for long periods of time can be tiring and stressful.

____ 12. Input is part of the information processing cycle.

____ 13. Storing is the last part of the information processing cycle.

____ 14. Law offices never use office workers.

____ 15. Office employees never have to worry about accidents happening on the job.

## Application Form and Employment Test

Maybe you have been thinking of applying for temporary work. You can prepare yourself by completing the employee application form on the next page and by taking the clerical test on the pages that follow.

# APPLICATION FORM

## ON-TIME TEMPS

| | | | | | APPLICATION DATE |
|---|---|---|---|---|---|

NAME—LAST    FIRST    MIDDLE

U.S. CITIZEN OR LEGAL RIGHT TO WORK

IN U.S.? ☐ YES ☐ NO

ADDRESS—STREET    CITY    STATE    ZIP

HOME PHONE    OTHER PHONE

ARE YOU PRESENTLY 18 YEARS OF AGE OR OLDER? ☐ YES ☐ NO

SOCIAL SECURITY NUMBER

HAVE YOU EVER HAD A U.S. SECURITY CLEARANCE RATING? ☐ YES ☐ NO

WHICH TYPE OF TRANSPORTATION DO YOU USE?
☐ CAR AVAILABLE
☐ PUBLIC TRANSPORTATION

NOTIFY IN CASE OF EMERGENCY    NAME    PHONE

HOW DID YOU HEAR OF ON-TIME?

HAVE YOU EVER BEEN CONVICTED OF A LEGAL OFFENSE OTHER THAN A MINOR TRAFFIC VIOLATION? ☐ YES ☐ NO

IF YES, GIVE DETAILS

| FROM | TO | NAME OF SCHOOL | CITY, STATE | MAJOR COURSE OF STUDY | DATE | CITY | STATE |
|---|---|---|---|---|---|---|---|

DIPLOMA/DEGREE ACHIEVED

| FROM | TO | EMPLOYER | CITY, STATE | TYPE OF WORK | FULL TIME OR PART TIME | SUPERVISOR | REASON FOR LEAVING |
|---|---|---|---|---|---|---|---|

MAY WE CONTACT?

REFERENCE CHECK

CHECK THE SKILLS AND BUSINESS AREAS BELOW IN WHICH YOU HAVE EXPERIENCE WITH TWO XX. IF TRAINING, USE ONE X.

INFORMATION PROCESSING

☐ W/P OPERATOR
☐ DEDICATED SPECIFIC EQUIPMENT USED:
☐ SPEC. APPL OPERATOR
☐ MINI-COMPUTER (SHARED) SPECIFIC EQUIP./SOFTWARE USED:
☐ MICRO COMPUTER P/C SPECIFIC EQUIP./ SOFTWARE USED:
☐ DE OPERATOR
☐ DATA ENTRY CLERK
☐ FAX OPERATOR
☐ ELEC. MAIL/COMM.
☐ ELECTRONIC TYPEWRITER SPECIFIC EQUIP. USED
☐ MAIN FRAME SPECIFIC EQUIP./SOFTWARE USED:

SECRETARIAL
☐ ADMINISTRATIVE
☐ GENERAL
☐ EXECUTIVE
☐ LEGAL
☐ MEDICAL
☐ SHORT-HAND
☐ MACHINE TRANSCRIPTION

TYPING
☐ GENERAL
☐ FORMS
☐ STATISTICAL
☐ LEGAL
☐ MEDICAL

SPECIFIC EQUIP. USED

GENERAL OFFICE
☐ GENERAL OFFICE
☐ FILING
☐ MAILROOM
☐ COPYING EQUIP.
☐ RECEPTIONIST
☐ SWITCHBOARD
☐ TELETYPE
☐ COLLATING

ACCOUNTING
☐ PAYROLL
☐ 10 KEY CALCULATOR
☐ CREDIT/ COLLECTIONS
☐ PAYABLE/ RECEIVABLES
☐ POSTING
☐ BOOK-KEEPING
☐ BANKTELLER

SALES/MARKETING
☐ SALES
☐ DEMOS
☐ SHOPPER
☐ HOST/HOSTESS
☐ TELEPHONE SALES/SURVEY
☐ DETAILER/ MERCHANDISER
☐ SAMPLER/ COUPONER

APPLICANT SIGNATURE    DATE

FOR OFFICE USE ONLY

APPEARANCE:    ATTITUDE:

| TYPING | SPEED | ACCURACY | ERRORS | WPM | RATING |
|---|---|---|---|---|---|

# ON-TIME TEMP SERVICES
## EMPLOYMENT TEST

Your Name _____    Time Begun _____

Date _____    Time Stopped _____

## Part I. Math

1. 497.3 + 6.2 + 30.5 + 7 + 92.34 = _____

2. 6389.45 − 23.6 = _____

3. 25 × 15 = _____

4. $7.80 × 5 = _____

5. 2400 divided by 25 = _____

## Part II. Checking

On the answer lines to the right, write "C" if the addition of the following problems is correct and "I" if it is incorrect.

| #1 | #2 | #3 | #4 | #5 | #6 | |
|----|----|----|----|----|----|----|
| | | | | | | 1. _____ |
| | | | | | | 2. _____ |
| 7 | 9 | 6 | 0 | 8 | 3 | 3. _____ |
| 6 | 4 | 6 | 0 | 7 | 9 | 4. _____ |
| 1 | 3 | 6 | 5 | 7 | 6 | 5. _____ |
| 13 | 16 | 18 | 10 | 22 | 18 | 6. _____ |

## Part III. Spelling

If any of the following words are misspelled, write the correct spelling to the right of the word. If the words are spelled correctly, write the word *correct* to the right of the word.

a. personel _____    f. discused _____

b. advertising _____    g. ledger _____

c. engeneer _____    h. proceed _____

d. supercede _____    i. excede _____

e. bussines _____    j. invoice _____

(continued on next page)

## Part IV. Alphabetic Filing

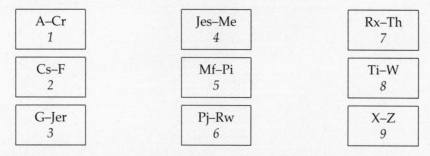

| A–Cr 1 | Jes–Me 4 | Rx–Th 7 |
| Cs–F 2 | Mf–Pi 5 | Ti–W 8 |
| G–Jer 3 | Pj–Rw 6 | X–Z 9 |

In the file drawers above, customer files are filed alphabetically. Each drawer has a number (1–9). In which drawers would you place the files listed below? Write the correct drawer number on the line to the left of the name.

a. ____ Solano Bakery

b. ____ Yarnell Cheese

c. ____ Barnes Culinary

d. ____ Place & Place Products

e. ____ 5-Hour Deliveries

f. ____ Rennett Corporation

g. ____ Jerrett Pies

h. ____ Tin Recycled

i. ____ Kraft Dairy

j. ____ McMillan Bros.

k. ____ Modems For Less

l. ____ Customer Satisfaction

## Part V. Numeric Filing

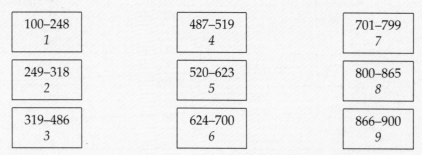

| 100–248 1 | 487–519 4 | 701–799 7 |
| 249–318 2 | 520–623 5 | 800–865 8 |
| 319–486 3 | 624–700 6 | 866–900 9 |

In the file drawers above, customer files are filed numerically. Each drawer has a number (1–9). In which drawers would you file the numbers listed below? Write the correct drawer number on the line to the left of the customer file number.

a. _____ 251      e. _____ 157      i. _____ 675

b. _____ 273      f. _____ 503      j. _____ 888

c. _____ 625      g. _____ 824      k. _____ 380

d. _____ 432      h. _____ 612      l. _____ 732

## Word Processing Applications

The purpose of this activity is to practice typing legal documents.

After an employment test and an interview, you are offered and accept a one-day assignment typing at a law firm.

You are given a Word Processing Job Request form (below). Read the form carefully and then complete the work. After completing the work, remember to fill in the bottom of the Word Processing Job Request form. Fill in the date, the time you started and finished the projects, and your initials.

---

**Word Processing Job Request**

Date: *Today*          Deadline Date: *Today*

Time: *AM*             Deadline Time: *PM*

From: *REC*

Rough Draft _____          Final Form _X_

Type of Paper:

Regular _X_  Bond _____  Letterhead _____

Envelope _____     Mailing Label _____  Other label _____

Special Instructions:

*We lost the four forms that follow. Please type new originals for us.*

Charge to (Account Name and Number): *Adm. 4691*

| Date | Time Started | Time Completed | Operator |
|------|--------------|----------------|----------|
|      |              |                |          |
|      |              |                |          |
|      |              |                |          |

---

(continued on next page)

## DECLARATION PARAGRAPH

I have personal knowledge of the facts stated above except as to those which are stated on information and belief, and as to those, I am informed and believe that they are true. If called as a witness, I could and would testify competently to the foregoing in a court of law. I declare under penalty of perjury under the laws of the State of California that the foregoing is true and correct.

Dated this ____ day of _____, 19 ____.

Save this file named DECLAR.PAR

# PARTNERSHIP ACKNOWLEDGMENT

STATE OF CALIFORNIA     )
                               )    ss.

COUNTY OF _____   )

    On this ___ day of _____, 19 ___, before me, the undersigned Notary Public, personally appeared _____, personally known to me (or proved to me on the basis of satisfactory evidence) to be the person who executed the within instrument on behalf of the partnership, and acknowledged to me that the partnership executed the same.

    WITNESS my hand and official seal.


_____

NOTARY PUBLIC



Save this file named PART.ACK

## SUBSCRIBING WITNESS ACKNOWLEDGMENT

STATE OF CALIFORNIA     )
                               )   ss.
COUNTY OF _____  )

    On this ____ day of _____, 19 ____, before me, the undersigned Notary Public, personally appeared _____, personally known to me (or proved to me on oath of _____ who is personally known to me) to be the person whose name is subscribed to within instrument as a witness thereto, and who swore or affirmed before me that _____ personally knows _____ to be the individual whose name is subscribed to the within instrument as principal and witnessed that individual sign the same and acknowledge signing it freely for the purposes therein contained.

    WITNESS my hand and official seal.

_____
NOTARY PUBLIC

Save this file named SUBWIT.ACK

# VERIFICATION OF ATTORNEY

I, the undersigned, declare:

I am an attorney at law duly admitted to practice before all courts of the State of California, and I have my office at One Market Plaza, 23rd Floor, San Francisco, California 94105.

I am _____ of Wong, Hing & Low, attorneys for in the above-entitled matter.

The _____ is absent from the county in which I have my office and for that reason I make this Verification on behalf of said _____.

I have read the foregoing _____ and know the contents thereof, and am informed and believe that the matters therein are true and on that ground allege that the matters stated therein are true.

I declare under penalty of perjury, under the laws of the State of California, that the foregoing is true and correct.

Executed this ____ day of _____, 19 ____.

Save this document named VERIFI

## ACTIVITY 1-3

### Word Processing

1. Using word processing software, keyboard accurately the following paragraphs, save, and print a copy of the document.

   Screen Face Angle. The face of the screen should be tilted back about ten to twenty degrees for easier viewing—provided this does not increase the glare on the screen.
   Screen Height. The top of the screen should be no higher than eye level to minimize eye movement.
   Viewing Distance. For comfortable viewing, the screen should be about eighteen inches from the eyes.
   Backrest Position. The backrest of the chair should fit comfortably at the small of the worker's back to give the back good support.

2. Edit the document in the following ways and print a second copy:

   A. Move paragraph ''Backrest Position'' from last paragraph to first paragraph.
   B. Use search and replace feature to replace the word screen with the word monitor throughout the document.


## ACTIVITY 1-4

### Word Processing

1. Keyboard, save, and print in single space an evaluation of an office you've visited recently. The office could be a local bank, a travel agency, or a school administrative office. After you have evaluated the office, keyboard full-sentence answers to the following questions:

   A. Is the office environment cheerfully decorated? If so, how? If not, what does it look like?
   B. Are the employee work areas divided to provide privacy and to allow employees to concentrate on work?
   C. Do the workstations allow for the storing of materials and manuals as well as holding the necessary office equipment?
   D. Does the lighting appear to be adequate for the total work environment?

2. Use a spelling dictionary during the editing process and set a ten-space paragraph indent tab.

## Word Processing

1. Prepare a letter in response to an inquiry from Mr. Ashcraft's letter below.

2. Keyboard your response letter using block style and mixed punctuation, save, and print one copy.

Dear Ms. Chen,

I am designing an office for a new business called Stan's Word Processing Services. An employee of mine attended a seminar in office design that you recently conducted at the local community college.

I wish I had attended. I am hoping you will be able to help me. Generally speaking, what general ideas should I follow when deciding on the office environment I should provide for my four employees?

Thank you for any ideas you may be able to share with me.

Sincerely,

Stanley Ashcraft

# Computer Systems in the Office

## Objectives

After completing this chapter, you will be able to do the following:

1. List the three classifications of computers and describe the differences between them.
2. Discuss the advantages of an office computer system compared with an electric or electronic typewriter.
3. Describe the four operational steps in the information processing cycle.
4. Identify the hardware devices that can be used in the input and output steps of the information processing cycle.
5. Describe the functions of primary storage and secondary storage.

## New Office Terms

auxiliary storage
central processing unit
computer system
data
disk drive
diskette
hard disk
input
keyboard
mainframe
microcomputer

minicomputer
monitor
optical character recognition
   (OCR) scanner
output
primary storage area
printers
processing
program
software

*Before You Begin . . .*

*Using an electronic typewriter or a microcomputer, answer the following questions to the best of your ability:*

1. *What might a computer system in an office look like?*
2. *What are two advantages to businesses of using a computer?*

---

When you walk into your first office, you will probably see many information processing systems already in place, like a phone system and a copying system. The most obvious system and the one that will likely immediately affect how you work, however, will be your company's computer system. Millions of dollars are invested each year by large companies to upgrade their computer capabilities. Such companies, in particular, realize that their use of computers will streamline the work flow for employees and save many dollars, which ultimately become profit.

As an office specialist working with a computer system, you will be able to process and complete tasks far more quickly and accurately than will the worker equipped only with an electric or electronic typewriter. Once you've worked with a computer, you may soon realize its value as a silent, dependable partner. You can rely on your computer to provide speed and efficiency you didn't think was possible. Computers increase both the amount and the quality of work you are able to produce because they allow you to work smarter, not harder. They do this with their speed of operation, high accuracy, reliability, and almost unlimited storage capabilities. They can help you become the professional office specialist you want to be.

Your on-the-job success can be greatly influenced by the computer knowledge and skills you possess. There is much to know about computers. They come in different sizes and capacities. In addition, they can perform many functions. Every office worker will need to have a minimum knowledge about computers. Most office workers will learn a little more—but those who most expand their knowledge will secure their jobs and advance in an organization.

Employers usually hire and promote individuals who use good judgment and who can think through the steps involved in making decisions. Computers can promote the development of these needed skills. To use a computer, you often must think through a sequence of operations and decide how to complete the job. For example, in completing a three-page report, you decide the order of steps to follow. You might decide to first key in the entire text and then format and design final copy with indents, proper margins, boldface, and italics. On the other hand, you might choose instead to format and design as you enter the text. The point is that the originator of the text is concerned only with the final product—the three-page report. You decide how to go about the task of preparing it in the most efficient manner.

Computers can perform the dull, noncreative, and repetitive tasks often found in the office work environment. By minimizing your time on these tasks, you will have more time to exercise creativity and good

O F F I C E   T I P

Exercise caution and do not eat food or drink beverages around any computer system. An unexpected spill or food particle could damage the computer. More important, such a mishap could keep the office from completing an important job on time.

judgment. You will be a more valuable employee when you are able to work on your own in deciding how to attractively format a document. Workers who know how to accurately edit a document to say exactly what they want it to say, and how to professionally lay out and print the final copy of important documents, are in demand for today's office.

You have probably already observed computers being used daily in business, government, hospitals, schools, and homes. You may have taken a computer literacy course or produced a term paper in your school's computer lab. But are you familiar with the many different kinds of computers you may work on when you actually walk into your first office job? Do you know why certain computers meet the needs and standards of business better than others?

## ■ COMPUTER SYSTEM CLASSIFICATIONS

What is a computer? A computer is an electronic device operating under the control of instructions stored in its own memory unit. It can accept data in the form of words and numbers, process data arithmetically and logically, produce usable output from the processing, and store the results for future use.

The term system implies organization and order. A **computer system,** therefore, is a group of computer devices that are connected, coordinated, and linked together in such a way that they work as one to complete a task. You will find relatively small and simple computer systems composed of only one or two small computers serving an entire office of ten people. In contrast, you will find large computer systems consisting of large amounts of data and information that everyone in an organization can access by simply using a keyboard-type device on his or her desk.

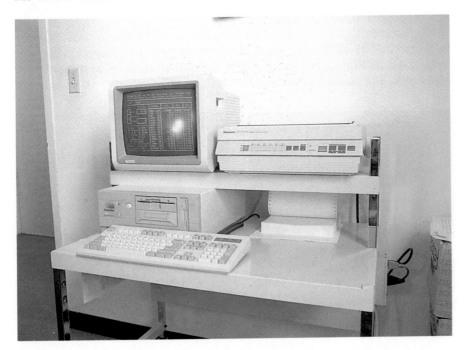

*The basic hardware devices for most computer systems include a monitor, a keyboard, a printer, and a computer system unit containing memory.*

The electronic computer devices that make up a computer system are called hardware. In its most simple form, hardware consists of anything you can physically touch on your computer system. You may already be familiar with the monitor, printer, and keyboard.

In an up-to-date office, you will see, and possibly have an opportunity to work on, one of three types of computer hardware systems: microcomputers, mainframe computers, and minicomputers.

### Microcomputers

Of the three types of systems used in offices, the **microcomputer**—also called the personal computer (PC)—will probably be the type you operate. Why? Simply because it is widely available and popular. It is also the type you've likely been using in school. Just like you, many office workers are already familiar with a microcomputer and have some idea how it works.

When operating a microcomputer system, you will have several components at your disposal. These are a computer system unit containing memory, a keyboard for entering data, a monitor for displaying what you're entering through the keyboard, one or two disk drives for storing files on disks, and a printer for producing final copy.

You can purchase a home microcomputer for as little as a few hundred dollars, or you may pay many thousands of dollars for more sophisticated microcomputer systems used in business. One variable that affects how much you pay for a microcomputer is the internal memory size. Today, standard memory size is no longer measured in kilobytes (K) but in megabytes (MB) of data.

Microcomputers can be purchased through mail order catalogs, in your local department stores, or from professional salespersons representing computer stores and manufacturers. In most cases, within an hour of being unpacked, your microcomputer can be operational and ready to work for you.

Microcomputers are widely used in the small-business environment by personnel at all levels. Many microcomputers are powerful enough to be used as the only computer in a small business. In advertising for office jobs, the small-business owner will usually try to recruit someone

*The IBM (left) and Macintosh (right) microcomputers are used in many offices.*

who is already familiar with the company's microcomputer system and with popular software packages like those for word processing, accounting, data bases, and spreadsheets.

However, microcomputers are not exclusive to the small office or home environment. They solve many paperwork needs, even in large offices with large computers available, because they are small-yet-versatile desktop units. This idea emphasizes a main difference between the three kinds of computers. That is, most microcomputers are single-user systems. With a single-user system, you will probably not share equipment or files with another co-worker. With a multiuser system, files, equipment, and memory are shared. Mainframe and minicomputer systems are best described as multiuser systems.

## Mainframes

**Mainframe** computers are powerful, large computers that can handle many users at the same time. They are able to process large volumes of data at incredibly high speeds. Most mainframe systems can store millions of characters in primary memory. Because of their size and capacity, you will usually find these computers in large organizations such as corporate home offices, hospitals, universities, and government agencies.

For example, a large bank needs a large computer like the mainframe. It is the only machine with the processing power to allow hundreds of tellers and other employees to access thousands of accounts daily. The Internal Revenue Service (IRS) is another organization that needs mainframes. The IRS must provide access for data contained on the tax records of all the taxpayers in the United States for auditing and other purposes. For these types of applications, where large volumes of data are required and numerous users need access to the same centralized computer, large computers like mainframes are used.

Because of their sophistication, mainframes require special physical accommodations. Cooling systems must be installed to handle the heat that is generated, special electrical wiring is needed, and platforms must be built to house the wires and cables beneath the computer system. These adjustments increase the cost of purchasing mainframes. Depending on the needs of an organization, the price of a large mainframe can range from as little as two hundred thousand dollars to as much as several million dollars.

Mainframes have a great capacity for work and storage. Often, companies buying or leasing them do not initially have enough work to keep them operating at a cost-effective level. Such companies, therefore, sell computer time to other, usually smaller, organizations. The organizations that buy this time have computer needs but choose not to invest in a computer system of their own. This process of selling and buying mainframe computer time is called time share.

If you work in a small office, you may find only a monitor and a keyboard at your desk. With these devices, however, it is possible to prepare and transmit work to a computer across town to be finalized.

When you identify employers who can use your computer skills, don't rule out the small companies. Keep in mind that small companies also have information processing needs and that these needs can be met by computer systems located outside your immediate work environment.

## Minicomputers

Originally, the **minicomputer** was developed in the mid-1960s to perform specialized tasks such as word processing or to produce architectural blueprints and drawings. Today, minicomputers are multiuser systems that can support a number of users performing different tasks at the same time. Their abilities are similar to those of the mainframe, but on a smaller scale. The minicomputer is smaller in size, is less expensive, and has less storage capacity than the mainframe.

Consider, for example, how a minicomputer might be used by office workers in the administrative area of A-Plus Technical School. During registration, computer terminals are placed on the desks where information is used and operations take place. Any office worker can access the same student data, like name or social security number. This data is needed when a student selects and registers for particular courses, pays for the courses, withdraws from or adds more courses, and receives a final grade report.

You might be asking yourself what types of companies use a minicomputer when the mainframe can do the same types of data processing activities. The answer is that medium-sized companies use minicomputers. Minicomputers meet not only their processing and growth needs, but their pocketbooks, as well. Midsize companies need computers that are less expensive than mainframes and that can easily be expanded to meet the needs of a growing organization.

*The minicomputer meets the needs of a growing, medium-size organization.*

|  | MICROCOMPUTER | MINICOMPUTER | MAINFRAME |
|---|---|---|---|
| Users | small businesses<br>home<br>schools | medium businesses<br>colleges | large corporations<br>government<br>banks |
| Memory Capacity | 256,000 to<br>1 million +<br>characters | millions of<br>characters | many millions of<br>characters |
| Cost | $200–$4000 + | $30,000–$200,000 + | $200,000–many<br>millions of<br>dollars |

The cost of a minicomputer ranges from as little as thirty thousand dollars to as much as two hundred thousand dollars—considerably below the cost of a mainframe. Minicomputers are easy to install by comparison with mainframes. They take up less floor space, require few special environmental conditions, and can be plugged into standard electrical outlets.

Today, the future of the minicomputer is uncertain. As the increased capabilities and wide usage of the microcomputer grow, many see the market for the minicomputer as vulnerable. In short, you are more likely to work in offices with mainframes or microcomputers than in offices with minicomputers.

Prepared office workers will know how to operate more than one computer system (see table 2–1). In addition, they will keep up to date on current trends and technology. On your first job, you may find that at your own desk and with needed devices and proper instructions, you and your microcomputer or mainframe terminal can complete many diverse tasks. These tasks will likely include preparing letters, budgets, inventory reports, business charts and graphs, and newsletters.

## Recall Time

*Answer the following questions:*

1. Define the term computer.
2. What are the three classifications of computers?
3. What are two reasons offices today are buying and using more microcomputers and fewer electric typewriters?

## SOFTWARE

Unless you are a computer programmer, your computer hardware will be useless without some software. **Software** is the set of sequenced instructions that directs the computer hardware in performing assorted tasks.

Software, often called a **program,** is written by computer programmers. Programmers write software instructions for computers, not humans, to follow. The two basic types of computer programs are system programs and application programs. You will need to understand both types of programs. However, you will actually use and become more familiar with certain application programs in your daily office activities.

## System Programs

System programs control the operations of computer hardware and directly affect the way a computer works. For most microcomputers, the operating system program is contained on a floppy disk and comes with the computer when it is purchased. The operating system instructions direct all internal activities. Therefore, they must be "loaded," or entered, into the computer before beginning a task such as typing a letter with a word processing program. If you are using a computer with a hard disk drive, your operating system instructions have probably already been permanently put on the hard disk.

When you go out on your first job, chances are the operating system will have been loaded into the computer. If this is not the case, you have an option before beginning actual typing tasks. You can choose to either load the disk operating system before your application program or put the disk operating system commands on the application program disk. The instructions to complete these tasks are in the manuals that accompany the application software you will be using.

Several disk operating systems are in use today. Among the most common are MS-DOS (Microsoft Disk Operating System), PC-DOS (Personal Computer Disk Operating System), and OS/2 (Operating System 2).

## Application Programs

The Windows software environment is changing the way computer operators use the computer. With Windows, developed by Microsoft, users can run multiple applications and more easily move data from one application to another.

Programmers write many different kinds of software called application programs to solve particular problems for the computer user.

Word processing software enables the computer to do word processing tasks such as producing letters and reports. Graphics software creates business graphs such as pie, line, and bar charts. Other kinds of software include desktop publishing, data base management, spreadsheet, telecommunications, and integrated software packages. Table 2–2 shows examples of popular commercial software packages.

Application software can be written in different ways. If you use a microcomputer, you will probably be asked either to make selections from a menu or to press certain keys to give the computer a command, such as Shift F7. In both cases, you are requiring the computer to do a particular action, such as printing out what has been entered. Software, therefore, can be written as menu driven or command driven. Both have advantages, and you may have already developed a preference for the kind of software you enjoy using.

| WORD PROCESSING | DATA BASE | SPREADSHEET |
|---|---|---|
| WordPerfect | dBase IV | Lotus 1-2-3 |
| Microsoft Word | PFS: Professional File | Microsoft Excel |
| PFS: Professional Write | | VP-Planner Plus |
| **DESKTOP PUBLISHING** | **INTEGRATED SOFTWARE** | |
| PageMaker | PFS: First Choice | |
| Ventura Publisher | AppleWorks | |
| PFS: First Publisher | Microsoft Works | |

■ TABLE 2–2

*Examples of popular commercial software packages.*

**Menu-driven Software** Often, menu-driven software packages are considered the most user friendly, meaning they are easy to learn and to use. Menu-driven software is easy to use because it prompts you with a list of choices or options to select from in instructing the computer. Many office workers prefer using menu-driven software because the chances for making errors are reduced.

**Command-driven Software** On the other hand, command-driven software packages, though slightly more difficult to learn, are preferred by many experienced office workers. This is because commands are performed faster when no wait time is needed for choice selection, as it is with a menu. Once a command is given, the activity or action occurs.

A wide selection of computer hardware and software is available to buy. Nevertheless, all computer systems accomplish tasks using the same process, called the information processing cycle.

# Recall Time

*Answer the following questions:*

1. What is meant by the terms *hardware* and *software?* Give examples of each.
2. How is an application program different from a disk operating system program?
3. What is menu-driven software? How is it different from command-driven software?

# ■ THE INFORMATION PROCESSING CYCLE

Computer systems help office specialists prepare usable *information* in the form of documents, charts, and tables. This usable information doesn't just happen, however. No magic is involved. Instead, all computers, regardless of their size, follow a continuous and orderly process to convert raw **data** (unorganized facts) into usable information.

## LARGE OFFICE/SMALL OFFICE: What's Your Preference?

### Computer Equipment

Mainframe computers are usually found in large offices because of their size and capacity. Large offices usually need to process large volumes of data at high speeds. A mainframe computer is the answer to this need. In addition, mainframes are so powerful that they allow many employees to use one mainframe computer at the same time. Many different employees can access information from or input information into a mainframe at the same time. Having mainframes also means having more job opportunities for individuals who enjoy working in data processing. Companies with mainframes need employees to maintain these computers.

Mainframe computers are usually not found in small offices. The employees in small offices usually work with microcomputers or with a minicomputer. Microcomputers or minicomputers meet the needs of a small office because it usually does not have a demand for large volumes of data to be processed. Also, it is not usually necessary for all employees to have access to the same information at the same time. Therefore, small offices have less need for a data processing department and fewer opportunities for individuals who enjoy working with the mainframes.

*If you are interested in a data processing career, will you apply to a large or small company for employment? Why?*

---

Ultimately, that information helps a business make decisions that are important to its continued operation and financial success. Computer systems lessen the amount of wasted time; and as a result, goals are reached more quickly. In the end, the customer is rewarded with a quality service or product, and the organization enjoys the financial rewards of repeat business.

The four operational steps in this information processing cycle are input, process, output, and storage.

## Input

The first step in information processing is **input.** To input means to put data into a computer's memory. Unless a computer has data already in its memory when asked to process new data, it will just sit there and blink at you.

**Source Documents** Documents from which data is taken are called source documents. For example, scores from your chapter test papers may become input into your instructor's computer to determine your average grade. In this case, the source documents are your graded tests. For another example, your boss may ask you to type a letter from a handwritten rough draft. The rough draft copy is the source document from which you type.

The operator's accuracy in entering data from a source document directly affects the overall accuracy of subsequent computer-generated information. Your keyboarding skill at this input step is vital. Can you type accurately? Further, can you prepare documents with accuracy and speed when you are working under the pressure to complete a rush job? Would your boss be consistently proud to sign documents you typed, or would typographical corrections need to be made periodically? Perhaps you've heard the term GIGO, or garbage in, garbage out. Simply put, this means that the computer will produce results that are as accurate, or inaccurate, as the data it receives from the operator.

Your ability to consistently type with speed and accuracy in meeting deadlines is important to your success. Data that is entered inaccurately costs organizations millions of dollars each year. Operator time is needed to proofread and rekey corrections. In addition, errors in business decisions often result from errors in computer-processed data. Such errors can also cost an organization in ways not easily measured, such as in losses to its image and reputation. These are intangible elements that are important to a company's customers. Because such errors are important to customers, they are also important to you. Your security and advancement as an employee depend on your company's success.

**Input Devices** Input devices are used to enter data into your computer. A wide range of input devices are used to input data and instructions into the computer. However, the office environment uses one type in particular. Can you name it? If you said a **keyboard** or terminal, you were right. As you enter or type data on the keyboard, it is simultaneously displayed on your monitor screen and stored in the computer's main memory. Another input device now being used in more offices is the optical character recognition scanner.

*Keyboard* Let's briefly examine your computer typing tool—the basic keyboard. Different keyboard models are available, with keys located in different places and with varying numbers of keys. Most keyboards consist of three distinct sections: the typewriter keypad, the cursor movement–numeric keypad, and the function keypad. Three common keyboard types that you will encounter in the office are the IBM standard, IBM enhanced, and Macintosh enhanced keyboards.

The *typewriter keypad* section is located in the center of the computer keyboard. It contains the standard typing keys, just as on a typewriter.

The *cursor movement–numeric keypad* section is located on the right side of the computer keyboard. It serves two purposes. As a cursor movement keypad, it controls the whereabouts of your cursor. As a numeric keypad, it allows you to type the numbers shown on the keys.

If you have already developed the touch method in using a ten-key adding machine, you may prefer to enter numbers more quickly using the cursor movement–numeric keypad rather than the top row on the typewriter keypad. The procedure to follow in developing the ten-key touch method will be described in a later chapter.

O F F I C E   T I P

Disks are sturdy enough to be used and reused many times, but you must treat them with due care. Follow the dos and don'ts usually printed on disk boxes and disk envelopes. A disk itself is not that valuable, but your time to rekey the contents certainly is!

The Num Lock key controls whether you're using the cursor movement–numeric keypad for moving the cursor or for typing numbers. The Num Lock key is a toggle switch. When it is active, the keypad inserts numbers. When it is pressed again, the keypad returns to a cursor movement keypad.

Depending on your keyboard, the *function keypad* section sits either on the left with keys labeled F1 through F10 or on the top with keys labeled F1 through F12 or F15. You can press a function key either by itself or in combination with the Ctrl (Control), Alt (Alternate), or Shift key. This commands the computer to use special features of the software package that you have loaded and are using.

When using a different software package, the same keys may initiate entirely different functions. For example, when WordPerfect software is loaded into an IBM microcomputer, you must press the Shift and F6 keys simultaneously to center a line. In comparison, while using MultiMate Advantage II software on an IBM, you simply press the F3 key to center a line. In summary, function keys are software dependent; their function depends on how the programmer selects them to perform.

*Optical Character Recognition Scanner* Improved technology has given offices another way to get data from a source document into the computer. This increasingly popular device is called the **optical character recognition (OCR) scanner.** An OCR device scans the shape of a character on a document and compares it with a predefined shape stored in its memory. It then converts this shape into a computer character, which it places in storage in the computer's main memory. The advantage of this technique is that this transfer is done without the operator having to reenter the information.

OCR scanners are cost-effective in the office. They are able to read a wide range of printed material. They can also link different types of equipment that ordinarily cannot "talk" with each other.

The communication ability of OCRs makes it possible to transfer information between unlike systems, which can save time and money. For example, suppose you are working in a small office where you

Abigail and Missy are good friends. They took secretarial courses like typing, speedwriting, and accounting together at Monument Technical Institute and made about the same grades. Since beginning their secretarial careers, both have been making almost the same amount of money using their acquired skills. Over lunch one day, they have the following conversation:

Abigail: The most wonderful thing just happened, Missy. Ms. Edwards, my boss, said the office was getting a new microcomputer system with accounting and word processing software in a few weeks, and she asked me if I wanted to be the first one in the office to be trained on it.

Missy: Well, what did you tell her?

Abigail: I said yes, of course.

Missy: What? You're out of your mind. Your job is great now. Aren't you afraid of what will happen when you start working on the computer? What if the computer is too hard to learn, or what if you train someone who becomes better at the computer than you? What will you do then, Abigail? Boy, if it were me, I sure wouldn't rock the boat. I'd help Ms. Edwards find someone else to do it.

Abigail: Well, I'm going to give it a try. I've been giving a lot of thought to going back to Monument Technical Institute and getting a computer skills certificate. I've been putting it off, but tonight I'm going to find out more about it. Want to go with me?

Missy: No, I'm happy just the way I am. Thanks anyway.

1. Can you predict the type of work life Abigail and Missy may each have in five years by the attitudes they express now? Explain your prediction.
2. What does *lifelong learning* mean? Does it apply to all workers today? Explain.

frequently use a typewriter. You also share a microcomputer and OCR scanner with four other members of the office staff. In this situation, you can take a multipage report prepared on your typewriter and scan the text into the computer's memory. You can then make whatever editing changes are necessary at the computer, and print out the final report at a high-quality printer. In this way, you will not delay your co-workers' projects by remaining at the computer while you type in the entire text.

OCR scanners are also fast readers. Many can scan more than one thousand words per minute, or more than three hundred pages per hour. So, the tedious task of inputting data into the office computer is becoming easier for the office worker, thanks to advances in technology.

OCR technology is being improved upon to better accommodate the office environment. However, office workers can benefit now because it presents a more efficient way of entering data than do keyboards. Faster completion of work and more freedom for revision are possible with OCRs. One effective use of OCRs is in helping ease peak work loads. It is often difficult to find temporary word processing operators for peak work load periods. Temporary typists can be hired instead and paid less per hour. The material they type at typewriters can be scanned by the OCR and revisions can then be made by the word processor.

## Process

Once programmed, the computer will, on its own, process whatever data you give it. But what is computer processing and how is it done?

**Processing** at a computer means manipulating data by performing mathematical calculations on numbers, or by logically organizing word or number data for output. The processor unit, sometimes called the **central processing unit** (CPU), contains the electronic circuits that actually cause the processing of data to occur. Once a computer has data stored in its memory, it can then process that data and new data at incredibly high speeds to produce the desired result.

To get an idea of how fast this processing occurs, consider the following situation. Suppose your school enrollment is nine hundred students, and information pertaining to each student is already in the school's computer. With the help of data base manager software, you can instruct the computer to sort out all students who are under twenty-five years of age. This task, which would take the average person thirty minutes to an hour to perform, will take the computer merely a second or two.

The CPU is much like the human brain in that certain parts of it are responsible for functioning a certain way and performing certain tasks (see figure 2–1). Briefly, the computer's "brain" consists of the following:

■ FIGURE 2–1

*Components of the Central Processing Unit*

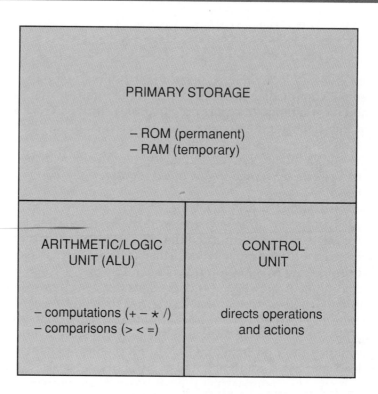

PRIMARY STORAGE

– ROM (permanent)
– RAM (temporary)

| ARITHMETIC/LOGIC UNIT (ALU) | CONTROL UNIT |
|---|---|
| – computations (+ − ★ /)<br>– comparisons (> < =) | directs operations<br>and actions |

**Martha Moyer**
*Supervisor, Training, General Services*
*Chevron USA*

Q: Mrs. Moyer, to what extent are microcomputers used in today's electronic office?

A: Microcomputers have become such a vital tool for text processing, it is hard to imagine operating without them. Analysts, managers, and supervisors use them to draft text for letters, memos, and reports—they are really an electronic "yellow pad." The support staff then finalizes the draft, checks format and handles distribution. A part of that distribution may be electronic, as many of our microcomputers are attached to the host network which helps to speed documents to many parts of the world.

Local area networks [LANs] are providing a means of sharing files among members of a work team. Eventually, we hope to have the LANs linked to the host so that work sharing can take place among several networks.

Q: What makes a successful word processing operator?

A: In addition to having excellent keyboarding skills and English skills, the successful word processing operator is also excited about trying new things. Today, technology is changing so fast that you've got to experiment constantly to see how projects can be done better or faster. A good word processing operator needs to be a good problem solver—looking for the best way to get a job done for the customer.

---

- the control unit, which maintains order and controls the activity that occurs in the CPU during processing
- the arithmetic/logic unit (ALU), which performs all arithmetic computations on data—such as adding, subtracting, multiplying, and dividing—and also performs all logical operations involved in organizing data into information
- the **primary storage area** or main memory area, which electronically stores data and program instructions as they are being processed in the main memory, is located inside the computer, and contains two parts called read-only memory and random-access memory.

**Read-Only Memory**  The read-only memory (ROM) portion of primary storage performs specific but commonly used functions of a computer. The contents of ROM are considered permanent because they have been permanently placed in memory by the manufacturer and cannot be changed or deleted by the operator. ROM instructions are always in the computer's memory, even when you turn the computer off.

**Random-Access Memory** The random-access memory (RAM) is located inside the computer. It is the part of primary storage that is lost if a power outage or a strong power surge occurs or if you simply turn off the computer. That is why RAM is considered temporary.

RAM is used by the computer as a temporary holding area for data that you keyboard or program instructions that you enter in solving particular problems. When the computer's power is off, the contents of RAM are as empty as a blank sheet of paper. When the computer is on, you can access RAM many times without ever destroying its contents. The way the computer uses information in RAM is determined by the commands you supply while using the software program.

## R ecall Time

*Answer the following questions:*

1. Define the term data.
2. What happens at the input, processing, and output stages of the information processing cycle?
3. What hardware devices are most often used for the input step? What determines when each could best be used?

## Output

*(Left) Hard copy is printed on paper.*

*(Right) Soft copy is seen on a monitor screen.*

Assume that you input a handwritten letter into the computer's memory. You then organize it, edit it, and save it to disk. The next step is to see what the output or finished document looks like.

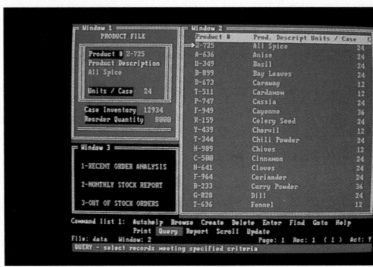

**Soft Copy and Hard Copy** Output from a computer can be presented as soft copy or hard copy. Soft copy output from a monitor gives you immediate but temporary access to processed information. For example, suppose you need to verify that an address on a letter is correct. To do this, you only have to see the letter on the screen. On the other hand, hard copy output created at a printer gives you a permanent printed copy of the processed information. A printed copy of a letter that you can hold in your hands is an example of hard copy.

**Output Devices** In business applications, the two most commonly used output devices are the monitor and the printer. The needs of the user determine the best output device to be used. For example, if an office person needs only to verify that information is correct or to locate a customer's phone number, then the monitor's visual output is adequate. On the other hand, if the operator needs a permanent record of the information as a paper copy to be mailed or edited, then the printer is used.

*Monitors* A **monitor** resembles a television set in that it displays output on a screen. In fact, television sets can be used as computer monitors. Monitors range in cost from less than one hundred dollars to several hundred dollars. The more expensive monitors have extra features such as color and high resolution, which produce more attractive and clearer images on the screen. Graphics software, for example, displays better on a color monitor with high resolution. Many offices pay the extra money for this upgraded quality.

*Printers* Numerous types of **printers** are available, with price tags ranging from one hundred dollars to many thousands of dollars. The two that you are most likely to use in the office are the dot matrix and laser printers.

*(Left) A monochrome monitor is found in most businesses.*

*(Right) A color monitor is more expensive and is usually found in offices that use graphics software.*

DOT MATRIX  The technology used in dot matrix printers has improved greatly in recent years. These printers can now provide excellent, near-letter-quality (NLQ) office printing. Letter-quality printing is top-quality printing that is usually associated with the consistent print of a typewriter. In addition, it can be done with a variety of fonts or type styles to fit the mood and tone of almost any business situation. Some common type styles or fonts used in business are Courier, Letter Gothic, and Script. Although typewriterlike printers with typing elements, print wheels, and thimbles are available, their use in offices is declining. Dot matrix printers are affordable and versatile, and have an acceptable speed for most office printing needs.

LASER  The technology of laser printers is replacing or supplementing the slower, near-letter-quality of dot matrix printers. Why is this happening? Because with laser printing, a sharper, more appealing page results. Documents simply look better.

Companies realize many advantages by using laser printers. Of primary importance are the following: (1) Proportionally spaced fonts are available. These produce quality output that is comparable to professional printing. (2) The cost of laser printers has been reduced, causing them to be inexpensive enough for small offices to afford.

The laser printer is fast becoming an affordable "must" in any office today. Some models can be purchased for less than one thousand dollars, although sophisticated models can carry a price tag of more than twenty-five thousand dollars.

## Storage

The final step in the information processing cycle is secondary storage or **auxiliary storage.** In this case, *secondary* means another kind of computer data storage that is separate from and outside of primary storage. Storage mostly occurs at the processing step. However, it can also follow the output step, if revisions are made to the original copy and you choose to replace the original copy with its revision.

Steven and Dolly work with you in the sales department of Kinko's Products. Although each has a microcomputer on his or her desk, they share the newest office dot matrix printer. For the past few weeks, tension has existed between them over the use of the printer.

Dolly has told you, "Steven doesn't know how to use the printer correctly. He never uses the proper buttons to eject his printouts. Then when I put my paper in the printer, it starts printing halfway down the paper and I must throw that copy away. This is happening more and more. Steven makes me waste so much time and paper—I wish he had his own printer!"

Steven, on the other hand, has told you, "Dolly thinks she knows so much and is always telling me what to do. She's not perfect, you know. Dolly never leaves the near-letter-quality switch set where it should be. She is changing it all the time from draft to NLQ and back again. I never know where the setting is going to be when I start printing. In addition, she prints out envelopes using the printer, and the paper guide setting is never where I expect it. I don't have the time to check the printer each time I print. I haven't mentioned these things to Dolly, but if she stays on my case, I just might blow up and get this printer business off my chest!"

1. Do printers present special operating problems for office staffs?
2. As a friend to both Steven and Dolly, how might you go about solving this problem and easing the tension in the office?

---

Floppy disks and hard disks are types of secondary storage devices that are used to save information and data that is contained in primary storage.

A key benefit of using a computer rather than a typewriter is that once you've prepared a document, it can be saved, or "captured" from main memory onto a secondary storage device for use at a later time. For example, you may want to use the same basic letter with various customers. That basic letter can be stored on disk and revised slightly each time you use it with a different recipient. Or you might want to update a monthly budget by typing in just the new numbers over the old numbers in last month's budget.

**Floppy Disks** A common device used in processing data for storage on microcomputers is a disk drive. A **disk drive** is a mechanical device that rotates disks during data transmission. The disk drive acts like a tape recorder. It deposits data as magnetic spots on a small circular, flexible, magnetically coated plastic disk called a floppy disk, or **diskette.** Because this storage is outside the computer's primary memory, these disks make the computer's storage capacity unlimited.

Many offices use floppy disks for numerous reasons. They are inexpensive, reusable, lightweight, and easy to file and store.

The most popular disk sizes for office use are 5¼ inches and 3½ inches. Don't be misled by size! Even though the 5¼-inch disk is larger in diameter than the 3½-inch disk, it can hold only about half the number of files or documents. As you might have guessed, the smaller disk is the newer one and owes its increased storage capacity to improved technology. More and more, you will be working with the smaller disks.

*3½-inch and 5¼-inch floppy disks.*

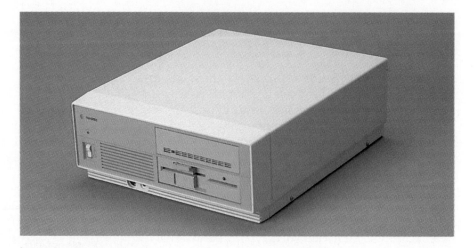

**Hard Disks** Depending on the amount and type of work you do in an office, you might use a **hard disk.** This is a metal storage device that is usually built right into your computer and can hold a large amount of data.

A hard disk system is preferred over a floppy disk because it stores much more data on a smaller area. It is also preferred because it's faster and, therefore, takes less time to store and locate data. Data retrieval is quicker simply because no disk handling is involved. With no disk handling comes the added plus of further protecting the data contents on the disk.

Hard disk drives are available for all sizes of computers. Common storage capacities used on most office computers range from ten to in excess of one hundred megabytes (MB) of data.

When you are working on an office microcomputer equipped with both a hard disk drive and a floppy disk drive, play it safe. Back up your hard disk data files to a floppy disk frequently. Sometimes exposure to heat, magnetic impulses, jarring, or some other physical abuse will cause your hard disk to "crash," or lose its memory. When files are lost from a hard disk, sometimes office work comes to a standstill until those important files are replaced. It is better to back up a disk than to be sorry!

## R ecall Time

*Answer the following questions:*

1. What are two types of printers used in the output step? Discuss the differences in their features.
2. Why is RAM called temporary memory? Why is ROM called permanent memory?
3. Why are hard disk drives becoming popular in offices today?
4. Why is it necessary to back up data from hard disks to floppy disks?

# SUMMARY

Computers are affecting the way office specialists work. For that reason, it is imperative to develop computer skills and knowledge to be prepared for tomorrow's jobs.

Computer systems are classified into three types: (1) mainframes, which are powerful, large computers equipped to handle many users at the same time; (2) minicomputers, which operate like a mainframe computer, but on a smaller scale; and (3) microcomputers, which are the most popular computers found in the office today because they are small-yet-versatile desktop units.

Software programs provide the necessary step-by-step instructions to tell the computer what type of activity to perform. The information processing cycle describes how the computer goes about doing its job. It consists of four steps: input, process, output, and storage.

Do you remember the following points about computer systems in the office?

- System programs control the operations of the computer hardware.
- Application programs solve particular problems for the computer user.
- Menu-driven software is more user friendly than command-driven software.
- Command-driven software is preferred by experienced computer office workers.
- The information processing cycle consists of four steps.
- Input is the first step of the information processing cycle. This is where information is put into the computer's memory.
- Process is the second step of the information processing cycle. This is when data is manipulated by the computer.
- Output is the information processing cycle step that displays the results of the first two steps.
- Storage is the information processing cycle step that saves information to be edited or used later.

## In Conclusion . . .

*When you have completed this chapter, use an electronic typewriter or a microcomputer to answer the following questions:*

1. *What might a computer system in the office look like?*
2. *What are two advantages to businesses of using a computer?*

# Review and Application

Match the following by writing the letter of each vocabulary word in the space to the left of its description.

____ 1. first step in the information processing cycle that puts data into the computer's memory

____ 2. a group of computer devices that are connected, coordinated, and linked together in such a way that they work as one to complete a task

____ 3. written by computer programmers and often called software

____ 4. also called personal computer or PC

____ 5. unorganized facts that will be processed and converted into usable information

____ 6. the set of sequenced instructions that directs the computer hardware in performing assorted tasks

____ 7. very powerful, large computers that can handle many users at the same time

____ 8. its abilities are similar to the mainframe computer but on a smaller scale

____ 9. also called a terminal that is used to enter or type data into the computer

____ 10. contains the electronic circuits that cause the processing of data to occur

____ 11. resembles a television set in that it displays output on the screen

____ 12. a device that scans the shape of a character on a document and compares it with a predefined shape stored in its memory

____ 13. stores data and program instructions as they are being processed in the main memory

____ 14. manipulating data by performing mathematical calculations on numbers, or by logically organizing word or number data for output

____ 15. can be presented as soft copy or hard copy

____ 16. examples are the dot matrix and laser

____ 17. is a mechanical device that rotates disks during data transmission

____ 18. a metal storage device that is usually built right into a computer and can hold a large amount of data

____ 19. also called secondary storage that is separate from and outside of primary storage

____ 20. a small circular, flexible, magnetically coated plastic floppy disk

a. auxiliary storage
b. central processing unit
c. computer system
d. data
e. disk drive
f. diskette
g. hard disk
h. input
i. keyboard
j. mainframe
k. microcomputer
l. minicomputer
m. monitor
n. optical character recognition (OCR) scanner
o. output
p. primary storage area
q. printers
r. processing
s. program
t. software

## DISCUSS AND ANALYZE AN OFFICE SITUATION

1. Students in the modern office procedures class at Regional Adult Technical Skills Center have been given an assignment. They are to conduct interviews and prepare a report describing the use of computers at three local businesses.

In doing the assignment, Richard finds out that the first business he interviewed never uses a computer—preferring to use an electronic typewriter instead. Further, the secretary he spoke to really doesn't care whether she ever learns the computer. Office workers at the second business he interviewed complained that the office doesn't have enough computers and therefore, time is lost waiting for a computer to become free. The legal secretary at the third business told Richard he would quit his job if he could not have the use of a computer with software that drives an OCR scanner.

In looking over his notes, Richard is wondering why the responses are so varied. Can you help him? Why do people have such different opinions of computers?

## PRACTICE BASIC SKILLS

### Math

1. Think like a computer. Do the processing steps necessary to correctly complete the following mathematical calculations. Remember that a computer will do first the calculations within parentheses, then any multiplication or division tasks, and finally addition or subtraction tasks. Also, "+" means to add, "−" to subtract, "*" to multiply, and "/" to divide.

   a. $37 + 22 - 16 =$
   b. $45 - 30 + 15 =$
   c. $10 * 4 + 12 =$
   d. $40 / 8 + 13 =$
   e. $(2 + 2 + 2) * 6 =$
   f. $4 + (72 / 9) =$
   g. $(5 * 8) * 2 =$
   h. $(100 - 60) * (30 - 20) / 2 =$
   i. $200 * (18 / 6) + 72 + 33 =$
   j. $(1 + 2) * (4 / 2) + (55 - 35) / 2 =$

### English

1. *Rule:* When the day follows the month, do not include the ordinal ending *st, nd, rd,* or *th.* When the day precedes the month or stands alone, use the ordinal ending or write the date in words.
   *Examples:* We plan to get together before June 15. The 8th of January is Jim's birthday.
   *Practice Exercise:* For the following, if a sentence is correct, write OK beside it. If a sentence is incorrect, rewrite it correctly.

   a. My birthday is on the 11 of December.
   b. Spring break begins March 12th.
   c. You must buy tickets before Monday, July 23.
   d. Don is scheduled for his health exam on October 20th.
   e. Gina will be inducted into the National Honor Society on Friday, April 22.
   f. November 5 is Darrin's birthday.
   h. Ice skating lessons for Charles are scheduled to begin on November 26th.

### Proofreading

1. Retype or rewrite the following paragraph, correcting all errors:

The computer is the key system of a companie's informaation sestem. It consiss of a central procesing unit where processing is carryed out, an inputt devise, and an outputt devise. Although computer systems very in sofistication, the input-processing-output cycle remanes the same.

## APPLY YOUR KNOWLEDGE

1. Part of the comfort level, and even pleasure, you will experience in operating any computer will come from understanding the parts of that computer, how and why those parts behave as they do, and how you can make the parts behave as you want them to. Now visualize a computer, and identify whether each of the following components is located on the outside or inside. Place a check mark in the appropriate column.

| Feature | Inside | Outside |
| --- | --- | --- |
| RAM | | |
| Printer | | |
| CPU | | |
| Monitor | | |
| Keyboard | | |
| Arithmetic/logic unit | | |
| Diskette | | |
| Hard disk | | |
| Control unit | | |
| Hard copy | | |
| Source document | | |

# QUIZ

*Write a **T** if the statement is true or an **F** if the statement is false.*

_____ 1. You are more likely to use a microcomputer in an office than the other two types of computer systems.

_____ 2. The minicomputer is larger in size, is more expensive, and has more storage capacity than the mainframe computer.

_____ 3. Trained office workers only need to know how to operate one computer system.

_____ 4. Software is the set of sequenced instructions that directs the computer hardware to perform assorted tasks.

_____ 5. Examples of application programs are MS-DOS, PC-DOS, and OS/2.

_____ 6. All computers, regardless of size, follow a continuous and orderly process of converting raw data into usable information.

_____ 7. Source documents are used in the processing step of the information processing cycle.

_____ 8. Examples of output devices are monitors, laser printers, and dot matrix printers.

_____ 9. Hard disk capacity is measured in megabytes (MB) of memory.

_____ 10. Primary storage uses floppy disks and hard disks to save data.

_____ 11. The computer term OCR scanner stands for "optical computer recognition" scanner.

_____ 12. Computers can perform the dull, noncreative, and repetitive tasks often found in an office work environment.

_____ 13. As an office worker, you only need to understand how to use application programs, not system programs.

_____ 14. WordPerfect software is a desktop publishing package.

_____ 15. Menu-driven software is easy to use because it prompts you with a list of choices or options to direct the computer.

## Computer System Classifications

Circle the computer classification on the left that correctly matches the description on the right.

Micro   Mini   Mainframe    1. widely used in schools and small businesses

Micro   Mini   Mainframe    2. requires special physical accommodations like cooling systems and special electrical wiring

Micro   Mini   Mainframe    3. most expensive system

Micro   Mini   Mainframe    4. primarily a single-user system

Micro   Mini   Mainframe    5. sometimes referred to as a "PC"

Micro   Mini   Mainframe    6. multiuser systems used by midsize companies

Micro   Mini   Mainframe    7. can be expanded to meet the needs of a growing company

Micro   Mini   Mainframe    8. typically uses disk drives

Micro   Mini   Mainframe    9. smaller in size, less expensive, and less storage capacity than the mainframe

Micro   Mini   Mainframe   10. time share is possible with this system; fast speed and great storage capacity

Micro   Mini   Mainframe   11. small, but versatile desktop units

Micro   Mini   Mainframe   12. uses popular software packages like word processing and spreadsheets

Micro   Mini   Mainframe   13. the largest multiuser system

Micro   Mini   Mainframe   14. abilities are similar to a mainframe, but on a smaller scale

Micro   Mini   Mainframe   15. uses large volumes of data during processing and is available to numerous users who need access to the same centralized computer

## Types of Computer Storage

Circle the type of storage on the left that correctly matches or describes the item listed on the right.

primary     secondary       1. known as main memory area of CPU

primary     secondary       2. contains read-only memory (ROM)

primary     secondary       3. also known as auxiliary storage

primary     secondary       4. uses a disk drive during data transmission

primary     secondary       5. contains random-access memory (RAM)

primary     secondary       6. uses floppy disks that come in different sizes

primary     secondary       7. RAM is erased when power outage occurs

primary     secondary       8. uses a metal storage device called a hard disk

primary     secondary       9. backing up disks is encouraged with this type of storage

primary     secondary       10. used to complete the information processing cycle during the processing step and following the output step of the information processing cycle

## Word Processing

1. Contact two businesses in your community to determine how each uses computers. Using the following list of questions as a guide, interview each business over the phone or in person.

   Questions:
   1. Do you use computers in your business?
   2. If so, what types of computer hardware do you have?
   3. Do you use word processing software? If so, which software package? What documents do you process using your software package?
   4. Do you use spreadsheet software? If so, which software package? What financial documents or forms do you process using your software package?
   5. Do you use data base management software? If so, which software package? What lists do you prepare using your software package?

2. From your interview responses, keyboard a two-column table (similar to the example below) that attractively displays how each business uses computers in business and what type of computer hardware each has installed.

|  | Business #1 Name | Business #2 Name |
| --- | --- | --- |
| Hardware |  |  |
| Software |  |  |
| Word Processing |  |  |
| Spreadsheet |  |  |
| Data Base |  |  |

3. Save and print a copy.

## Word Processing

1. Research information about two types of computer hardware systems (example, IBM and Macintosh) in current computer magazines. Assume that your research will result in a purchasing decision for a home computer that you will use for educational and personal purposes.

(continued on next page)

2. Keyboard a two-page, double-spaced research report. Your research should find answers to the following questions:

   A. What type of monitor would you select for each system?

   B. What type of keyboard would you select for each system?

   C. What would the control unit and disk drives look like?

   D. What type of printer would you buy that would best meet your current needs?

   E. Describe the type of computer system hardware you are currently using in your classroom.

3. Save and print a copy of the report.

---

## ACTIVITY 2–5

### Word Processing

1. Keyboard double-spaced the following paragraphs describing the information processing cycle.

   The four operational steps in the information processing cycle are input, process, output, and storage. The first step is input. To input means to put data into a computer's memory. Keyboards and optical character recognition scanners are examples of input devices.

   The process step uses a processor unit sometimes called the central processing unit. At the output step, an operator can create either a paper copy or screen copy of the computer's memory. There are various quality levels for printed copy. The laser printer provides letter quality printing, while the dot matrix printer provides near-letter-quality print.

   The final step in the information processing cycle is secondary storage using floppy disks and hard disks. A hard disk is preferred over a floppy disk because it stores much more data on a smaller area.

2. Save and print a copy.

3. Edit the document in the following ways and print a second copy:

   A. Use boldface type to enhance the four words that describe the steps in the information processing cycle (input, process, output, and storage) each time they are used.

   B. Change the line spacing from double to single.

# The Information Processing Cycle

Assume you have been hired to work in a travel agency. The agency has generated questions according to the information processing cycle to help train you. A client walks in the door of Global West Travel Agency and wants to book travel plans. Using the sample data from your agency's Trip Record source document (on the next page), answer the following questions.

Keep in mind the four steps of information processing are: input, process, output, and storage. Write your answers on the page provided.

## INPUT
1. How do you receive the information in order to complete the Trip Record form?
2. What other sources will provide additional information?
3. Is the Trip Record form the only one used?

## PROCESS
1. What happens once the trip record is filled in?
2. Is it likely that this information will be changed by the client? If so, how often and in what ways?
3. When are airline travel, car rental, and room reservations made?

## OUTPUT
1. What documents do you prepare for the client from this trip information?
2. At what point do you print out the tickets and itinerary?

## STORAGE
1. Do you file the Trip Record form?
2. Do you transfer any of the information to a data base in order to keep travel information on customers?

(continued on next page)

# GLOBAL WEST TRAVEL AGENCY
## TRIP RECORD

For _Thomas Calvin_      Date _4-12-92_

Consultation Notes:

- non-smoking rooms
- on ground floors, if possible
- first-class travel
- travel between 8 AM & noon

| Travel Agent | Passenger(s) |
|---|---|
| Christine | Thomas |
| | Marion (wife) |

## AIR TRAVEL

| Date | From | To | Dep Time | Arr Time | Airline | Flight # |
|---|---|---|---|---|---|---|
| 7/20 | El Paso | Wash DC | 9:30 | 11:30 | Am | #103 |
| 7/23 | Wash DC | NYC | 10:04 | 10:50 | (Shuttle) | # 8 |
| 7/30 | NYC | El Paso | 9:00 | 10:30 | Am | #411 |

## ACCOMMODATIONS

| Hotel | City | Arr Date | Dep Date | # Nights |
|---|---|---|---|---|
| Embassy | Wash DC | 7/20 | 7/23 | 3 |
| Plaza | NYC | 7/23 | 7/30 | 7 |

## CAR RENTAL

| Company | Type | Pick Up City/Date | Drop Off City/Date | Days |
|---|---|---|---|---|
| Budget | Sedan | NYC 7/23 | NYC 7/30 | 7 |

## OTHER SERVICES

Delivered Ticket on _4/15/92_ at _10:30_ (AM) PM.

## INPUT

1. _____

_____

2. _____

_____

3. _____

_____

## PROCESS

1. _____

_____

2. _____

_____

3. _____

_____

## OUTPUT

1. _____

_____

2. _____

_____

## STORAGE

1. _____

_____

2. _____

_____

## Computer Hardware Devices

Prepare the following memorandum to the office staff at Global West Travel Agency. After you have keyed the memorandum, prepare and attach a response to the memo that lists questions you might ask during the computer equipment demonstration.

---

MEMORANDUM

TO:        OFFICE STAFF
FROM:      GAIL HODGE, OFFICE MANAGER
DATE:      JANUARY 29, 19___
SUBJECT:   COMPUTER HARDWARE DEVICES—DEMONSTRATION AND TRIAL

On Monday, February 3, at 8:00 a.m., Mr. Walter Blue of Computer Equipment, Inc. will be in our office to demonstrate the hardware computer devices used in travel agencies. If we want to test the equipment on a one-week trial basis, he will leave a demonstration system with us. As you know, the computer system we use to book travel for clients does not allow us to do normal correspondence, brochures, reports, listings, or spreadsheets. The results of last week's survey indicate to me that you feel an investment in a microcomputer and software system would be cost justified. It would save you time and present the professional image Global West Travel Agency wants to project to customers and prospects.

When you see the demonstration, please be ready to question Mr. Blue in the following areas:

A. INPUT DEVICES (to include keyboards and OCR Scanners) and

B. OUTPUT DEVICES (to include monitors and printers—laser and dot matrix)

Please jot down at least two questions on each area and return these questions to me before 3:00 p.m. Friday. I expect to make a buying decision within the month on an office computer system, so your understanding and input of the type of system we should buy is most important. Thank you.

---

## Computer vs. Electronic Typewriter

Assume you are a receptionist at Global West Travel Agency and have a microcomputer (equipped with word processing and desktop publishing software packages) and an electronic typewriter near your desk area. Indicate on the lines following each item: a) which equipment you would choose to complete the following documents, and b) why you made that choice.

1. A preprinted form that contains a client's itinerary information (only four blanks per form must be filled in)

    Equipment: _____

    Why: _____

2. Ten file folder labels for folders in a geographic filing system

    Equipment: _____

    Why: _____

3. A travel brochure that is being prepared that describes a European Summer Tour Package (expect at least two or three revisions before final)

    Equipment: _____

    Why: _____

4. A form letter that will be personalized to ten clients giving departure details about an Alaskan Cruise Tour that Global West Travel Agency has arranged and booked

    Equipment: _____

    Why: _____

5. A three-page report to the owners of Global West Travel Agency from the office manager detailing a recent confrontation with a dissatisfied customer (expect revisions)

    Equipment: _____

    Why: _____

(continued on next page)

6. A brief 4" × 6" thank you note to a client for booking around-the-world trips through Global West Travel Agency

   Equipment: _____

   Why: _____

## Word Processing

1. Keyboard single-spaced three of the office tips mentioned in chapter 2 that represent new and important office hints for you. Use a dictionary disk, if available, to check for spelling or other keyboarding errors.

2. Save and print a copy.

3. Using the three tips you have just keyboarded,

   A. restate each of them in your own words while at the computer, and
   B. describe an office situation where each office tip would apply.

4. Print a copy of this revision.

# Processing Information with Computers

# O bjectives

After completing this chapter, you will be able to do the following:

1. List the four types of information processed in offices.
2. Describe the goals of word processing.
3. List the essential equipment needed for a word processing system.
4. Define word processing and describe the three steps in the word processing cycle.
5. Describe methods used at the input step of the word processing cycle.
6. Distinguish between traditional, centralized, and decentralized information processing settings.
7. List important word processing skills.
8. Describe career opportunities in word processing.
9. List and describe common features found in word processing software.
10. List and describe common features found in spreadsheet software.
11. Identify the types of accounting software used in offices today.
12. Describe the purpose of data base management software and explain how office information is maintained and accessed with this system.
13. Describe the purpose of analytical business graphics and presentation graphics.
14. Describe desktop publishing software in relation to the business documents it produces.
15. List the advantages of using integrated software.

# N ew Office Terms

accounting software
centralized information processing
  approach
compatibles or clones
data base management software
decentralized information processing approach
desktop publishing software
field
file
graphics software

integrated software
local area networks (LANs)
record
spreadsheets
stand-alone software
telecommuting
word processing
word processing center
word processing cycle
word processing system
WYSIWYG

## Before You Begin . . .

*Using an electronic typewriter or a microcomputer, answer the following questions to the best of your ability:*

1. *What does the term* word processing *mean? Are word processing and desktop publishing the same or different? Explain.*
2. *What types of software can you use to process information with computers?*

Have you ever heard of the term *information overload?* Information overload is a reality that businesspeople are increasingly aware of. Today, the problem in running a successful business is not a lack of information but rather an abundance of it.

Computers make information readily available to businesses. As a result, a business can learn the status of its operations at a moment's notice. Examples of questions answered daily by business computer systems are: How much money do customers owe us right now? How much money do we owe creditors right now? What is our current inventory level? What does our cash flow look like this month? Answers to these questions are important to any business. A timely response to both business problems and opportunities is possible through computer information processing.

If business information is organized, current, and prepared in an easy-to-understand format, its value is priceless and it will be used. Organizations make sound decisions and maintain their competitive edge with, for example, computer-generated reports, statistical tables, and pie charts. When you learn to use various information systems, you contribute to the future prosperity of an organization.

Why do companies need employees who are willing to continue to learn how to use technological advances? Offices are becoming more technologically advanced. At the same time, office workers who are most capable are assuming positions with greater control over a company's information systems. These employees often suggest more creative ways of working more efficiently.

In selecting a company to work for, you will want to choose a progressive business. A progressive business has learned how to harness, organize, and put to profitable use information of all types that come from many sources. Today's businesses get information in four ways—text, data, image, and voice. In the office, you will work with all these types of information.

Much of your job success will depend on your employer's success. You want to work for an employer who is keeping up with the latest methods for processing information. If you want to become a valued employee in today's computer age, you'll want to read more about types of office information and how it is processed.

Office information is processed in many ways using computers. Knowledgeable office workers have a good understanding of the importance and scope of word processing in the office environment. The

*Computers process information in order to answer questions and solve problems.*

most common major software packages you will use to process various office information are spreadsheet, accounting, data base management, graphics, desktop publishing, and integrated.

## ■ WORD PROCESSING

Simply defined, **word processing** (also known as text processing) is the efficient processing of words or text. Word processing relieves you of time-consuming and routine paperwork tasks. It therefore increases the amount and accuracy of work you can produce and the overall quality of a document's appearance.

Word processing evolved because it's natural for humans to look for easier ways to get things done. Word processing equipment is to the typewriter what the typewriter was to the pen and pencil.

The typewriter was invented about 1873, and since that time, people have been finding fast and more efficient ways of putting words on paper. The manual typewriter evolved into the electric typewriter, and then into the electronic typewriter. Today, computers and their word processing software are the basis for most office automation activities.

A tremendous volume of paperwork is processed in today's offices. This paperwork requires high-quality text that can easily be revised any number of times before printing final copies. Furthermore, the need to produce personalized letters over and over still exists.

Word processors, or personal computers using word processing software, reduce the time it takes to process paperwork. They enable you to write, edit, format, and professionally print text. In addition, other compatible software programs check your spelling, punctuation, and grammar and offer alternative word choices, as a thesaurus would do.

OFFICE TIP

Always update old data in a computer with new or correct data as soon as it comes to your attention. For example, an incorrect phone number or address is as worthless to the user as not having it in the first place.

## Goals of a Word Processing System

To make a word processing system operational is not an easy task. A **word processing system** requires the careful coordination of people, machines, procedures, and environment. The entire organization must have a real commitment to change. Further, people throughout the organization must genuinely support the change.

When a company installs a word processing system, what are the expected benefits? They are the following:

- increased speed and accuracy by means of improved document turnaround time with no errors in typing, grammar, spelling, punctuation, or word usage
- improved, more professional presentation by means of effectively written documents that are properly formatted and attractive
- limited physical and mental effort from users due to a lack of extra keystrokes, retyping, and unnecessary decision making
- greater cost-effectiveness through wiser use of people's time

In summary, a word processing system allows everyone in the organization to "work smarter, not harder." Word processing makes writing tasks easier. It promotes an organized and efficient approach to handling any document from start to finish. It provides you with the power to type at your rough draft speed because you do not have to slow down and type for control in order to prevent making typing errors. Then it gives you the flexibility to revise a document any number of times or to individualize the same letter to hundreds of people in a short amount of time.

*Shown here are examples of specific pieces of equipment that make up a word processing system.*

## Parts of a Word Processing System

When you use a word processing system to produce written communication, you must have specific pieces of equipment and software. The basic configuration includes the following:

- a computer with enough RAM in primary storage to accommodate and run the software
- a hard disk drive with two floppy disk drives or one floppy disk drive
- a monitor to view the document as it is typed and edited
- a printer to receive the text from the computer and print it on paper
- a word processing software package to do your word processing

# R ecall Time

*Answer the following questions:*

1. What does the term *information overload* mean?
2. What are three documents that are processed in an office?
3. What are three benefits to the company that installs a word processing system?
4. What is the essential equipment that makes up a word processing system?

# Word Processing Cycle

Let's say you are now ready to process a letter. How will you proceed? The **word processing cycle** describes the way a document flows through the office from the time an idea begins through the final storage of that document. This cycle is also called the document production cycle or simply work flow. It includes the input, processing, and output steps, as shown in figure 3–1. In chapter 2, the information processing cycle was discussed using the same terms. Don't become confused. The meanings of these terms are the same. The difference is that here the functions are specific to processing words.

**Input**  The input step begins the document processing because it is here that ideas originate. Most of the time, someone will provide you with the material to type. However, one day someone in your company may ask you to compose letters, memos, or reports yourself. Then you will become an originator of documents.

You can use various methods to input ideas. New methods include inputting from rough draft copy or from copy scanned by an optical character recognition scanner. However, many originators still use the traditional methods of longhand, shorthand, and machine dictation.

Which method is most used and preferred? Well, it depends. The reasons originators might prefer one method over another are often as different as the originators' personalities.

*Rough Drafting*  Today, most originators who have access to a keyboard and computer prefer composing their thoughts quickly as rough draft copy. Using a microcomputer is fast. Typing errors are easily corrected, and typing speed is relatively unimportant. What is important is to capture an idea so it is not lost.

A document's draft copy is saved to disk and the input step is completed. This disk is often then handed to an office worker to finalize (process, print, and store).

*Optical Character Recognition Scanning*  In offices, you can use an optical character recognition (OCR) scanner to convert the printed characters from one machine into a form that can easily be read and saved by another machine.

As an example, suppose you work in a legal office. An attorney who is new to the firm is preparing a fifteen-page legal document for a client. The attorney asks you to begin with a similar document that he used at his old firm. Ninety percent of the old document will be the same in the new one. You take a printed copy of the old document to your OCR scanner and scan the characters into your computer's memory. The fifteen pages now in memory can easily be edited, proofread, stored, and printed. You have to type only between one and two pages. The time it takes you and the attorney is minimal.

*Longhand*  The most popular traditional way to input is still longhand. Why? Because paper and a pencil are usually available. The main advantage of using this method is that no one else needs to get involved

---

■ FIGURE 3–1

*WORD PROCESSING CYCLE*
*(Involves Processing Words)*

**Input**
Rough Drafted Copy
OCR Scanned Copy
Longhand
Shorthand
Machine Dictation

**Processing**
Revisions to Documents

**Output**
Printing
Photocopying
Distributing

Modern Office Procedures

Leslie has just been hired as a computer operator in an old-established real estate office in town. She wants to do her best and learn as much as she can on this job. Leslie hopes someday to get her real estate license and sell residential properties herself. She views the job as a way to learn the business from the ground up.

Almost immediately, Leslie senses something is wrong when she asks the other three office workers questions to clarify her work assignments and office procedures. Two of them, Tracy and Craig, seem to intentionally withhold important information from her. It appears to Leslie that they are only going to dole out information when it is needed.

The third office worker, Kim, is more helpful. Leslie finds herself feeling closer to Kim and using her as a role model.

1. Why do some office workers have the attitude that they must keep, rather than share, certain knowledge and special procedures?
2. The attitude practiced by Tracy and Craig leads to human relation problems. What are some other outcomes that businesses can expect when employees practice this attitude and are allowed to get away with it?
3. Some people work with the attitude "As soon as I learn something new, I give it away." What does this mean? How can this attitude help the organization and the office worker?

in the process. Though longhand is the least efficient and most time-consuming method, it offers the advantage of convenience to originators.

*Shorthand* The need for the study of shorthand is highly debated. Your school may not offer shorthand and transcription courses. It might instead offer notehand or speedwriting, or it might offer nothing along these lines.

Still, many originators prefer dictating to an office worker who can take shorthand. The office worker can help with the right idea or phrase and remember correct dates, times, and addresses. Those who have used this method to dictate letters and other documents find it difficult to input any other way.

Shorthand is an expensive way to input because it ties up two people's time. That is why usually only top managers are allowed to work one-on-one with a secretary in this way. For example, a secretary might take shorthand dictation but go back to the desk, quickly keyboard a rough draft copy of the dictation, and save the copy on a disk. Then this disk can be given to any office specialist to finalize the document.

*Machine Dictation* Research shows that machine dictation is a more cost efficient input method than shorthand. What contributes to this efficiency? For one thing, machine dictation involves only one person. For another, people speak their thoughts about five times faster than they write them.

Using a machine to dictate has two important drawbacks. One, many originators do not like to talk to a machine. Two, the task of preparing to dictate is time-consuming, and originators often consider it just one

**Dwight W. Clark**
*Industry Consultant*
*IBM Corporation*

Q: Mr. Clark, what is the relationship between data processing and word processing?

A: Both data processing and word processing use electronic technology. Data processing is the act of a computer handling information to produce results based on a given set of internally stored instructions. Data processing provides a number of functional uses of computers. Word processing is an example of functional use. Word processing is the act of using a computer to prepare documents.

Q: How knowledgeable should secretaries be in this area?

A: One goal is to work more effectively with less effort or "work smarter." One of the means to achieve that goal is to use computers to your advantage. You should have a conceptual or basic understanding of data processing. Due to the intensity of use, you will need substantial knowledge about word processing. Sharpen your [reasoning] skills to recognize and [think of] other ways to use the technology to work for you.

---

more thing to do. However, a person who prepares for machine dictation by first jotting down on paper some key ideas in a logical sequence is successful with this input method.

Chapter 4 will provide more complete information on automated voice processing using machine dictation and transcription equipment.

**Processing** Once a document has been originated or input in some form, the next step is processing. During this step, you first keyboard at your rough draft speed and later edit for content and typing errors. It is rare for a document to be typed directly onto good letterhead paper. Corrections are easy and are often necessary to make. In most offices, one or more revisions occur.

With each revision, you resave the document to disk using an appropriate file name. Completing a log sheet by noting file name, keyboarding time, and any special instructions at this point makes good sense.

Log sheets were initially developed in the late 1960s to measure productivity. In some large word processing centers today, they are still used to manage, track, and coordinate the work flow into and out of the center. At the processing step, however, a disk or document log sheet is used at an individual workstation to keep track of documents that have been saved.

Log sheets indicate on which disk and under which file name a particular document is stored. This is important because often documents stored on disks become the basis for new documents that must be created. (This situation was illustrated in the example of a legal document that was scanned by an OCR.) If a previous document is used, then a printout of it is made, marked up, edited, stored under a different file name, and printed. A log sheet should always be tailored to the individual needs of an office.

**Output**  In the output step, a document is completed by printing and distributing it. If what appears on the monitor screen is what you want, send the document to the printer and get the final copy. You can then make photocopies for distribution.

Originals and paper copies are usually distributed through either the U.S. Postal Service or interoffice mail. Today, distribution is more likely to occur through telecommunication technology that uses phone systems. Facsimile (fax) and electronic mail (E-Mail) are two examples of these new distribution methods, which are discussed more in chapter 4. Telecommunications devices are popular because they transmit data, text, and images quickly, simply, and relatively inexpensively compared with other traditional mail services.

# R ecall Time

*Answer the following questions:*

1. What are the three steps in the word processing cycle?
2. Why is machine dictation more efficient than shorthand?
3. Why would an originator prefer to input using the shorthand skills of an office worker?
4. If you were processing a letter, which input method would you prefer to work from? Explain your preference.

## Word Processing Settings

When you picture yourself working, what kind of setting do you see yourself in? You can choose your work environment from the many that are available. Job satisfaction and work environment are connected, so this choice is an important one. One caution: Don't become too content. Stay flexible. Recognize that office settings will continue to change as new technologies are introduced, and workers must continually adapt to those changes.

The three most common office settings in which people process information are traditional, centralized, and decentralized. The setting often determines the procedures and methods used to process information.

**Traditional** In the traditional office setting, you work for one or two managers. Your desk is equipped with an electronic typewriter or possibly a microcomputer, and it usually sits near or directly outside the manager's office.

The important consideration in processing work in a traditional setting is keeping the flow of work orderly. Your job description is lengthy. It usually includes taking dictation (either machine or shorthand), typing, proofreading, filing, greeting clients, scheduling appointments, preparing itineraries, and reproducing materials.

**Centralized** When IBM introduced word processing equipment in the late 1960s, many companies reorganized the traditional office and created office workers who were specialists. This reorganization was done primarily to justify purchasing new and expensive automated equipment.

The **centralized information processing approach** specializes and combines like tasks in the office. In this way, hiring for future growth is controlled. In addition, fewer people are needed to do routine, often repetitive tasks like word processing. For example, a task that used to require three secretaries with typewriters can now be produced by one specialist using automated equipment. The savings in labor costs offset the cost of the equipment.

A specialist is an office worker whose job description contains one type of duty. For example, in a centralized approach, a specialist performs either administrative (nontyping) or correspondence (typing) activities. If your job title is administrative specialist, you probably will not have a typewriter at your desk because you will not need one. You will perform all tasks except typing. If an envelope or preprinted form has to be typed quickly, a nearby typewriter will be shared by perhaps as many as five other administrative specialists.

If your job title is correspondence specialist, you will work in a word processing center. A **word processing center** is a centrally located area where all typing activities are performed. It is equipped with state-of-the-art equipment and is staffed with office specialists who are thoroughly trained on and use that equipment. Today, the word processing center is likely to be called the information processing center because word processing and data, image, and voice processing are performed there.

Many organizations have moved away from the centralized information approach. Nevertheless, you will still find centralized information processing in some large companies. Companies that have a centralized system claim that it provides for a more controlled supervision over cost, employees, equipment, and procedures.

**Decentralized** Decentralized information processing combines the best characteristics from the traditional and centralized settings. Because of this, you are apt to find a type of decentralized approach in most offices today. In the **decentralized information processing approach,** documents are processed in different locations throughout the company, rather than in one centralized location. These locations are usually in close proximity to a few or several executives or managers.

This approach is flexible. Therefore, many variations exist. Typically, however, this is how it might work when comparing it with a traditional setting:

Burt has just changed jobs. His last job, at the Williams School District, was traditional. He worked for three assistant superintendents and always felt busy and under pressure. He did administrative tasks such as scheduling appointments, answering phones, and helping the superintendents prepare for their numerous meetings each week.

At any given time, Burt had several reports in progress at his microcomputer. He often felt rushed and stressed because these reports were never finalized by a superintendent until the last minute, and he was the only one in the office to do them. Often Burt worked beyond five o'clock. He liked the superintendents and knew they depended on him. However, money for hiring an additional secretary to help him was not in the budget, so he chose to leave the district.

Burt now works for Horizon Property Management. Horizon has adopted a type of decentralized approach and has minicenters throughout the company. A minicenter or satellite center is often a small information processing center that is geographically removed from a large information processing center in a company.

Horizon has two minicenters and one information processing center. Burt is an information processing specialist in the public relations and marketing minicenter. He prepares documents for as many as six executives. He likes this job. He does not do administrative tasks; he only does keyboarding tasks. Because he can plan his work and is rarely interrupted, he gets more work done and always leaves the office on time.

The managers in Horizon's public relations and marketing departments like the decentralized minicenter approach as well. They appreciate that Burt knows the formatting requirements and work flow procedures. They consider Burt to be an expert in the specialized software and automated equipment used in both departments. Horizon considers him as part of the team and a vital link to its overall success.

The decentralized approach provides for a flexible, responsible, and loosely structured environment that can be tailored to the needs of individual users. It is gaining in popularity as the cost of microcomputers decreases and local area networks become more commonplace in the work environment.

**Local area networks (LANs)** are often found in decentralized settings. They include communication software and wire cables that physically link computers in the same general area. LANs reduce hardware and operating costs. Several computers and users can share data files, software, and equipment such as laser printers, hard disk drives, and modems.

How does a LAN work? Imagine yourself working at your desk with only a monitor and keyboard, yet with access to all the data files in the company's computer that is located no more than one thousand feet from you. The number of computers in a LAN varies widely. Small LANs typically connect two or twenty-five computers: large LANs can connect as many as ten thousand computers.

## Important Word Processing Skills

Office work is fun and exciting if you are prepared to accept the challenge of change. Change in the office happens when new technologies

*Local area networks allow users to share data files, software, and other equipment such as laser printers.*

are introduced and procedures that you normally follow must alter. To be successful, you need to be adaptable and demonstrate up-to-date work skills in the word processing environment. Employers will recognize, through promotion or an increase in salary, an employee who shows a willingness to learn new equipment and update job skills.

If you were interviewing for a job, the employer might want to know the following about your office skills:

1. Can you maintain your composure while typing with speed and accuracy in meeting production deadlines?
2. Are you able to plan and organize your work load in meeting deadlines?
3. Are you flexible in your thinking and able to adjust to new ideas as they are introduced?
4. Can you proofread accurately for typing errors and changes in spelling, punctuation, and grammar?
5. Can you correctly edit the content of typewritten material and business documents?
6. Can you operate the computer using word processing software as comfortably as you can operate an electric or electronic typewriter?
7. Are you able to read, understand, and use equipment and software manuals in completing job tasks?
8. Can you follow written and spoken directions?
9. Do you ask questions if you don't understand what someone has said to you?
10. Are you willing to be trained in new technologies and equipment that save time, reduce errors, and end much routine work?

You may be saying to yourself, "I won't have those skills when I apply for my first job." And you'll be right—so don't worry; it's OK. Not all skills you may need on your first job can be learned or perfected in the classroom. Employers recognize this. You learn skills, proper work techniques, and shortcuts in the classroom. Then, as you work on the job, these improve and are reinforced. Most employers will agree that the two most important qualities you bring to your first few jobs are your positive attitude and your willingness to learn and do a good job.

## Career Opportunities in Word Processing

Career opportunities in word processing are abundant, and additional growth is projected. An office worker has traditional and nontraditional word processing career opportunities in business. These opportunities include office, telecommuting, and secretarial service careers.

**Office** The size of the business you work for and the office setting in which work is processed will determine your job title. Most jobs will involve the processing of common office documents like the letter, memorandum, report, and statistical table.

You may be the only office specialist in a small office situation. Or you may be one secretary out of hundreds working in a word processing center or a minicenter of a large corporation. Regardless of the job title you're given upon employment, you've chosen a profession in much demand when you prepare to be an office worker. You're especially lucky because a wide number of career choices are available within the traditional, centralized, and decentralized work settings.

In a traditional environment, your career moves often depend on your manager's ability to be promoted. When managers are promoted, they sometimes choose to take their secretary. The advantage of the traditional office setup is that you have a variety of experiences to bring to your next job because you've had to do every task—administrative and typing.

In a centralized environment, career paths for employees may be limited owing to a lack of advancement opportunities within a center. Some specialized job titles and job descriptions in a centralized approach are as follows:

- *lead operator.* A lead operator is responsible for formatting, producing, and revising complicated documents. This person exercises independent action when interpreting instructions to produce a quality document, understands proofreader marks, and assumes full responsibility for the accuracy and completeness of documents. He or she can use all technological devices in a center with proficiency.
- *word processing specialist.* A word processing specialist possesses adequate typing skills and a good knowledge of grammar, punctuation, spelling, and formatting. This person can use dictionaries, handbooks, and other reference manuals in completing projects. She or he is responsible for routine transcription and text processing as assigned.
- *proofreader.* A proofreader is responsible for proofreading typed copy for text content, style consistency, spelling, punctuation, grammar, and typographical errors.
- *word processing supervisor.* A word processing supervisor is responsible for the overall operation of a center. This person schedules and coordinates work flow and helps word processing personnel produce documents. He or she establishes and maintains quality standards while analyzing production data and procedures.
- *administrative assistant.* An administrative assistant is responsible for providing administrative support functions such as filing and photocopying; maintaining calendars, records, and lists; and providing special secretarial services to executives.

In a decentralized environment, you will find career opportunities similar to those described in both the traditional and centralized approaches.

Now let's consider some office settings other than traditional, centralized, and decentralized. Most office workers get their first experiences at a business location. However, lots of unique opportunities are available if you have salable skills and good work attitudes. What are some? Telecommuting and owning a secretarial service are two popular suggestions.

# LARGE OFFICE/SMALL OFFICE: What's Your Preference?

### Word Processing

Many large offices have word processing centers to handle the large volumes of correspondence done within a company. Individuals from different departments within an office send their letters, memos, reports, and other documents to this center to be processed. The center may have only one or many operators to do the word processing. It often has a lead operator to coordinate the work and a proofreader to proofread the finished product.

In a small office, word processing duties are usually only one part of the total job description for each secretary or other office support person. However, sufficient equipment and software are available for the word processing to get done. In addition, a secretary or support person is totally responsible for the finished product including the proofreading.

*Are you interested in doing word processing only, or do you want to do a variety of office tasks, including word processing? Would you choose to be a word processing operator in a large company, or to have word processing duties be part of your job in a small company? Why?*

**Telecommuting Telecommuting** refers to the ability of individuals to work at home and communicate with their office by using personal computers and communication lines. With a personal computer, an employee can access the main computer at the office. Electronic mail allows an employee to read and answer mail and messages. Company data bases are accessed to complete projects at home and then transmit those completed projects back to the office.

Would you like to work out of your home one day? Some argue against the benefits of this approach, but the trend toward increased telecommuting is growing. It is predicted that by the end of the 1990s, more than 10 percent of the work force will be telecommuters. Most of these people will probably arrange their schedule so they can telecommute two or three days a week.

The biggest advantage of telecommuting is that it provides flexibility. It allows companies and employees to work out arrangements that can increase productivity and at the same time meet the personal needs of individual employees. Other advantages include the following:

- reduces the time needed to commute to the office each week
- eliminates the need to travel during poor weather conditions
- provides a convenient and comfortable work setting for disabled employees or workers recovering from injuries or illnesses
- allows employees to combine work with the personal responsibilities of family, home, and further schooling

### OFFICE TIP

Set some realistic short- and long-term goals for yourself now. For example, it may be unrealistic to expect that within two years, you'll be running your own secretarial service. But ten years from now, circumstances might be right for this to happen. By setting goals, you become committed to making them happen.

*Telecommuting provides a unique option for workers who prefer to work for companies from their homes.*

Not all employees would enjoy telecommuting; some disadvantages exist. Often employees realize they are not disciplined in completing tasks on time. They may need a more formal work environment to stay on a task. Additionally, they may need social interaction with co-workers to be happy. Working out of their home may not meet these employees' needs.

**Secretarial Service** Perhaps your dream is to become your own boss. Owning your own secretarial business is a natural choice for a few veteran office specialists. With a one-person operation, you could start modestly and stay that way or choose to expand by adding office staff later (see figure 3–2). All you need to begin with is a personal computer, a word processing software package, a desk, some office supplies, a telephone, and most of all, your up-to-date skills.

Where would you get work to do? Could you earn enough money to survive? If careful attention is given to surveying secretarial needs in your community, the answers to these questions are easy.

For example, often secretarial services are located close to a university or community college. These services are equipped with a microcomputer and laser printer. They process school documents like term papers, research reports, and theses for students and faculty.

Secretarial services are also located in large office building complexes. Small offices within these complexes either may be unable to afford a full-time secretary or may have chosen not to invest at this time in a microcomputer and software. These offices will welcome the services you can provide.

Depending on your circumstances, it may be appropriate for you to run your secretarial service out of your home. For example, Rita has

---

# Melissa's Secretarial Services

"Word Processing You Can Afford"

Specializing in:

| | |
|---|---|
| Business Letters | Repetitious Letters |
| Business Forms | Reports |
| Indented Typing | Resumes |
| Mailing Labels | Specifications |
| Manuscripts | Statistical Typing |
| Newsletters | Term Papers |
| Proposals | Theses/Dissertations |

Accuracy Guaranteed
Professional Quality
IBM Computer—Laser Printer
Free Estimates
Pickup & Delivery Available

900-9090 by appointment only

*Background: B.A. in Business Education (Secretarial Subjects)
Word Processing Instructor for North Community College*

---

two small children and she wants to stay home with them. Rita's home is located near hotels and resorts. She provides excellent secretarial services to business travelers. She will even pick up and deliver business reports and correspondence. The hotels recommend her services to guests because she has earned a reputation of dependability and consistent quality service—true marks of a professional.

Why is operating a secretarial service appealing to many? You can set your priorities, work whatever hours of the day or night you choose, and accept or reject work depending on your personal schedule and choice. Often, two or more secretarial services will help each other by referring clients to each other if one gets overbooked or wants to take some time off.

If you have the technical skills combined with the desire and drive to do professional work, career opportunities will always be available. You will find, over the years, that your work options are many. The problem will be in selecting the right opportunity for you. Remember that often professional careers begin with a secretarial position. So when you work, try to work in occupations that interest you.

# R ecall Time

*Answer the following questions:*

1. What is the difference between the traditional, centralized, and decentralized information processing settings?
2. Why are local area networks gaining in popularity?
3. What are the top five word processing skills all office workers should possess? Defend your choices.
4. What are three benefits to telecommuting? Would you like to telecommute? Why or why not?

## ■ INFORMATION PROCESSING SOFTWARE

You will use several major software packages with your computers to process office information. Seven types used in today's offices are word processing, spreadsheet, accounting, data base management, graphics, desktop publishing, and integrated packages.

### Word Processing

A wide selection of word processing software is on the market today. In most cases, you will work in an office where the software is already there and in use on a microcomputer. You will, therefore, need to learn and use whatever package the office has chosen.

On the other hand, you might be asked to select the word processing software to use. How do you decide which software package to buy? You will need to gather some information and answer questions such as the following before making the right choice:

- What are some common features among word processing programs?
- Do I need certain pieces of equipment to make the software work?
- What are the most popular software packages in use today?
- How much will a package cost?

Before you make a buying decision, first assess your word processing needs. Do you need word processing just to do simple letters and memos? Or will you use it for lengthy and sometimes technical reports that must be published? It is not practical to buy a fancy sports car (other than for satisfying the desire to own one) if your needs and your pocketbook can't support the decision. The same is true of computer equipment and software. A sensible guideline to follow is to buy as much as you can afford, based on your known needs.

**Features** Once needs have been identified, then you can begin to look at the features required to meet them. The most practical feature for any

word processing package is that it be user friendly. A user-friendly software package is easy to learn and to use. The other basic word processing features can be broken down into three types: writing and editing, formatting and printing, and supplementary.

*Writing and Editing* Writing and editing features allow you to control what happens on the screen while you are typing or editing your document. Common features include word wrap, word inserting and deleting, block operations, scrolling, and the ability to search and replace words or groups of words. These features also include special type enhancements like boldface, underlining, and italics.

*Formatting and Printing* Formatting features allow you to arrange written material so it is presented attractively on a page. Setting tabs, margins, and line spacing are among these features. Printing features can create headers and footers, do page numbering, and control the placement of line endings on a page.

*Supplementary* You may want to splurge and consider other abilities contained in certain word processing packages. These include a spelling check program, a thesaurus, the mail-merge option, drawing and math capabilities, and help features.

Table 3–1 describes some word processing features. As in most purchases, the more features you choose, the more it will cost you. That is why you must decide first which word processing features you must have, and which features would be nice to have but are not necessary.

| WORD PROCESSING FEATURES | | |
|---|---|---|
| Writing and Editing | Formatting and Printing | Supplementary |
| word wrap | setting tabs | spell-check |
| word inserting | setting margins | thesaurus |
| word deleting | line spacing | mail merge |
| block operations | headers and footers | drawing |
| scrolling | page numbering | math |
| search and replace | line endings | help features |
| type enhancements | | |

**Cost and Compatible Systems** Word processing software packages will range in price from as little as twenty dollars to over four hundred dollars. Among the most popular packages used in offices today are WordPerfect, PFS: Professional Write, Microsoft Word, and MultiMate Advantage.

These word processing packages and others are available for many brands of computers. Remember to specify which computer you will be using when buying any software. Why? Because each software package is written based on a computer's operating system instructions. No one standard operating system is used in the personal computer environment.

When the IBM Personal Computer (IBM PC) became the industry standard, many other microcomputer manufacturers introduced their version of the IBM PC design. These other versions are called **compatibles** or **clones.** They have the distinction of using the same operating system instructions as the IBM PC. Some popular clones are COMPAQ, Leading Edge, and Tandy computers.

The most popular operating systems in use today are the MS-DOS and PC-DOS, which are compatible; the Macintosh; and OS/2. Software written for Apple's Macintosh computer, for example, will not be understood when loaded into an IBM PC system (see figure 3–3). Sometimes the same software package—Microsoft Word, for example—is written for more than one operating system. Then you must buy two separate packages if you have an IBM PC and a Macintosh computer.

For example, Sharon and Bob work in the same office. Sharon has a Macintosh computer and Bob works on an IBM OS/2 computer. If Sharon is out ill, Bob cannot use his IBM computer to take over some work on one of Sharon's disks. Bob has to continue what Sharon started on Sharon's Macintosh. This is cumbersome and inefficient.

Can you see why if you were the boss, you would want to hire someone who knew both operating systems? How is the company's business affected if Bob only knows how to operate software that runs on IBM? How is the company's business affected if he knows how to operate both systems?

Without a standardized operating system, software selection must be made very carefully. Many offices are buying only one brand of office equipment to avoid problems like those faced by Bob and Sharon.

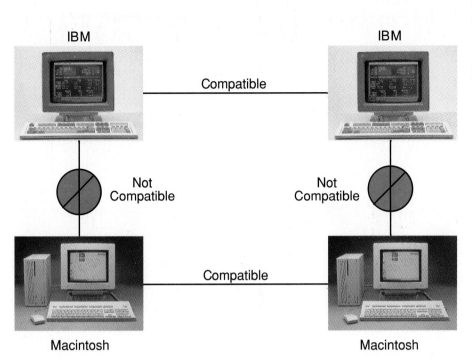

IBM     Compatible     IBM

Not Compatible     Not Compatible

Macintosh     Compatible     Macintosh

One last reminder: When buying software, be sure to ask for the most current version or update.

## Spreadsheets

**Spreadsheets** are financial planning tools that perform mathematical calculations. Electronic spreadsheets replace accountants' columnar pads, pencils, and calculators.

An electronic spreadsheet software program makes it easy to calculate depreciation, prepare financial statements, plan budgets, manage cash flow, and analyze alternatives. When businesses need to calculate and analyze figures quickly and easily, they use spreadsheets. Spreadsheets were one of the first business applications processed on the microcomputer.

A spreadsheet consists of columns and rows made up in a grid pattern. The location where a column and row intersect (for example, A3 or E13, with letters representing columns and numbers indicating rows) is a cell on the spreadsheet. The average spreadsheet has thousands of cells. A label (name), value (number), or mathematical formula is written at a cell location.

Suppose you are a member of a formal dance committee. You are responsible for keeping track of the budget. You have fifteen hundred dollars to spend on the dance. How can you spend the money in the most efficient way?

*Changes to financial statements can be entered easily at a moment's notice when offices use spreadsheet software.*

*Financial plans and budget tasks are easier to do with the aid of spreadsheet software.*

| A | B |
|---|---|
| DANCE BUDGET | |
| DECORATIONS | $ 300.00 |
| REFRESHMENTS | 520.00 |
| DJ OR BAND | 250.00 |
| DANCE FAVORS | 120.00 |
| INVITATIONS | 210.00 |
| PROGRAMS | 100.00 |
| TOTAL | $ 1,500.00 |

An easy way to determine how you should spend the money is to create an electronic spreadsheet. Type the expense categories you anticipate—like decorations, refreshments, DJ or band, favors, invitations and programs—in the first column, called column A. In column B, type the amounts that were spent in each category for last year's dance. As the last entry in column B, write a formula to add up all the expense amounts in that column. This is your starting point.

As the committee chooses the decorations and determines the cost, replace last year's figure with the new amount. Here you can see a spreadsheet's power. Because you used a formula to total column B amounts, the computer will automatically recalculate a new total expense amount with each change you make. In this way, as your plans develop, you can always make sure you will not go over the budgeted amount of fifteen hundred dollars (see figure 3–4).

The value in one cell of your spreadsheet may depend on the value in another cell. Therefore, you can use the spreadsheet for forecasting. This process is called what-if analysis. You can change the value in one cell and immediately see how it affects the values in other cells. Suppose you go over budget. If your cost for refreshments is based on serving soft drinks, alter the figure and base it on serving a less expensive punch drink. The computer will show through a projection how much closer to the budget you can get.

Table 3–2 shows features of spreadsheet software. Some common features are variable column width, recalculation, and formatting and copying of cells. Lotus 1-2-3 is the most popular business spreadsheet. Other popular packages include VP-Planner and SuperCalc5. Spreadsheets can be purchased for as little as thirty dollars and as much as five hundred dollars.

| SPREADSHEET FEATURES | | |
|---|---|---|
| variable column width | ranges | graphics |
| inserting rows and columns | copy | automatic spillover |
| deleting rows and columns | recalculation | windows |
| formatting cells | locking cells | titles |
| sorting | hiding cells | |

## Accounting

**Accounting software** packages are a variation of a spreadsheet program. Using computers does not change basic accounting concepts. Only the tools and methods change. Many accounting activities are routine and repetitive. Money transaction activities require the accuracy and speed that the computer gives. Accounting software is popular in both small and large companies because management decisions depend on accurate and up-to-date accounting information about each phase of a business.

You might be called upon to use an accounting package to keep your company's general ledger. A general ledger software package contains a set of all accounts for a particular business. These may include the following:

- *accounts payable*—the amounts that must be paid to creditors for items purchased.
- *accounts receivable*—the amounts that are owed by customers from credit transactions.
- *expense accounts*—the amounts that are owed for other expenses, including utilities and rent.

These accounting terms and procedures are discussed in chapter 8.

General ledger software generates bills or statements of accounts from the data contained in the accounts payable files. All the expenses of a company are totaled from the individual accounts, and the income is totaled from all the revenue accounts. From this instant summarization, the computer gives the overall income picture—profit or loss—for the company within a few minutes.

Other popular accounting software packages are payroll and inventory control. For example, payroll applications are an efficient use of a computer's ability to accomplish repetitive tasks quickly. A payroll package automatically calculates gross pay, adds any bonuses, subtracts the necessary deductions, totals the net pay, and even prepares the paycheck for each employee.

## Data Base Management

**Data base management software** computerizes record keeping and information tasks. It is often called an electronic file cabinet. Data base management involves using a computer rather than a manual system

O F F I C E   T I P

When you first open a new software package and before you start to use it, read and follow the installation procedure carefully. Most software companies will allow you to legally make one backup copy of the original set of disks. Do this immediately. Then put your originals away in a safe location and use the set of copied disks.

to store, manipulate, retrieve, and report on information. Data managers allow you to enter information once, perform a complex calculation or sorting routine on that information, and then produce three different reports drawing on the results.

What kind of information goes into a data base? If you work for a nonprofit organization, you might create a mailing list data base consisting of names, addresses, and phone numbers. If you work for a small business like a video store, you might want to set up an inventory data base that tracks videos on hand and checked out, rental prices, and money received. Schools, hospitals, restaurants, and in fact all types of businesses have to store and manage data.

Large organizations collect great volumes of data that different people may want to access in different ways. Thus, computerizing can yield enormous gains. These gains result from better use of information and from a more efficient means of processing raw unorganized data into useful reports.

**Functions** In general, most data base managers carry out the following functions:

- enter data according to a predefined format
- retrieve specific data to be viewed or printed
- change or delete data
- search a file for certain data
- sort or rearrange data into different order, as needed
- produce printed reports that provide meaningful and organized information

**Terminology** The three most important terms you must understand when using any data base system are field, record, and file (see figure 3–5). Each unit of information is called a **field.** A set of fields that describes one logical unit of information is called a **record.** In the video store example, a logical unit of information is a videotape. On each videotape record, you might have five fields: title, length, actors, rental cost, and rating. A collection of records that share the same format—that have the same fields—is called a **file.** If the store has twenty-five hundred videotapes, for example, the videotape data base or file will have twenty-five hundred records, with each record containing five fields.

Offices create data base files to maintain employee records, customer records, inventory, and invoice information. In addition, data managers are often used with word processors to prepare mass mailings by supplying names and addresses while creating form letters.

Why do businesses use data base management software? How does data base management software help the office worker? The ability to retrieve, sort, and analyze data quickly can make the difference between a company's success and failure. It can also improve an employee's ability to work more efficiently. With a manual system, file cabinets use a lot of space. In addition, often several departments may keep the same data. This duplication of data adds up to a waste of time, effort, and space. In addition, it can lead to confusion or errors when data must be updated.

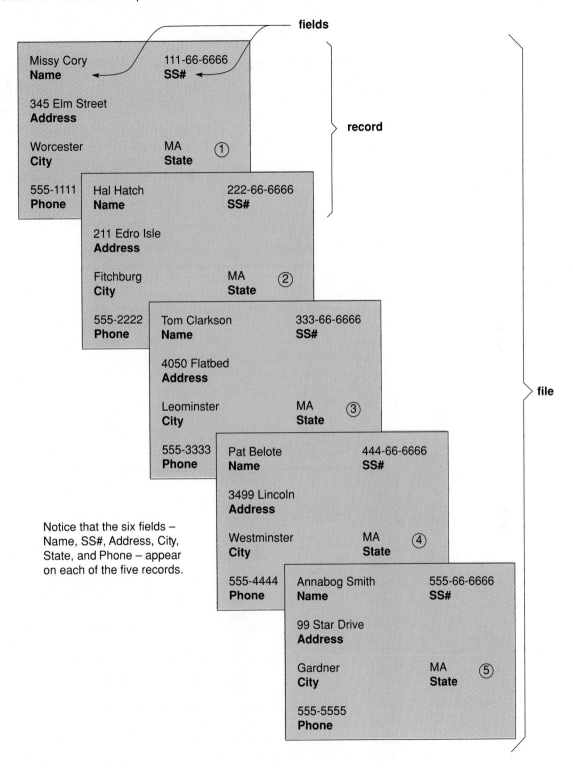

fields

Missy Cory
**Name**

111-66-6666
**SS#**

345 Elm Street
**Address**

Worcester
**City**

MA
**State**

①

record

555-1111
**Phone**

Hal Hatch
**Name**

222-66-6666
**SS#**

211 Edro Isle
**Address**

Fitchburg
**City**

MA
**State**

②

555-2222
**Phone**

Tom Clarkson
**Name**

333-66-6666
**SS#**

4050 Flatbed
**Address**

Leominster
**City**

MA
**State**

③

555-3333
**Phone**

Pat Belote
**Name**

444-66-6666
**SS#**

3499 Lincoln
**Address**

Westminster
**City**

MA
**State**

④

555-4444
**Phone**

Annabog Smith
**Name**

555-66-6666
**SS#**

99 Star Drive
**Address**

Gardner
**City**

MA
**State**

⑤

555-5555
**Phone**

file

Notice that the six fields –
Name, SS#, Address, City,
State, and Phone – appear
on each of the five records.

# Recall Time

*Answer the following questions:*

1. What are five features common to word processing software? Describe the function of each.
2. What are three common examples of how businesses use spreadsheet software?
3. How are accounting software packages useful to most businesses?
4. What is the purpose of data base management software in the office?
5. What is the relationship between the data base terms *field, record,* and *file?*

## Graphics

**Graphics software** presents numerical data clearly and quickly in visual form on a computer. In business, one way to communicate the meaning of numerical data is with graphs and charts. Business professionals and administrative support workers use graphs to define and analyze problems, summarize and condense information, and spot trends or trouble spots. Further, business reports that summarize ideas graphically are more interesting to read and more persuasive with customers.

When you use a graphics software package, you will be able to do the following:

■ convert data into a variety of charts and graphs such as line, bar, and pie forms

*Line and pie graphs are shown here using Microsoft Excel software.*

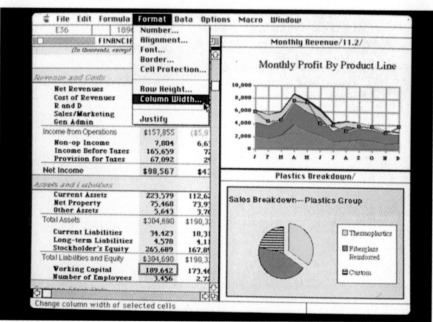

- customize a graphic by changing text sizes and styles
- provide options to add legends, titles, labels, shadings, and horizontal or vertical grids

To produce professional-looking documents using graphics software, your computer system must have a few additional hardware devices. The computer, for example, will need a graphics memory card to display graphs. Most users will then be able to display a graphics image on a monochrome (one-color) monitor or preferably on a color monitor. A graphics image is formed by sectioning a monitor screen into thousands of individual row and column positions. These positions are called picture elements, or pixels. Each pixel represents a tiny dot on the computer screen.

Most office professionals agree that the final printouts of computer graphics are only as good as the output devices that prepare them. You can print graphs using most printers such as dot matrix, laser, and ink jet printers, and plotters. The highest-quality output, however, will result from a high-resolution monitor and printer. The term resolution refers to the clarity of an image or graph. The cost of graphics equipment often reflects in direct proportion the quality of high or low resolution.

As an office worker, you will prepare either analytical graphics or presentation graphics with a graphics software package. Analytical business graphics view and analyze data and present this information as line, bar, and pie graphs and charts. These graphics show important relationships between numbers. They also reduce the amount of paper used for printing long, hard-to-read statistical reports. Presentation graphics impress those attending meetings or conferences by making a presentation more interesting, clear, and persuasive.

*A bar graph can be created, displayed, and printed using software like Lotus 1-2-3.*

# Desktop Publishing

In the early 1980s, most people thought of computers primarily as machines for word processing. Today, word processing and graphics capabilities are united in one software package called desktop publishing. **Desktop publishing software** combines text and graphics in various sizes and styles to create an attractive document. These documents are of such high quality that they rival professionally published works.

In the late 1980s, many businesses became intensely interested in desktop publishing. An important part of success in business is the ability to communicate your message clearly. A great deal of business communication is written. Therefore, a clean, crisp, and professional-looking document increases the chances of a business's message being read. Good ideas have to create immediate impact to cut through the flood of messages people receive daily.

Have you ever received four or five different items to read at once? Why did you read particular ones first? The overall appearance of some documents is better than that of others at inviting your eyes to read. Today, desktop publishing software combined with laser print technology turns ordinary facts into influential business communication.

With desktop publishing software, the same person who writes a text can typeset and design final pages complete with graphics. Publishing in-house (within a company) with desktop publishing provides greater freedom and more control over the entire process. No longer is a businessperson at the mercy of professional artists. Last-minute text editing and formatting changes are fast and easy to make. These changes are simple to make because in desktop publishing, **WYSIWYG,** or "what you see is what you get." Your printed page will be essentially the same as what you see on your computer screen.

**Components** What do you need to make desktop publishing work? Components of a desktop publishing system include page composition software; a computer; system software; and devices for display, input, and output.

Desktop publishing uses special software to convert text prepared under word processing programs into typeset text. The text is combined with computer-generated illustrations to produce finished pages. Two examples of desktop publishing software are PageMaker and Ventura. In addition, desktop publishing requires a microcomputer equipped with a graphics card and large amounts of both primary and secondary storage.

**Terminology** When you use desktop publishing, you will use unique typesetting terminology (see figure 3–6). To meet the challenge of using desktop publishing, become familiar with the following terms:

- *typeface design*—a particular style or shape of letters; a family of type that has a common design, such as Courier, Helvetica, or Times Roman.
- *font*—a complete set of letters, numbers, and symbols of a specific typeface.

■ FIGURE 3–6

*TYPESETTING TERMINOLOGY*

Typeface Design
Font
Point Size
Type Style
Portrait Fonts
Landscape Fonts
Leading
Kerning

Suppose you are an office worker at Mel's Image Production Company. The company creates and produces printed documents for publications and local businesses. Mr. Owen, the owner, has asked you to help him with a software-buying decision. He knows that you've studied desktop publishing in school. He wants you to make a list of the benefits and limitations of this software compared with a word processing package.

The office manager, Ian, is already familiar with a leading word processing package that boasts of being able to produce printed documents for publications. Ian is pressing to buy a word processing package instead of desktop publishing. But you sense that Mr. Owen feels the company needs to jump on the bandwagon and get with desktop publishing.

1. What benefits and limitations are on the list you prepare for Mr. Owen? In other words, if you were making the decision, what would convince you to buy desktop publishing software over word processing software?
2. What is involved in installing and using desktop publishing on a microcomputer system, compared with installing and using word processing software?

- *point size*—a measure of the height of characters where one point equals 1/72 of a vertical inch. The type you are reading now, and most of the type in this book, is 10½-point type. The main headings in each chapter are set in 12-point type.
- *type style*—a variation of a typeface, like boldface or italics, used to add contrast or emphasis.
- *portrait fonts*—print across the width of a page for vertical documents like letters and reports.
- *landscape fonts*—print across the length of a page for horizontal documents such as spreadsheets and organization charts.
- *leading*—the amount of space between lines. This book uses two points of space between the lines of type.
- *kerning*—the process of reducing the amount of space between letters or symbols to improve readability.

**Benefits**  Using desktop publishing within a company is much less expensive than going to an outside printer. For a businessperson, desktop publishing helps to present ideas powerfully and dramatically. Charts, diagrams, drawings, and even photographs can be added to documents for enhancement and clarity. Also, the ease of merging text and graphics gives a professional look to newsletters and proposals. Today, the technology for producing these documents is a part of the total integration of information systems in an office.

Many office microcomputer systems include desktop publishing software and laser printers. Desktop publishing applications are more complex than word processing applications, but you may find them stimulating and fun. Often, months of training and practice are necessary for you to reach a level of practical efficiency. However, learning the skill is worth the investment because businesses want workers knowledgeable in desktop publishing.

| Examples of Standalone Output | Versus | Example of Integrated Output |

**Word Processing**

Dear Customer,

Thank you for your order dated October 2.  I am sorry to inform you that we have no tennis uniforms in the size you request at the present time.

We are, however, expecting a shipment within the week and will be able to fill your order at that time.

Sincerely,

James Frederick
Sales Manager

**Data Base**

| Uniform Description | | | Inventory |
|---|---|---|---|
| Blue | – | Large | 20 |
| Blue | – | Medium | 100 |
| Blue | – | Small | 5 |
| Red | – | Large | 150 |
| Red | – | Medium | 29 |
| Red | – | Small | 65 |

**Spreadsheet**

Income from Sales of Uniforms

| Blue | – | Large | $ 400 |
|---|---|---|---|
| Blue | – | Medium | 170 |
| Blue | – | Small | 566 |
| Red | – | Large | 350 |
| Red | – | Medium | 175 |
| Red | – | Small | 635 |
| Total | | | $2296 |

**Letter** →

Dear Customer,

Thank you for your order dated October 2.  I am sorry to inform you that we have no red tennis uniforms in the medium-large and extra large sizes you requested.  Below is what we currently show in inventory.

**Report** →

| Red | – | Large | 150 |
|---|---|---|---|
| Red | – | Medium | 29 |
| Red | – | Small | 65 |

**Letter** →

Please let us know if we can fill your order from our existing stock.

Sincerely,

James Frederick
Sales Manager

Integrated software combines in one document a letter and inventory report.

## Integrated

**Integrated software** combines several independent software packages—such as word processing, spreadsheet, graphics, and data base—for coordinated use in one package. With integrated software, you can perform a variety of tasks uniformly and simultaneously. In comparison, **stand-alone software** performs only one task at a time—for example, word processing or graphics. You therefore cannot share information between packages. Figure 3–7 shows results of integrated versus stand-alone software.

Integrated software allows you to pass information freely and easily between tasks. This is possible because you use the same commands to perform all tasks in a similar way. Integrated software gives you the power to combine output from two or more separate application programs that normally cannot be used. For example, you can easily create a letter with a budget forecast in it.

Three examples of popular integrated software programs used in business are Microsoft Works, PFS: First Choice, and Appleworks. Some of these programs have as many as five applications within the package—word processing, spreadsheet, data base management, communications, and graphics.

# R ecall Time

*Answer the following questions:*

1. What is the difference between preparing graphs for presentations and preparing graphs for business analysis?
2. Why is desktop publishing often described as being one step beyond word processing?
3. What issues would you consider in deciding whether to use desktop publishing software instead of word processing software?
4. What are the advantages of using integrated software?

# ◼ SUMMARY

Processing information with computers makes information readily available for business use. Computers allow information to be organized, current, and prepared in an easy-to-understand format.

Word processing is the efficient processing of words or text. Some goals of word processing include increased speed and accuracy and overall improved document quality. The word processing cycle includes the input, processing, and output steps. Word processing can take place in traditional, centralized, or decentralized settings. Local area networks that physically link computers in the same general area promote the decentralized approach.

Software must be user friendly, which means it must be easy to learn and use. Word processing software helps process words or text material efficiently. Electronic spreadsheets are financial planning tools that perform mathematical calculations and are used to analyze financial data. Common accounting software packages in business today include general ledger, payroll, and inventory. Data base management software uses a computer rather than a manual system to store, manipulate, retrieve, and report on information.

Other software includes graphics to produce graphs and charts; desktop publishing, which combines text and graphics to create attractive, professionally prepared documents; and integrated packages, which combine two or more independent software packages.

Can you recall the meaning of the following points about processing information with computers?

- A word processing system consists of a computer, printer, and software.
- New methods to input in the word processing cycle include rough drafting copy at a computer and scanning with OCR readers.
- Telecommuting and secretarial services present two popular job opportunities attracting office workers.
- Before buying any software package, identify why and how you intend to use it.
- Accounting software packages are a variation of a spreadsheet program.
- Graphics software requires a few additional hardware devices to work properly.
- Desktop publishing will rival word processing, as it goes one step beyond and produces higher-quality documents.
- Data base management software processes raw unorganized data into useful reports or listings.
- Integrated software uses the same commands to perform tasks of combined software.

## In Conclusion . . .

*When you have completed this chapter, use an electronic typewriter or a microcomputer to answer the following questions:*

1. *What does the term* word processing *mean? Are word processing and desktop publishing the same or different? Explain.*
2. *What types of software can you use to process information with computers?*

# Review and Application

## REVIEW YOUR VOCABULARY

Match the following by writing the letter of each vocabulary word in the space to the left of its description.

____ 1. a set of fields that describes one logical unit of information in a data base system

____ 2. the efficient processing of words or text

____ 3. copies or versions of a personal computer design that use the same operating system instructions

____ 4. presents numerical data clearly and quickly in visual form on a computer

____ 5. requires the careful coordination of people, machines, procedures, and environment

____ 6. describes the way a document flows through the office

____ 7. a variation of a spreadsheet program

____ 8. computerizes record keeping and information tasks

____ 9. specializes and combines like tasks in the office

____ 10. include communication software and wire cables that physically link computers in the same general area

____ 11. the ability of individuals to work at home and communicate with their office by using personal computers and communication lines

____ 12. combines text and graphics in various sizes and styles to create an attractive document

____ 13. a centrally located area where all typing activities are performed

____ 14. "what you see is what you get" on your computer screen

____ 15. combines several independent software packages for coordinated use in one package

____ 16. processing of documents occurs in different locations throughout the company, rather than in one centralized location

____ 17. financial planning tools that perform mathematical calculations

____ 18. a unit of information in a data base system

____ 19. a collection of records that share the same format

____ 20. performs only one task at a time

a. accounting software
b. centralized information processing approach
c. compatibles or clones
d. data base management software
e. decentralized information processing approach
f. desktop publishing software
g. field
h. file
i. graphics software
j. integrated software
k. local area networks (LANs)
l. record
m. spreadsheets
n. stand-alone software
o. telecommuting
p. word processing
q. word processing center
r. word processing cycle
s. word processing system
t. WYSIWYG

## DISCUSS AND ANALYZE AN OFFICE SITUATION

1. Cecilia is a new secretary in the accounting department's minicenter at Federated Foods. This is her third job this year. She is sure this is a nice place to work because the people here seem to like her.

   Cecilia uses a microcomputer to do word processing tasks for the first two weeks. She is looking forward to soon entering accounting transactions using the general ledger accounting software.

   Ms. Ziede is manager of the accounting department. She is concerned. Almost one-fourth of the correspondence Cecilia has completed so far has been returned because of spelling or general typing errors. What is most perplexing to Ms. Ziede is that Cecilia doesn't see any problems with her skills. It is almost as though she doesn't care. Cecilia's normal response is that mistakes are easy to fix with a computer, and if she doesn't see an error, someone else will point it out to her.

   Ms. Ziede is sure that Cecilia will not be entering accounting data in the computer. But the immediate problem is, should she keep her? Cecilia is a nice person, but she is not observant and fails to recognize errors or problems. Ms. Ziede knows that this attitude cannot be allowed in the accounting department.

If you were Ms. Ziede, what actions would you take? If Ms. Ziede decides to counsel Cecilia, what should she say?

## PRACTICE BASIC SKILLS

### Math

1. Help Parker compute his summer budget as an electronic spreadsheet would. Compute the June, July, and August totals for his revenue (income) sources and expenses. Also total each line across. If Parker meets his budget, how much will he have left over each month that can go into his savings account?

Summer Budget for Parker

|  | June | July | August | Total |
|---|---|---|---|---|
| Revenue |  |  |  |  |
| Park job | 200 | 200 | 200 |  |
| Allowance | 50 | 50 | 50 |  |
| Baby-sitting | 100 | 50 | 100 |  |
| Total revenue |  |  |  |  |
| Expenses |  |  |  |  |
| Snacks | 75 | 75 | 75 |  |
| Clothes | 100 | 25 | 75 |  |
| Movies | 30 | 30 | 30 |  |
| Vacation | – | 250 | – |  |
| Gifts, miscellaneous | 50 | 50 | 50 |  |
| Total expenses |  |  |  |  |
| Savings |  |  |  |  |

### English

1. *Rule: Can* implies ability; *may* indicates permission. *Examples:* Can you prepare a budget using Lotus 1-2-3? May I help you proofread your term paper? *Practice Exercise:* Apply the rule to each of the following sentences. If a sentence is correct, write OK. If a sentence is incorrect, rewrite it correctly.
   a. Can I go with you to the computer demonstration?
   b. Gina may not be allowed to use the terminal to enter data after 5:00 p.m.
   c. Can you figure the payroll this week?
   d. I may put the headings in boldface type.
   e. I can run the spelling check using WordPerfect.
   f. Can you organize your work in the next five minutes?
   g. May we have your name printed legibly on the form?
   h. OCR scanners can be used as an input method.
   i. Can I be trained at the same time you are?
   j. Can you proofread and edit accurately?

### Proofreading

1. Retype or rewrite the following paragraph, correcting all errors.

   You can't learn all the skills you'll need in the class room. Some skils will haf to be lerned on-the-job. The skills you must learn in the classroom are; 10-key touch methid, composing at the keybord, editting and proof reading, spelling, and punctuatation.

## APPLY YOUR KNOWLEDGE

1. Which software would you use to process the following office applications? On a separate sheet of paper, write *WP* if the description describes a word processing activity, *SS* if spreadsheet, or *ACC* if accounting.
   ____ a. payroll records
   ____ b. budget
   ____ c. multipage report
   ____ d. spelling check
   ____ e. accounts receivable
   ____ f. general ledger
   ____ g. financial predictions
   ____ h. letter and memo
   ____ i. legal brief document revisions
   ____ j. current grade point average calculation
2. What are your word processing skills today? Complete the following steps to identify them:
   a. List eight important word processing skills.
   b. Put a star next to the skills you are strong in right now.
   c. Put a question mark next to any two skills you want to improve.
   d. Describe in two or three paragraphs how you plan to accomplish this improvement goal.
3. You decide. . . . Which software package would you use to process the following office applications? On a separate sheet of paper, write *DTP* if the description is a desktop publishing activity, *GR* if graphics, *DB* if data base management, or *ITG* if integrated software.

_____ a. bar graph comparing the manufacturing costs of four products

_____ b. company newsletter to five thousand employees

_____ c. office equipment inventory lists

_____ d. letter to stockholders showing profit and loss statement

_____ e. customer mailing list

_____ f. line graph showing profit trends over the last five years

_____ g. sales letter promoting new laser printer to potential customers

_____ h. company's marketing plan with budget projections

_____ i. pie chart showing cost breakout of miscellaneous expenses

_____ j. new sales order form

## QUIZ

*Write a **T** if the statement is true or an **F** if the statement is false.*

_____ 1. Word processing is the efficient processing of words or text.

_____ 2. The two steps in the word processing cycle are processing and output.

_____ 3. Local area networks are often found in centralized word processing settings.

_____ 4. Telecommuting refers to the ability of individuals to work at home and communicate with their office by using a computer.

_____ 5. The abilities to type quickly and proofread carefully are the only skills office workers need.

_____ 6. A sensible guideline to follow when buying software is to buy as much as you can afford, based on your known needs.

_____ 7. When businesses need to calculate and analyze figures quickly and easily, they use data base management software.

_____ 8. The three terms—field, record, and file—are associated with data base management software.

_____ 9. Graphics software presents alphabetical data clearly and quickly in visual form on a computer.

_____ 10. Desktop publishing software unites in one package word processing and graphics capabilities.

_____ 11. For most office workers, word processing is easier to learn than desktop publishing.

_____ 12. Integrated software combines several software packages for coordinated use in one package.

_____ 13. Secretarial services are owned by large companies.

(continued on next page)

____ 14. Most office workers work in similar physical settings and environments.

____ 15. There are only two methods used to input ideas—longhand and shorthand.

## Word Processing

1. Using word processing software, keyboard the following paragraphs accurately. Single-space, save, and print a copy of the document.

Benefits of a Word Processing System

1. Increased speed and accuracy by means of improved document turnaround time with no errors in typing, grammar, spelling, punctuation, or word usage
2. Improved, more professional presentation by means of effectively written documents that are properly formatted and attractive
3. Limited physical and mental effort from users due to a lack of extra keystrokes, retyping, and unnecessary decision making with reference to documents
4. Greater cost-effectiveness through wiser use of people's time in processing documents

2. Edit the document in the following ways and print a second copy:

A. Move paragraph #1 from the first paragraph to the third paragraph, and renumber the paragraphs accordingly.

B. Use the search and replace feature to replace the word "documents" with the words "text copies."

C. Change the initial letter for each word that starts each paragraph from upper case to lower case.

D. Use boldface type for the title.

E. Use double-spacing between each paragraph.

## Word Processing Cycle

The purpose of this activity is to understand the word processing steps applied to an office-document processing procedure.

Part I. Below is a list of several procedures describing steps to follow when preparing client letters at the Global West Travel Agency.

On the line to the left, indicate which step is being described:

I  for output
P  for processing or
O  for output.

**Answers**

____ 1. Revise the client letter, as needed.

____ 2. Listen carefully to instructions when taking machine dictation from a travel agent.

____ 3. When possible, scan a similar letter from a source document file and make appropriate revisions.

____ 4. Print an original on letterhead and mail it to the client.

____ 5. Log in the document to show the disk and file name used.

____ 6. Copy the original letter and file it in the client's folder.

____ 7. Keyboard the document at your rough draft speed.

Part II. On the blank lines, re-order the seven steps from Part I so they represent a more logical and sequential procedure to follow.

1. _____

_____

_____

(Continued on next page)

2. _____

_____

_____

3. _____

_____

_____

4. _____

_____

_____

5. _____

_____

_____

6. _____

_____

_____

7. _____

_____

_____

## ACTIVITY 3–3

## Word Processing Careers

Assume you are thinking about career opportunities in word processing. Indicate on the lines following each item: a) which career setting (office, telecommuting, or secretarial service) you would select at that stage of your life, and b) why you made that choice.

1. Your first job out of school.

   Career Setting: _____

   Why: _____

   _____

2. You are very self-motivated and prefer to work on your own with little interaction with others. In addition, you prefer not to dress up, but instead prefer to work comfortably and at your own pace.

   Career Setting: _____

   Why: _____

   _____

3. For twenty-two years, you have held numerous office jobs in six different organizations. You are tired of working for others, and you have begun to wonder if you can make a living being self-employed.

   Career Setting: _____

   Why: _____

   _____

4. You are interested in going into office management someday but know you need to be "groomed" in many aspects of that career. You're twenty-five years old, just got married, and are seriously thinking about your long-term career plans.

   Career Setting: _____

   Why: _____

   _____

## ACTIVITY 3–4

### Word Processing

1. Suppose you were given a three-page research assignment. Using the three steps in the word processing cycle described in the text, explain how you would use the cycle at each step as you prepare the assignment. In other words,

   A. What would you do and how would you do the input step?

   B. What would you do and how would you do the processing step?

   C. What would you do and how would you do the output step?

2. Keyboard in two or three double-spaced paragraphs the process you would use, save, and print a copy.

## ACTIVITY 3–5

### Word Processing

You read about important word processing skills office workers should have. Given the following job advertisement, prepare an application letter in response to the job advertised. Be sure to mention the word processing skills you've acquired.

Wanted. A top-flight travel receptionist. No experience necessary, will train. Must have good office, computer, and people skills and be able to work in a large office with over 20 travel agents. Salary commensurate with abilities. Contact Gail Hodge, Office Manager, at Global West Travel Agency, 555-8314.

## ACTIVITY 3-6

### Word Processing

1. Use the following six questions about word processing skills as a guide while you compose at the computer. Then evaluate your skills in paragraph form.

   A. Can you maintain your composure while typing with speed and accuracy in meeting production deadlines?

   B. Are you able to plan and organize your work load in meeting deadlines?

   C. Can you proofread accurately for typing errors and changes in spelling, punctuation, and grammar?

   D. Can you follow written and spoken directions?

   E. Do you ask questions if you don't understand what someone has said to you?

   F. Are you able to read, understand, and use equipment and software manuals in completing job tasks?

2. Keyboard two paragraphs double-spaced. Center the heading, MY WORD PROCESSING SKILLS, over the text in boldface type.

3. Save and print a copy of the evaluation.

## ACTIVITY 3-7

### Word Processing

1. Using the sample secretarial service flyer shown in figure 3-2 on page 93 in the text, keyboard a flyer that advertises secretarial services you might offer. Call the business (Your Name) Secretarial Services. It is possible that your services might be similar to those for Melissa's Secretarial Service.

2. Use as many style features of your software as you can to enhance the appearance of your flyer. Some features to consider using are:

   — boldface                  — centering
   — italics                   — caps lock
   — underlining               — margin and line space changes

3. Save and print a copy of the flyer.

## Word Processing vs. Desktop Publishing Software

Circle WP (word processing) or DTP (Desktop Publishing) to indicate which one correctly matches the description on the right.

| WP | DTP | 1. text processing |
| WP | DTP | 2. PageMaker |
| WP | DTP | 3. spell check program |
| WP | DTP | 4. thesaurus |
| WP | DTP | 5. WYSIWYG |
| WP | DTP | 6. word processing cycle |
| WP | DTP | 7. search and replace |
| WP | DTP | 8. combines text and graphics |
| WP | DTP | 9. in-house publishing |
| WP | DTP | 10. revision typing |
| WP | DTP | 11. typesetting terminology used |
| WP | DTP | 12. WordPerfect |
| WP | DTP | 13. point size |
| WP | DTP | 14. personalized letters or mail merge |
| WP | DTP | 15. requires more training time |

## Computer Software

Circle SS for spreadsheet, DBM for Data Base Management, GR for graphics, or INTG for integrated software to indicate which description on the right correctly matches that software.

SS   DBM   GR   INTG       1. an electronic file cabinet

SS   DBM   GR   INTG       2. image formed by thousands of picture elements, or pixels

SS   DBM   GR   INTG       3. consists of columns and rows in a grid pattern

SS   DBM   GR   INTG       4. presents numerical data in visual form on a computer

SS   DBM   GR   INTG       5. unit of information is a field

SS   DBM   GR   INTG       6. cell locations can contain a value, label, or mathematical formula

SS   DBM   GR   INTG       7. word processing and spreadsheet on same software package

SS   DBM   GR   INTG       8. a collection of records is called a file

SS   DBM   GR   INTG       9. converts data in a variety of charts and graphs such as line, bar, and pie forms

SS   DBM   GR   INTG       10. opposite of stand-alone software

SS   DBM   GR   INTG       11. uses same commands to perform all tasks in a similar way

SS   DBM   GR   INTG       12. includes accounting packages

SS   DBM   GR   INTG       13. used to store, manipulate, retrieve, and report on information

SS   DBM   GR   INTG       14. used to maintain employee records and inventory information

SS   DBM   GR   INTG       15. what-if analysis

# More Automation for Information Processing

# Objectives

After completing this chapter, you will be able to do the following:

1. Describe the capabilities of electronic typewriters.
2. Use the touch method in operating an electronic calculator.
3. List skills needed and procedures to follow when transcribing documents.
4. List skills needed and procedures to follow when dictating documents.
5. Define reprographics and describe the advantages of centralized and decentralized copying environments.
6. Identify the uses for and advantages of using the facsimile machine in an office.
7. Identify the uses for and advantages of electronic mail in an office.
8. Define teleconferencing and list four methods used to accomplish it.
9. Describe the function of voice mail and voice recognition systems in an office.
10. Describe the term *integrated information system* as it relates to an office.

# New Office Terms

centralized reprographics
decentralized reprographics
electronic calculator
electronic calendaring
electronic mail
electronic office
electronic typewriters
facsimile
integrated information system

modem
photocopying
reprographics
telecommunications
teleconferencing
telephone tag
voice mail
voice processing
voice recognition systems

Much is written about computers today. At times, it is easy to forget that other automated systems are just as vital in helping an office run smoothly. You'll be expected to know some other automated equipment and procedures when you begin your first job.

Today's office is very automated. Most office tasks like typing, copying, and communication have been affected by innovations in automation. In fact, office experts suggest that modern offices will operate at an optimum level when people, processes, and equipment perform as one integrated information system. An **integrated information system** shares the same information with all departments by blending computer and automated functions with modern telecommunications technology and devices.

You will use automated office systems when you take and transcribe (make a written copy of) machine dictation, use electronic calculators and electronic typewriters, or make reduced-size copies of original documents. Other uses of automated systems include the popular trend toward using telecommunications equipment (telephonelike devices) to process information. Examples of these devices are the facsimile machine and electronic mail, voice mail, and teleconferencing equipment.

Today's office is called an electronic office. An **electronic office** consists of several electronic and automated systems that increase office productivity and efficiency. Faster, more efficient equipment will make your work hours more productive and more stimulating than ever before. Clerical and administrative employees like yourself will have within reach an abundance of data and information to manage and use effectively.

Readily accessible information is now available throughout companies. As a result, sound decision making has never been so solidly based on facts as it is now and will continue to be. Computers and other automated systems contribute to sound decision making because they are flexible, efficient, and cost-effective. They are also increasingly necessary to handle the growing volume of data in today's information society.

## ▉ OTHER AUTOMATED OFFICE EQUIPMENT

In processing office information, you can expect to use equipment other than computers to get a job done. For example, you will use an electronic typewriter to fill in preprinted forms, an electronic calculator

when you determine petty cash amounts, and dictation and transcription machines when you prepare business letters and reports.

## Electronic Typewriters

Since most typing classes use **electronic typewriters** to instruct on, chances are you have already used one. Electronic typewriters have far more automatic capabilities than do most electric typewriters. These additional automatic features help you center and underline words and phrases, align decimal tabs, and use automatic carriage returns to align text within paragraphs.

Internal memory capacity is also available on most electronic typewriters. Memory can range from one-line recall to the storing of multipage documents. With memory, an office worker can key (type) in, proofread, and edit text copy before a final document is printed.

## Electronic Calculators

Through the use of electronic technology, almost all calculating machines use the ten-key keypad. The **electronic calculator** is a ten-key machine with the capacity to solve problems at an incredibly fast speed. Calculators can be either printing or display machines. Printing calculators print numbers on a paper tape. Display calculators display numbers as illuminated figures on a screen. It is possible to combine and use both abilities as a printing-display calculator.

When you learn to operate an electronic calculator with the touch system, the technique, speed, and accuracy you develop can easily be

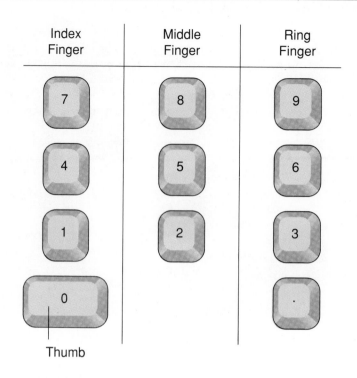

transferred to other machines. For example, most microcomputer keyboards have special ten-key sections on the right side. If you were a computer data entry clerk at a local bank, you would probably be paid based on the number of keystrokes entered from a ten-key pad.

The basic rule for learning touch operation is not to look at your fingers while depressing the number keys. The ten-key pad is operated with the four fingers and thumb of the right or left hand. The home keys are 4, 5, and 6. These are the starting positions for any key from 1 to 9. You make your reaches up or down from the three home keys. Many businesspeople consider being able to touch operate with a ten-key pad as important as being able to touch-type at a typewriter.

Here is a quick lesson on touch operation. Place your fingers on the home keys, as shown in figure 4–1. On most calculators and computers, key 5 has a raised dot, which can easily be felt. This dot makes the home row easily identified by touch.

The finger used to depress home key 4 is used to reach up to key 7 and down to key 1. The second finger is used to depress home key 5 and is also used to reach up to key 8 and down to key 2. And finally, the finger used to depress home key 6 reaches down to key 3 and up to the key 9. The fourth finger and thumb usually operate the plus key, the minus key, and the zero key.

When you are practicing this new technique, develop your accuracy first. Speed will naturally improve with practice, but only if your technique is correct.

## Transcription and Dictation Machines

Machine dictation is an input method in the word processing cycle. To transcribe accurately from machine dictation, you will need to develop good transcription skills and learn the proper procedures to follow. It is also important to learn how to dictate using good techniques. Pointers on proper machine dictation techniques could be helpful someday if you need to train someone or use dictation equipment yourself.

**Transcription Skills and Procedures** Machine transcription goes beyond just listening to words and typing them. You must also know how to properly listen for and interpret instructions from the person dictating a message. Good dictators give instructions before, during, and after dictation. Ask the person providing dictation how instructions will be given during machine dictation.

Through the use of good transcribing skills, you will be able to prepare a professional-looking document. Any professional-looking document must be free of spelling, punctuation, grammar, and keyboarding errors. To achieve this, you need to develop and use good proofreading techniques. When you proofread, watch for format, style, and typographical errors, in addition to the meaning of a message. You may have to proof a document more than once.

Become familiar with the speed and volume controls on your transcription unit. Good transcribers keep the typing rhythm smooth, not jerky, as they listen and keyboard dictated words.

**Dictation Skills and Procedures** Even if you never dictate documents in an office situation, you still need to know how the dictation

*Office workers who transcribe must be able to listen well, follow instructions, and produce error-free documents.*

Beth is frustrated and has a problem that needs a solution fast. She works in the centralized typing area of Atlas Insurance Agency. Her day is spent keyboarding at her rough draft speed into a micro-computer while transcribing dictation from as many as ten different departmental managers.

Beth prides herself on being a fast typist with strong skills in spelling, punctuation, and general proofreading. In the last three years, while working for another insurance company, she always received compliments on letters she typed from dictation. In fact, she never had any problems with her work un-til she moved to Atlas.

In the past month, at least five letters have been returned to Beth each week for retyping. She is sure it's not her fault. The problem, she feels, is poor dictation techniques. For instance, three dic-tators give her hardly any instructions on dictation tape. Some dictators speak as though they have food in their mouths. And though most letters make sense, a few dictators could use some improvement.

Beth is tired of taking the blame for the poor dic-tation habits of the people she transcribes for. If peo-ple at Atlas dictated like those at her last job, there would be no problems at all, she feels.

1. If you were Beth, how would you go about changing the situation and solving the problem?
2. If you were asked to develop a thirty-minute Art of Dictation seminar, what would you cover in the presentation?

---

process works. With this understanding, you may become a better tran-scriber because you will know what to expect. Good dictation skills can be developed with training and fine-tuned with practice. Persons using machine dictation need to be trained in two areas: (1) how to prepare for dictation, and (2) how to give clear instructions to the transcriber.

Good dictators think about what they are going to say first before they speak. They organize key ideas in some logical order with a defi-nite purpose in mind. Some dictators may even prepare a rough outline of these ideas before speaking into the microphone.

Good dictators also effectively instruct a transcriber to produce final copy that will be signed and mailed. Clear instructions must be given before, during, and after a dictated message.

Before dictating, a dictator should give the following basic informa-tion: her or his identity (if appropriate), the type of document to be typed (letter, memo, report), the type of copy that is preferred (rough draft or final), the number of copies needed, and any special instructions such as how to mail or what to enclose.

During dictation, a dictator should spell out unusual words and all proper names of people and businesses. Some dictators are able to in-dicate correctly where punctuation and paragraph sections should be. Experienced transcribers prefer that dictators vary the pitch or loudness of their voices and maintain normal talking speed.

After dictation, a dictator should mark an indicator slip and state any instructions he or she may have forgotten. The transcriber knows to check any special instructions noted on the indicator slip before begin-ning to transcribe.

*Dictation machines can be portable units, as shown here, or desktop models.*

# Recall Time

*Answer the following questions:*

1. What additional features do electronic typewriters have compared with electric typewriters?
2. What are three types of electronic calculators used in today's office?
3. What are the three home keys on the ten-key pad? How are your fingers positioned on them?
4. What are some proofreading reminders you should follow when transcribing documents?
5. What kind of instructions do machine dictators give before dictation begins?

## ■ REPROGRAPHICS

What one office information system will panic most office staffs if it is unavailable or becomes inoperative? Did you guess the copying system? If so, you are probably right. The copying or reprographics system has become such a convenient necessity in most offices that most people are unable to think of not being able to make a copy on demand.

The term **reprographics** refers to the process of reproducing or copying documents using copiers, duplicators, and electronic printers. Office reprographics systems may be responsible for over 90 percent of the output copy in many organizations. They are an important and costly

*Small, but effective, desktop copiers (left) are popular because of their convenience; centralized large-size copiers (right) are cost-effective.*

Charlene is a new receptionist at the local newspaper. She has many tasks to do. She runs copies, answers phones, receives visitors, hears complaints from customers on poor delivery service, and does overload typing on particularly busy days. The front desk is challenging for even the best of workers, and Charlene does a good job staying on top of crisis situations.

The problem is Charlene's attitude. She is overbearing. It appears to many co-workers that she thinks her job is the only important one at the newspaper. Charlene is not a kind person. For example, she will tie up the copy machine and be snippy in telling others they'll just have to wait. Co-workers have remarked that most of the time, she sounds as though she is talking down to them. As a result, few like to be around her. Charlene has no friends and always sits alone at lunch in the break room.

1. Are attitudes like Charlene's typical in office situations?
2. If you wanted to be a friend to Charlene and help her fit in, what steps would you take?
3. Can Charlene's attitude be changed? If so, how would you go about helping her do so?

consideration of every integrated information system. For that reason, reprographics should not be taken for granted. A system must be carefully selected and managed.

When selecting a reprographics system, a company should base its decision on desired copy quality, equipment reliability, cost-effectiveness, and productivity. The quality and reliability of the output is determined by the equipment. Nevertheless, it is still up to people in an organization to use the equipment in a productive and cost-effective way.

Reprographics includes technologies such as photocopying, phototypesetting, offset printing, and duplicating. Of these four technologies, **photocopying** is the most common one used in offices today. Photocopiers produce copies of uniform quality. They also offer many capabilities, including duplexing, or copying on both sides of the paper; reducing or enlarging the image of an original document; copying in color or on colored stock; making transparencies, and sorting and stapling multipage documents.

What determines where copiers will be located? Usually, most copier location decisions are based on overall office efficiency. Further considerations are the frequency with which the equipment is used, the number of people using the equipment, the amount of space the equipment takes up, and the volume of work the equipment generates.

Reprographic functions may be centralized, decentralized, or both. In general, production-type systems are usually centralized. In contrast, low-volume systems are often decentralized.

## Centralized

A **centralized reprographics** operation is sometimes called a copy center. It serves an entire company or office and may even serve branch offices in other buildings. Requests for copies are usually picked up and delivered to a reprographics area through a company's internal mail system. Large organizations are able to control their departments' usage of equipment and copies with this approach. In addition, the amount of paper used is easily monitored and requests for copies are scheduled in order of priority.

## Decentralized

With copies becoming less expensive and equipment more sophisticated, many offices are purchasing additional individual copiers. In a **decentralized reprographics** environment, copiers are conveniently located throughout a company. Employees do not have to walk far to reach the machines, and they can make copies whenever they need them. This kind of "on-demand" system works well in small offices where the volume of copies does not justify a centralized system.

The biggest advantage to a decentralized approach is convenience. The major disadvantage is lack of control. Often, offices will require copy logs at scattered copiers, or provide special locks with counters to prevent unauthorized copying by employees.

Some companies combine a centralized and decentralized system. However, the recent trend is to decentralize the copying functions.

# R ecall Time

*Answer the following questions:*

1. Define the term reprographics.
2. Why is the reprographics or copying function important in an office environment?
3. What issues would you consider in designing an effective copying system?
4. What features make the photocopying process popular?

# TELECOMMUNICATIONS

**Telecommunications** combines the use of automated office equipment with telephone systems and communications technology. For example, messages, appointments, blueprints, photographs, and even meetings are telecommunicated in offices today. Sophisticated and integrated telecommunications systems serving entire organizations distribute large amounts of information every day. Four types of telecommunications that you will use are facsimile, electronic mail, teleconferencing, and voice mail.

## Facsimile

A **facsimile** (fax) machine translates copies of text or a graphics document into electronic signals. These signals are then transmitted over telephone lines or by satellite. A facsimile machine can send and receive

*A small office or home fax (above) takes up little desk space; larger offices may require more features and faster speed on their fax machines (below).*

exact copies of documents to and from any location in a matter of minutes. All that is required is telephone service and two compatible fax machines.

The trend toward using fax machines is changing the way businesses communicate. Order processing and the transmission of reports to regional offices are common uses of the fax. As a result, the fax is replacing the U.S. Postal Service and overnight express mail services in delivering business communications.

The future of the facsimile is already in the office with these advanced features:

- *cost.* Fax units range in price from six hundred dollars to over five thousand dollars, depending on the speed and features you select.
- *speed.* Depending on the sophistication and cost of a fax model, documents can be sent at speeds that range between four seconds per page and forty seconds per page.
- *copy quality.* New, expensive fax units provide bond paper printing. However, it is still possible to get good-quality transmission with the less expensive thermal (or coated) paper method. The sending fax unit determines the copy quality. It doesn't matter how well a receiving fax unit prints copy; it will get only the best that the sending fax unit sends.
- *speed dialing.* Speed dialing with a fax is similar to that with many phone systems. It saves time by providing for quick access to frequently dialed numbers.
- *multiple uses.* Some fax units also function as high-quality convenience copiers and pulse-tone telephones.

Operating a fax machine is easy. If you've never used a fax before, ask someone in the office to show you. One guided lesson can build your confidence in using the fax.

To fax a document, you simply place the paper document to be transferred in your fax scanner, enter the telephone number of the fax machine that is to receive the document, and press the start button. Within seconds, a facsimile of the original document emerges from the photostatic printer of a receiving fax machine anywhere in the world.

Recall that computers have special disk operating systems that prevent them from talking to one another. Unlike computers, nearly all facsimile machines speak the same electronic language. This international language transmits various documents that include computer-generated, printed, and handwritten copy, as well as pictures, graphs, and photographs. Important information gets where you want it with such clarity and detail that it is difficult to tell the fax copy from the original. With the speed and convenience of a phone call, fax machines speed up business communications in a relatively inexpensive way.

## Electronic Mail

Unlike the fax, electronic mail uses computer technology. Because computers are accessible and this telecommunications device is efficient, electronic mail is replacing the need for the internal office document

138

called the memorandum. **Electronic mail,** or E-Mail for short, uses computers to send messages to and receive messages from other computers. It is quick, economical, and accurate.

Why is E-Mail increasing in popularity? E-Mail speeds up the delivery of messages. It also reduces telephone, paper, and duplicating costs. Business professionals prefer it because faster transmission speed and quicker turnaround on replies are possible.

Most E-Mail systems are easy to use and involve only a few steps. For example, suppose you work for Mr. Tate, marketing vice president of Acme Toy Company. You must periodically add up the number of toy orders that have come into six remote sales offices since the beginning of the year. Mr. Tate expects you to prepare a summary report by the close of business on the days you do this.

Using E-Mail, here's a procedure you might follow. First, access your electronic mail system following the prescribed procedure.

Then, compose your message asking for this month's toy orders in dollars and units at the computer, taking care to be concise and to the point. Your message will be an internal document; that is, it will be kept within the organization. Therefore, you do not need to use extra words. Once your message is ready to send, post it in the computer's "out box."

Within minutes, the message arrives at the receiving computer's "in box." The computer beeps, or a pop-up window appears telling the receiver that "mail" is in the computer's in box.

Once a message is received and read, the remote sales office can choose to save, print, edit, or delete it. In this case, you've asked for a response before 4:15 p.m. Thus, the message you sent is read and returned for your comments.

Why can't you just phone each sales office instead of using electronic mail? You could. However, E-Mail reduces telephone tag.

**Telephone tag** is the ongoing annoyance where a series of telephone calls are made back and forth to talk with someone. Have you ever called a friend who wasn't home and left a message for him to call you, then been unable to come to the phone when he called you? This scenario is played out daily in offices across the United States.

In contrast to a phone call, E-Mail does not require you to be at your desk for completing a message. If you are away from your desk when a message comes in, the message will wait for your return. Once you return to the office, you can answer the message immediately and transmit it back, if appropriate.

Electronic mail systems can be set up in one of two ways, as shown in figure 4–2. One way is to use individual computers; the other way is to use a local area network.

When you use individual computers with electronic mail, a simple system will require only a microcomputer or terminal, a communications software package, and a modem to connect the computer terminal to the telephone lines. A **modem** is a device that sends computer-generated data over telephone lines.

Electronic mail functions without a modem when local area networks link computers by cable at one site. You can expect E-Mail usage to expand as the popularity of using local area networks to connect previously separate personal computers grows.

## FIGURE 4–2

*A remote electronic mail system requires a modem to connect distant computers over telephone lines while a local area network system uses cables to connect computers located in the same building.*

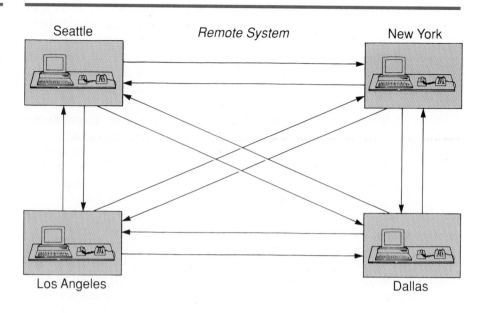

Seattle  Remote System  New York

Los Angeles  Dallas

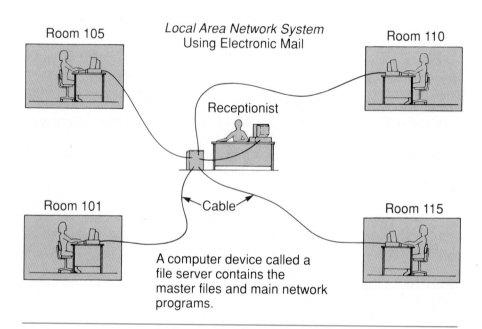

Room 105  Local Area Network System Using Electronic Mail  Room 110

Receptionist

Room 101  Cable  Room 115

A computer device called a file server contains the master files and main network programs.

Expanded electronic mail capabilities can result when you put an executive's calendar on the computer. This procedure is called electronic calendaring. **Electronic calendaring** uses software to record appointments, meetings, and travel plans through entries on screens that resemble paper appointment calendars. Electronic calendaring is yet another example of how traditional office functions are becoming automated.

Suppose you have to schedule a special meeting for an executive. Through electronic mail, you can review the calendars of persons who should attend. When you find an acceptable date, you electronically and automatically schedule the event for all parties at once. At the same time, you send any additional messages about the meeting.

## Teleconferencing

**Teleconferencing** is the process of using computers and telecommunications devices to conduct conferences and share information among people who are in remote locations. Businesses like teleconferencing because it enables people in different geographical locations to participate in the same meeting. As a consequence, it reduces a company's travel and saves money. Another advantage of teleconferencing is that it gives an executive more time to spend productively in the office.

As an office worker, you will likely assist in setting up teleconferences. A teleconference can be as simple as linking the audio among participants' telephones. Or it can be as complex as using television cameras to transmit video images and sound of conference participants to other participants with similar equipment at a remote location.

Organizations use teleconferencing in four ways. These are through a conference call, an audio conference, a video conference, and a computer conference.

A conference call simply connects multiple parties for joint conversations over the telephone.

*The video conference, a method of teleconferencing, effectively links remote locations; thereby reducing travel costs and promoting more effective use of people's time.*

Audio conferencing, on the other hand, gathers participants at different locations in meeting rooms. The rooms are equipped to amplify telephone conversations through speakers. Some community college courses are taught using this method when only a few students in outlying rural areas need a particular course to graduate.

A video conference involves two or more sites linked by video and audio systems. Some late-night newscasts feature this arrangement and it works extremely well.

Finally, a computer conference is a meeting in which participants work at a microcomputer. They respond to questions or problems through entries on their keyboards.

# R ecall Time

*Answer the following questions:*

1. Define in your own words the term telecommunications.
2. What office activities and tasks are processed using telecommunications?
3. What is the difference between using electronic mail and using facsimile machines?
4. Why might a large organization prefer to video conference a national sales meeting rather than physically gathering fifteen sales representatives together in some major city?

## Voice Mail

The function of **voice processing** in the office is to convey verbal messages. Chapter 5 will describe telephone procedures used in the office. Two automated voice processing technologies are voice mail and voice recognition.

**Voice mail** is used to send and receive messages through the telephone system without installing additional equipment such as telephone answering machines. A caller can leave a message that is stored within the telephone network itself and have it delivered at a designated time. The system will continue to dial the called party's number until the message is delivered. Some mail-order companies use voice mail to inform a customer that an order has been received or shipped.

Suppose you work for Davenport Marketing Agency and had a voice mail system installed. You are tied up taking shorthand dictation from Ms. Davenport when the telephone rings. The voice mail system answers Ms. Davenport's telephone automatically. The call is routed immediately to an electronic mailbox. When you and Ms. Davenport are through with the dictation, all messages can be scanned quickly by either of you.

One advantage of voice mail over standard answering machines is that it allows for longer messages. Longer messages minimize misinterpretation of a message. A second advantage of voice mail is that it reduces the dilemma of telephone tag.

An additional voice mail feature enables a user to send the same message to several different people. With just one phone call, for instance, a user can set up a sales meeting time and place in a matter of minutes.

In the office of the future, most messages and information will probably be sent or received by means of a type of "electronic mailbox." This electronic mailbox will receive voice, image, or text messages. For instance, a manager can dictate a message to you. Once edited and finalized, this message can be delivered to certain recipients by voice and to others in printed form, with a copy left over for electronic filing.

Today, computers cannot interpret fluent and continuous speech because doing so is an extremely complex task. **Voice recognition systems** are, however, an exciting technology for the office of the future. As with voice mail, speech is the input method. But unlike voice messaging equipment, voice or speech recognition equipment usually "understands" human speech. Voice-to-text machines can recognize human speech and change it into written words. These words are displayed on a screen as if they had been keyed on a keyboard.

For voice recognition systems to work, people will have to learn how to talk to a computer. They will need to know what a computer can and cannot understand. Speakers will need to identify themselves through some prescribed method before they can begin communicating.

In the future, intelligent machines may be able to record, transcribe, and deliver hard copies of letters, conversations, or meetings without anyone touching a recording device, typewriter key, or copying machine. Do you agree with the futurists who say it's only a matter of time?

## INTEGRATED OFFICE SYSTEMS

For an information system to be most effective in an organization, information of all types—text, data, image, and voice—should be integrated and blended together. That means all departments and workers in a company will have access to a centralized source of information, all data files, various types of computer and automated equipment, and detailed procedures explaining how to use and merge various information processing systems.

Fully automated offices use many types of equipment. Each piece of equipment performs a different function but all are linked electronically (see figure 4–3). Office equipment connected in this way is called an integrated information system or integrated office system.

To illustrate an integrated approach to completing a task, let's take the case of Woodrow. Woodrow is manager of new products at Kitten Products International. He is preparing a ten-page proposal about a new product that will be launched next month. The information for this proposal is "in the system."

Woodrow was just taught the proper procedures in how to access the information from his desk terminal. His proposal must be ready by

> **OFFICE TIP**
>
> When given a new assignment in the office, ask questions of others. Try to determine if a similar assignment has ever been done before. If so, perhaps you could save some time and effort by simply adding your creativity to an already good plan or idea. Remember, to be a smart worker doesn't mean you have to work harder.

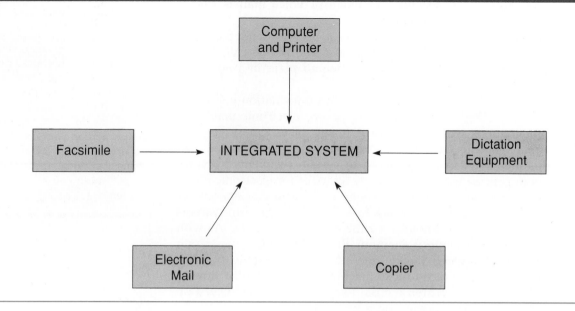

*An integrated system blends text, data, image, and voice information.*

9:00 a.m. tomorrow for a meeting with five other department managers. He feels he can get the job done himself; at least, he wants to try.

Woodrow has decided to include the following items in his proposal:

1. the new-product description, which can be copied from a recently developed brochure in a word processing file
2. the customer listing sorted to receive promotional literature, which is already in the customer data base file
3. the projected start-up costs, which were prepared on a spreadsheet; this data will be converted to a pie chart showing portions of the cost

Woodrow adds a few transition sentences and moves a few paragraphs using his word processing program. Otherwise, he uses existing data and creates the multipage proposal in just twenty minutes.

But before Woodrow runs a final draft, he wants his administrative assistant, Pat, to proof for errors and content. So, using electronic mail, he sends the report to Pat. He includes a message to please proof and return within the hour.

Pat is efficient. She has the report back within the hour with some suggestions for minor changes. Making those final revisions is easy.

The copier can make the few transparencies that will be used for the presentation directly from the proposal. It can also prepare five copies of the finished proposal for the managers attending the meeting.

Woodrow has everything ready. He feels especially good because it took just two hours from start to finish. The hardest part, he realizes, is knowing where to go for the information. With the integrated approach, the job was easy.

The need for instant access to information as in the above example is prompting the integration of office operations. Separate departments

## OFFICE TIP

When you initially take on a project, try to visualize what you want the final product to look like. Or try to imagine how good you will feel when you've finished the project and you know it looks good. Often, the hardest part of getting a job done is just starting it and convincing yourself that it is worth doing.

**Nancy Hillan**
*Market Research Analyst*
*Hewlett-Packard*

Q: Mrs. Hillan, what types of automation are becoming common-place in offices?

A: Our company has been using electronic mail for quite a few years; it is as common as the telephone. Fax machines are almost indispensable now. Some of our sites have electronic voice messaging systems. Voice mail has lifted some of the burden of answering the phones off the secretaries' shoulders. Teleconferences are starting to become more common, but they are quite expensive.

   The main change I expect in the near future is better integration of office automation tools—computers, telephones, printers, copiers, and who knows what else—talking to each other and working together without human intervention.

Q: How are the office workers accepting this change?

A: Most workers welcome the changes, as they usually make life easier. As with any change, new technologies often prompt changes in procedures. This requires flexibility on everybody's part.

---

such as data processing, word processing, telecommunications, and even reprographics are now being combined into a total system. This trend will continue.

In the future, incompatible devices will be standardized. Software that enables those devices to communicate and transfer data will be developed. The increased productivity provided by automated office devices will encourage more organizations to adopt them to help control costs and remain competitive. The key to the integrated office of the future will be the ability to link voice, graphics, document preparation, and data communications systems.

# Recall Time

*Answer the following questions:*

1. Define the term voice mail.
2. What are three advantages of using voice mail in the office?
3. What are some office information systems that can be integrated in today's office?

---

## SUMMARY

In addition to computers in the office, other automated equipment like electronic typewriters, electronic calculators, and dictation and transcription machines is used. An integrated information system shares information by blending all computer and automated equipment functions with modern telecommunications technology and devices. Examples of telecommunications methods include facsimile, electronic mail, teleconferencing, and voice mail.

Fax machines translate text or graphics documents into electronic signals that are transmitted via telephone lines or satellite.

Electronic mail uses computers to send messages to and receive messages from computer users.

Teleconferencing is the process of conducting conferences at remote locations by using computers and other telecommunications devices. A teleconference can be conducted as a conference call, an audio conference, a video conference, or a computer conference.

Voice processing in the office is used to convey messages. It can be in the form of voice mail, which is a step beyond phone answering machines, or in a developing form of voice recognition.

The reprographics function refers to the process of reproducing or copying documents using copiers, duplicators, and electronic printers.

An integrated system links all office functions to work as one fully automated office system.

The following items are important in automation for information processing. Can you recall their meaning?

- Electronic typewriters have more capabilities than electric typewriters.
- When you learn the touch operation of the ten-key pad, don't look at your hands.
- Good dictators give instructions to transcribers at the beginning of, during, and at the end of the dictation cycle.
- A transcriber has the ultimate responsibility for thoroughly proofreading all work that is typed.
- Centralized reprographics are often found in big companies.
- Fax machines have varying costs, speeds, and abilities.
- Electronic mail is replacing the typing of memorandums in offices.
- Office workers set up teleconference activities.
- Voice recognition systems, when developed and tested, will change the way office information is processed in the future.

### In Conclusion . . .

*When you have completed this chapter, use an electronic typewriter or a microcomputer to answer the following questions:*

1. *What are two automated methods or equipment, other than computers, used to process information in the office? Describe them.*
2. *What types of office activities use telecommunications technology?*

# Review and Application

Match the following by writing the letter of the vocabulary word that is described below.

_____ 1. settings where copiers are conveniently located throughout a company

_____ 2. combines the use of automated office equipment with telephone systems and communications technology

_____ 3. shares the same information with all departments by blending computer and automated functions with telecommunications technology and devices

_____ 4. uses software to record appointments, meetings, and travel plans

_____ 5. the process of using computers and telecommunications devices to conduct conferences and share information among people who are in remote locations

_____ 6. consists of several electronic and automated systems that increase office productivity and efficiency

_____ 7. the process of reproducing or copying documents using copiers, duplicators, and electronic printers

_____ 8. have more automatic capabilities than do most electric typewriters

_____ 9. uses computers to send messages to and receive messages from other computers

_____ 10. a process where a series of telephone calls are made back and forth to talk with someone

_____ 11. a device that sends computer-generated data over telephone lines

_____ 12. functions to convey verbal messages in the office

_____ 13. most common method of reprographics used in offices today

_____ 14. a copy center that serves an entire company

_____ 15. a ten-key machine with the capacity to solve math problems

_____ 16. used to send and receive messages through the telephone system without installing additional equipment such as telephone answering machines

_____ 17. a process that understands human speech

_____ 18. translates copies of text or a graphics document into electronic signals that are then transmitted over telephone lines or satellite

a. centralized reprographics
b. decentralized reprographics
c. electronic calculator
d. electronic calendaring
e. electronic mail
f. electronic office
g. electronic typewriters
h. facsimile
i. integrated information system
j. modem
k. photocopying
l. reprographics
m. telecommunications
n. teleconferencing
o. telephone tag
p. voice mail
q. voice processing
r. voice recognition systems

## DISCUSS AND ANALYZE AN OFFICE SITUATION

1. As part of a classroom assignment, students in an office practice class at East Technical School are required to visit at least two offices. They are also asked to prepare a report describing the types of automated information systems each office was using.

Cheryl has read the chapters on automated systems and feels knowledgeable to pursue the assignment. Miguel, on the other hand, has only skimmed the chapters on automated office systems. Though he doesn't fully understand automated systems, he isn't worried. He says, "It's better to really learn about automated systems in person."

Does Miguel have a point? Which student will prepare the better report? Why do some students approach assignments differently? Does this relate to how they might approach assignments on the job?

## PRACTICE BASIC SKILLS

### Math

1. In the following table, what is the total cost of copying items per month? What percentages of the monthly total are toner, paper, operator time, and copier rental?

| Copying Item | Cost per Month | Percentage of Monthly Total |
|---|---|---|
| Toner | $ 250 | |
| Paper | $ 350 | |
| Operator time | $1,000 | |
| Copier rental | $ 400 | |
| Total | | 100% |

2. If management says that the costs in question 1 must be cut by 10 percent, what do those costs become? Do their percentages change?

| Item | Cost per Month |
|---|---|
| Toner | |
| Paper | |
| Operator time | |
| Copier rental | |

### English

1. *Rule:* Whenever possible, avoid dividing a word at the end of a line. When word division is unavoidable, try to divide at a point that will least disrupt the reader's grasp of the word. Divide words only between syllables. If unsure, consult a dictionary.
   *Examples:* 1) automation   au-to-ma-tion
   2) information   in-for-ma-tion
   3) procedures   pro-ce-dures

*Practice Exercise:* Apply the rule to each of the following words. If a word is divided correctly, write OK. If a word is divided incorrectly, rewrite it correctly.
   a. elec-tron-ic
   b. facs-im-ile
   c. mod-em
   d. pho-tocopy
   e. busi-ness
   f. cal-cu-la-tor
   g. off-ice
   h. tele-phone
   i. in-te-gra-ted
   j. gra-phics

### Proofreading

1. Rewrite or retype the following paragraph, correcting all errors.

   A new generation of fax tecnology has just arived offering more higher levels of quality and performance. Advanced features makes even text and graphics combined come through crisp and clear. On top of each document you send, a page heder apears with your name and phone no.

## APPLY YOUR KNOWLEDGE

1. You decide. . . . Which office system would you use to process each of the following office activities? In the space to the left of each description, write the letters *EM* if it is electronic mail, *FAX* if facsimile, or *RPG* if reprographics.
   ____ a. pie chart sent from Los Angeles to Chicago
   ____ b. notice of sales meeting sent to ten sales representatives in a building
   ____ c. order for ten office chairs sent to a vendor one hundred miles away
   ____ d. memo about business ethics sent through an LAN
   ____ e. request for six copies of fifty pages to be collated and stapled
   ____ f. request for six overhead transparencies of a sales presentation
   ____ g. picture of a new product transferred to a branch office in the next city
   ____ h. replacement for expensive overnight delivery services
   ____ i. replacement for the U.S. Postal Service
   ____ j. request for four hundred copies of four original pages, reduced to fit on the front and back on one page

2. Practice the touch method by adding the following columns of figures using an electronic calculator. A good way to check each answer is to add the numbers again in the opposite direction.

| a. 45 | b. 55 | c. 656 | d. 333 | e. 444 | f. 7,878 |
|---|---|---|---|---|---|
| 33 | 66 | 333 | 222 | 234 | 5,896 |
| 65 | 35 | 456 | 654 | 699 | 4,485 |
| 58 | 47 | 699 | 411 | 544 | 8,644 |

# QUIZ

*Write a **T** if the statement is true or an **F** if the statement is false.*

____ 1. An electronic office correctly describes today's office.

____ 2. Electronic typewriters and electronic calculators are examples of equipment other than computers that are used in offices today.

____ 3. It is not necessary to learn the touch method of using an electronic calculator because you can key just as fast looking at the keys.

____ 4. Good dictators give instructions during the dictation process and at no other time.

____ 5. Office workers who transcribe must be able to listen well, follow instructions, and produce error-free documents.

____ 6. A copying or reprographics system must meet the needs of the office, as well as be reliable and cost-effective.

____ 7. Small, but effective, desktop copiers are popular because they are cost-effective.

____ 8. "On-demand" copying systems are best associated with a decentralized reprographics operation.

____ 9. A facsimile machine can only transmit copies of text, not graphics documents.

____ 10. Examples of telecommunications include facsimile, electronic mail, teleconferencing, and voice mail.

____ 11. Electronic mail uses computer technology; the fax machine does not.

____ 12. The device that sends computer-generated data over telephone lines is called a modem.

____ 13. Teleconferencing enables people in different geographical locations to participate in the same meeting.

(continued on next page)

_____ 14. There are no real advantages of using voice mail compared to the standard answering machine.

_____ 15. An integrated office system combines all types of information—text, data, image, and voice.

## Electronic Typewriters and Calculators

Using an electronic (or electric) typewriter and an electronic calculator, complete the following activities.

1. Prepare envelopes to mail itineraries and flight tickets to the following three clients of Global West Travel Agency.

Mary Brown
322 Swiss Road
Boulder, CO 80333

Rollie Greer
773 Empire Street
Denver, CO 80281

Hannah Larkin
45 Matterhorn Drive
Silverton, CO 80737

Using the touch operation of your electronic calculator, calculate the following columns and record your answers on the lines provided.

2. Addition.

| 548 | 864 | 159 | 753 | 559 | 628 |
| 788 | 544 | 825 | 654 | 714 | 213 |
| 338 | 441 | 658 | 900 | 705 | 430 |

a. _____ b. _____ c. _____ d. _____ e. _____ f. _____

3. Subtraction.

| 892 | 436 | 711 | 904 | 550 | 314 |
| −789 | −209 | −173 | −876 | −220 | − 39 |

a. _____ b. _____ c. _____ d. _____ e. _____ f. _____

4. Multiplication. (Note: * = to multiply)

11 * 34 _____

704 * 25 _____

65 * 41 _____

201 * 9 _____

841 * 90 _____

917 * 101 _____

5. Division. (Note: / = to divide)

4,400/11 _____

983/8 _____

77,777/65 _____

590/37 _____

170/45 _____

670/88 _____

## Dictation Procedures and Techniques

Assume you are a transcriber at Global West Travel Agency. The owner of the agency has asked you to prepare a handout, entitled Dictation Procedures and Techniques, that would help travel agents improve their dictation skill. Use these instructions to complete the activity:

1. On the lines below, jot down some suggestions you would include on the handout.
2. Prepare an attractive handout using word processing or desktop publishing software incorporating these ideas.

### DICTATION PROCEDURES AND TECHNIQUES

I. Be Prepared to Dictate

_____

_____

_____

II. Give Clear Instructions

   A. Before Dictation

_____

_____

_____

   B. During Dictation

_____

_____

_____

   C. After Dictation

_____

_____

_____

## Word Processing

1. Using word processing software, keyboard the following paragraphs accurately, save, and print a copy of the document.

Electronic Typewriters
   Electronic typewriters have far more automatic capabilities than do most electric typewriters. These additional automatic features help you center and underline words and phrases, and use automatic carriage returns to align text within paragraphs.

Electronic Calculators
   The electronic calculator is a ten-key machine with the capacity to solve problems at an incredibly fast speed. Calculators can be either printing or display machines. It is possible to combine and use both abilities as a printing-display calculator.

Transcription and Dictation Machines
   Machine dictation is an input method in the word processing cycle. To transcribe accurately from machine dictation, you will need to develop good transcription skills and learn the proper procedures to follow.

2. Edit the document in the following ways and print a second copy.

   A. Delete the last sentence in the electronic calculators paragraph.

   B. Use a thesaurus (on disk) and find an alternate word for "capabilities" in the first paragraph and an alternate word for "accurately" in the last paragraph.

   C. Change line spacing to double-spaced.

   D. Underline the three side headings.

## ACTIVITY 4–4

## Reprographics

After studying the reprographics section in chapter 4, indicate on the lines following each item: a) which copying environment (centralized, decentralized or a combination of both) you would select to meet the needs of the following office situations, and b) why you made that choice.

1. A small travel agency with only four agents who have partitioned offices and the owner who has a glass-enclosed room.

   Environment: _____

   Why: _____

   _____

   _____

2. A large travel agency with three branch offices located near downtown Chicago. Each office has no fewer than thirty travel agents and at least one office manager. Everyone has her or his own office. Flyers, brochures, itineraries, letters, memos, and reports all require the use of reprographics equipment. These documents are prepared by the three secretaries and one receptionist at each location.

   Environment: _____

   Why: _____

   _____

   _____

3. The owner of this travel agency is upset with the last six months' copying costs. He feels extra copies are being made and going unused. He determines that more control over "on-demand" copying is needed. There are fifteen employees.

   Environment: _____

   Why: _____

   _____

   _____

## Word Processing

1. Research and describe the reprographics system used at your school, at your place of work, or at an office you know. To guide your composition at the keyboard, consider the following questions:

   A. Is it a centralized or decentralized operation?

   B. What special capabilities does the photocopier have? (duplexing, enlarging, reducing, sorting, stapling)

   C. Is a log sheet kept to keep track of who makes copies and how many?

   D. Is the location of the copier adequate to meet the needs of the users?

2. Keyboard and carefully proofread a two-paragraph double-spaced description. Save and print a final copy.

## Telecommunications

Circle the telecommunications category on the left that correctly matches the description on the right.

Fax   E-Mail   Teleconf   Voice Mail      1. sends and receives messages through current phone system

Fax   E-Mail   Teleconf   Voice Mail      2. electronic calendaring is possible

Fax   E-Mail   Teleconf   Voice Mail      3. used to conduct conferences with people in remote areas

Fax   E-Mail   Teleconf   Voice Mail      4. need computer to transmit message

Fax   E-Mail   Teleconf   Voice Mail      5. translates graphics into electronic signals

Fax   E-Mail   Teleconf   Voice Mail      6. used in order processing

Fax   E-Mail   Teleconf   Voice Mail      7. is the basis for voice recognition systems

Fax   E-Mail   Teleconf   Voice Mail      8. examples are conference calls and computer conference

Fax   E-Mail   Teleconf   Voice Mail      9. uses modem device

Fax   E-Mail   Teleconf   Voice Mail      10. is reducing the number of internal memos

Fax   E-Mail   Teleconf   Voice Mail      11. used to teach college courses through speakers

Fax   E-Mail   Teleconf   Voice Mail      12. is replacing U.S. Postal Service and overnight express mail services

## Word Processing

1. Keyboard a description of a personal situation involving a friend or business associate that resulted in telephone tag. How could a telecommunications device have resolved the problem?

2. Proofread carefully and use a spell-check disk.

3. Save and print two copies.

## Integrated Office Systems

Refer to the Integrated Office Systems section beginning on page 143 of the text and answer the following questions on the lines provided.

1. React to the statement, "Increasingly, more managers like Woodrow will be preparing their own reports from many information sources." Do you agree or disagree and why?

_____

_____

_____

_____

_____

2. What aspects of the integrated office system approach do you like the most? What aspects do you personally like the least?

_____

_____

_____

_____

_____

3. Reread the last paragraph in the chapter describing future trends. Do you think that what is said will actually happen? If so, how will it affect jobs you may have in the future? Is there anything you can do now to prepare for this trend should it occur?

_____

_____

_____

_____

_____

# ACTIVITY 4-9

## Word Processing

1. Visit a store that sells computer equipment, software, and supplies. In particular, take note of the following ideas:

   A. What type of computer equipment is sold?

   B. What type of computer software is sold?

   C. What type of computer supplies are sold?

   D. Were you asked by a sales representative if you wanted a demonstration on equipment using particular software?

   E. If you had the money and were interested in making a computer-related purchasing decision soon, would you buy from this store? Why or why not?

2. Keyboard at least two paragraphs responding to the questions stated above. When preparing the copy

   A. place it within a four-inch line of writing

   B. use double-spacing, and

   C. center and boldface the title, EVALUATION OF A COMPUTER STORE.

3. Save and print.

# Telephone Procedures

## Objectives

After completing this chapter, you will be able to do the following:

1. List and explain the important qualities of a good telephone voice.
2. List and explain the steps necessary to answer, place on hold, and transfer a business telephone call.
3. List and explain the steps used to screen calls in a business office.
4. List the items necessary to record telephone messages for another person.
5. List and explain the types of outgoing telephone calls made in a business office.
6. List and explain the main telephone network systems used in business offices.
7. List and explain the special features of telephone equipment used in a business office.

## New Office Terms

call screening
Centrex
conference call
intercom

PBX
switchboard
time zone
WATS

## Before You Begin . . .

*Using an electronic typewriter or a microcomputer, answer the following questions to the best of your ability:*

1. *How important is the telephone in the business world?*
2. *What are the differences between answering the telephone at home and answering the telephone in a business office?*

Did you know that at this very minute, millions of office workers are doing business on the telephone? Did you know that the telephone is used in approximately 95 percent of all business transactions? It is estimated that more than 100 million calls are made each day to conduct business transactions. A customer calls to get information or to place an order. A customer service representative uses the telephone to service accounts and to sell a product.

Did you make a business call recently? Maybe you called to get your car repaired and an office worker had to make an appointment for you. Maybe you called to ask what time a store closed. These are all business calls. Did you get a polite answer?

Many people have been refused jobs because they cannot talk properly on the telephone. Sometimes when you answer an advertisement for a job, the preliminary screening will be done over the telephone. Individuals may pass all a company's tests, yet not be hired for the position owing to their telephone manners.

Some people have lost jobs because they cannot handle business calls on the telephone. A fast typist may be hired for a job, but may also be terminated if proper telephone procedures are not followed.

*Telephones have become an important part of the job for most office workers. They are used frequently both for incoming and outgoing calls.*

Using the telephone effectively is crucial to the success of the company you will work for. No company wants to lose business because of improper telephone techniques by its employees. If you appear rude or unconcerned, that will be the impression you give of your company. However, if you express enthusiasm and confidence in your telephone conversations, callers will view your firm in a positive way.

Potential clients make judgments about your competence and your company's abilities based on how you handle their calls. It is important that these potential clients feel valued and appreciated when you are handling their telephone calls. Do you remember being treated poorly when you made a doctor's appointment or when you called for information about a movie or a restaurant? Do you also remember being treated nicely when you made other calls? Which do you prefer?

In a speech to a group of business students, a personnel manager stated that all employees frequently use the telephone on a job. Telephones are on all office workers' desks. Some office workers are even required to relieve the main switchboard operator during breaks or at lunchtime. Someday, you may be the person to relieve an operator. Are you prepared for this?

## ▮ PROPER PROCEDURES

Answering the telephone in a business office is easy if you know the right procedures. The right procedures involve what you say and how you say it.

When the telephone rings, even before picking up the receiver, it is best to prepare yourself for the caller. You can do this as follows:

- Stop any work you are doing, so you can concentrate entirely on the caller.
- Always have a message pad or notepaper and pen or pencil ready.
- Set aside the problems of the day and have a positive attitude.

Did you know that the way you hold the telephone can affect the sound of your voice? Do not rest the telephone on your shoulder or chin. This will make your voice sound muffled. The listener may have to ask you to repeat or to speak louder. Hold the telephone about one inch from your lips and speak directly into the mouthpiece.

One important aspect of proper telephone procedures is concentrating on the quality of a good voice. A caller will not be able to see you smile or to see other friendly expressions. You must rely entirely on your voice and good telephone manners to create a positive impression for your company. Here are a few important qualities of a good telephone voice:

- Speak distinctly. Use clear, unmistakable words and sentences.
- Speak with a normal tone. Do not shout at the caller, yet speak loud enough to be heard.
- Speak naturally. Let your pleasing personality show.
- Speak politely. Be considerate and respectful to the caller.
- Speak courteously. Speak in a manner that will please the caller.

How you speak on the telephone in an office is quite different from the way you speak on the telephone at home. Talking to a client is different from talking to your friend or neighbor. When you speak on the telephone at work, remember the following:

- Never use slang. Avoid words such as *ain't* or *huh.*
- Never have something in your mouth. Avoid chewing gum.
- Never run words together. Avoid saying, for example, "Whadidya say?" instead of "What did you say?"

It is recommended that you use standard English when speaking on the telephone in an office.

## Recall Time

*Answer the following questions:*

1. What are three ways an office worker can prepare herself or himself to answer the telephone when it rings?
2. What are four important qualities of a good telephone voice?
3. Ari, an office worker, receives a call from a new customer who wishes to place an order. Ari has a radio broadcasting a football game on very softly so the customer cannot hear it.

   The customer begins giving the order, but Ari interrupts and puts her on hold because he cannot find anything to write with. Since the customer has a heavy accent, Ari talks very loud and almost shouts at times. He also needs to say "huh" quite a few times during the conversation. Ari concludes the conversation by saying, "Thanks for placing the order."

   What would you have done differently if you were Ari?
4. Make a telephone call to inquire about clerical job openings at a local business. Ask for the personnel department and request that job descriptions be sent to you. After you place the call, answer the following questions:
   a. Did the person at the personnel department appear to be concentrating on your conversation? If not, why not?
   b. Did the person at the personnel department have a good business telephone voice—distinct, polite?
   c. Did the person at the personnel department avoid slang expressions and avoid running words together?

Receiving and placing calls in an office are also different from at home. The following are business procedures for receiving and placing calls.

## Incoming Calls

Let's now look at the mechanics of answering a telephone in a business office. The following techniques can be used if you are answering a

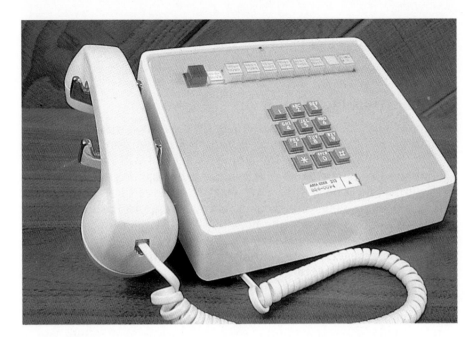

**switchboard** with many lines or a standard business phone on your own work desk with a few lines.

The main parts of the telephone that you will encounter on a job are the handset, the hold button, the incoming and outgoing lines, and the **intercom** line.

Most telephones in a business office have more than one line for incoming and outgoing calls. As this type of telephone rings, the button for the incoming call will begin to flash. To answer the call, push down on the button that is flashing and pick up the handset. Remember to push down on the button first; otherwise, you may cut into someone else's conversation.

Certain procedures are followed by most businesses when answering incoming calls. These procedures are as follows:

- Answer the call promptly; after the first or second ring is preferred.
- If the call came through a switchboard, answer by first giving the department name and then identifying yourself.
- If the call did *not* come through a switchboard, answer by first giving the company name and then identifying yourself.
- If you are answering your boss's telephone, identify your boss first, and then yourself.

For example, when customers call Rudy Yee, the calls are first answered by an operator at the switchboard and then transferred to Rudy. He answers like this: "Payroll Department, this is Rudy Yee."

When clients call Margo Gonzales, the calls go directly to her desk. She answers like this: "Good morning; Transworld Company, Margo Gonzales speaking."

Hugh Scott's boss usually answers her own phone. However, when she is away, Hugh answers like this: "Ms. Lopez's office, Hugh Scott speaking."

Some companies have special procedures to follow when answering the telephone. It is best to review company policies when beginning a new job.

## Hold or Transfer Calls

Once you have answered an incoming call, the next step may be to hold or transfer the call. If the call is for another person, say to the caller, "One moment, please" or "One moment, please, I will ring her office." Then press firmly on the hold or transfer button and release it.

If you have a hold button, after you press it, the line button for the line or extension you were speaking on will begin to flash on and off. Always remember to push the hold button, or your connection to the caller will be broken.

Let's assume the call is to be transferred to your boss. Once the caller is on hold, push down on the intercom button and key in your boss's extension. When he answers, tell him which line the call is on. Then hang up your handset. Your boss will push the flashing line button on his telephone set. He will then be able to talk to the caller.

If you have a transfer button, after you push it, you simply key in the extension you want the call transferred to. The call will ring on that person's telephone. When the person to receive the call answers, the light will stop flashing. If the light does not stop flashing, it means the person did not pick up the call. In that case, you return to the caller and take a message.

Some valuable points to keep in mind when holding or transferring calls are these:

- Ask permission before placing a caller on hold.
- If you return to a call, thank the caller for waiting.
- Never leave a caller on hold for more than thirty or forty seconds before returning to check on the caller.
- When transferring, give the caller the name and number of the person to whom you are transferring the call.

Cora is an administrative assistant for a travel agency. This is an example of how she would transfer a call: "Good morning. GO Travel Services, Cora speaking. . . . That would be handled by our international division. May I transfer you to that department? . . . In case you get disconnected, I am transferring you to Harold Price at extension 42."

Have you ever been left on hold for a long time? This is annoying. Leaving someone on hold for a long time is a common mistake made by many office workers. Do not make the same mistake. Keep checking back with a caller who is on hold. You can tell a caller is still on hold if the line continues to have a flashing light. Get back to a caller who is on hold and say, "Do you still wish to hold or may I take a message?"

Many executives like their calls screened before a transfer is made. This means they would like you to find out who is calling before you put that person on hold. It is important that you screen calls in a polite way so as not to offend a caller. Some common phrases used in **call screening** are "May I ask who is calling, please?" and "May I tell Mr.

Partel who is calling, please?'' Check with your employer to see if calls should be screened.

## Messages

Many times, your boss may not be able to take a telephone call. In these cases, politely tell the caller why your boss cannot take the call. Then ask if you can take a message. For example, say "I am sorry, she is not at her desk right now. May I take a message?" or "I am sorry Ms. Chavez is out of the office right now. May I take a message?" It would also be helpful to say when your boss is expected back and to ask if you or someone else can be of help.

Never say, "She is busy right now." This may offend the caller by implying that the caller isn't important enough to speak to. Your company does not want to offend any customers.

Sometimes, your boss will be available, but will not wish to speak to a particular caller. In that situation, you may use the same phrases you would use if your boss were unable to take the call: "I am sorry, he is not at his desk right now. May I take a message?" or "I am sorry, he is out of the office right now. May I take a message?"

One executive secretary in an advertising firm has a special way of screening calls for her boss, Mr. Perkins. Mr. Perkins is particular about which calls he wants to answer. The secretary handles it this way:

Caller: Asks for Mr. Perkins.
Secretary: I am not certain if Mr. Perkins has returned from his meeting. Let me check. May I have your name, please?

*To* _____

*Date* _____ *Time* _____

## WHILE YOU WERE OUT

_____

**of** _____

**Phone** _____

| STOPPED BY | | PLEASE RETURN CALL | |
|---|---|---|---|
| TELEPHONED | | WILL CALL AGAIN | |
| RETURNED YOUR CALL | | | |

**Message** _____

_____

_____

**Message received by** _____

In this situation, the secretary can tell Mr. Perkins the name of the caller and he can decide if he wishes to speak to the person. If he does not, the caller will be told Mr. Perkins has not returned from the meeting. This is a good way to avoid offending a caller.

If you need to take a telephone message, you can use a standard form (see figure 5–1). This type of form is usually contained in a telephone message pad. The forms may vary a little, but you will always need to record who the message is for, the date, the time, who the message is from and the name of that person's company, a return phone number, the message itself, and your signature or initials.

Recording the correct information is very important. Here are some helpful hints for you:

- If you cannot hear, ask the caller to speak louder.
- If you do not understand, ask the caller to repeat.
- Always get the caller's telephone number. This saves looking it up.
- If you cannot spell the caller's name, ask the caller to spell it for you.
- Before you hang up, read back the information to the caller. This will ensure that your message is accurate.

Have you ever answered the telephone at home and the caller said, "Sorry, I dialed the wrong number"? Well, maybe the caller dialed the wrong number because he or she was given the wrong number. It is extremely important that you record the correct telephone number onto the message pad. Too many wrong numbers could mean a loss of business for a company. It could also mean the loss of a job for you.

It never hurts to be extra polite when taking messages. For example, you can make a caller feel important by using her or his name during the conversation. Let's assume you are taking a message for Ms. Huff. The caller is Mr. Carver. To be really polite, say, "I will give Ms. Huff the message, Mr. Carver" or "I will be certain she receives the message, Mr. Carver."

Professional secretaries care enough about their jobs to put extra effort into helping callers. They recommend that you try to help a caller receive the correct information or be transferred to the right person who can help. Avoid telling a caller that you cannot be of any help. If it is necessary, tell the caller you will find the answer and return the call yourself.

Finally, it is considered good business practice to let the caller end the conversation and hang up first. You do not want to offend the caller or have the caller think you are rude and want to end the call in a hurry. This is also a good time to practice courtesy and to use the caller's name when ending the conversation. For example, say, "Thank you for calling, Ms. Harris."

The following list is given to all new employees at a county office in northern California. It is a helpful list for reviewing tactful telephone phraseology.

| Do not say . . . | Do say . . . |
| --- | --- |
| "Who is this?" | "May I ask who's calling, please?" |
| "What's your name?" | "May I have your name, please?" |
| "What's your phone number?" | "May I have your number, please?" |
| "Speak up, please." | "Excuse me, I am having trouble hearing you." |
| "You didn't talk to me." | "I cannot remember talking with you." |
| "What do you want to talk to him about?" | "May I ask what your call is in reference to?" |

## Outgoing Calls

When you work in an office, you will not only receive calls, you will also have to place calls. The first important point in placing an outgoing call is to prepare yourself for the call. You do this as follows:

- Make a checklist of subjects you wish to cover.
- Have all the necessary information needed to ask or answer questions. This may include file folders, notes, and a calendar.
- Be certain to have the correct phone number. If in doubt, look it up.
- Try to call during business hours and avoid lunchtimes.

Now you are ready to make the outgoing call. Remember that when the buttons on a telephone are lighted, it means someone is talking on those lines. Therefore, when placing an outside call on some phone systems, you must find a button on your telephone that is not lighted.

Once you have found an open line (one that is not lighted), push down on the button for that line, pick up the handset, and key in the number you are calling. After the number is keyed, give the person enough time to answer—eight or ten rings.

When the party answers, identify yourself before starting the conversation. In some cases, it will save a lot of time if you also identify your company. For example, when the party answers, you could say: "This is Saul Neal calling. May I speak to Ms. Lew?" or "This is Sally Perez from Fresno Travel Service. Is Mr. Allen in, please?"

Sometimes, your boss may want to speak to a person but will ask you to dial the number and get the person on the telephone. If this happens, be certain your boss is close by and will be ready to talk to

### OFFICE TIP

Sometimes when you wish to speak with your boss or another office employee, that person is on the telephone, so you have to wait. Stand far enough back so you do not hear the conversation. If it is a private office, stay outside the office until the call is finished.

Olga works as an administrative assistant for a public relations firm. She enjoys word processing and finds it interesting to type the proposals for new clients. She works for three bosses and is kept busy most of the day.

In this public relations firm, all the administrative assistants must take turns relieving the receptionist at lunchtime one day each week. During this time, the telephones are very busy, so there is no time for any other work.

Tuesday is Olga's day to relieve the receptionist. One Tuesday, the receptionist says she has an im-portant lunch date, so she must leave on time. On that same Tuesday, one of Olga's bosses gives her a proposal that must be typed and sent to a client by 1 p.m. At 12 noon, when the receptionist wants to leave, Olga still has a few pages to complete.

Olga begins to get nervous. She must finish the proposal, yet it is her turn to relieve the receptionist.

1. Explain at least three actions that Olga could take in this situation.

---

the person when you place the call. For example, Mr. Castle asks his secretary, Kay, to get Ms. Butler of Invest Savings on the phone for him. Kay keys in the telephone number. Ms. Butler answers and the conversation is as follows:

Kay: Ms. Butler, this is Kay West from Castle & Curl. Bill Castle would like to speak with you. May I put him on the line now?
Ms. Butler: Yes, please do.
Kay [As she signals her boss]: Here he is, Ms. Butler.

Another time-saver when making outgoing calls is to spell uncommon words or names when leaving a message. If your name or your company's name is easily confused, it is best to spell it. For example, Orv is a secretary at the Weinberg and Heller law firm. When people hear the name Weinberg, they may think Wineberg, or Weinburg, or another spelling. When Orv must leave messages, his conversation is similar to the following:

"This is Orv Fletcher from Weinberg and Heller. I would like to leave a message to remind Ms. Reiser of our meeting. . . . Yes, Orv F-l-e-t-c-h-e-r of W-e-i-n-b-e-r-g and Heller. Thank you very much."

## ■ OTHER IMPORTANT PROCEDURES

Similar procedures are followed by most offices when using the telephone.

### Personal Calls

All companies have a policy on personal telephone calls. Most companies do not allow them, except in the case of an emergency.

Ralph has been an office support person in the office of an architect's firm for three years. His attendance record is good and the quality of his office work is very good.

Ralph comes from a family of seven brothers and sisters. It seems as if the brothers and sisters are always having problems and relying on Ralph for advice. Therefore, Ralph is constantly on the telephone at work answering calls from his family.

Ralph was raised with a strong family commitment, so he believes all the personal family problems can be given attention during work time. Besides, his production work is always done with few errors.

1. What do you think of Ralph's attitude?
2. Should family calls be allowed at work? Is there a limit?
3. Should other personal calls be allowed?

With current technology, it is possible for companies to identify calls made from all telephone extensions. This allows employers to charge calls to departments or special accounts. This also allows employers to separate business calls from personal calls and trace each call to the person who made it.

Check for company policy on personal calls. It is considered good business ethics not to make personal calls from work.

### Disconnected Calls

Have you ever been disconnected when talking on the telephone? When this happens in a business office, it is the custom for the person who made the call to call back immediately.

### Wrong Number Calls

It is not uncommon for a person to get a wrong number when making a call. If this happens on a long-distance call and you hang up immediately, you may dial the operator and not be charged for the call.

### Telephone Coverage

When leaving your desk for a period of time, ask someone to answer the phones for you. In many companies, you can ask the main switchboard operator to answer for you. If you are a receptionist or in charge of answering many lines, it is crucial that you arrange for phone coverage when you are away from your desk.

# Recall Time

*Answer the following questions:*

1. What are four major parts of a telephone?
2. You are an employee working for Alex Auto Supplies. When calls come to you, they go directly to your phone; there is no switchboard. How should you answer the calls?
3. You are an employee in the accounting department of Garcia Advertising Company. All calls are first answered by a receptionist and then transferred to your desk. How should you answer your calls?
4. Your boss is Ms. Seville. She is not available, so you answer her telephone. What do you say when you answer the phone, and what do you tell the caller?
5. Your boss, Mr. Woo, wants all his calls screened. What does this mean, and how do you do it?
6. What are seven items of information that need to be recorded when taking telephone messages?

## TYPES OF TELEPHONE CALLS

You can save time and money for yourself and your company if you are familiar with different types of calls that can be made or received on the telephone. A *station-to-station call* is made to a distant point. The caller will speak to anyone who answers. This type of call is made without the help of an operator.

A *person-to-person call* is made to a particular person at a distant point. The caller must give an operator the name of the person being called. This type of call can be dialed direct by keying in the number 0, the area code, and then the telephone number. An operator will cut in to ask the name of the person being called.

A **conference call** allows more than one party to participate in the call from more than one location. The caller first tells the operator the names and phone numbers of those taking part in the conference call and the time of day he or she would like to hold the call. Conference calls may be local or long distance.

Before placing long-distance calls, make sure your company permits them. Also consider the time of day. This is important because long-distance telephone calls are cheaper at certain times during the day. It is also important because times differ across the United States. You only want to make calls when you know people are in their offices.

It is helpful for you to refer to a **time zone** map before placing long-distance calls. Most of the United States is divided into four time zones: Eastern, Central, Mountain, and Pacific. Each zone changes by one hour as you move through the zones. Figure 5–2 is a sample of a time zone map. The map would be used in the following way:

Reprinted with permission of the copyright owner, U.S. WEST Direct, Publishers of the White and Yellow Pages.

**FIGURE 5–2**
*Sample of a Time Zone Map*

| When it is . . . | it is . . . |
|---|---|
| 4 a.m. in Wyoming | 6 a.m. in New York |
| 10 a.m. in Kansas | 11 a.m. in New York |
| 7 p.m. in Nevada | 10 p.m. in Massachusetts |
| 9 p.m. in Virginia | 7 p.m. in Arizona |
| 11 a.m. in Texas | 9 a.m. in California |

As you view the map in figure 5–2, notice that in addition to time differences, it also lists the various three-digit area codes. This is handy when you need to place a call to a number outside your area code.

*Directory assistance* is sometimes necessary when you cannot find a number in your telephone directory. To call directory assistance outside your area code, key in the number 1, then the area code, and then 555-1212. If you do not know the area code, you can refer to the time zone map. The map would be used in the following way:

| For directory assistance in . . . | dial . . . |
|---|---|
| New Mexico | 1-505-555-1212 |
| Maine | 1-207-555-1212 |

| | |
|---|---|
| Duluth, Minnesota | 1-218-555-1212 |
| Springfield, Missouri | 1-417-555-1212 |
| Alabama | 1-205-555-1212 |

## ◼ REFERENCE MATERIALS

You will find the same type of telephone books in an office that you keep in your home. In addition, most offices have several local directories, copies of the Yellow Pages for various geographic areas, and other directories that relate to their type of business.

When you want to find the phone number for an individual or a company, or sometimes a government agency, you refer to the White Pages of the telephone book. The names are listed in alphabetical order. Most telephone books also have a separate section for government agencies—divided into their classifications of federal, state, county, and city. For example, to find a phone number for the Navy, you would look under United States Government, Navy Department.

The local Yellow Pages of a telephone directory contain an alphabetic listing of businesses only. The businesses are arranged by subject area or according to the service they provide or the product they sell. For example, to find the number of the local Hyatt Hotel, you would look in the Yellow Pages under Hotels.

Company telephone directories list the telephone numbers or just the telephone extensions of employees within a company. They list the various departments and the employees within each department. They also contain an alphabetic listing of all employees. In figure 5–3, you will find the telephone number for Gene Ott by looking under Marketing.

◼ FIGURE 5–3
*Sample Company Telephone Directory*

---

**Brimmer Associates**
**Company Telephone Directory**

Accounting

Anderson, Henry ................2308
Chew, Dennis .....................2310
Dios, Gloria ........................2312
Franklyn, Henrietta ............2314

Contract Sales

Alvarez, Walter ..................5612
Wong, George ....................5614

Mail Room

Guisto, John .......................3367

Marketing

Bascom, Theresa ................4810
Ott, Gene ...........................4812

Word Processing

Singh, Lu ............................6678

---

# ■ TELEPHONE EQUIPMENT

The computer-controlled telephone equipment used in businesses today is very sophisticated. It is set up in various networks and can provide a variety of features for both large and small companies.

## Main Networks

The main networks used within companies are the Private Branch Exchange system and the Centrex system. The Private Branch Exchange, or **PBX,** has many incoming lines that are answered by an operator or receptionist. This operator or receptionist then transfers the calls to the appropriate individuals within the company. With the PBX system, employees can place their outgoing calls directly—they do not need to go through the operator.

The major difference with the **Centrex** system is that incoming calls can go directly to individuals because each telephone has its own seven-digit telephone number. However, companies using this system have one general number listed in telephone books in case a caller does not have an individual employee's number. People calling the general number do go through an operator. As with the PBX, outgoing calls can be dialed directly by individuals.

Businesses, like homes, use telephone answering machines that will record messages when workers are not available to answer the telephones. Just as you do not want to miss a friend's call, an employer does not want to miss a customer's call.

Companies that receive frequent calls from within their own network of telephones may purchase a liquid crystal display (LCD). This is a display terminal that can be connected to their telephone set. This feature displays the telephone number of an incoming call. It can also display the names of callers from within an office.

## Special Features

Once the equipment is decided upon, a company may subscribe to one or to several of the following features:

**Night Service** When the main switchboard or PBX is turned off, individuals can access incoming calls from their own desk. After the telephone rings, an individual must key in a certain code to access the call.

*Example:* You are working at your office desk at 8 p.m. The switchboard operator has gone home, and the switchboard is set for night service. The telephone rings. You key in a preset code, and the call comes to your desk.

**Automatic Callback** When you call a busy number, the automatic callback feature "remembers" the number and dials it for you automatically after you hang up.

*Example:* You dial a number and it is busy. Your preset program will continue to redial until the line is clear.

**Call Forwarding–Busy Line–Don't Answer** The call forwarding–busy line–don't answer feature automatically reroutes calls to a designated answering station if your line is busy or if you do not answer after so many rings.

*Example:* Your phone rings five times (the number of rings is set by you); no one answers. The call is automatically transferred to another person's desk.

**Call Hold** The call hold feature lets you put a caller on hold and make another call. It also allows you to switch back and forth between on-hold calls. It is different from the hold button because it gives you access to the dial tone while a call is held.

*Example:* You are speaking to a party on the telephone. You need to get some information for the person. You press a special key to put the person on hold. With the same line, you now place a call to another department to get the information.

**Call Waiting** The call waiting feature lets a caller reach you even when your line is busy. A gentle signal alerts you to an incoming call.

*Example:* You are speaking on the telephone. You hear a soft beep in your ear. This means another call is coming in.

**Distinction Ring** The distinctive ring feature signals the source of an incoming call. One ring means it is an inside call; two rings mean it is an outside call.

*Example:* The telephone rings once. You have a call from inside the company. The telephone rings twice (with two close rings). You have a call from outside the company.

## LARGE OFFICE/SMALL OFFICE: What's Your Preference?

### Telephone

The PBX telephone system has many incoming lines that are handled by a receptionist or operator. This system is often found in large offices where many workers are employed. The operator or receptionist spends most of the workday handling the incoming calls. A minimum amount of the operator's workday is spent doing other miscellaneous office tasks, such as light typing and mail processing.

A small office with few employees has no need for the PBX system and no need for an operator. In this situation, each person answers his or her own telephone, or one employee may have the responsibility to answer calls for other people in the office. However, the handling of the calls takes up only a minimum amount of that one worker's day. Most of the workday is spent in other office tasks.

*Would you accept a job as a receptionist in a large office? What skills would you need? Would you prefer answering phones in a small office? Why?*

**Speed Calling** The speed calling feature saves time and avoids wrong numbers by dialing frequently called numbers with a fast one-or-two-digit code that you have programmed into the system.

*Example:* You frequently dial the same client. A preset code will dial the number for you after you dial two digits.

**Wide-Area Telecommunications Service** The Wide-Area Telecommunications Service, or **WATS,** feature provides a way for companies to cut costs if they make frequent long-distance calls to the same area. A company receives a volume discount service for these outbound calls. In a given office, some phones may have WATS and some may not.

*Example:* You work for a company that has its headquarters in Oregon. It has a marketing office in New York. By subscribing to WATS, the Oregon headquarters can call its New York office at reduced rates.

**800 Service** The 800 service feature provides a cost-free service to callers. Charges for calls are automatically reversed to a company at a volume discount rate.

*Example:* You work for a company that sells computer software. Many of your customers call when they have problems with the software. You install an 800 number so your company will pay for the calls.

**Intercom** The intercom feature provides a fast, one-way connection to another preselected station. An intercom has a separate speaker. An intercom may be equipped with a hand-free feature that allows you to speak on the intercom without holding a button or a handset.

Modern Office Procedures

**William J. Gerard**
*Manager, Transmission Control Systems Development*
*US Sprint*

Q: Mr. Gerard, why do you feel proper telephone procedures are important for your employees?

A: In modern office technology, the telephone is one of the most sophisticated tools utilized by the largest number of employees. This tool is utilized to generate revenue, provide services, and resolve problems all in the course of a normal business day. Conversely, the telephone can also be the vehicle by which revenue is lost and problems created.

In face-to-face business dealings, first impressions are both visual and physical in nature. The proper attire, a warm smile, and a firm handshake are the entrée to the business activity. In telephone business dealings, abrupt or improper greetings are virtually impossible to recover from because the caller holds the ultimate power in the telephone business deal by his or her ability to simply hang up and call someone else.

In addition, the incorrect telephone salutation has led to the demise of many promising careers. While it is technologically possible to identify the number of the party calling, the use of such devices in most office environments is not common. Therefore, *all* calls must be answered properly and courteously in case it is the boss or the boss's boss instead of a customer calling.

Q: What are some personal comments of yours in training employees at US Sprint?

A: Always identify yourself when answering *or* placing a business call.

Never say . . . "Who's calling?" Use a phrase such as . . . "May I tell him/her who's calling?"

No matter how bad your day is going, do not take it out on the caller. Always try to take a deep breath and answer the telephone properly.

Do not place a person on hold and allow them to wait forever without coming back on the line to report progress.

If the call has reached the wrong number (within the company), assist them in getting to the right number.

---

*Example:* Your boss has a speaker on his telephone. He wants to be reminded of a 3 p.m. appointment. From your desk, you push the intercom button, key in his extension, and say the message. He hears it through his speaker without picking up a receiver.

## R ecall Time

*Answer the following questions:*

1. Which is more expensive, a station-to-station call or a person-to-person call?
2. If it is 4 a.m. in Wyoming, what time is it in New York?
3. If it is 9 p.m. in Virginia, what time is it in Arizona?
4. What is the phone number for directory assistance?
5. What is found in the Yellow Pages of a telephone book?

## ■ SUMMARY

Employers will continue to give top priority in hiring and keeping individuals who are polite, efficient, and cost conscious when handling the telephone. Achieving the proper telephone procedures for an office takes a certain amount of awareness and preparation. A large corporation in Silicon Valley, California, asks its employees to complete a telephone self-critique on the following points. How would you rate if you worked for this firm? Would you do each of the following?

- Answer on the first or second ring.
- Answer using your full name.
- Answer giving your department.
- Use the caller's name during a conversation.
- Sound pleasant and agreeable.
- Make a checklist to cover before placing a call.
- Have reference material available.
- Take notes of needed facts as they are given.
- Ensure accuracy by confirming spelling, numbers, and message.
- Write complete and legible messages.
- Ask permission to place a caller on hold.
- Give a caller the name and number of the person to whom you are transferring a call.
- Let the caller say good-bye first.
- Arrange for phone coverage when away from your desk.
- Call long distance during the cheapest hour of the day.
- Use WATS whenever possible.

### *In Conclusion . . .*

*When you have completed this chapter, use an electronic typewriter or a microcomputer to answer the following questions:*

*1. How important is the telephone in the business world?*

*2. What are the differences between answering the telephone at home and answering the telephone in a business office?*

# Review and Application

## REVIEW YOUR VOCABULARY

Supply the missing words by choosing from the new office terms listed below.

1. When working in an office, you may be asked to relieve the main _____ operator at break times.
2. _____ stands for Private Branch Exchange.
3. If you want to know the time difference in another state, you would refer to a _____ _____ map.
4. You may speak to an employee in another office by using the _____.
5. Two or more people in different locations may all speak together by participating in a _____ _____.
6. The new secretary was asked to use _____ _____ for her boss whenever she answered the telephone.
7. With the _____ system, incoming calls can go directly to the individuals because each individual telephone has its own seven-digit telephone number.
8. Subscribing to the _____ feature provides a way for companies to cut costs if they make frequent long-distance calls to the same area.

   a. call screening     e. PBX
   b. Centrex           f. switchboard
   c. conference call    g. time zone
   d. intercom          h. WATS

## DISCUSS AND ANALYZE AN OFFICE SITUATION

1. Glenda telephones a company to ask about a clerical job. Someone from personnel speaks with Glenda for a few minutes. Glenda is trying to save time, so she is combing her hair while talking on the telephone. To do this, she has to place the handset on her shoulder while talking. But Glenda is not worried because the personnel worker cannot see her. Glenda also has her television on fairly loud to catch the daily news.

    Glenda is never called in for an interview. What may be the reason?

## PRACTICE BASIC SKILLS

### Math

1. Your boss wants you to compute last year's telephone expenses for your department. To be extra-cautious, add both vertical and horizontal figures in the following report and check the totals.

Advertising Department
Yearly Telephone Expense

| MONTH | MESSAGE UNITS | WATS | SERVICE | MONTHLY TOTAL |
|---|---|---|---|---|
| January | $23.78 | $876.90 | $1,876.00 | |
| February | 12.78 | 65.32 | 2,345.78 | |
| March | 18.56 | 643.76 | 2,266.00 | |
| April | 22.00 | 58.21 | 2,177.83 | |
| May | 20.90 | 883.77 | 1,966.45 | |
| June | 19.20 | 78.44 | 2,045.55 | |
| July | 19.60 | 75.45 | 2,099.65 | |
| August | 12.90 | 777.80 | 2,350.88 | |
| September | 23.87 | 768.09 | 1,678.00 | |
| October | 18.60 | 436.45 | 1,880.75 | |
| November | 23.00 | 830.75 | 2,280.55 | |
| December | 19.22 | 80.10 | 1,950.00 | |
| Yearly Total | | | | |

2. Referring to the following report, what is the total amount of telephone calls for extension 6411?

CFEB Company
Telephone Usage Report

| DATE | TIME | DURATION | EXTENSION | COST |
|---|---|---|---|---|
| 06/11 | 08:14A | 1:12 | 6433 | $0.80 |
| 06/11 | 08:30A | 10:00 | 6444 | 2.18 |
| 06/11 | 08:33A | 4:15 | 6411 | 1.24 |
| 06/11 | 10:20A | 2:60 | 6455 | 1.10 |
| 06/11 | 10:55A | 12:56 | 6411 | 4.70 |
| 06/11 | 11:48A | 3:40 | 6444 | 1.90 |
| 06/11 | 01:45P | 4:00 | 6411 | 1.00 |
| 06/11 | 03:30P | 13:40 | 6411 | 5.80 |

## English

1. *Rule:* Use capital letters when an adjective is derived from a proper name.
   *Example:* Japanese art, Mexican food
   *Practice Exercise:* Rewrite the following sentences using capitals where necessary.
   a. There will be a special exhibit of american indian art.
   b. We always enjoy portuguese food.
   c. I will be starting a spanish class next month.
   d. The movie has english subtitles.
   e. There is a new thai restaurant on the block.

## Proofreading

1. Retype or rewrite the following paragraphs, correcting all errors.

   Any telephone system can conect you from point A to point B. But todays businesses demand more—more capacity, more capabilities, more flexability. This makes our system the logical choice for allmost any company on the move. Wheather you need single station featurers or inhanced software for high-level network control, our system delivers.

   To help your become famliar with these features and learn what they can do for you, heres a breif guide. Making you business better is our aim.

## APPLY YOUR KNOWLEDGE

1. Arrange the following words into alphabetic order. Using a microcomputer or an electronic typewriter, tabulate the words in three columns.

   | | |
   |---|---|
   | operator | switchboard |
   | telephone | hold button |
   | dial | voice |
   | incoming | outgoing |
   | handset | transfer |
   | flashing | caller |
   | message | screen |
   | disconnected | network |
   | automatic | ring |
   | service | intercom |
   | information | |

*Write a **T** if the statement is true or an **F** if the statement is false.*

_____ 1. All office employees must use the telephone sometime during their working day.

_____ 2. The way you hold the telephone can affect the sound of your voice.

_____ 3. It is easier to be understood if you shout at the caller when speaking on the telephone.

_____ 4. It is suggested you wait for the fifth ring before answering the telephone.

_____ 5. It is good business practice that you ask permission before placing a caller on hold.

_____ 6. Once a caller is on hold, it is good business practice to keep checking back on the caller.

_____ 7. Screening calls is out of date and not used by business executives today.

_____ 8. When ending a conversation, it is considered good business practice to let the caller end the conversation and hang up first.

_____ 9. Once you place an outgoing call, it is suggested you wait for eight or ten rings before hanging up.

_____ 10. For business calls, it does not matter what time of the day you place the call.

_____ 11. When leaving your desk for a period of time, ask someone to answer the phones for you.

_____ 12. A conference call allows more than one party to participate in the call from more than one location.

(continued on next page)

____ 13. The telephone number for directory assistance is the same all over the country—1, area code, 555-1212.

____ 14. PBX stands for Private Business Enterprise.

____ 15. WATS stands for Wide-Area Telecommunications Service.

## ACTIVITY 5-1

## Word Processing

1. Keyboard accurately the following paragraph, save, and print a copy of the document:

    One important aspect of proper telephone procedures is concentrating on the quality of a voice. Here are a few important qualities of a good telephone voice:

    1. Speak distinctly. Use clear, unmistakable words and sentences.
    2. Speak naturally. Let your pleasing personality show.
    3. Speak courteously. Speak in a manner that will please the caller.
    4. Speak with a normal tone. Do not shout at the caller, yet speak loud enough to be heard.

2. Edit the document in the following ways and print a second copy.

    A. Move item 3 to item 1 and renumber the listing.

    B. Replace the word "speak" each time it appears with the word "converse."

    C. Boldface the word "converse" throughout the document.

## ACTIVITY 5-2

## Word Processing

The objective of this activity is to evaluate your telephone skills as rated by someone other than yourself. Even though talking to a client is different from talking to your friend or neighbor, qualities of a good telephone voice can be evaluated.

1. Give the following set of five questions to a friend, family member, or someone with whom you converse frequently on the phone and ask them to briefly supply the answers.

    A. Do you speak distinctly?
    B. Do you speak with a normal tone?
    C. Do you speak naturally?
    D. Do you speak politely?
    E. Do you speak courteously?

2. Keyboard the five questions and their answers using complete sentences. Underline each question before supplying the answer. Save and print one single-spaced copy.

## Telephone Messages

You have been called for an assignment from On-Time Temps. Because you did such a good job on the last assignment, you are sent back to the same law firm. In addition to your typing duties, you must answer the telephone for Attorney Grace Fong.

In order for you to experience the constant ringing of the telephone, you are to stop typing every five minutes and simulate that the telephone rings. You are to record these messages for Grace Fong each time you stop. Remember, stop every five minutes and record the following messages on the message pad including the date, time, and message for Grace Fong.

| FROM | COMPANY | MESSAGE |
|------|---------|---------|
| Judge Molinari | Superior Court | Reminder of meeting of the Bar Association this evening. 692-2900 |
| Carlos Unoz | Apple-Five | Please call 626-3940 |
| Roberta Borghi | Borghi Imports | Returned your call. 367-8181 |
| Brian Williams | The Best Imports | Need to speak with you as soon as possible concerning tomorrow's court case. 755-1776 |
| Judge Sing | Superior Court | Will you be a guest speaker at the Asian Law Association luncheon next month? 937-8081 |
| Andrea Munos | Latin Imports | Please call 544-4518 |

(continued on next page)

### (IMPORTANT MESSAGE)

FOR_____

DATE_____TIME_____ A.M. / P.M.

M_____

OF_____

PHONE_____
AREA CODE — NUMBER — EXTENSION

| TELEPHONED | | PLEASE CALL | |
| CAME TO SEE YOU | | WILL CALL AGAIN | |
| WANTS TO SEE YOU | | RUSH | |
| RETURNED YOUR CALL | | SPECIAL ATTENTION | |

MESSAGE _____
_____
_____
_____
_____
_____

SIGNED _____
LITHO IN U.S.A.

TOPS FORM 3002P

---

### (IMPORTANT MESSAGE)

FOR_____

DATE_____TIME_____ A.M. / P.M.

M_____

OF_____

PHONE_____
AREA CODE — NUMBER — EXTENSION

| TELEPHONED | | PLEASE CALL | |
| CAME TO SEE YOU | | WILL CALL AGAIN | |
| WANTS TO SEE YOU | | RUSH | |
| RETURNED YOUR CALL | | SPECIAL ATTENTION | |

MESSAGE _____
_____
_____
_____
_____
_____

SIGNED _____
LITHO IN U.S.A.

TOPS FORM 3002P

---

### (IMPORTANT MESSAGE)

FOR_____

DATE_____TIME_____ A.M. / P.M.

M_____

OF_____

PHONE_____
AREA CODE — NUMBER — EXTENSION

| TELEPHONED | | PLEASE CALL | |
| CAME TO SEE YOU | | WILL CALL AGAIN | |
| WANTS TO SEE YOU | | RUSH | |
| RETURNED YOUR CALL | | SPECIAL ATTENTION | |

MESSAGE _____
_____
_____
_____
_____
_____

SIGNED _____
LITHO IN U.S.A.

TOPS FORM 3002P

---

### (IMPORTANT MESSAGE)

FOR_____

DATE_____TIME_____ A.M. / P.M.

M_____

OF_____

PHONE_____
AREA CODE — NUMBER — EXTENSION

| TELEPHONED | | PLEASE CALL | |
| CAME TO SEE YOU | | WILL CALL AGAIN | |
| WANTS TO SEE YOU | | RUSH | |
| RETURNED YOUR CALL | | SPECIAL ATTENTION | |

MESSAGE _____
_____
_____
_____
_____
_____

SIGNED _____
LITHO IN U.S.A.

TOPS FORM 3002P

## IMPORTANT MESSAGE

FOR _____

DATE _____ TIME _____ A.M. P.M.

M _____

'OF _____

PHONE _____
AREA CODE          NUMBER          EXTENSION

| TELEPHONED | | PLEASE CALL | |
| CAME TO SEE YOU | | WILL CALL AGAIN | |
| WANTS TO SEE YOU | | RUSH | |
| RETURNED YOUR CALL | | SPECIAL ATTENTION | |

MESSAGE _____
_____
_____
_____
_____
_____

SIGNED _____
LITHO IN U.S.A.

TOPS ♦ FORM 3002P

---

## IMPORTANT MESSAGE

FOR _____

DATE _____ TIME _____ A.M. P.M.

M _____

OF _____

PHONE _____
AREA CODE          NUMBER          EXTENSION

| TELEPHONED | | PLEASE CALL | |
| CAME TO SEE YOU | | WILL CALL AGAIN | |
| WANTS TO SEE YOU | | RUSH | |
| RETURNED YOUR CALL | | SPECIAL ATTENTION | |

MESSAGE _____
_____
_____
_____
_____
_____

SIGNED _____
LITHO IN U.S.A.

TOPS ♦ FORM 3002P

---

## IMPORTANT MESSAGE

FOR _____

DATE _____ TIME _____ A.M. P.M.

M _____

OF _____

PHONE _____
AREA CODE          NUMBER          EXTENSION

| TELEPHONED | | PLEASE CALL | |
| CAME TO SEE YOU | | WILL CALL AGAIN | |
| WANTS TO SEE YOU | | RUSH | |
| RETURNED YOUR CALL | | SPECIAL ATTENTION | |

MESSAGE _____
_____
_____
_____
_____
_____

SIGNED _____
LITHO IN U.S.A.

TOPS ♦ FORM 3002P

---

## IMPORTANT MESSAGE

FOR _____

DATE _____ TIME _____ A.M. P.M.

M _____

OF _____

PHONE _____
AREA CODE          NUMBER          EXTENSION

| TELEPHONED | | PLEASE CALL | |
| CAME TO SEE YOU | | WILL CALL AGAIN | |
| WANTS TO SEE YOU | | RUSH | |
| RETURNED YOUR CALL | | SPECIAL ATTENTION | |

MESSAGE _____
_____
_____
_____
_____
_____

SIGNED _____
LITHO IN U.S.A.

TOPS ♦ FORM 3002P

## ACTIVITY 5-4

### Word Processing

1. Suppose you were asked to immediately call all customers who had recently purchased a product from your company. You now learn that the product is defective, and for safety reasons it must be replaced by your company. Keyboard two short paragraphs at the computer:

   A. Describing the procedure you would follow in preparing to place an outgoing call of this type, and

   B. Describing what words you would use to explain the problem to the customer in such a way that you can retain the customer for future purchases.

2. Save and print one double-spaced copy.

## ACTIVITY 5-5

### Word Processing

1. Consult a local telephone directory and answer the following questions at the computer.

   A. On what page(s) in the directory will you find:

      — local and long-distance information
      — area codes
      — local zip codes
      — maps
      — indexes

   B. How does the directory set up special listings for U.S. government offices, state government offices, county government offices, and city government offices?

2. Keyboard the answers to these questions and save.

3. Print one double-spaced copy.

## Word Processing Applications

The purpose of this activity is to practice typing legal documents.

You receive a call from On-Time Temp Services and they ask if you will accept another assignment for two days at a different law firm. You accept and report to the new firm, Fong & Family, Attorneys-at-Law, the following morning.

Lying on your desk is a different Word Processing Job Request form, but it still serves the same purpose. It outlines one of your work assignments. Read the form carefully and then begin the work.

---

### WORD PROCESSING ORDER

RUSH _____

DATE _Today_____     DEADLINE _none_____

TO _temp_____     FROM _Laura Fong_____

CLIENT _____     JOB # _____

COPIES TO _____

_____

_____

FAX TO _____ AT _____

OVERNIGHT _____ NEXT DAY _____

PRINT:   DISK # _____ DOC # _____ PAPER _____

SPECIAL INSTRUCTIONS _____

_Please type, save and print this form. Include the names and changes I made._

_____

---

(continued on next page)

   

*2. I understand and it is my intention that this power of attorney shall not be affected by my subsequent incapacity.*

# DURABLE POWER OF ATTORNEY
# FOR HEALTH CARE

## 1. Appointment of Attorney-in-fact

I, *Alfred Louis Anderson*, of *21-88th St., San Francisco, CA* do hereby designate and appoint *Robert William Curtis*, of *21-88th St., San Francisco, CA* telephone number *808-055-1148* as my attorney-in-fact to make health care decisions for me as authorized in this document.

## ~~2.~~ Statement of Authority Granted

Subject to any limitations set forth in this document, I hereby grant to my attorney-in-fact full power and authority to make health care decisions for me to the same extent that I could make such decisions for myself if I had the capacity to do so. In exercising this authority, my attorney-in-fact shall make health care decisions that are consistent with my desires, as set forth in this document.

## ~~3.~~ Inspection and Disclosure of Medical Information

*Remember*

My attorney-in-fact shall have the power and authority to request, receive, and review all information (verbal or written) regarding my physical or mental condition, including (but not limited to) all medical, hospital, and billing records. My attorney-in-fact shall have authority to execute any release or authorizations required to obtain medical, psychological, or psychiatric information. My attorney-in-fact shall, in addition, have authority to consent to the disclosure of this information.

## ~~4.~~ Visiting Principal

With regard to visiting me while I am hospitalized or a resident in any health care facility, my attorney-in-fact shall be entitled to priority under the patient visiting regulations of such health care institution.

## ~~5.~~ Duration

This durable power of attorney shall expire and shall cease to be in force or effect seven years from the date hereof.

(continued on next page)

## 7. Revocation of Prior Designations

By this document, I revoke any durable power of attorney for health care I may have executed prior to this date.

IN WITNESS WHEREFOR, I have signed and acknowledged this Durable Power of Attorney for Health Care this _13th_ day of _March_                    , 19__.


ALFRED LOUIS ANDERSON

## Time Sheet

After completing the two-day assignment, you are required to complete a time sheet for On-Time Temps. Use the following information to complete the time sheet.

Write this week's date.

The customer order number is **29845.**

Tuesday you began work at 9 a.m., took one hour for lunch, and left work at 5 p.m.

Wednesday you began work at 9 a.m., took only thirty minutes for lunch, and left work at 5:30 p.m.

(continued on next page)

ON-TIME TEMPORARY
TIME SHEET

Client Customer Name (Please Print)

Department

Employee Name (Please Print)

Employee Social Security Number

Week ending Sunday:      /      /

Customer Order #_____

| Date | Time Started | Time Finished | Less Lunch | Total Time Worked |
|------|--------------|---------------|------------|-------------------|
|      |              |               |            |                   |
|      |              |               |            |                   |
|      |              |               |            |                   |
|      |              |               |            |                   |

Total Hours Worked (nearest 1/2 hour)  _____

Has this assignment been completed?  Yes  _____ No _____

I certify that the hours shown above were worked by me during the week indicated.

Employee signature

Client signature

# *Filing and Managing Records*

# Objectives

After completing this chapter, you will be able to do the following:

1. List the purposes for maintaining records.
2. Give examples of classification of records.
3. Give examples of filing systems.
4. List the steps taken to file a record.
5. List paper storage systems.
6. List electronic storage systems.
7. List advantages and disadvantages of electronical storage systems.
8. Give examples of basic indexing rules.
9. Give examples of basic alphabetizing rules.
10. Give examples of a record retention system.

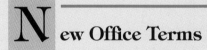

alphabetic filing system
centralized filing system
chronological filing system
cross-reference
geographic filing system
hard copy
indexing

lateral files
mobile files
numeric filing system
open files
rotary files
subject filing system

## Before You Begin . . .

*Using an electronic typewriter or a microcomputer, answer the following questions to the best of your ability:*

1. *What are the five basic filing systems? Explain them.*
2. *What are three examples of equipment used for filing records?*

Have you ever heard about the paperless office? Does one really exist? Will one ever exist?

In the 1980s, microcomputers became commonplace in businesses, and employers began to talk about the paperless office. Many people thought that storing information in a computer would eliminate the need for paper.

So far, this has not proven true. Individuals still want to see information on a hard copy. **Hard copy** means information printed onto paper, as opposed to saved on a computer disk.

What are all these pieces of paper that people are expecting to disappear? Here are some examples:

- a purchase order for a new desk
- the mortgage papers on a building owned by a business
- personnel records of all employees
- all financial papers for tax purposes
- advertisements
- copies of letters
- copies of contracts
- copies of memorandums

*As you can see, the paperless office has not arrived for most businesses. Filing continues to be an important part of the clerical employee's work.*

It is important to maintain records for a business to function effectively. Records are also kept for legal reasons, such as for tax reports or to comply with state and federal labor laws.

For example, consider a rental agreement between the owner of a small business that rents an office and the owner of the office building. This record is important for tax purposes, for rent increases, and to prove the responsibilities for maintaining the property.

Records should be stored and maintained in an orderly fashion so that past information can be located and used when needed. Storing and maintaining records is known as records management.

Records management involves developing a filing system that will meet the needs of a particular office. This system must allow you to store records. It must also allow you to easily retrieve the records when needed.

Many office workers will tell you that the simpler a filing system, the more efficient it will be. In the above example of a rental agreement, the simplest method would be to file the agreement under the address of the property. That is because more than one tenant occupies the building.

##  FILING SYSTEMS

The basic filing systems used in offices are alphabetic, subject, geographic, numeric, and chronological. Some offices use just one system. Other offices use a combination of two or more systems.

### Alphabetic

The **alphabetic filing system** is the most conventional and widely used system. It consists of arranging files in order beginning with *A* and ending with *Z*. Files may be records for individuals, businesses, or government agencies.

The following is an example of names listed in alphabetic filing order:

Acme Bread Company
Andrews, Harold
Danford Hauling and Storage
Justine's on the Park
Kirk, Ronald

### Subject

The **subject filing system** involves arranging files by topics or by subjects. An office worker should be careful when establishing this type of system. It is important that meaningful topics or subjects be chosen.

For example, the personnel department in a hospital may use the following topics for a subject filing system:

Professional
    Doctors
    Nurses
    Administrative Employees

Nonprofessional
    Clerical Workers
    Grounds and Maintenance Workers
    Cafeteria Workers

Within each subject area is an alphabetic listing of the employees in the company. If you need to locate the personnel file for a word processing operator named Loretta Ramas, for example, you go to the Clerical Workers subject section and then proceed to the letter *R*. Can you see how arranging the files first by subject can simplify and speed up the process of retrieving records as compared with using a totally alphabetic system?

It is wise to keep an alphabetic listing of the subjects if you use a subject filing system. This listing will prevent you from adding a new subject when one is already on file. For example, in the above listing you already have Nurses as a subject, so you would not add that word again to your list. It will also help new employees who need to use the files. You can keep the alphabetic list on sheets of paper, on a card index, or in a computer.

## Geographic

The **geographic filing system** arranges, or groups, records according to geographic location. The locations are categorized by international, national, state, and regional boundaries. The names within each group are then listed alphabetically.

For example, a trucking firm may use the following geographic system:

East
    Maine
    New York
    Rhode Island

South
    Alabama
    Georgia

Midwest
    Ohio

West
    California
    Oregon
    Washington

Within each geographic area is an alphabetic listing of the clients of the company. For example, suppose you need to retrieve the file for

Sonic Freight Service of Georgia. You look in the drawer that contains the files for the South. You then look under the letter *S* for Sonic.

As with other filing systems, the geographic system also needs some type of cross-index. *Cross-index* means related information found in another location. In the above examples, the client names are cross-indexed alphabetically on paper, on cards, or in a computer.

## Numeric

The **numeric filing system** arranges records in numeric order according to numbers that were assigned to the files. This is considered an indirect method of filing, since you must know what name a number represents. The name is usually found through an alphabetic listing.

The following is an example of a numeric system using consecutive numbers in ascending order:

104358921
105345643
121339564

## Chronological

The **chronological filing system** arranges records in order by date. This system is used in addition to, not in place of, another filing system. For example, a letter from Roger Craig dated June 11 is filed alphabetically under Craig. In addition, a copy of the letter is filed chronologically under the date June 11. This is a way to locate information when a worker has forgotten the contents of a record.

Another example of the chronological system is a monthly binder with sections separated by days. Copies of all correspondence are filed into the binder under the date they are written.

A chronological file is a quick way to review the activity of a company over a certain period of time. For example, Paul is a marketing representative. He was recently transferred to a position in a different state. Paul used the "chron" file to become familiar with the activity of his new district over the past six months.

# Recall Time

*Answer the following questions:*

1. What is meant by hard copy?
2. You are looking at a letter on a computer monitor. Is this considered hard copy?
3. How will the following be listed if arranged in alphabetic order?
   Lake Street Hardware
   Harris, Thomas
   Mandel, Laura
   Blue Bird Cafe
   Harris, Marian
4. How will the following be listed if arranged in numeric order?
   454213355
   219570311
   219564133
   535892110
   134351221
5. You have just opened a women's clothing store. You decide to set up a subject filing system. What topics could you use for the filing systems?
6. A new company decides to use only a chronological filing system. Is this a wise decision? Explain.

# PREPARATION OF RECORDS FOR FILING

Carole is a general office clerk for a graphics firm located in the South. Carole sets aside time each day for her filing. She uses the following routine to prepare her records for filing.

Recall that a record could be a letter, a contract, an invoice, or other documents to be processed.

## Checking

Carole first inspects the record to see that it has been released for filing. This means that her boss has made a stamped or handwritten notation on the record that indicates the record is ready to be filed.

Susan is working in a department where she and all the other employees are from the same country and have the same cultural background. It has been this way for almost a year. The employees get along well and enjoy breaks and lunches together.

A new person named Teng is hired. He is not from the same country as the other employees and has a much different cultural background. Teng has good clerical skills, and all the required work continues to get done adequately.

All the employees are polite to Teng, but that is where it stops. Teng joins the group only occasionally for breaks and never for lunch.

1. Do you think Teng will be happy in this new environment?
2. If you were an employee in this group, would you make an extra effort to make Teng feel comfortable with the other employees?

## Stapling and Mending

Carole realizes that paper clips are not to be used for permanent storage of records. So, she removes paper clips and staples the required pages together. She also uses tape to repair areas that need mending.

## Deciding

Carole must now make a decision on where the record is to be filed. For example, her company is using the alphabetic system for filing. She has a letter from Ana Lewis, a client. She must file the letter in the location from which it can most easily be found in the future. Carole decides to file it under Lewis.

## Marking

In a previous job, Carole learned that it was necessary to mark directly on a record where the record is to be filed. For this process, she underlines the key word to be used for filing. In the letter from Ana Lewis, Carole underlines the word *Lewis* using a colored pencil. Some office workers may write the word in the upper right-hand corner of the paper.

## Cross-referencing

Sometimes, you will have material that can be filed under one or more names or subjects. For example, suppose you receive a letter from Ms. Simpson and the subject of the letter relates to Ms. Morgan. You file the letter under Morgan, and put a **cross-reference** sheet under Simpson. Figure 6–1 is an example of a cross-reference sheet.

A permanent cross-reference sheet is prepared when a company or a person changes her or his name. For example, Ana Lewis has been a client of Carole's firm for many years. However, her last name became

```
CROSS-REFERENCE SHEET

NAME OR SUBJECT:

DATE:

REGARDING:


                              SEE:

NAME OR SUBJECT:
```

Lewis just recently when she married. Carole maintains a folder under the name of Lewis with all past and future records. Under Gable, Ana Lewis's maiden name, Carole prepares a cross-reference sheet or guide and files it in its alphabetic location with the rest of the folders. A cross-reference guide can be the same as a cross-reference sheet, but you fasten it onto sturdy material, such as an old file folder.

### Arranging

As the last step in preparing to file, Carole arranges the documents to be filed in a way that the filing will go quickly. This means she places them in alphabetic order and in groups if the file drawers are in different locations.

## ■ CLASSIFICATION AND RETENTION

Carole did not realize there was so much to know about filing until she began working for this graphics company. She soon realizes that companies have many different kinds of records. Some are vital to keep, some are important to keep, some are useful to keep, and some need not be kept at all. For example, Carole discovers the following:

- The graphics firm owns the building it is located in. The mortgage papers are *vital records* to keep.
- Businesses must pay taxes, just as individuals must pay taxes. All files relating to taxes are *important records* to keep.
- The graphics firm recently purchased Carole a new desk. The purchase order for the desk is a *useful record* to keep.
- Carole's boss received an announcement of a luncheon meeting sponsored by a graphics club. He has a meeting that day and cannot attend. There is no reason to keep the announcement. This is a *nonessential record*.

Once Carole has decided which records are vital and important to keep, her next question to her supervisor is, "Do we keep these records permanently? If not, for how long?" This decision is usually made at the time of the first filing and is based on a record retention schedule set up by each company. A record retention schedule is a listing of all the classification of records and how long each should be retained. Carole's supervisor, Mr. Lloyd, is an active member of the Association of Records Managers and Administrators (ARMA). Thus he is able to give her an accurate answer.

A nationwide survey has been conducted on the subject of record retention. Figure 6–2 is a partial listing of the results of the survey. The schedule in this figure was determined by surveying the record retention schedules recommended by leading authorities on record storage and by businesses with established procedures.

The schedule in figure 6–2 reflects current business thinking. However, the retention periods shown are not offered as final authority, but as guideposts. States have statutes of limitations, laws on how long records must be kept, and federal agencies have regulations that must be followed. Each company must make the final decision on how long to retain records.

■ FIGURE 6–2
*Partial Listing of Nationwide Survey on Records Retention*

### Retention Schedule

(P = permanent; O = optional; numbers represent suggested years)

| | |
|---|---|
| Accounts payable ledger | P |
| Accounts receivable ledger | 10 |
| Building permits | 20 |
| Government audit reports | P |
| Annual reports | P |
| Checkbook orders | O |
| Check records | 7 |
| Employee service records | P |
| Pension plan | P |
| Sales invoices | 7 |

## INDUSTRY FOCUS

**Richard L. Lechnar**
*Manager*
*Corporate Record Systems*
*Syntex (USA), Inc.*

Q: Mr. Lechnar, how important is filing in the business world?

A: When we think of filing procedures, we tend to think of paper documents. However, in today's changing environment, the files might be in different media—for example, electronic, magnetic, optical, or photographic—but, the principles of efficient filing remain the same. Therefore, it is extremely important that the techniques and methods of files management be learned and followed. Without these basics, we will have systems anarchy rather than systems organization.

Q: Any personal experiences where mismanagement of filing has caused problems?

A: I have experienced a number of occasions where the loss of documents through poor files management practices has caused both economic loss and reduction of customer satisfaction. The failure to produce required documents in litigation, in many cases, resulted not only in financial embarrassment but also in directed guilty verdicts, particularly in product liability matters.

Q: What advice would you give to a student who is planning on an office career?

A: The major contribution—in my opinion—students can bring to the business world is an open mind and a willingness to pitch in and help. Skills can be learned—a good attitude opens the door to learning.

## ■ LOCATION OF PERMANENT RECORDS

Carole is concerned about space for all the records that must be kept on a permanent basis. She also wonders if enough space is available for records that must be kept for long periods and yet are not being used. She asks Mr. Lloyd about this.

Mr. Lloyd explains that at their graphics firm, records pass through three stages:

- *Stage 1.* These records are active and should be close at hand. They are referred to frequently, and Mr. Lloyd must have immediate access to them.

216

- *Stage 2*. These records are only occasionally needed by Mr. Lloyd. They are only semiactive and can be placed in storage.
- *Stage 3*. These records are no longer needed by the graphics firm but must be kept owing to government regulations. They are usually held in permanent storage, often in another location.

Carole later learns that these procedures are followed by many firms, not just her current employer.

# ■ FILING EQUIPMENT

Choosing the proper equipment in which to store records is an important part of records management. Choose equipment that will protect the records from damage and that is efficient to use. For example, you can use vertical, lateral, open, rotary, mobile or portable, or card files.

## Vertical Files

Vertical filing equipment is usually made of metal and sits upright with one or more drawers. The files face the front of the drawer, making it easy to locate documents.

## Lateral Files

Lateral filing equipment is also made of metal, but the drawers rest sideways. The files are arranged vertically, from side to side, inside the drawers. Cabinets for **lateral files** require less aisle space than do vertical cabinets.

*Vertical filing cabinets are the most commonly used filing equipment by businesses.*

*Lateral file cabinets are also commonly used by businesses.*

## Open Files

Open filing equipment resembles open bookshelves. The file folders are placed on an open shelf. Equipment for **open files** saves on space. Many employees use color-coded files for quicker location of records.

## Rotary Files

**Rotary files** may be contained in a small unit that sits on the desk or in a large unit that operates on the floor. A small unit may simply be a rotating wheel that holds business cards of all the clients. A large floor unit may be electronically operated and may contain standard file folders and guides. The files rotate in a circular motion similar to that of a carousel.

## Mobile or Portable Files

When files must be shared on a regular basis, it is easiest to locate them in portable cabinets. These portable cabinets are known as **mobile files.** They are usually one-drawer cabinets that are on wheels allowing them to be moved from one location to another. The drawer normally has a lid to pull up, as opposed to being the pullout style.

## Card Files

Many office workers keep card files even when other filing equipment is used within the company. A card file is normally a small desktop box or tray that is used for quick reference of frequently needed information. Card files can also be located in a cabinet drawer when more space is needed and quick reference is not needed.

 **BASIC INDEXING RULES**

When preparing a new folder or card for filing purposes, you must decide in what order to type the name of the person or company. This is called **indexing.** Once you have indexed the name on the folder, then you will file the folder alphabetically with the rest of the files.

## Individual Names

Individual names are indexed by first the surname (last name), next the first name or initial, and then any middle names or initials. For example:

| The name . . . | is indexed as . . . |
| --- | --- |
| Ann E. Delgardo | Delgardo, Ann E. |
| T. C. O'Neil | O'Neil, T. C. |
| J. Linda Singh | Singh, J. Linda |

## Company Names

Company names are indexed in the order that they appear. However, when a company name is composed of an individual's name, follow the rules for indexing individual names. For example:

| The name . . . | is indexed as . . . |
|---|---|
| Westamerica Bank | Westamerica Bank |
| Applied Biosystems | Applied Biosystems |
| C. Martin, Inc. | Martin, C., Inc. |
| Rita Ramos & Sons | Ramos, Rita & Sons |

## ◼ BASIC ALPHABETIZING RULES

Lorie began working as a temporary office worker six months ago in a large midwestern city. Lorie could not type, so most of her assignments were filing jobs. Lorie began to compare the filing rules she learned in school with the systems she found on the various assignments. She found many deviations in the filing systems used. Nevertheless, Lorie did realize that secretaries all followed the same basic filing rules.

*These folders are arranged in alphabetic order. This will help make the filing go quickly.*

### Basic Filing Rule

Arrange files in alphabetical order by the first word. The first word is the first word you decided to type when you did the indexing. For example:

| Out of Filing Order | In Filing Order |
|---|---|
| Erickson, Barbara | Alioto, Martin |
| Clark, Tyler | Clark, Tyler |
| Alioto, Martin | Erickson, Barbara |
| Wiggins, Heloise | Wiggins, Heloise |

### Similar Names of Unequal Length

When two or more names are the same up to a certain letter, the shorter name is filed first. For example, Clark is filed before Clarke. A good way to remember is to memorize "nothing comes before something." For example:

| Out of Filing Order | In Filing Order |
|---|---|
| Lowe, Georg | Low, Charles |
| Low, Charles | Lowe, Georg |
| Smithe, Lucy | Smith, Sara |
| Smith, Sara | Smithe, Lucy |

### Hyphenated Names

Hyphenated names are treated as one word. For example Debbie Wilson-Tobin is filed under Wilson-Tobin. Also for example:

| Out of Filing Order | In Filing Order |
| --- | --- |
| Lee-Harris, Shelly | Harris, Carol Lee |
| Harris, Carol Lee | Lee-Harris, Shelly |
| Perkins-Millan, Inez | Millan, Flora |
| Millan, Flora | Perkins-Millan, Inez |

## Abbreviations

Abbreviations are spelled out in full. For example, Robt. is filed using Robert. Also for example:

| Out of Filing Order | In Filing Order |
| --- | --- |
| Portillo, Wm. | Burrell, Charles |
| Burrell, Chas. | Pembroke Rental Company |
| St. Veronica's School | Portillo, William |
| Pembroke Rental Co. | Saint Veronica's School |

## Surnames with Prefixes

If an individual surname is compounded with prefixes, it is treated as one word. For example:

| Out of Filing Order | In Filing Order |
| --- | --- |
| O'Neil Richard | Del Rosario, Rima |
| Del Rosario, Rima | D'Martini, Christine |
| D'Martini, Christine | Los Robos Lodge |
| Los Robos Lodge | O'Neil, Richard |

## Articles, Prepositions, Conjunctions

Articles, prepositions, and conjunctions are *not* considered part of a filing unit. Disregard them. The exception is if a preposition comes as the first word of a company name, such as At the Top of the Hill Restaurant. For example:

| Out of Filing Order | In Filing Order |
| --- | --- |
| The Fashion Center | (The) Fashion Center |
| Hospice of Marin | (The) Haswell Group |
| Top of the Bay Hotel | Hospice (of) Marin |
| The Haswell Group | Top (of the) Bay Hotel |

## Names Containing Numbers

When a name contains a number, the number is spelled out both on the folder and when alphabetizing. For example:

| Out of Filing Order | In Filing Order |
| --- | --- |
| 50 Sutter Place | Fifty Sutter Place |
| 1 Market Plaza | First American Title |
| 9 Months Only | Nine Months Only |
| 1st American Title | One Market Plaza |

# Recall Time

*Answer the following questions:*

1. What is the marking process when records are prepared for filing?
2. When is a cross-reference sheet used?
3. What is the difference between indexing and filing?
4. What is the result when you index the following?
   Donald Hammond
   Stephen Wong
   J. Alice Goldstein
   Sunrise Hill Associates
   Union City Tire & Brake
5. What is the result when you arrange the following in alphabetic order?
   Garcia Bakery
   Cox, Ben
   Day Hour Mini Mart
   Apple Annie's
   Cox, Chas.
   Smith-Hawkins, Paula
6. What is the result when you arrange the following in alphabetic order?
   The Kraftsman Group
   Del Rose, Teresa
   25 Moller Plaza
   Society of Brothers

##  PREPARATION OF FILING SUPPLIES

Blanche is excited. She has been hired as a receptionist by an architect who has been in business for only a year but who has a good reputation and quite a few clients. Since the architect's business is new, not much work has been done in setting up files for the clients. Blanche decides to attack this as one of her first projects. She first purchases a new vertical filing cabinet. She then purchases a secretary's handbook from a local bookstore, reviews the section on techniques of record management, and begins to set up the files. Her procedure involves preparing folders and labels, inserting correspondence, and placing folders into a file drawer.

### Preparing Folders and Labels

Blanche sets up a business-size 8½×11 manila folder for each client. She types a label for the folder using the largest type possible, by typing in uppercase letters.

While preparing the folders, Blanche is faced with the following problems. She is able to solve them with help from her office handbook.

---

### Maintaining Records

Most large offices use a **centralized filing system** for their records. This means that a company's general files are stored in one central location. Under this system, employees are hired to work exclusively in the centralized filing area. These employees are responsible for maintaining all the centralized files including developing a method to know where the records are at all times. The equipment used in large offices with a centralized filing system is lateral or open files as opposed to vertical files.

Small offices may also use a centralized system, but it is more common for them to use a decentralized filing system. This means that records are stored in different locations within an office. Each secretary or other clerical employee is responsible for the storage and retrieval of files pertaining to her or his specialized work. Vertical filing cabinets, rather than lateral files, are most often used in small offices.

*Would you like to begin your office career as a file clerk in a large office with a centralized filing system? Why or why not? If you work in a small office, will you remember to set a time aside for filing on a regular basis?*

---

- She finds two clients with the exact same name. Her solution is to use labels of different colors for these two clients. In this way, she can identify the folders quicker.
- She discovers that one client already has so many reports that they cannot all fit into one folder. Her solution is to prepare two folders for the one client and separate them by date headings.

## Inserting Correspondence

Once the folders are prepared, Blanche takes all the correspondence for each individual client. She arranges the correspondence in the appropriate folder by date with the latest date on the top. She is extra cautious that the right papers go into the right file folders. She remembers that her boss told her that new business prospects can be lost if the necessary papers are not available when needed for the clients.

## Placing Folders into a File Drawer

Blanche places the folders in alphabetic order in a drawer of the vertical file cabinet. She then refers to her secretary's handbook and reads the section on file guides. File guides divide the file drawers into sections making it easier to locate a folder. For example, one guide can be labeled A and all the folders behind it can begin with the letter A. If you have only a few clients, the guide can be labeled A–D and all the folders behind it can begin with the letters A, B, C, and D. Both examples are

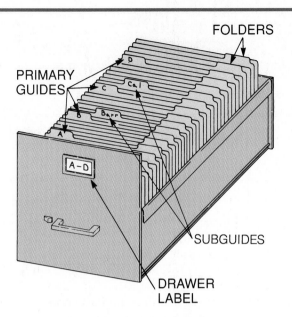

FOLDERS

PRIMARY GUIDES

D

C

Ca,l

B

Barr

A

A–D

SUBGUIDES

DRAWER LABEL

**VERTICAL FILE DRAWER**

primary guides because they represent major divisions within the drawers.

Blanche completes the project by setting up the primary guides. She also reads about secondary guides, which divide the folder even further, into subdivisions. However, she does not believe this procedure is necessary for her situation. She does not yet have enough files to make subdivisions useful.

Refer to figure 6–3 for an example of a file drawer with both primary and secondary guides. File guides may be purchased at stationery stores.

## ■ WHERE'S THE FOLDER?

No matter how efficient your filing system, it will not work if you cannot find a folder when you need it. One cause of folders being misplaced is that another employee may take them from the file drawer from time to time. In this case, some notation must be made stating which employee has a particular folder. This is done by an out card.

An out card is the same height as the file folders. It may be a different color with the word *OUT* printed in all capital letters on the top tab of the card. On the front of this out card are ruled columns for an employee to record the date, a description of the file or material removed, when the item is to be returned, the name of the person the item is charged to, and other remarks. See figure 6–4 for a sample of an out card.

The out card is placed in the exact spot from which a folder or material is removed. A secretary will not use an out card every time a file

OUT

| DATE | MATERIAL | DATE REMOVED | TO BE RETURNED | REMOVED BY | COMMENTS |
|------|----------|--------------|----------------|------------|----------|
|      |          |              |                |            |          |
|      |          |              |                |            |          |
|      |          |              |                |            |          |
|      |          |              |                |            |          |
|      |          |              |                |            |          |

is pulled. An out card is used only when someone outside the immediate office wants a file or if a secretary or a boss wishes to remove a file for a long period of time.

## ■ ELECTRONIC STORAGE

Most records are still stored on paper. However, two electronic methods of storing files are also common in the business world. These are storing on computer disk or tape, and storing on microfilm or microfiche.

### Microcomputer Disk

Bo uses a microcomputer to do word processing for four bosses. All his files are saved on disk. He must give these files a name before they are saved. His word processing program only allows him to use eight letters plus a three-letter extension. Since Bo has four bosses, he keeps several disks for all his files. He has a disk for each boss, plus a separate disk for each client. Therefore, when he names a file, he uses the name of the addressee plus the disk number as the extension.

For example, Bo is working with data disk number 102 in his microcomputer, and he has just finished inputting a letter to Arnold Alvarez. When Bo saves the file, he names it ALVAREZ.102. He also types that file name at the bottom of the letter. He keeps a hard copy of the letter. If his boss needs to make changes on the letter, Bo puts disk 102 back into the computer and retrieves onto his computer screen the file ALVAREZ.102.

Bo could also have named his file ALVAR102.LTR. The first letters identify the addressee, the number of the disk follows, and the extension LTR denotes the file is a letter. Under this system, Bo would use MEM as an extension when he saves a memorandum, and RPT when he saves a report.

At the end of each day, Bo makes a backup copy of all his disks. He has learned from past experience that the disks may get damaged or files may get deleted by mistake. Having a backup copy means he will have a second disk copy of all his files if something happens to the original. Backup copies are done on a daily basis.

Bo stores his disks in cases that were purchased at a local stationery store. These cases are specifically made to store disks. They are flat trays with plastic lids to protect from static, dust, and debris.

## Mainframe Tape

Ed works for a money market fund firm in California. The company files all its records on a mainframe computer in Chicago. It rents time on the mainframe from the computer company in Chicago. All the transactions are done through telephone lines that connect Ed's computer terminal to the mainframe in Chicago.

Ed works in the customer service department. He frequently adds new customers to the computer files. To do this, he must (1) activate the program, (2) log on with his password, (3) call onto the screen the New Customer File, and (4) input the information.

After the new information is added, Ed must again store the files onto magnetic tape that is in the mainframe. Magnetic tape is similar to a cassette tape in a tape recorder. It can be removed from the mainframe, and erased and reused if necessary. Saving files on this magnetic tape is preferred to saving files on floppy disks because the tape has room to store more files.

Remember, files are given names that relate to their contents. When Ed wants to retrieve the New Customer File onto the screen, he has to type NEWCUST.FIL as the name of the document.

A password is used for security purposes. Only the employees in Ed's department who know the names of the files can access them. Unless you know the password, you cannot get into the files.

## Microfilm

Pamela works as a chief assistant in the traffic department for a municipal court. She has an entirely different filing system than the disks used by Bo and the tapes used by Ed. All the traffic tickets and records for her department are stored on microfilm. Microfilm is used for filing when companies need to reduce the size of file space. This is done by making copies of the records onto rolls of film.

At Pamela's traffic department, the traffic tickets are first put into batches of two hundred to three hundred tickets. A Canon camera is then used to take the microfilm pictures. At this point, the tickets are given a cartridge and frame number. The cartridge is a container for the film when it is put into storage. The frame is the location of the individual ticket on the film.

All the cartridges are labeled on the outside and stored on lazy Susan–type shelves. The filing numbers written on the cartridges are in groups representing year, cartridge, and frame. For example, 91-0078-4488 represents the year 1991, cartridge 78, and frame 4488.

Rowland is a data entry operator in the traffic department of a large city in the West. He is one of five operators who enters traffic citations into the computer.

One day, Rowland hears two other operators, Martha and Rick, talking. Rick tells Martha how he was able to fix a ticket for his neighbor by not entering it into the computer.

1. If you were Rowland, what would you do? Say something to Rick? Tell a supervisor? Do nothing?

When Pamela needs information about a traffic ticket, she views the film on a screen. The screen is about the size of a computer monitor. The ticket is magnified so all the information can easily be viewed. About three full-size traffic tickets fit on the screen at one time. The original hard copies of the tickets are kept for two months and then destroyed. Hard copies can be made from the microfilm if needed.

### Microfiche

In the same building where Pamela works, the tax department uses a filing system similar to Pamela's. The tax department, however, stores its microfilms on sheets or cards. These are called microfiche. They are rectangular-shaped sheets with small squares of microimages (reduced images) on them. When information is needed, the microfiche are viewed on a screen. Hard copies can also be made.

*This employee is using a microfiche reader to view information that is stored on microfilm.*

# ADVANTAGES AND DISADVANTAGES OF ELECTRONIC FILES

Diskette, magnetic tape, microfilm, and microfiche are examples of electronic filing storage. The major advantage of these electronic files is that they need less storage space than do hard copy files. It is also easier to retrieve files from them than from hard copy systems.

A major disadvantage of electronic files is their sensitivity to heat and dust. The files can be damaged much more easily than can hard copy files. Electronic filing systems are also more expensive to install and maintain.

## R ecall Time

*Answer the following questions:*

1. You are setting up file folders. How do you solve the following dilemmas?
   a. You need folders for two different clients with the same name.
   b. One client has too many papers to fit into one folder.
2. What are file guides used for?
3. What is the difference between primary and secondary file guides?
4. What is an out card used for?
5. What are one advantage and one disadvantage of using electronic filing as opposed to paper filing?

## SUMMARY

Filing is a task that is performed by all office workers. Some do more than others, but files must be maintained by all workers. Standard basic filing systems are used by most workers to make filing tasks more efficient.

Basic indexing rules are also used by most office workers. Once these rules are mastered, filing systems become fairly easy to maintain.

In some companies, electronic filing systems are used in addition to hard copy systems. In a few companies, electronic systems replace hard copy systems.

Look at the following list of filing methods and systems. Do you understand all of them? If not, which ones need further study?

- alphabetic filing system
- subject filing system
- geographic filing system
- numeric filing system
- chronological filing system
- preparation of records for filing
- retention of files

- selection of filing equipment
- basic alphabetizing rules
- electronic filing methods

---

## *In Conclusion . . .*

*When you have completed this chapter, use an electronic typewriter or a microcomputer to answer the following questions.*

*1. What are the five basic filing systems? Explain them.*
*2. What are three examples of equipment used for filing records?*

---

# Review and Application

## REVIEW YOUR VOCABULARY

Supply the missing words by choosing from the new Office Terms listed below.

1. There is a document that can be filed under more than one name. You file the document under one name and _____ _____ under the other.
2. If information is printed on paper, you have a _____ _____ .
3. A _____ _____ _____ arranges records according to location.
4. A _____ _____ _____ arranges names by topics.
5. A _____ _____ _____ arranges records by date.
6. A large company keeps all its files in one central location. This is called a _____ _____ system.
7. When preparing a new folder or card for filing purposes, you must decide in what order to type the name of the person or company onto the folder or card. This is called _____ .
8. _____ files are contained on a wheel that rotates in a circular motion.
9. _____ files are portable and shared on a regular basis.
10. _____ files resemble bookshelves.
11. _____ files have drawers that rest sideways and the files are arranged from side to side.

a. alphabetic filing system
b. centralized filing system
c. chronological filing system
d. cross-reference
e. geographic filing system
f. hard copy
g. indexing
h. lateral files
i. mobile files
j. numeric filing system
k. open files
l. rotary files
m. subject filing system

## DISCUSS AND ANALYZE AN OFFICE SITUATION

1. Diane and Ruth are file clerks for a large corporation. Their entire workday is spent in the file room. They are the only two employees doing the filing.

   They have little contact with other employees except when someone calls for a lost file. The file room employees have no dress code.

   Diane has noticed a strong odor coming from Ruth the past few days. Ruth is a clean person and bathes every day. However, Diane has noticed that Ruth wears the same clothes every day. Diane is guessing the odor is coming from the clothes.

   The smell is beginning to bother Diane. Should Diane say something to Ruth? If so, how should she approach Ruth?

## PRACTICE BASIC SKILLS

### Math

1. Your boss asks you to total the following expenses charged to the filing department.

| ITEM | AMOUNT | PRICE |
| --- | --- | --- |
| Hanging folders | 3 boxes | $14.79 per box |
| Hanging folder labels | 5 packages | 4.59 per package |
| Hanging folder frames | 6 boxes | 4.20 per box |
| Tab inserts | 8 packages | 1.05 per package |
| File jackets | 9 packages | 4.19 per package |

2. Your boss receives a catalog of discount supplies. He asks you to calculate how much would have been saved if the items in exercise 1 had been purchased at the following discount prices.

| ITEM | DISCOUNT PRICE |
|---|---|
| Hanging folders | $6.79 per box |
| Hanging folder labels | 2.49 per package |
| Hanging folder frames | 1.99 per box |
| Tab inserts | 0.69 per package |
| File jackets | 2.29 per package |

3. Compute the total amount that will be charged to the filing department for use of temporary help during the last six months. Use the following information:

### Temporary Help
### Six-Months Report

**January**

| | |
|---|---|
| Advertising department | $375.00 |
| Filing department | 235.00 |
| Accounting department | 680.00 |

**February**

| | |
|---|---|
| Advertising department | 375.00 |
| Filing department | 460.00 |
| Accounting department | 680.00 |

**March**

| | |
|---|---|
| Advertising department | 235.00 |
| Filing department | 375.00 |
| Accounting department | 680.00 |

**April**

| | |
|---|---|
| Advertising department | 800.00 |
| Filing department | 1,275.00 |
| Accounting department | 1,490.00 |

**May**

| | |
|---|---|
| Advertising department | 775.00 |
| Filing department | 1,030.00 |
| Accounting department | 1,490.00 |

**June**

| | |
|---|---|
| Advertising department | 800.00 |
| Filing department | 1,490.00 |
| Accounting department | 1,275.00 |

### English

1. *Rule:* Use a hyphen sometimes when *self, vice,* and *ex* are joined with another word.
   *Examples:* He was a self-made man. His ex-boss was in the building

*Practice Exercise:* Rewrite the following sentences, placing hyphens where needed.
   a. It was viewed by all the people as self imposed exile.
   b. The woman was elected vice chair of the committee.
   c. The meeting was scheduled for 3 p.m. between the attorney and his ex wife.
   d. He has always been a self supporting person.
   e. He furnished a new office for the vice president.

### Proofreading

1. Retype or rewrite the following, correcting all errors.

BOOKS FOR SALE

ACTIVE FILNG FOR PAPER RECORDS by Dr. Ann Bennick, CRM

Active Filing for Paper Records focuses on three bacis topics related to the managemnt of paper records: file systems development, filing equipment, and filing suplies. Implementation and conversion procedures is presented within the context of systems development techniques and ,where appropriate, as the relate to a discusion of spesific procedures, equipment, and supplies.

OPTICAL DISK SYSTEMS FOR RECORDS MANAGEMENT
By William Saffady

Optical Disk Systems for Records Management is divided into two parts. Section One provides an overview of optical disk technology. It defins the various types of storage media and breifly reviews their records management significance. Section Two provides a detailed discusion of optical filing systems, computer-based hardware and software configurations which store digitized document images on opticl disks for on-demand retreival. The discussion emphasises characteristics which influence the evaluation and selection of optical filing systems for records management applications.

### APPLY YOUR KNOWLEDGE

1. Arrange the following words into alphabetic order. Using a microcomputer or an electronic typewriter, tabulate the words into three columns.

storage
chronological
lateral
vertical
rotary
centralized
records
financial
paperless
vital
alphabetic
index

geographic
numeric
digit
important
reference
business
retrieval
folder
tabs
labels
supplies
drawer

*Write a **T** if the statement is true or an **F** if the statement is false.*

_____ 1. Hard copy means information printed onto paper, as opposed to saved on a computer disk.

_____ 2. The geographic filing system is the most conventional and widely used system.

_____ 3. The subject filing system involves arranging files by topics or by subjects.

_____ 4. The chronological filing system arranges records in order by numbers.

_____ 5. A cross-reference sheet is used in filing when material can be filed under more than one name or subject.

_____ 6. Mortgage papers are an example of nonessential records and need not be kept for a long period of time.

_____ 7. ARMA stands for the Association of Records Managers and Administrators.

_____ 8. Indexing is deciding in what order to type the name of a person or company on a new folder.

_____ 9. C. Martin, Inc. would be indexed as Martin, C., Inc.

_____ 10. In filing order, George Lowe would be filed before Charles Low.

_____ 11. Burrell, Wm. would be filed as Burrell, William.

_____ 12. In filing order, Hyatt Hotel would be filed before The Fashion Center.

_____ 13. In filing order, 1 Market Plaza would be filed as Market Plaza 1.

_____ 14. File guides divide file drawers into sections making it easier to locate folders.

_____ 15. A major advantage of using electronic filing over paper filing is that electronic filing requires less storage space.

## Word Processing

1. Keyboard the following paragraphs and correct all errors according to the proofreader's marks.

   The alphabetic filing system is the most conventional and widely used system. It consists of arranging files in order beginning with A and ending with Z.

   The subject filing system involves arranging files by topics or by subjects. The geographic filing system arranges, or groups, records according to geographic locations.

   The numerical filing system arranges records in numeric order according to numbers that were assigned to the files. The chronological filing system arranges records in order by date.

2. Save and print one copy.

3. Edit the corrected document in the following ways and print a second copy.

   A. Underline each of the filing systems (example: <u>alphabetic filing system</u>).

   B. Double-space the copy and indent each paragraph ten spaces.

   C. Move the last paragraph to the second paragraph.

### Word Processing

1. Using the basic indexing and alphabetizing rules covered in this chapter, keyboard the correct index name for the following listing:

   A. Midnight Moving and Storage

   B. Darrell C. Williams

   C. Mary Dawn-Jones

   D. Edward O'Henry

   E. The Pharmacy

   F. Mary Dawn Jones

   G. St. Michael's Church

   H. 1 Wilshire Place

   I. J Parker Phillips

   J. Murphy Elementary School

2. Save and print a copy.

3. With the correctly indexed listing, keyboard a second list in correct filing order. Print a copy.

## Word Processing Applications

The purpose of this activity is to practice placing lists of words in alphabetic order.

You receive a call from On-Time Temps asking if you would be able to work for four hours to help Fong & Family Attorneys-at-Law get caught up with its work. You receive the following job request form when you report to work.

---

### WORD PROCESSING ORDER

RUSH ____

DATE _today_    DEADLINE _ASAP_

TO _temp_    FROM _Grace_

CLIENT _____    JOB # _____

COPIES TO _____

_____

_____

FAX TO _see instructions_    AT _____

OVERNIGHT _____ NEXT DAY _____

PRINT:    DISK # _____ DOC # _____ PAPER _____

SPECIAL INSTRUCTIONS _____

_Please complete the attached. I have_

_typed instructions at the top of each_

_Thank you,_

_Grace_

---

(continued on next page)

I will be giving a workshop for legal secretaries next week and need the following list alphabetized and tabulated into three columns.

WORDS AND PHRASES COMMONLY USED IN THE LEGAL PROFESSION

Execute
Set forth
Therefore
Duly sworn
Hereto
Parties hereto
Aforesaid
Notwithstanding
Herein
Hereafter
To wit
In witness whereof
Witnesseth
Whereas
Above-entitled
Just and proper
Foregoing
Wheresoever
Undersigned
Insofar as
Waive
Thereof
Hereby
Thenceforth
Deems
Thereafter
Certify
Resolved
Affix
Thereto

(continued on next page)

I will need the same done to these Latin words for the same workshop. Please use two columns with headings, one for the words and one for the meanings. Please also put in alphabetical order.

## LATIN WORDS COMMONLY USED IN THE LEGAL PROFESSION

| | |
|---|---|
| Lex | Law |
| Ex officio | Powers given by virtue of the office |
| Ad interim | In the meantime |
| Caveat | A warning |
| Situs | Location |
| Caveat emptor | Let the buyer beware |
| Per diem | By the day |
| Alias | Also known as |
| Pro rata | Proportionately |
| In to | Completely |
| De facto | In fact |
| In loco parentis | In the place of a parent |
| Prima facie | At first sight |
| Corpus juris | Body of law |
| Ante | Prior to |
| Per annum | By the year |
| Sine | Without |
| Subpoena | An order to appear in court |
| Modus | Method |

(continued on next page)

I need to have a master copy of my personal legal files. Please type the attached list in alphabetical order. Please use uppercase. Please also fax to Janie Ross at 367-8081. Bill to admin.

Boland Litigation Consultants
Bank of San Francisco
Patel Paralegal Services
Newquist & Keough, Attorneys-at-Law
James Gibson, Attorney-at-Law
Investigative Services
Western Investigative Services
Dunn Properties
Empire Bank
Carroll Legal Secretarial Services
PC Experts
Nina Sanchez, Attorney-at-Law
Nakamura Temporary Services
Thornton Temporary Services
Muranishi Temporary Services
Video Sound by McCall
Bay Area Court Reporters
Janie Ross, Attorney-at-Law
Legal Support Group
Law Office Consulting Services
Hamasaki and Company
On-Line Thru Garcia

(continued on next page)

## FONG & FAMILY ATTORNEYS-AT-LAW

### FAX COVER

DATE: _____     TRANSMITTED BY: _____

TIME: _____

TO:          _____

FROM:        _____

NO OF PAGES (INCLUDING THIS COVER): _____

BILL TO:

_____

If you do not receive all pages, call 815.055.8225

ADDITIONAL MESSAGES:

_____

_____

_____

_____

_____

### Word Processing Applications

The purpose of this activity is to practice typing legal documents.

---

WORD PROCESSING ORDER

RUSH _____

DATE _today_____          DEADLINE _ASAP_____

TO _temp_____          FROM _Grace_____

CLIENT _Import Specialists_____          JOB # _10436_____

COPIES TO _____

_____

_____

FAX TO _____ AT _____

OVERNIGHT _____ NEXT DAY _____

PRINT:     DISK # _____ DOC # _____ PAPER _____

SPECIAL INSTRUCTIONS _____

_This is only a part of this document._
_Try to get it all typed today so we can_
_add to it in the morning. Thanks_
_Please o/s it._

---

(continued on next page)

## POWERS OF TRUSTEE

The Trustee shall have with respect to any and all property, which may at any time be held under this Trust, including any property held for a minor, whether constituting principal or accumulated income, the following rights and powers which may be exercised in Trustee's discretion at any time during the continuance of any trust created herein:

(A) To enter into transaction with the estate of either Settlor or any trust in which they, or their issue, have a beneficial interest, even though any Executor of such estate or the trustee of such other trust is also fiduciary under this Trust.

(B) To hold any property and to operate at the risk of the Trust Estate any business that the Trustee receives or acquires under this Trust for so long as the Trustee deems advisable.

(C) To vote and to give proxies to vote on any securities, or to pay any assessment levied upon stock. The Trustee shall exercise any right, option of subscription or otherwise which may attach or be given to the holders of any securities forming part of the Trust Estate. To join in any plan of lease, mortgage, consolidation or reorganization of any Trust property, including but not limited to, the deposit of any securities with any holders or protective committee, or to take and hold any securities issued under any such plan. The Trustee shall be entitled to enter into any margin account with securities of the Trust Estate, or to enter into options or commodity transactions. Securities shall be deemed to include, but not be limited to, property such as stocks, bonds, or other instruments of a similar nature.

(D) To invest or reinvest in stocks, bonds, notes or mortgages on property in or outside the State of California; in real property whether or not it is productive at the time of investment; in common trust funds established by a bank or trust company, including any bank or trust company which may be acting as the Trustee hereunder; in life insurance, annuity, health or disability insurance on any beneficiary or on anyone in whom a beneficiary has an insurable interest; and generally, in such property as the Trustee may deem fit and proper, without being restricted by any statutory limitations on investments by the Trustee not in effect at the date hereof. When purchasing property, the Trustee may purchase on any terms and conditions that the Trustee deems to be in the best interests of the Trust Estate, including, but not limited to, the use of private annuities.

(E) To control, sell at public or private sale, convey, exchange, partition, divide, improve and repair Trust property. When selling Trust property, the Trustee may sell on any terms and conditions that the Trustee deems to be in the best interests of the Trust Estate. The Trustee may grant options on Trust property, or lease for terms within or extending beyond the term of any trust created herein.

(F) To purchase securities or other property from, and/or make loans and advancements, secured or unsecured, to the Executor or other representative of either Settlor's estate.

(G) To lend or advance Trust funds. Any such loan or advance of Trust funds shall be a first or second lien against any such property and shall be repaid therefrom.

(H) To enforce any mortgage or deed of trust hereunder, and to purchase at any sale thereunder any property subject thereto.

(I) To carry such insurance as the Trustee may deem advisable as an expense of the Trust Estate. To pay premiums on any life insurance contract which may at any time be held hereunder.

# Processing Business Documents

# Objectives

After completing this chapter, you will be able to do the following:

1. List the major parts of a business letter.
2. Describe how a block letter is typed.
3. Describe how a modified block letter is typed.
4. Explain the difference between mixed punctuation and open punctuation.
5. List the major parts of a memorandum.
6. List three different styles used for memorandums.
7. Prepare business envelopes.
8. Make corrections using proofreaders marks.
9. List the major parts of business reports.
10. List the rules for the typing of business reports.
11. Prepare an itinerary.
12. Prepare an agenda for a meeting.
13. List the contents of the minutes of a meeting.
14. Type legal forms.
15. Set up a tickler file.

# New Office Terms

agenda
appendix
attachment notation
bibliography
block style
body
closing
default margins
enclosure notation
greeting

inside address
itinerary
leaders
memorandums
minutes
mixed punctuation
modified block style
open punctuation
proofreaders marks
tickler file

*Before You Begin . . .*

*Using an electronic typewriter or a microcomputer, answer the following questions to the best of your ability:*

1. *What are the major parts of a business letter? How should one be typed on company letterhead?*
2. *What are the major parts of a business report? What are the rules used for typing one?*

For clerical workers in business offices, typing is a major part of their job. What do these workers type?

If you were to survey these workers on typing tasks most frequently performed, you would find the answer to be envelopes, letters, and memorandums (memos). File clerks and mail room personnel do light typing, including the typing of envelopes and letters. Receptionists perform the same typing functions. Most secretaries and word processing operators spend many hours typing letters and memorandums.

Companies want to make a good impression by the appearance of their correspondence. Therefore, it is important for clerical workers to know the correct form to use when typing correspondence.

## ■ BUSINESS LETTERS

If you type a letter at home, you likely type and print it on plain typing paper. However, when you begin working in an office, your business letters will be typed and printed on company stationery, called company letterhead. This means that the name of a company, its address, and its telephone number are preprinted on the paper.

When your business letters are finished and printed, they must be properly spaced on the letterhead stationery. They should not be too high on the paper, nor should they be too low. They should be evenly placed with equal left and right margins. When a client receives the letters, they must be "pleasing to the eye."

The following section describes procedures used by office workers when setting up letters.

### Major Parts

Figure 7–1 shows some of the parts of a business letter, which include the date, inside address, greeting, body, closing, signee's name, typist's initials, enclosure notation, attachment notation, copies notation, and file name.

**Date** Type the date 2 to 3 lines below the bottom of the letterhead. If you are not using letterhead paper, begin 12 to 14 lines from the top of the paper. Type the date using a word for the month followed by numbers for the day and year. An example is June 11, 19—.

**Inside Address** The **inside address** includes the name, title, company, and address of the person receiving the letter. It is typed 4 to 8 lines below the date. The number of blank lines between the date and the inside address is determined by the length of the letter. Long letters require fewer blank lines; short letters require more.

**Greeting** Type the **greeting** double-spaced after the inside address. The greeting usually begins with the word *dear* followed by the name of the person receiving the letter. A sample of a greeting is "Dear Mr. Wong:."

**Body** The **body** of the letter begins double-spaced after the greeting. This is the major part of the letter. It tells the reason for the letter and is usually at least two paragraphs long.

**Closing** Type the **closing** double-spaced after the ending of the body of the letter. The two most common closings used in business are as follows:

Very truly yours,
Sincerely,

**Signee's Name** Type the signee's name (the name of the person signing the letter) 4 lines after the closing. This leaves enough room for the person to sign the letter. Usually, you will type the person's title on the line after the typed name.

CFEB COMPANY
PO BOX 795
DALY CITY CA 94017
(415)755-8251

Date

Name, Title
Company
Street
City, State, Zip Code

Greeting

Body

Body

Body

Closing

Signee's Name
typist's initials
enclosure
c:
file name

**Typist's Initials** Type your own initials at the left margin double-spaced after the signee's name. Your initials are always typed in lowercase.

**Enclosure Notation** The **enclosure notation** is double-spaced after the typist's initials. If this notation appears on the letter, it means something is being enclosed with the letter. You type this only if something in addition to the letter is in the envelope. For example, a company may enclose a refund check with a letter in an envelope.

**Attachment Notation** The **attachment notation** is used in place of the enclosure notation when something is stapled or attached to the letter. It is typed in place of the word *enclosure*, double-spaced after the typist's initials.

**Copies Notation** Sometimes you may need to send a copy of a letter to another person. If any copies are to be made for other people, notation is made double-spaced after the enclosure notation or, if nothing is enclosed, double-spaced after the typist's initials.

For example, suppose you are sending a letter to Harry Basset and you will be sending a copy of the letter to Sylvia Chow. You will type the following on the letter:

c: Sylvia Chow

**File Name** Type the file name at the very bottom of the letterhead paper. This is the name given to a file when stored on computer disk. Using a hard disk, an example is PLEADINGS\GARY.122.

## Other Parts

The attention line, the subject line, and information for letters of more than one page occasionally appear on letters. It is important for you to know where to type them.

**Attention Line** Type the attention line within the inside address, on the line below the company name. Use the attention line when you address a letter to a company but want the letter to be directed to a particular department or person. For example:

Angle Hook Company
Attn: Accounts Payable
45 Spooner Street
Boston, MA 02390

ProServ
Attn: Harold Gerard
One Spear Street
Oakland, CA 94233

**Subject Line** If you use a subject line, type it double-spaced after the greeting. Many people prefer to type the subject line all in capital letters. This is the preferred way in the business world.

A subject line is sometimes named a reference line. It is used so a reader can immediately know the purpose of a letter. It is usually a short phrase referring to the contents of the letter. For example:

SUBJECT: INVOICE #345
SUBJECT: DATE FOR ANNUAL MEETING
RE: YOUR LETTER OF MARCH 18

**Information for Letters of More Than One Page** If a letter is longer than one page, all pages after page one should contain the following:

> ### OFFICE TIP
>
> Sometimes you will be asked to send a copy of a letter to someone other than the recipient of the letter without the recipient's knowledge. This type of copy is called a *blind copy* (bc). The letters bc should be typed only on the copies, not on the original letter.

- the name of the person the letter is addressed to
- the date
- the page number

The placement of this information can be either blocked at the left margin or spaced across the page all on one line. It is typed in all capital letters. For example:

ERIC JOHNSON
SEPTEMBER 17, 19—
PAGE 2

ERIC JOHNSON          PAGE 2          SEPTEMBER 17, 19—

## Form

Preferred letter styles vary from company to company. The two most common styles, however, are the block style and the modified block style. In recent years, block style has become the most popular because it saves time. When you start a new job, before you type your first letter, check with your supervisor to see which letter style your boss prefers.

**Block Style**  In **block style,** the entire letter is typed even with the left margin. This is the most commonly used style in industry. It is faster because you save time by not indenting.

**Modified Block Style**  In **modified block style,** or semiblock style, the date and closing begin at the center. This style sometimes looks better with certain letterhead. Even though the date and closing are indented, it is not necessary to indent paragraphs.

## Punctuation

Different rules apply for mixed versus open letter punctuation in the greeting and closing.

**Mixed**  When using **mixed punctuation,** a colon goes after the greeting and a comma goes after the closing. This is the most popular rule, preferred by the business world.

**Open**  For **open punctuation,** no punctuation is used after the greeting and no punctuation is used after the closing.

## Margins

When using word processing programs, office support staff typically use **default margins,** or margins that are preset in the program. If margins need to be set, most office workers leave a one-inch margin on both sides of the letter.

# MEMORANDUMS

**A memorandum,** or memo, is the correspondence that stays within a company (see figure 7–2). The style of a memo is set up in various ways, but usually contains the headings To, From, Date, and Subject. The following are samples of the styles office workers use for memorandums:

TO:
FROM:
DATE:
SUBJECT:

        TO:
      FROM:
       DATE:
    SUBJECT:

TO:                       DATE:
FROM:                SUBJECT:

When typing memorandums, keep the following points in mind:

- Memorandums are informal; never use titles. This holds true even for the titles Mr., Mrs., Miss, and Ms., which should not be included.
- Do not use a salutation or closing.
- Use the block style.
- Triple-space between the subject line and the body of the memo. The body is the message part of the memo.
- Type the typist's initials, enclosure notation, and copy notation in the same locations as they are typed on a letter.

**FIGURE 7–2**
*Parts of a Memorandum*

CFEB COMPANY
PO BOX 795
DALY CITY CA 94017
(415)755-8251

M E M O R A N D U M

TO:
FROM:
DATE:
SUBJECT:

Body

Body

typist's initials

# ■ LEGAL-SIZE ENVELOPES

Business envelopes have two major parts, and certain business rules are used when typing these onto envelopes.

## Parts

The main parts of the information you type onto a business envelope are the return address and the main address (see figure 7–3). Sometimes special notations are included.

**Return Address** Most companies have their own envelopes with a printed return address. However, if you must type the return address yourself, begin to type two lines down from the top and three spaces in from the left margin.

**Main Address** An experienced typist, using an electronic typewriter, puts the envelope in the machine and turns the roller to the correct spot for typing the main address. If you have not typed envelopes before, locating the correct spot can be a problem. Therefore, the rule to remember is to begin fifteen lines down from the top and five spaces left of the center of the envelope. Set a margin or tab at this location.

**Special Notations** Common notations typed on envelopes include the attention notation and the personal or confidential notation.

*Attention* In the attention notation, the word *attention* and the name of the person or department are typed in the address itself, on the line after the company name.

*Personal or Confidential* In the personal or confidential notation, the word *personal* or the word *confidential* is typed approximately 3 lines below the return address.

■ FIGURE 7–3
*A Legal-Size Envelope*

```
CFEB COMPANY
PO BOX 795
DALY CITY CA 94017




            IRMA LOPEZ
            TRANSWORLD EXPORTS
            45 FIRST STREET     ROOM 203
            SAN FRANCISCO CA 94013
```

# Typing Rules

Some points to remember when typing envelopes are as follows:

- Always single-space.
- Type all states with two capital letters and no periods.
- Leave at least six lines at the bottom of an envelope. Current post office regulations state that the bottom of an envelope must be free of all notations so that the envelope can go through the post office's electronic scanning machines.
- When typing the main address, most office workers use upper- and lowercase letters. However, the post office would prefer all uppercase letters with no punctuation. The following are some samples of both methods:

| Method Used by Most Companies | Method Preferred by the Post Office |
|---|---|
| The Noodle Corporation<br>Attention Ms. Shirley Gonzales<br>2399 Palm Avenue<br>Burlingame, CA 94060 | THE NOODLE CORPORATION<br>ATTN MS SHIRLEY GONZALES<br>2399 PALM AVE<br>BURLINGAME CA 94060 |
| Mr. Paul Wong<br>131 Battery Street<br>Portland, OR 93616 | MR PAUL WONG<br>131 BATTERY ST<br>PORTLAND OR 93616 |
| Ms. Julia Singleton<br>Buy-Rite Company<br>9 Almond Way<br>Boston, MA 02368 | MS JULIA SINGLETON<br>BUY RITE CO<br>9 ALMOND WAY<br>BOSTON MA 02368 |
| Ms. Rose Marie Frazier<br>Personnel Department<br>Save Now Bank<br>34 Montgomery Street<br>San Francisco, CA 94115 | MS ROSE MARIE FRAZIER<br>PERSONNEL DEPARTMENT<br>SAVE NOW BANK<br>34 MONTGOMERY ST<br>SAN FRANCISCO CA 94115 |

When deciding which method to use, check the preference of your boss. If she or he has no preference, use the post office's preferred method.

---

# R ecall Time

*Answer the following questions:*

1. What are three typing functions that most all office clerical workers perform?
2. What are the main parts of a business letter?
3. What is the difference between block-style and modified-block-style letters?
4. What four headings are used in memorandums?
5. Where is the word *attention* typed on an envelope?

## ■ BUSINESS REPORTS—MANUSCRIPT TYPING

At a public relations firm in New York, the executives frequently create proposals to present to new clients. As the executives compose their reports, they do all their own keyboarding directly into microcomputers. The office support staff then makes typing corrections and prints the final copies, which are referred to as business reports. This means that the office support staff must know the parts of a business report as well as what typing rules to use in formatting a final copy.

### Parts

The main parts of a business report are the title page, table of contents, body, appendix, and bibliography.

**Title Page** The title page is usually the front cover of the report. It includes the title of the report, the name of the person the report is for, the author of the report, the company name, and the date.

**Table of Contents** The table of contents includes the titles of the topics in the report and the page number that each topic begins on.

**Body** The body is the main part of the report. It usually includes an introduction, major statements, and a conclusion.

**Appendix** Some business reports have supplementary information that supports the statements in the body of the reports. This supplementary information is located in the **appendix,** usually following the body of the report. The appendix can be in the form of a chart, a graph, or a table. A report can have more than one appendix.

**Bibliography** The **bibliography** is a listing of all sources used to write the report. It includes books, magazines, and newspaper articles. It usually appears at the end of the report.

## Typing Rules

Certain procedures are followed by office workers when typing the various parts of business reports.

### Title Page

- Center each line horizontally.
- Leave several blank lines between each item (title, name of person the report is for, author, company name, and date). Center the typed lines vertically on the page.

### Table of Contents

- Center the titles and page numbers both horizontally and vertically.
- Depending on the size, either double- or single-space.
- Beginning at the left margin, first list the topic number, usually as a roman numeral. On the same line, follow with the name of the topic. On the same line, end with the page number at the right margin.
- Use **leaders** (periods) across the space between the topic name and the page number.

### Body

- Usually, double-space the body of the report. However, sometimes you will space-and-a-half a report, leaving one-half blank line between typed lines. You will seldom single-space a report.
- Use a 2-inch top margin for the first page and a 1-inch top margin for all other pages, a 1-inch bottom margin for all pages, and 1-inch side margins for all pages.
- Type the headings and subheadings at the left margin, in all capital letters.
- Type the page number in the center of the page, 3 lines up from the bottom.

### Bibliography

- Prepare items in alphabetic order.
- For each item, include the name of the author, publication, publisher and the publication date.
- Begin the first line of each item at the left margin, and indent all other lines.
- Single-space lines.
- Use the same margins as in a report.

You arrive for work one morning and find a letter that you must type to Lee Baxter. Your boss, who has gone on a business trip, left the letter for you to type. The letter must go in that day's mail.

You begin the letter by typing the date and the inside address. You get to the salutation (greeting) and you stop. You do not know if Lee Baxter is a man or a woman. No one in your office knows.

1. What do you do?

## ■ TRAVEL ARRANGEMENT DOCUMENTS

Angelina is an administrative assistant in the corporate office of a large oil company located in San Francisco. Her boss has to go on a business trip. This is Angelina's first experience in making travel arrangements for her boss.

Angelina learns from another company employee that business executives within the company make travel arrangements through a travel agent. The company already has an account established with the travel agency.

Before Angelina calls the travel agent, she writes down the following information:

- where her boss is to go
- date of departure and date of return
- class of travel
- if a rental car will be needed

Angelina also looks in her files to learn her boss's preference for seating on the airplane.

Now Angelina is ready to prepare an itinerary for her boss. When her boss returns, she will complete an expense account form for him.

### Itinerary

An **itinerary** is a record of travel plans. It is neatly typed and includes date and time of departures and arrivals, location of departures and arrivals, transportation means, and hotel accommodations. It may also include information on car rentals and time and location of business meetings. See figure 7–4 for a sample of an itinerary. Some travel agents will prepare the itinerary for you.

### Expense Account Form

When Angelina's boss returns from the business trip, Angelina is asked to complete an expense account form for him. This form is completed when a businessperson wishes to be reimbursed (paid back) for money spent during a business trip.

*The assignments for some clerical workers include making travel arrangements and creating and typing travel itineraries.*

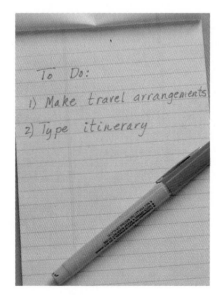

Most companies reimburse employees for transportation, hotel accommodations, meals, business entertainment, and miscellaneous expenses incurred on a business trip. It is necessary for an employee to keep receipts for proof of all the expenses.

Angelina must complete a form similar to the one shown in figure 7–5 for her boss to be reimbursed for the travel expenses. Once the form is completed, all receipts are attached to the back, it is signed by her boss, and it is sent to the accounting department for processing. In some cases, it may also require an additional signature of approval before being processed.

■ FIGURE 7–4
*Sample Itinerary*

ITINERARY
LYDIA DELOSARDO
MAY 3, 19— TO MAY 5, 19—
CHICAGO TO BOSTON

**Monday, May 3**

| 8:30 a.m. | Leave Chicago | WA Flight #347 | Breakfast |

| 10:40 a.m. (Boston Time) | Arrive Boston Taxi to Tremont Plaza Hotel (confirmation #S783012) |

| 2:00 p.m. | Meeting with Lum Video, Inc. 678 Bolyston Street (864-8251) |

**Tuesday, May 4**

| 9:00 a.m. | Meeting with Lum Video, Inc. |

| 1:00 p.m. | Meeting with Lacey Disk Company 9 Fremont Avenue (755-3929) |

| 7:30 p.m. | Dinner meeting One Sutter Place Association of Entrepreneurs |

**Wednesday, May 5**

| 10:20 a.m. | Leave Boston | WA Flight #743 | Breakfast |

| 2:00 p.m. (Chicago Time) | Arrive Chicago |

FIGURE 7–5 *Sample Expense Account Form*

**EXPENSE REIMBURSEMENT CLAIM**

This section must be TYPED or PRINTED LEGIBLY, or form will be returned. Submit Original and two copies to Accounting Dept.

FILED BY: _____ VENDOR NO. _____

DEPT.: _____ (OR) ADDRESS: _____

FOR MEETING HELD:  FROM _____ , 19____   TO _____ , 19____

AT: _____

DEPARTURE DATE: _____ TIME: _____   RETURN DATE: _____ TIME: _____

PURPOSE OF MEETING: _____

REFER TO REGULATIONS on the back of this form BEFORE COMPLETING this section.

| DATE | MEALS | | | TOTAL MEALS | OTHER EXPENSES* Lodging / Transportation / Incidentals (Description/Explanation) | TOTAL OTHER EXPENSE | TOTAL CLAIM |
|---|---|---|---|---|---|---|---|
| | B | L | D | | | | |
| | | | | | | | |
| | | | | | | | |
| | | | | | | | |
| | | | | | | | |
| | | | | | | | |
| | | | | | | | |
| | | | | | | | |
| | | | | | | | |
| | | | | | | | |
| T O T A L S | | | | | //////////////////////////////////////////////////////////////////////////////////// | | |

I HEREBY CERTIFY that the above claim represents a true cost and full accounting of all expenses incurred by me in attending the above-named meeting.

SIGNATURE: _____

LESS: ADVANCE

NET CLAIM

ADDITIONAL INFORMATION (or) EXPLANATION:

OTHER EXPENSES(S) PAID BY EMPLOYER: (List PO# and Amount)

TRNSPTN: _____

HOTEL: _____

OTHER: _____

_____

ACCOUNT NO. | AMOUNT

_____ $_____

_____ _____

_____ _____

TOTAL _____

SUPERVISOR
APPROVAL: _____

*If personal car is used, include mileage reimbursement on this claim form—NOT on Monthly Mileage Reimbursement form.

Some companies will give an employee a cash advance before the employee leaves on a business trip. If this is done, the cash advance must be subtracted from the amount due on the expense form. Note where this is located on the sample expense form in figure 7–5.

## ■ MEETING DOCUMENTS

When Angelina's boss was away on the business trip, she had time to do work for other supervisors. One supervisor asked her to prepare an agenda for the monthly meeting of the company's Computer Software Advisory Committee. Angelina was also asked to attend the meeting and to take the minutes.

### Agenda

The **agenda** is a listing of what is to take place during the meeting. It usually includes the committee name, meeting date and place, call to order, roll call, approval of minutes of last meeting, old business, new business, announcements, date of next meeting, and adjournment (see figure 7–6).

### Minutes

The **minutes** of the meeting are a record of who attended the meeting and what took place at the meeting. It is important that you take accurate and complete minutes of the meeting, but it is not necessary to repeat the meeting word for word. It is helpful for you to read minutes of previous meetings, make a seating chart as the meeting begins (unless you know all the members), record the names of persons who make motions, and record the meeting on a tape recorder.

After the meeting, while it is fresh in your mind, type a rough draft of the minutes from your notes. Then compare the rough draft against the tape recording. From this rough draft, type the final copy using the following typing guidelines:

1. Type the name of the committee and the date of the meeting at the center of the paper.
2. Type the time and place of the meeting.
3. Type the name of the person leading the meeting.
4. Type a list of the names of persons attending the meeting.
5. Type the body of the minutes using single-spacing and the same margins as for manuscripts. Set up sections for corrections to previous minutes, old business, and new business.
6. Type the time and place of the next meeting.
7. Type the time the meeting adjourned.
8. Type a solid line at the end of the minutes for the signatures of the chairperson and secretary.

See figure 7–7 for an example of minutes of a meeting.

AGENDA
COMPUTER SOFTWARE ADVISORY COMMITTEE MEETING
ALLSTATE CONFERENCE ROOM C
JULY 15, 19—

I. CALL TO ORDER

II. ROLL CALL

III. MINUTES FROM LAST MEETING

IV. OLD BUSINESS

      Final bid on spreadsheet software

      Evaluation results of NetCheck

V. NEW BUSINESS

      New word processing software

      State Computer Users Conference

VI. ANNOUNCEMENTS

VII. DATE OF NEXT MEETING

VIII. ADJOURNMENT

## ■ ROUGH DRAFTS AND PROOFREADERS MARKS

Many letters, reports, minutes, and other business documents are revised one or more times before printing a final copy. When these documents are in rough draft format, **proofreaders marks** are often used to denote the changes to be made.

Proofreaders marks are standard symbols used by most office workers. They make it easier to understand the corrections that need to be made. The following is a sample of proofreaders marks used on a paragraph:

FIGURE 7–7
*Sample Meeting Minutes*

COMPUTER SOFTWARE ADVISORY COMMITTEE
MINUTES OF MEETING
JULY 15, 19—
ALLSTATE CONFERENCE ROOM C

The meeting was called to order by _____ at 12 noon.

In attendance: _____ _____    _____ _____
_____ _____    _____ _____
_____ _____    _____ _____
_____ _____

The following corrections were made to the June minutes:
_____
_____
_____

Old Business:
_____
_____
_____
_____

New Business:
_____
_____
_____
_____
_____
_____
_____

The next meeting is scheduled for _____.

The meeting adjourned at 2:30 p.m.
_____

Customer Service Quality customer service begins with how weell employees understand their role in teh organization and how much they feel they
contribute to its success. EMployees with a positive self-image aremore likely
to provide quality service to internal and external customers.

Refer to table 7–1 and you will see that you are to do the following:

■ Type "Customer Service" in uppercase (all capital letters).
■ Delete the extra *e* in "weell."

O F F I C E   T I P

When you are typing letters on
the job, many bosses will want
you to correct spelling or
punctuation errors. However,
never change the wording (the
content) of a letter without
checking with your boss.

| MARK | MEANING | EXAMPLE |
|------|---------|---------|
| ℓ | Delete | We will ~~not~~ be on time. |
| ∼ | Transpose | She sent teh fax. |
| ¶ | Start a new paragraph | .... at the office. After it .... |
| ⌒ | Close up | She was al ready late. |
| # | Insert a space | She arrived;we started. |
| lc | Lowercase | Be there at 9 A.M. |
| uc | Uppercase | Call senator Kennedy. |
| ∼∼∼ | Boldface | The meeting is Monday. |
| STET | Leave words in | We will ~~not~~ attend. |
| · · · · · | Leave words in | We will ~~not~~ attend. |
| ⊙ | Insert a period | The meeting is 9 a m. |
| ∧ | Insert something | It will be the hall. |

- Transpose the *e* and *h* in "teh."
- change the uppercase *M* to a lowercase *m* in "EMployees."
- Leave a space between *are* and *more* in "aremore."

## ■ LEGAL DOCUMENTS

Legal contracts or documents are written agreements between individuals. The document may be a printed form such as a rental lease, a sales agreement, or a form to be completed for small claims court.

Electronic typewriters are often used to complete these printed forms. When filling in the information on such a form, the typist uses the same margins as those set by the size of the form. When completing forms with blanks indicated by printed lines, it is advisable to type slightly above the lines.

Some law firms repeatedly process many of the same forms. In this situation, they may type a full form and store it as a file on a computer disk, or have the form printed on continuous-feed paper for use with their printers.

Procedures for the typing of other legal documents, such as complaints or motions, for criminal and civil courts vary from state to state. In California, for example, the courts require legal documents to be typed on 8½×11 paper, double-spaced, with single-spacing for quotations. This size paper is desired simply for filing purposes, to save on space.

Procedures for the typing of other legal documents, such as wills or right-to-die agreements, are not determined by the courts. The typing style for these documents is dictated by the legal profession. These documents are often typed on 8½ × 14 paper, double-spaced, with indented paragraphs. In some cases, special legal paper is used. This type of paper is numbered on the side and has vertical lines down the sides. See figure 7–8 for a sample of this paper.

FIGURE 7–8
*Sample Special Legal Paper*

# TICKLER FILES

As you can see from the previous examples, secretaries and administrative assistants such as Angelina must keep track of meetings, reports to do, business trip dates, and many other clerical tasks. Some secretaries find it helpful to use a **tickler file** as a reminder for these tasks.

A tickler file is set up by dates. Its main purpose is to remind a secretary of important deadlines. For example, see the file in figure 7–9. This file has twelve folders, one for each month of the year. Within each folder are thirty-one folders representing the days of the month. When a secretary wants to be reminded of an important project, deadline, or date, he or she puts a reminder note in the appropriate folder a few days *before* that date. Do you see why the reminder is placed a few days before the due date?

Tickler files can be set up by using cards, an accordion pocket file, or a file drawer with file folders. They need not be as elaborate as the system illustrated in figure 7–9.

A tickler file can also be set up on a computer. You can purchase software that includes a type of tickler file as part of its program, or you can create your own by simply setting up a file for each month. The file can be printed onto hard copy on a monthly basis, or it can be retrieved onto the computer screen when needed.

■ FIGURE 7–9

*File drawer with file folders being used as a tickler file.*

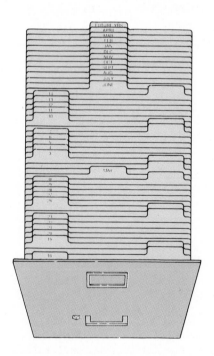

Modern Office Procedures

Julian is a secretary to the office manager of an advertising firm. You and five other secretaries work in the same office. All the secretaries have the same job description and report to the same supervisor.

All the office staff must share one photocopy machine, so it is a busy location. When deadlines are to be met, it becomes even busier. Many times, two or more secretaries are waiting in line to use the copy machine.

One day, you are the second person in line and desperately needing to get copies for your boss. Julian cuts to the head of the line and says, "Excuse me for cutting in. My boss needs this for a meeting in fifteen minutes, and I only need a few copies." Julian runs his copies and goes on his way.

As you think back, you realize Julian frequently cuts to the head of the line.

Should Julian be allowed to do this? Does it make a difference that he works for the office manager? What can you do in this situation?

# Recall Time

*Answer the following questions:*

1. What are the five parts of a business report?
2. What five items are usually on a title page?
3. What are leaders?
4. Do businesses prefer to single- or double-space business reports?
5. What is an itinerary?
6. How is an itinerary formatted? Prepare one using the following information:

   Amy Nygard, vice president of SaveAll Software, is traveling from Boston to Atlanta and San Francisco. She leaves Boston on United Flight #1127 on May 16 at 8:00 a.m. She arrives in Atlanta at 11:00 a.m. That evening, she stays at the Atlanta Regency Hotel. She leaves on May 17 on United Flight #2217 at 10:00 a.m. and arrives in San Francisco at 1:00 p.m. She stays at the Hotel Union Square that night. She leaves San Francisco on May 18 on United Flight #1130 at 7:30 a.m. and arrives back in Boston at 5:30 p.m..

# SUMMARY

Certain procedures are frequently used by office workers when typing business documents. Furthermore, particular forms and styles are preferred by office workers when setting up business documents.

Just before putting a letter in an envelope, give it one last look and ask yourself the following questions:

- Is the letter typed too high on the paper?
- Is the letter typed too low on the paper?
- Are the left and right margins even?
- Is the finished letter "pleasing to the eye"?

After completing a business report, give it one last look and ask yourself the following questions:

- Is a title page included and is it centered?
- Is a table of contents included and is it centered?
- Is the body double-spaced?
- Are the margins set according to rules for the typing of business reports?
- Is an appendix included? If so, is it located directly after the body of the report?
- Is a bibliography included and is it prepared in alphabetic order?

## *In Conclusion . . .*

*When you have completed this chapter, use an electronic typewriter or a microcomputer to answer the following questions.*

1. *What are the major parts of a business letter? How should one be typed on company letterhead?*
2. *What are the major parts of a business report? What are the rules used for typing one?*

# Review and Application

## REVIEW YOUR VOCABULARY

Supply the missing words by choosing from the new Office Terms listed below.

1. A _____ _____ has all parts of the letter typed at the left margin.
2. A _____ _____ _____ has the date and closing typed at the center.
3. In word processing, _____ _____ are the margins preset in the program.
4. The main part of a business letter is the _____ of the letter.
5. The word Sincerely is used in the _____ of a business letter.
6. The word Dear is used in the _____ of a business letter.
7. The word _____ typed on a business letter means you are enclosing something with the letter.
8. In a business report, the _____ lists the sources used to write the report.
9. In a business report, the _____ contains supplementary information.
10. A _____ contains the words To, From, Date, Subject.
11. An _____ is a record of travel plans.
12. Periods that are used in a table of contents are called _____ .
13. A _____ _____ is a file that is set up by dates.
14. Using _____ _____ in a business letter means to put a colon after the greeting and a comma after the closing.
15. Using _____ _____ in a business letter means to put no punctuation after the greeting and no punctuation after the closing.
16. What is to take place during a meeting is listed on an _____ .
17. What actually takes places at a meeting is recorded in the _____ of the meeting.

a. agenda
b. appendix
c. attachment notation
d. bibliography
e. block style
f. body
g. closing
h. default margins
i. enclosure
j. greeting
k. inside address
l. itinerary
m. leaders
n. memorandum
o. minutes
p. mixed punctuation
q. modified block style
r. open punctuation
s. proofreaders marks
t. tickler file

## DISCUSS AND ANALYZE AN OFFICE SITUATION

1. It is Pierre's first day on the job, and he is given some letters to type. Pierre wants to impress his employer by not asking questions, just getting the work done. He types the letters in block style because he remembers his teacher in school saying, "All companies use the block style for letters."

   At the end of the day, Pierre is told by his supervisor that the company does not use block style for letters because of the setup of its letterhead. Pierre is asked to redo the letters.

   How could this have been avoided?

## PRACTICE BASIC SKILLS

### Math

1. Your boss is planning a meeting for all company supervisors that will be held at a local hotel. Refer to the hotel's Conference Price List given below as you answer these questions:
   a. How much should the breakfast budget be if you order the following:
   2 gallons of coffee
   1 gallon of tea
   40 whole wheat muffins
   3 trays of fresh fruit
   b. How much should the evening budget be if you order the following:
   25 petits fours
   3 dozen Danish cookies
   10 mud pies
   30 soft drinks

c. You can get 12 slices from the zucchini bread. How much is saved by ordering 4 loaves of zucchini bread instead of 48 whole wheat muffins?

d. A gallon of coffee serves 16 cups. How many gallons would you order to plan for 70 cups?

e. A pitcher of orange juice serves 12 glasses. How many pitchers would you order to plan for 90 glasses?

### Conference Price List

**MORNING COMBINATIONS**

| Item | Quantity | Price |
|------|----------|-------|
| Coffee | Gallon | $20.00 |
| Tea | Gallon | 20.00 |
| Orange juice | Pitcher | 16.00 |
| Fresh fruit | Tray | 19.50 |
| Date nut bread | Loaf | 17.50 |
| Zucchini bread | Loaf | 17.50 |
| Whole wheat muffins | Each | 2.25 |

**EVENING COMBINATIONS**

| Item | Quantity | Price |
|------|----------|-------|
| Fresh fruit | Bowl | $15.00 |
| Petits fours | Each | 1.50 |
| Soft drinks | Each | 1.75 |
| Danish cookies | Dozen | 8.00 |
| Fruit punch | Gallon | 18.00 |
| Mud pies | Each | 1.75 |

### English

1. *Rule:* Use a comma to separate dependent clauses.
   *Examples:* With your help, we will get the task completed by Wednesday. As soon as the machines are repaired, we will return to work.
   *Practice Exercise:* Rewrite the following sentences placing commas where needed.
   a. For further information call the toll-free number.
   b. During the committee meeting a minor earthquake rattled the room.
   c. If you need any further help you may call our service representative.
   d. In order to get the job done we will need to call a temporary service.
   e. As mentioned last week we will need three reports typed in 12 pitch.

### Proofreading

1. Retype the following, making the changes noted by the proofreaders marks.

EARTHQUAKE RECOVERY GUIDELINES

self-help techniques

1. Don't push thoughts and memories of the event away, it is critical to talk about them.

2. Don't feel embarrassed about a repetitious need to talk to people. Try family, friend, co-workers, church and social groups. Ask what others are doing to cope.

3. Keep your life in balance. There are practical things you can do to regain a sense of control over your life.

   a. Know what practical things you can do to be prepared for on-going earthquake stress.

      1. Duck and cover

      2. Stand under a door way

      3. Know emergency routes

      4. Sleep in your clothes, put flashlights, wallets, shoes, etc. closeby

      5. Follow emergency preparation guidelines in the phone book

   b. Resume your normal program of activities asquickly as you can.

   c. Pay careful loving attention to your self—eat nutritional foods, get plenty of rest, drink liquids, and increase other selfnurturing activities.

4. Write about your experiences.

5. Increase physical activity.

6. Practice relaxation, meditation or prayer activities.

1. Arrange the following words into alphabetic order.
   Using a microcomputer or an electronic typewriter,
   tabulate the words into three columns.

| | |
|---|---|
| memorandum | letter |
| envelope | greeting |
| closing | enclosure |
| block | punctuation |
| proofreader | manuscript |
| contents | bibliography |
| appendix | itinerary |
| travel | agenda |
| meeting | minutes |
| leaders | default |
| modified | salutation |
| copies | attachment |

*Write a **T** if the statement is true or an **F** if the statement is false.*

_____ 1. If you were to survey clerical workers on typing tasks most frequently performed, you would find the answer to be accounting statements and minutes of meetings.

_____ 2. The inside address of a letter includes the name, title, company, and address of the person receiving the letter.

_____ 3. The most common closing used in businesses today is "Cordially yours."

_____ 4. Secretaries never type their initials on a letter.

_____ 5. The attachment notation is used in place of the enclosure notation when something is stapled or attached to the letter.

_____ 6. The subject line of a letter is usually typed immediately after the date.

_____ 7. Modified block style is still the most common form of letter style used in businesses today.

_____ 8. Default margins are the margins preset in the word processing program.

_____ 9. Never type the date on a memorandum.

_____ 10. The post office would prefer that envelope addresses be typed in all lowercase letters.

_____ 11. The appendix in a business report lists the supplementary information that supports the statements in the body of the report.

_____ 12. Business executives never use travel agents for travel arrangements.

_____ 13. An itinerary is a record of travel plans.

(continued on next page)

_____ 14. An agenda is prepared after a meeting to record what took place in the meeting.

_____ 15. Legal secretaries use a type of paper that is numbered on the side and has vertical lines down the sides.

## Word Processing

1. Keyboard the following unarranged letter in block style and open punctuation.

   RETURN ADDRESS: 3497 West Lincoln Street; San Diego, CA 92002; May 5, 19—

   LETTER ADDRESS: Ms. Beth Haglin; Del Personnel Agency; 767 Seventh Street; Escondido, CA 92025

   Dear Ms. Haglin

   This letter will contain a brief explanation of some of the major parts of a business letter.

   Date. Type the date 2 to 3 lines below the bottom of the letterhead. If you are not using the letterhead paper, begin 12 to 14 inches from the top of the paper.

   Inside Address. The inside address includes the name, title, company, and address of the person receiving the letter and is typed 4 to 8 lines below the date.

   Body. The body of the letter begins double-spaced after the greeting. It is at least two paragraphs long.

   Closing. Type the closing two lines or double-spaced after the last typed line in the body of the letter.

   Signee's Name. Type the signee's name (the name of the person signing the letter) 4 lines after the closing.

   Sincerely yours; Ms. Marcia Cropp; Student Body Secretary

2. Save and print one copy.

## Word Processing

1. Keyboard the following unarranged letter in modified block style and mixed punctuation.

   RETURN ADDRESS: 37 West Washington Street; Phoenix, AZ 95009; September 15, 19—

   LETTER ADDRESS: Ms. Betty Lou Davis; 3767 University Drive; Tempe, AZ 85024

   Dear Ms. Davis

   This letter will contain a brief explanation of some of the special notations at the end of a business letter.

   <u>Closing</u>. Type the closing double-spaced after the ending of the body of the letter.

   <u>Signee's Name</u>. Type the signee's name (the name of the person signing the letter) 4 lines after the closing.

   <u>Typist's Initials</u>. Type your own initials at the left margin double-spaced after the signee's name in lowercase.

   <u>Enclosure Notation</u>. The enclosure notation is double-spaced after the typist's initials.

   <u>Attachment Notation</u>. The attachment notation is used in place of the enclosure notation when something is stapled or attached to the letter.

   <u>Copies Notation</u>. If any copies are to be prepared for other people, notation is typed double-spaced after the enclosure notation or, if nothing is enclosed, double-spaced after the typist's initials.

   Very truly yours; Emogene Edam

2. Save and print one copy.

## Word Processing Applications

The purpose of this activity is to practice typing legal documents.

You receive a call from On-Time Temps asking if you would be able to work for an afternoon to help Fong & Family Attorneys-at-Law get caught up with its work. You receive the following job request form when you report to work.

---

### WORD PROCESSING ORDER

RUSH _____

DATE _*today*_           DEADLINE _*tomorrow*_

TO _*temp*_               FROM _*Grace*_

CLIENT _*Heart*_         JOB # _*97*_

COPIES TO _____

_____

_____

FAX TO _*Attorney Steiner*_ AT _*162 - 4459*_

OVERNIGHT _____ NEXT DAY _____

PRINT: DISK # _____ DOC # _____ PAPER _____

SPECIAL INSTRUCTIONS _____

_*Type including the added names.*_
_*Where you see initials, type in full*_
_*names. Also complete fax cover.*_

_____

---

(continued on next page)

1  *Harriet Winer*

2  *9 Mint Ave #66*

3  *San Francisco CA 94103*
   *007-6400*

4  Defendant In Pro. Per.

5

6          MUNICIPAL COURT OF THE STATE OF CALIFORNIA

7          CITY AND COUNTY OF SAN FRANCISCO

8

9                                    ) No.
                                     )
10  *Mimi L. Heart*                  )
                                     )
11  Plaintiff,                       ) NOTICE OF DEMURRER OF
                                     ) DEFENDANT *Harriet Winer*
                                     ) TO COMPLAINT OF PLAINTIFF
12                                   )
                                     ) *Mimi R. Heart*
13                                   ) MEMORANDUM OF POINTS AND
                                     ) AUTHORITIES
14  v.                               )
                                     )     Date: March 12, 19
15  *Harriet Winer*                  )     Time: 9:00 a.m.
                                     )     Dept: Law and Motion
16     *et al.*                      )           Dept. 5, Room 379
    *Defendants*                     )
17  _____      )

18  TO PLAINTIFF *MH* AND HIS ATTORNEY OF RECORD:

19  PLEASE TAKE NOTICE that the hearing on the demurrer of defendant,  *HW*

20  will be held on March 12, 19*92* at 9:00 a.m. or as soon thereafter as the matter can be

21  heard in the Law and Motion Department of the above-entitled Court, Department 5,

22  Room 379, City Hall, San Francisco, California. Defendant demurs to the complaint on

23  the grounds that:

24              1. The complaint fails to state a cause of action. This demurrer is

25  based on this notice, the attached memorandum of points and authorities, all papers

26

278                                                        Modern Office Procedures

1 and records on file herein, and such evidence, both oral and documentary, as may be

2 presented at the hearing of this motion.

3 Dated: *Feb 18, 1992*

4

5 _____

*Harriet Winer*

6 (signed) Defendant In Pro. Per.

7

8                    MEMORANDUM OF POINTS AND AUTHORITIES

9 I. STATEMENT OF FACTS

10 The present action is one for unlawful detainer. The complaint is based upon a three-

11 day notice to pay rent or to quit. The notice specifically states the rent due for the

12 months of December, January, and February, each respectively $~~380~~ *560*. However, it is

13 unclear as to what month the fourth amount of $~~380~~ *560* is due. The notice indicates that

14 the month of November was paid, which seems to be the month for which the amount

15 for the fourth month of rent is requested.

16 I. THE COMPLAINT FAILS TO ALLEGE FACTS SUFFICIENT TO

17 CONSTITUTE A CAUSE OF ACTION OR IN THE ALTERNATIVE, IS

18 UNCERTAIN

19              Code of Civil Procedure section 430.10(e) provides that a complaint is

20 subject to demurrer where it does not state facts sufficient to constitute a cause of

21 action. Code of Civil Procedure section 430.10(f) provides that a complaint is subject to

22 demurrer where the complaint is uncertain. Uncertain includes ambiguous and

23 unintelligible.

24              Statutory notice requirements for unlawful detainer actions are strictly

25 construed, and one who seeks the summary remedy of unlawful detainer must bring

26 himself strictly within its terms. Horton-Howard v. Payton (1919) 44 Cal.App. 108 112

1 *Harriet Winer*
  *9 Mint Ave #66*
2 *SF 94103*

3             PROOF OF SERVICE BY MAIL

4 CASE NAME: *Heart v. Winer*     CASE NO.:

5 I, *Alfred Garza* _____, declare:

6 That I am employed within the City and County of San Francisco; that my business

7 address is *16 Powell St 14th Floor San Francisco Calif 94102*     ; and

8 that I am over the age of eighteen (18) years of age and not a party to the within action.

9

10 That on *Feb 18, 1992*                    I served the following:

11

12 Demurrer, Points and Authorities

13

14

15 upon *Mimi Heart*                    by putting the same in an envelope,

16 first class postage affixed thereto and depositing the same in a United States Post Office

17 mailbox in the City and County of San Francisco, California, addressed as follows:

18

19 *Mimi Heart*
  *47 Oak Street*
20 Oakland, CA 94612

21

22 I declare under penalty of perjury that the foregoing is true and correct and that this

23 declaration was executed on *2/18/92*     at San Francisco, California.

24                              _____

25

26

# FONG & FAMILY ATTORNEYS-AT-LAW

## FAX COVER

DATE: _____     TRANSMITTED BY: _____

TIME: _____

TO: _____

FROM: _____

NO OF PAGES (INCLUDING THIS COVER): _____

BILL TO:

_____

If you do not receive all pages, call 815.055.8225

ADDITIONAL MESSAGES:

_____

_____

_____

_____

_____

## Time Sheet

Complete a time sheet for the four hours you worked. Use the following information to complete the time sheet.

Write this week's date.

The customer order number is **29845.**

You began work at 2 p.m. and left at 6 p.m.

(continued on next page)

(ACTIVITY 7–4 continued)

ON-TIME TEMPORARY
TIME SHEET

Client Customer Name (Please Print)

Department

Employee Name (Please Print)

Employee Social Security Number

Week ending Sunday:      /      /

Customer Order # _____

| Date | Time Started | Time Finished | Less Lunch | Total Time Worked |
|------|--------------|---------------|------------|-------------------|
|      |              |               |            |                   |
|      |              |               |            |                   |
|      |              |               |            |                   |
|      |              |               |            |                   |

Total Hours Worked (nearest 1/2 hour)   _____

Has this assignment been completed?   Yes _____ No _____

I certify that the hours shown above were worked by me during the week indicated.

Employee signature

Client signature

# 8

# *Accounting and Record Keeping*

# Objectives

After completing this chapter, you will be able to do the following:

1. List accounting and record-keeping activities that are performed by an office worker.
2. Discuss the purpose of a balance sheet.
3. Interpret the accounting equation Assets = Liabilities + Capital.
4. Discuss the purpose of an income statement.
5. Interpret the accounting equation Net income = Revenue − Expenses.
6. Distinguish between the purposes of accounts receivable and accounts payable.
7. Distinguish between the methods used in periodic inventory and perpetual inventory.
8. Describe the order-processing procedures when merchandise is ordered, received, sold, and returned.
9. Calculate net pay based on yearly salary, hourly wages, and straight commission.
10. Describe the proper banking procedures to follow in depositing, endorsing, and writing checks.
11. Describe the steps to follow in reconciling a bank statement.
12. Describe how an office petty cash fund is set up and maintained.

# New Office Terms

accounting cycle
accounts payable
accounts receivables
assets
balance sheet
capital
expenses
financial statements

income statement
inventory
liabilities
net income
payroll
petty cash payments
reconciliation
revenues

## ACCOUNTING ACTIVITIES

Business organizations of all types must keep financial records. Salesclerks, farmers, factory workers, and owners of businesses all must keep records. Regardless of where you work or the position you accept when you graduate, you will probably have to keep some records as part of your job. Why? One reason is that the government requires businesses to keep records so that certain information is reported to the Internal Revenue Service (IRS) on a periodic basis. Another reason is that accurate records are the basis for sound business decisions.

Maintaining accounting records will probably become an important responsibility of yours at some point in your office career. Financial activities you could do range from taking care of small amounts of cash needed to run an office on a day-to-day basis to helping an accountant prepare financial statements essential to the success of a business.

Accounting activities may be done by hand and stored on paper or done with a computer and stored on disk. The same financial information is kept in either case. A manual accounting system (one done by hand) is still popular in today's offices. With manual accounting, you perform calculations using an electronic or ten-key calculator.

Today, however, because of the many records that businesses must keep, the use of computers to complete and store records is growing in popularity. The availability of economical, user-friendly accounting software packages has encouraged both businesses and families to easily computerize records.

Businesses thrive as a result of maintaining accurate, up-to-date records in usable form. This is because competition in business rewards maximum efficiency. Inaccurate accounting records often contribute to business failure and bankruptcy. As business owners and managers strive for economic success, sound decisions and plans require the use of complete and accurately prepared accounting cycle information.

An **accounting cycle** involves recording, classifying, and summarizing financial information for owners, managers, and other interested parties. Performing the accounting cycle in a consistent, timely, and accurate manner is important in all businesses.

The series of procedures in the accounting cycle is repeated for each *accounting period.* The length of an accounting period depends on the needs of a business and how often financial information needs to be summarized. Though an accounting period is usually one year long, it can be as short as a month, or it can be three months long on a quarterly basis.

To compare like information, specific times for a financial review need to be established and those same periods compared. For example, sales from December of this year will be compared with sales from December of last year. This allows for historical data to be used for making informal future plans.

The four accounting activities office workers assist in most often are: 1) preparing financial statements, 2) accounting for credit transactions in accounts receivable and accounts payable, 3) managing merchandise inventory and order processing tasks, and 4) preparing payroll activities.

## Financial Statements

Changes in financial information are reported for a specific period of time in the form of **financial statements.** Financial statements permit owners, managers, and accountants to analyze business activities and interpret their effectiveness. Answers to questions such as How do sales and profits from this year compare with sales and profits from the last two years? or What is our cash flow this month? are provided by analyzing financial statements.

All businesses should prepare financial statements on a regular basis so that any changes or trends can be noted immediately. The two most common financial statements used to answer these types of questions are the balance sheet and the income statement.

**Balance Sheet** A **balance sheet** shows the financial condition of a business at a particular time, for example on December 31, 1993, or June 30, 1994. In reality, the details of a company's financial condition change constantly. Every day, a company pays bills and receives payments. Every day, some inventory is used and must be replaced with new purchases.

Even though the financial picture is in constant motion, periodically every business must take a snapshot of its finances to get some idea of its value or net worth at that particular time. Only an accurate, up-to-date balance sheet can provide this view of a business's finances. The balance sheet shows the assets, liabilities, and capital, or net worth.

All balance sheets must satisfy the following accounting equation:

$$\text{Assets} = \text{Liabilities} + \text{Capital}$$

To understand accounting, you must understand the three basic terms in this equation.

**Assets** are everything of value that a company owns. They can include such things as cash, buildings, and land. As a person, you have assets. Some examples of your personal assets are your clothes, money in your wallet or bank account, and any jewelry that you've purchased or that has been given to you.

**Liabilities** are a business's financial obligations or debts. All businesses acquire debts and obligations as they buy goods and services from others. Suppose you borrow money from a friend and promise to pay it back in a week. This is an example of a liability or debt you owe to someone else. Examples of typical business liabilities are mortgages on buildings and charge accounts established with suppliers for materials or services purchased to operate a business.

**Capital,** or owner's equity, is the claim that an owner has against a firm's assets. To better understand capital, let's look at an example. Suppose Sharla owns and operates Quick Business Services and wants to sell it. She and her accountant value the assets at $70,000. But Sharla owes suppliers money; her liabilities amount to $40,000. If Sharla finds a buyer and sells her business for $70,000, she will receive $30,000. This $30,000 represents her owner's equity because it is the difference between the assets and the liabilities of Quick Business Services.

With reference to this example, remember two things:

- You can figure owner's equity easily because a variation in the accounting equation is the following equation:

$$\text{Owner's equity, or capital} = \text{Assets} - \text{Liabilities}$$

- In the accounting equation, you must keep the sections before and after the equal sign in balance or equal at all times. In other words, Sharla's owner's equity is $30,000 because assets of $70,000 minus liabilities of $40,000 equal $30,000.

Let's prepare a balance sheet. Suppose you and four friends start a business selling baseball caps. You call your business the Cap Company. On October 1, 19—, the five of you invest a total of $500 into the business. A week later, you enter into an agreement with the Top Cap Manufacturing Company to make the caps for you to your specifications.

In early November, the Top Cap Manufacturing Company sends you an initial shipment of printed caps. A few days later, you receive a bill for $250 payable in thirty days. As a result, your balance sheet as of November 15 looks like this:

The Cap Company

Balance Sheet, November 15, 19—

| | | |
|---|---|---|
| Assets | | |
| Cash | $500 | |
| Merchandise | $250 | |
| *Total Assets* | | <u>$750</u> |
| Liabilities | | |
| Top Cap Manufacturing Co. | $250 | |
| Capital | | |
| Paid-in Capital | $500 | |
| *Total Liabilities and Capital* | | <u>$750</u> |

Business activities such as buying and selling goods and services, receiving money, and paying bills cause continual changes in a company's assets, liabilities, and capital accounts. These activities, called *business transactions*, involve the exchange of one item of value for another.

For example, notice that the November 15, 19—, balance sheet shows assets to be greater than the amount of money you and your friends invested. But the $250 increase is not really all yours. It occurs because you bought $250 worth of caps on credit. This $250 in merchandise is an asset that is "balanced" by the $250 bill from the Top Cap Manufacturing Company.

If you pay for the merchandise the next day, before you sell any hats, you will have $250 less in your cash account and a zero balance in Top Cap Manufacturing Company's account. As a result of this one transaction or exchange, the balance sheet changes considerably in just one day's time, as shown below:

The Cap Company

Balance Sheet, November 16, 19—

Assets

| | |
|---|---|
| Cash | $250 |
| Merchandise | $250 |

*Total Assets*                $500

Liabilities

| | |
|---|---|
| Top Cap Manufacturing Company | $ 0 |

Capital

| | |
|---|---|
| Paid-in Capital | $500 |

*Total Liabilities and Capital*           $500

Keep in mind that a balance sheet shows what the values of certain accounts are at a given time. In other words, it shows the status of a company's different accounts. This is the source of the term *accounting*.

**Income Statement** An **income statement** is a summary of all income and expenses for a certain time period, such as a month or year. It is probably the most frequently studied of all financial statements. Owners study income statements to determine how much profit they are making. Bankers study income statements to decide whether or not to approve a business loan.

Unlike a balance sheet, which presents a stationary financial picture, an income statement reflects a business's profitability over a given time period. The accounting formula for income statements is as follows:

$$\text{Net income} = \text{Revenue} - \text{Expenses}$$

**Revenues,** or income, are all funds an organization raises from the sale of its goods and services. They are generally received in the form

### Accounting

In a large office, accounting duties are usually shared by many employees. Usually, one department or individual is responsible for one area of the accounting process. For example, one department or individual may be responsible for accounts payable and another for accounts receivable. All the work of a department or individual will relate to that one specific area of accounting.

In a small office, one individual is usually responsible for many areas of the accounting work. Many times, this one person functions more as a bookkeeper for the company. It is also common for a small office to hire an outside accountant to do the company taxes and other financial reports. The bookkeeper will then simply record the day-to-day transactions, accumulating and maintaining the data as needed by company managers and the outside accountant.

*Do you enjoy bookkeeping and accounting tasks? If so, should you specialize in these areas and work in a large office, or would you prefer to work in a small office where bookkeeping and accounting might represent just one part of your total job description?*

of cash payments. Cash, as used in business, may mean currency (bills and coins) or a check drawn on a business or personal checking account.

**Expenses** are the costs a business incurs as it buys the resources it needs to produce and market its goods and services. They are classified as the cost of goods sold (for manufacturing firms) and as operating expenses, such as salaries, rent, supplies, and utilities.

**Net income** is the amount of money that remains after expenses are subtracted from revenues. It is commonly called the "bottom line." If an income statement shows that revenues were greater than expenses, the company made a *net profit*. If expenses were greater than revenues, however, the company suffered a *net loss*.

Businesses detect the reasons for increases or decreases in net income by comparing current and previous income statements. This comparison is helpful in making management decisions about future operations and money management, in general.

Suppose the Cap Company has been in business for one year. Over the past year, it has ordered more caps on three occasions and sales are continuing to increase at a steady pace.

These transactions are included on the Cap Company's income statement covering the period November 15, 19—, to November 15 of the following year, as shown on the top of the next page.

The Cap Company

Income Statement

For Year Ended November 15, 19—

Revenue:

    Sales                                                $1,500.00

Expenses:

| | | |
|---|---|---|
| Caps Purchased | $450.00 | |
| Advertising Expense | $ 95.00 | |
| Postage Expense | $ 37.50 | |
| Miscellaneous Expenses | $ 96.00 | |
| Less: Total Expenses | | $678.50 |
| Net Income | | $821.50 |

# Recall Time

*Answer the following questions:*

1. How is the term *accounting cycle* related to the term *accounting period?*
2. Why does a business prepare financial statements?
3. How is the function of a balance sheet different from the function of an income statement?
4. What do the terms *asset* and *liability* mean? Give a business example of each.
5. What types of business transactions can affect a balance sheet?
6. What do the terms *revenue* and *expense* mean? Give an example of each.

## Accounts Receivable and Accounts Payable

You may work for a business that sells its products on credit. Credit transactions are best accounted for through the use of accounts receivable and accounts payable accounts (see figure 8–1).

When a business sells something and accepts payment later, it is in a way giving the buyer a loan. Such a transaction creates transactions called **accounts receivables,** which represent an accounting of money that credit customers owe to a business. If, for example, the Cap

*Accounts Receivable*

4/1
Made Credit Sale (30 days) to:

| | |
|---|---|
| J. Martin | $5 |
| J. Carney | 5 |
| M. Hampshire | 5 |

4/2
Set Up Account Receivable Cards for:

J. Martin
2315 Hemberg
Glendale, AZ 85030
Balance due                    $5

J. Carney
34 Cropp Road
Peoria, AZ 85032
Balance due                    $5

M. Hampshire
980 Greenfield
Tolleson, AZ 85045
Balance due                    $5

5/1
Received Payment in Full from:
J. Martin
2315 Hemberg
Glendale, AZ 85030
Balance Due                    –0–

M. Hampshire
980 Greenfield
Tolleson, AZ 85045
Balance due                    –0–

5/2
Sent invoice to J. Carney

5/11
Received Payment in Full from:
J. Carney
34 Cropp Road
Peoria, AZ 85032
Balance due                    –0–

*Accounts Payable*

Made Credit Purchases from:

| | | |
|---|---|---|
| 12/4 | Top Cap Mfg. Co. | $200 |
| 12/5 | Caps & Things Wh. | 100 |
| 12/11 | Baseball Caps Sales | 150 |

12/12
Set Up Account Payable Cards for:

Top Cap Mfg. Co.
711 Buster Street
Chicago, IL 38602
Balance due                    $200

Caps & Things Wh.
345 Spring Street
Los Angeles, CA 90502
Balance due                    $100

Baseball Caps Sales
737 Bay Road
Oakland, CA 98767
Balance due                    $150

Made Payments to:

| | | |
|---|---|---|
| 1/6 | Top Cap Mfg. Co. | $100 |
| 1/8 | Caps & Things Wh. | 50 |
| 1/18 | Baseball Caps Sales | 150 |

1/18
Updated Account Payable Cards:
Top Cap Mfg. Co.
711 Buster Street
Chicago, IL 38602
Balance due                    $100

Caps & Things Wh.
345 Spring Street
Los Angeles, CA 90502
Balance due                    $50

Baseball Caps Sales
737 Bay Road
Oakland, CA 98767
Balance due                    –0–

O F F I C E    T I P

Once an error gets into a computer, it may not be noticed until it appears on a customer's bill. You can prevent many errors by carefully proofreading information as it is displayed on your computer's monitor.

Company sells caps to its customers and allows thirty days to pay for the caps, then an accounts receivable account will be established.

As an office worker processing accounts receivable, you will check, record, and post purchase transactions related to sales and cash received for payment. You may use a microcomputer to maintain and store the accounts receivable records. However, whether you use a manual system or a computerized system, the basic tasks will not change; only your tools and methods will differ.

Accounts receivable accounts involve money owed to a company. **Accounts payable** accounts, on the other hand, refer to money a company owes to its creditors when it buys supplies or materials on credit, rather than paying cash. If, for example, the Cap Company buys caps from more than one source, an accounts payable system will keep track of how much is owed to the various cap manufacturers.

As an office worker processing accounts payable, you will check, record, and post transactions related to purchases your company makes on credit and cash payments made to suppliers for those purchases.

## Inventory Control and Order Processing

An **inventory** is an itemized list showing the value of goods on hand in a business. The term *inventory* also refers to the actual goods. For example, a shoe salesperson might tell a customer, "Our inventory is low," meaning that the store doesn't have a lot of shoes to sell. Inventory is an asset because it can be sold to customers for a certain amount of money—it can be converted to income.

Businesses that sell merchandise such as office supplies or equipment realize that inventory is a costly asset. It is also a difficult asset to manage.

Inventory represents money that could be used to acquire other assets. The money used to produce, store, and keep track of inventory is money "lost" for other purposes. Thus, inventory represents opportunity costs or money that is unavailable should other profitable opportunities arise.

Why is managing a merchandise inventory difficult? For many reasons. First, a merchandise inventory can consist of thousands of items; keeping records on this many items can be time-consuming and error prone. Second, inventory is subject to theft by customers and employees. Third, space used to store inventory is expensive. And fourth, often businesses must borrow money to purchase inventory, which results in interest payments and reduced profits.

You may be able to see why it's important to avoid excess inventory. It is, however, equally important not to let inventory get too low. If inventory is too low, out-of-stock conditions may occur where customers are unable to find the product to buy on the shelves. The consequences of an out-of-stock condition are lost sales, loss of customer confidence, and reduced profits. Thus, a well-managed inventory system keeps inventory levels as low as possible, while still maintaining enough inventory to meet customer demand. A good inventory system is vital because it helps a business know when and how many inventory items to reorder.

The key to solving inventory problems is a good record-keeping system that provides accurate and timely information when reordering decisions must be made. Although inventory records today are maintained both manually and by computer, the trend is to computerize the

STOCK RECORD CARD

Caps — blue

ITEM size small Maximum 5C

STOCK No. C-BS Minimum 1C

UNIT Each

| Date | | Quantity Received | Quantity Issued | Balance |
|------|---|-------------------|-----------------|---------|
| 19—DEC | 1 | 5C | | 5C |
| | 4 | | 2C | 3C |
| | 11 | | 2C | 1C |
| | 23 | 4C | | 5C |
| | | | | |
| | | | | |
| | | | | |
| | | | | |
| | | | | |
| | | | | |
| | | | | |

inventory and order processes. If one of your jobs is to keep inventory records, you are involved in an important part of a business. How well you and others working with you do this job can affect the success or failure of your company.

**Inventory Methods** When you monitor inventory, you determine for each product the quantity on hand that is available to sell. Businesses use two manual methods to monitor inventory: periodic and perpetual. A business can use either method or a combination of both to determine the quantity on hand.

When the *periodic inventory method* is used, the quantities of each product are physically counted, weighed, or measured at a given time. This periodic inventory, also called a physical inventory, is usually taken only once or twice a year. For example, when you see an advertisement that reads Closed for Inventory or Come to our Preinventory Sale, it is talking about performing a periodic inventory.

When the *perpetual inventory method* is used, an up-to-date, continuous record of increases and decreases of merchandise is maintained for each item in an inventory. The form used to record this information is a *stock record card* (see figure 8–2). Each time a business sells a product, that item is immediately deducted from an existing balance. Each time a business buys more product; those new items are added to the existing balance.

The advantage of using the perpetual method of keeping inventory is that current quantity is always accessible for ready reference. Inventory levels are checked frequently. For example, they are checked when it's time to reorder products and also when large orders are received.

Because of the many items and high volume of transactions involved in merchandise inventory, manual record keeping can become a time-consuming, cumbersome process. Consider the necessity of a computer system for an auto parts store that may have millions of different items in inventory.

Computerized inventory systems are programmed to perform similarly to the perpetual inventory method. When someone buys an auto part, for example, the item is automatically deducted from inventory when the amount is rung up at the cash register terminal. Computer inventory control is efficient for businesses to use because it automatically monitors stock levels as sales are made and can easily be programmed to alert management when supplies must be reordered or manufactured.

Computers are capable of storing and retrieving data and of making computations quickly and accurately. They sort, organize, and report information and then store the inventory on a diskette. The availability of inexpensive microcomputers now makes it possible for even a small retail business to use a computer to keep records and control inventory. Maintaining inventory records is likely an important task you will perform if you work on an office staff in a retail business.

**Order Processing** Order-processing transactions affect inventory records. When merchandise is ordered, received, sold, or returned, the balance in the inventory account changes. When inventory changes are recorded, it is only after certain documents authorizing those changes have been properly completed. These documents are called *source documents*.

*Ordering Merchandise* When a business orders merchandise, it completes a *purchase order* and sends it to the company selling the merchandise, which is called the vendor. For example, when the Cap Company orders more caps, it must complete a purchase order specifying how many caps in different sizes it wants to order, as shown in figure 8–3. A purchase order must be correctly completed because it becomes a contract that is legally binding. The business that places an order retains a copy of the purchase order.

*Receiving Merchandise* A *packing slip* from the vendor usually accompanies merchandise when it is shipped to a purchaser. For example, when the Cap Company receives the caps it orders, taped to the box or inside the box will be a packing slip similar to the one shown in figure 8–4.

The packing slip shows the quantity of each item shipped. Receiving clerks compare this slip against the items in the package and against the purchase order to be sure that all items ordered were shipped. An invoice or bill indicating the cost for the goods received will arrive separately.

As an office worker, you will compare the packing slip to the invoice when you receive it from the vendor. This comparison is your way of verifying that all items billed were received.

OFFICE TIP

Many forms used in order processing contain dollar amounts and quantities that you must add, subtract, multiply, or divide. Learn to estimate the answers before you figure them out. Estimating and developing good math proofreading skills will help you prevent costly errors.

**PURCHASE ORDER**

**THE CAP COMPANY**
Box 4050
Phoenix, AZ 85020

ORDER NO. 3
DATE Mar 1, 19—
SHIP VIA Truck
DATE WANT Mar 16 19—
TERMS 30 days

TO: Top Cap Manufacturing Company
711 Buster Street
Chicago, IL 38602

| QUANTITY | DESCRIPTION | UNIT PRICE |
|---|---|---|
| 20 ea | C-BS: Caps—Blue, Size Small | $3.00 |
| 30 ea. | C-RM: Caps—Red, Size Medium | $3.00 |

By_____*Jayne Wilson*_____
Purchasing Agent

■ FIGURE 8–3
*Sample Purchase Order*

FIGURE 8–4
*Sample Packing Slip*

**PACKING SLIP**

**TOP CAP MANUFACTURING COMPANY**
711 Buster Street
Chicago, IL 38602

Sold To  The Cap Company
Box 4050
Phoenix, AZ 85020

INVOICE NO.   60
DATE   Mar 10, 19—
OUR ORDER NO.   201
CUSTOMER'S ORDER NO.  3

TERMS  30 days

SHIP   Via Truck

| QUANTITY | STOCK NO. | DESCRIPTION | UNIT PRICE | TOTAL AMOUNT |
|---|---|---|---|---|
| 20 ea. | C-BS | Caps—Blue, Size Small | | |
| 30 ea. | C-RM | Caps—Red, Size Medium | | |

---

FIGURE 8–5
*Sample Completed Sales Slip*

The Cap Company
Box 4050
Phoenix, AZ 85020

NO. 29

Wayne Gibson   Jan 18  19 —
Sold To

1127 W. Brown Street
Street

Phoenix, AZ 85020
City State Zip

| Sold by | pgc | Cash XX | | Charge | |
|---|---|---|---|---|---|
| Quantity | Description | | | Unit Amount | Total Amount |
| 2 ea | Caps—blue, size large | | | $5.00 | $10.00 |
| 1 ea | Cap— red, size large | | | $5.00 | 5.00 |
| | | | | | |
| | | | | | |
| | | | | | |
| | Total Due | | | | $15.00 |

This slip must accompany all returns

Customer's Signature
for charge sales

*Selling Merchandise* Whenever a company sells merchandise, it makes a record of the transaction. That record is commonly called a *sales slip*. It may be prepared manually or produced automatically by a cash register. An example of a sales slip for the Cap Company is shown in figure 8–5.

*Returning Merchandise* Customers sometimes return merchandise because it is defective or it is the wrong size. When merchandise is received, customers can get a cash refund, can get credit to their charge account, or can exchange the item for other merchandise. When merchandise is returned, a *return slip* is completed. An example of a return slip used by the Cap Company is shown in figure 8–6.

## Payroll

A **payroll** is the total amount paid to all employees for a pay period. Various methods of figuring and recording payroll are used by different companies. If you work in a payroll office, the method you will use depends on the number of employees and the type of office equipment you have available. To speed up the preparation of a payroll, businesses of all sizes use their own computers. Many large companies, however, turn the task over to other companies that have sophisticated payroll programs. Like most accounting activities, the procedures to perform the payroll function are the same should a manual or computerized method be used.

■ FIGURE 8–6
*Sample Return Slip*

```
                The Cap Company
                    Box 4050
                Phoenix, AZ 85020

                  Return Slip

Customer's Name: Wayne Gibsen        Account No.: _____
Address: 1127 W. Brown Street        Date: Jan 22, 19—
         Phoenix, AZ  85020
─────────────────────────────────────────────────────────
THIS IS A CREDIT FOR MERCHANDISE RETURNED
1 ea.   Cap—blue, size large                      5.00



       K. Cappelli
_____
Approved by:
```

Although employees are paid by many methods, the most common include yearly salary, hourly wages, and straight commission. The most frequent method of paying white-collar and management personnel is by yearly or annual salary. A *salary* is a fixed amount of money paid to an employee for certain assigned duties. Salaries are stated as gross pay per year, such as $28,000 per year.

*Wages* are paid based on the number of hours worked. Straight hourly wages are easy to calculate. To determine an employee's gross pay, simply multiply the number of hours worked by the pay rate per hour. For example, if an employee works 40 hours per week and is paid $6 per hour, the gross pay is $240 (40 × $6).

Employees are paid at a higher rate per hour for overtime hours. *Overtime* is the time an employee works over 40 hours per week. The usual overtime rate is 1½ times the regular rate. If, for example, an employee earns $6 per hour, then the overtime rate is $9 (1½× $6).

Overtime wages are calculated using these three simple steps:

1. Multiply 40 by the regular rate.
2. Multiply the hours over 40 by the overtime rate.
3. Add the two totals together.

For example, if an employee making $6 per hour works 45 hours, the employee will earn $240 in regular pay (40 × $6) plus $45 in overtime pay (5 × $9). The employee will thus earn a total gross pay of $285 ($240 + $45).

A third procedure used to calculate wages is *commission*, which refers to a percentage of total sales. Salespeople are usually paid on a commission basis. Different types of commissions are used. The most popular and easiest to calculate is straight commission. In figuring straight commission, you multiply a percentage by the total sales.

For example, let's suppose that Eddie, who sells for Action Office Supply, is paid on a 10 percent commission basis. In other words, for every dollar in sales that Eddie generates, he is paid ten cents (10% × $1). In February, Eddie sells $20,000 worth of office supplies. His commission for February is $2,000 (10% × $20,000). In March, Eddie sells $31,000—he receives a large order of office supplies from a government account. Eddie therefore receives a $3,100 paycheck in March.

Commissions are good for some people and bad for others. Because the amount of money each month can vary, a person who works on commission must be a good money manager. In reality, many workers are not good money managers. This prompts businesses to offer salespersons the opportunity to receive a base salary of perhaps $1,500 every month plus a small commission of 4 percent of sales instead of just a large commission of 10 percent of sales.

Regardless of how an employee is paid, the first step in processing a company payroll is to determine an employee's gross pay. *Gross pay* is total earnings before deductions are made. Deductions include insurance and various federal and state taxes.

The second step is to adjust the gross pay amount by making various deductions so you can arrive at the take-home pay or *net pay* due an employee. A large deduction required by U.S. tax laws is federal income tax. Another required deduction is Federal Insurance Contributions Act

Darren is a good office worker at Zero Based Accounting Systems. The professional and accurate way he completes his work is the reason he is being groomed for a better position. Vi is a junior accounting clerk. In a few months, she will be moving to another town and her position will be open. Darren is hoping to be considered for that position. In fact, he is taking night courses in accounting at the community college and is doing well.

Darren likes Vi and has always admired the efficient and organized way she works. Lately, however, he has noticed that the quality of her work is lower. On two occasions, he has noticed math errors in her payroll calculations. When he tells her about the errors, she seems annoyed with him. Darren doesn't intend to accuse Vi of knowingly producing inaccurate payroll checks. Nevertheless, he worries about other math errors she might be making.

1. If you were Darren, what would you do about the situation?
2. Should Darren just keep a close eye on Vi's work, or should he tell his supervisor?
3. What other options, if any, does Darren have?

(FICA) tax, commonly known as Social Security tax. Other examples of deductions that affect net pay are state and city income taxes (where applicable) and miscellaneous voluntary deductions such as medical insurance payments, retirement plan payments, and union dues.

As an example, suppose Doris works for Top Flight Helicopter Company as a senior office worker making $20,000 per year. What is her monthly net pay if her annual deductions are as follows?

| | |
|---|---|
| Federal income tax | $2,400 |
| State income tax | 1,200 |
| Dependent medical insurance payment | 720 |
| Credit union loan payment | 600 |

Doris's monthly net pay is $1,257. It is calculated by following these steps:

1. Determine gross salary per month:

$$\$20,000 \div 12 = \$1,667$$

2. Determine total deductions per month:

| | |
|---|---|
| Federal income tax ($2,400 ÷ 12) | $200 |
| State income tax ($1,200 ÷ 12) | 100 |
| Dependent medical insurance payment ($720 ÷ 12) | 60 |
| Credit union loan payment ($600 ÷ 12) | 50 |
| Total deductions per month | $410 |

3. Calculate net pay per month:

$$\$1,667 - \$410 = \$1,257$$

When you perform accounting activities in a large office, you may use a computer system that operates from a sophisticated integrated accounting software package. This system may have the capabilities of incorporating the accounts payable, accounts receivable, payroll, and inventory control with the general ledger accounts.

In contrast, if you work in a small office, you will likely still use computerized accounting programs. But you may have only a payroll program or a type of inventory control software program, rather than an integrated package.

# R ecall Time

*Answer the following questions:*

1. In what way are the terms *accounts receivable* and *accounts payable* opposite in meaning?
2. How are the inventory process and the order process related?
3. What are the advantages of computerized inventory methods compared with manual inventory methods?
4. In order processing, what is the relationship between a purchase order and a packing slip?
5. In order processing, what is the relationship between a sales slip and a return slip?
6. What do yearly salary, hourly wage, and straight commission mean?
7. In calculating a payroll, what are four deductions that affect a person's net pay?

# ■ RECORD-KEEPING ACTIVITIES

As an office worker, you can expect to do some record-keeping activities. Among the activities you are likely to perform are banking tasks and petty cash fund maintenance tasks.

## Banking Tasks

Most businesses put cash receipts in a bank and make most cash payments by check. This practice occurs because money, consisting of bills and coins, is not as safe as many other assets. Care must be taken in handling money because money can be transferred easily from one person to another without any questions asked. Unfortunately, in some cases, ownership is usually determined by the person having the money.

For these and other reasons, businesses keep most of their cash-on-hand in a bank and use various banking services. Banking services are safe, are convenient, and provide great accuracy in maintaining cash records for businesses. Businesses depend on banking services to verify accounting records, to compare the businesses' records of checks written with the banks' records of checks paid, and to transfer cash electronically using *electronic funds transfer* (EFT). With EFT, businesses can elec-

At lunch one day, a discussion goes on that makes Justine feel very uncomfortable. Andy, Heather, Ron, and Shujian are sitting at her table. They are co-workers that Justine has grown to know over the past year while working at a large insurance company in Los Angeles.

The four co-workers are laughing and joking about how easy it is these days for employees to steal from companies and supplement a small paycheck. Heather says she heard on TV of how a computer programmer established a separate personal checking account that received all the half cents and lesser amounts from payroll checks. This programmer made more money than he could have imagined.

Shujian tells about a friend who works for a charity organization. This friend told Shujian that periodically, when cash is received through the mail, she will pocket the donation. Shujian agrees with her friend that it isn't that bad because the amounts are only five and ten dollars and are too small to help out the cause anyway.

Other examples are shared during the hour's lunch in Justine's presence. That afternoon, Justine can't get the discussion off her mind. It really bothers her.

1. Would the discussion have bothered you as it did Justine? If you were Justine, would you have said anything to the four co-workers about how you felt? Explain how you would feel.
2. What are some outcomes that this stealing attitude can produce? Is this attitude commonplace in today's society?

tronically make payments, deposits, and other banking transactions quickly and on a timely basis with this "paperless" transfer of funds.

Let's review some common banking terms you will encounter while processing banking tasks:

- Placing cash in a bank account is called *making a deposit*.
- A person or business in whose name cash is deposited is called a *depositor*.
- A bank account from which payments are ordered by the depositor is called a *checking account*.
- A *check* is a business paper used to make payments from a checking account.
- *Endorsing a check* is signing your name or a company's name on the back of a check in order to transfer the check to a bank or to someone else.

In an office, you may perform three common banking tasks. These tasks are depositing checks that have been properly endorsed, writing checks, and reconciling monthly bank statements.

**Preparing Deposits** Preparing deposits involves three steps: (1) endorse all checks to be deposited, (2) prepare the deposit slip, and (3) record the deposit in the check register.

When you deposit a check in a checking account, you must transfer it to your bank by signing your name on the back of the check. This procedure is called endorsing the check. You can use three endorsements: blank, restrictive, or full. A blank endorsement is a signature-only endorsement. A restrictive endorsement restricts the use of the check. Many businesses and individuals often write "for deposit only" to ensure that the check amount will only be deposited, not cashed. A

## FIGURE 8-7

*a) Paycheck for Patrick Reynolds*
*b) Sample Check Endorsements*

The Cap Company     No. 075
Box 4050
Phoenix, AZ 85020     Date __Nov. 5,__ 19___ 9022/2360

PAY to the
Order of __Patrick Reynolds__     $125.00

__One hundred twenty-five and no/100——__ Dollars

Valley of Sun Bank
200 Central     *Doug Fonner*
Phoenix, AZ 85008

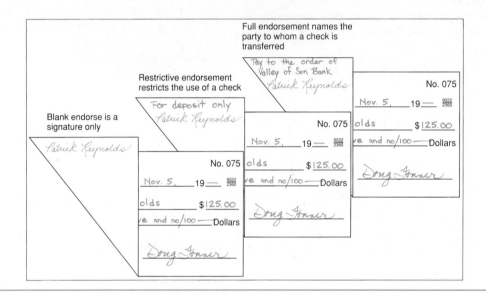

Blank endorse is a
signature only

Restrictive endorsement
restricts the use of a check

Full endorsement names the
party to whom a check is
transferred

---

## FIGURE 8-8

*Sample Deposit Slip with a Check Listed*

For DEPOSIT to the Account of     9022/2300
Patrick Reynolds
600 E. Oak Drive
Glendale, AZ 85099

Date __Nov 5,__ 19___

Valley of Sun Bank
200 Central
Phoenix, AZ 85008

⑆2360 74169⑈ 863ꞌ5290⑈

| | Dollars | Cents |
|---|---|---|
| Bills | | |
| Coins | | |
| Checks: | | |
| 9022 | 125. | 00 |
| | | |
| | | |
| | | |
| | | |
| Total Deposit | 125. | 00 |

full endorsement names the party to whom a check is transferred. Figure 8–7 shows examples of acceptable endorsements.

When you deposit a check, you must list it on a deposit slip along with any bills and coins to be deposited, as shown in figure 8–8. Be sure to enter the total amount of the deposit in the check register and add it to the old balance to find your new checkbook balance.

**Writing Checks** Some checks have two parts: the stub, which remains in the checkbook, and the check itself, which is sent to the person to whom you owe money. The stub gives a record of the important facts about a check. Careful people always fill out the stub first before writing a check. If they did not do this, they might mail the check and then find that they have no record of the details about it. You can record the details of checks you write on a stub or in a check register (see figure 8–9). A check register contains a record of each check that was written and each deposit made.

If many checks are written by a business, it's a good idea to use a machine known as a check writer or check protector. This machine prints the amount on a check in a way that makes changes to the check amount impossible without being detected. Other businesses may prepare their checks using a computer system.

**Reconciling Bank Statements** Reconciling a bank statement is a common task for an office worker. The purpose of this procedure is to bring your company's checkbook balance and a bank statement balance into agreement.

Usually, the bank sends a monthly bank statement. This statement summarizes all checking account transactions. It lists all checks processed and paid by the bank, deposits recorded, and any service fees charged.

When you receive a bank statement, compare either the check stubs or the check register entries against the bank's summary. This procedure

*Banks and other financial institutions often use a check writer, as shown here, to safeguard money amounts from being altered.*

■ FIGURE 8–9
*a) Sample Check Register*
*b) Sample Check Stub*

a)

| Check No. | Date | Check Issued to or description of deposit | Amt of check | √ | Amt of deposit | Balance forward | |
|---|---|---|---|---|---|---|---|
| | | | | | | Balance forward | 225.00 |
| 075 | Nov 5 | To Patrick Reynolds | 125.00 | | | Check or Deposit | 125.00 |
| | | For paycheck Nov 1-5 | | | | Balance | 100.00 |
| | | To | | | | Check or Deposit | |
| | | For | | | | Balance | |
| | | To | | | | Check or Deposit | |
| | | For | | | | Balance | |
| | | To | | | | Check or Deposit | |
| | | For | | | | Balance | |
| | | To | | | | Check or Deposit | |
| | | For | | | | Balance | |

b)

No. 075           $ 125.00

Date Nov 5, 19—

To Patrick Reynolds

For Paycheck Nov 1-5

| | Dollars | Cents |
|---|---|---|
| Bal Brought Fwd | 225 | 00 |
| Amt Deposited | 0 | 00 |
| Total | 225 | 00 |
| Amt this Check | 125 | 00 |
| Bal Carried Fwd | 100. | 00 |

| The Cap Company | | | | | |
|---|---|---|---|---|---|
| Bank Reconciliation Form | | | | | |
| December 31, 19— | | | | | |
| Checkbook balance. | 525 cc | Bank balance | | 607 00 | |
| | | Less: o/s checks | | | |
| | | # 129 | | 82 cc | |
| Adjusted chkbk balance | 525 00 | Adjusted bank bal | | 525 00 | |

is called **reconciliation.** Banks usually provide a reconciliation form on the back of the monthly statement. Figure 8–10 shows a sample reconciliation form for the Cap Company. In reconciling a bank statement, here are the steps to follow:

1. Compare the amounts of all deposits shown on the bank statement with the deposit amounts you recorded on the check stubs or in the check register.
2. Arrange the canceled checks in numerical order by check number.
3. Compare the amounts of the canceled checks with the amounts entered on the stubs or check register. Make a small check mark on the stub if a canceled check has been returned and the amounts agree. Stubs that are not checkmarked represent checks that were not returned by the bank. These are called *outstanding checks.*
4. Prepare the bank reconciliation form (usually on the back of the monthly bank statement).

## Petty Cash Fund Maintenance Tasks

Businesses must keep careful records of all money they spend. This is true for payments made by check and for payments made with currency. Although businesses prefer to make payments by check, it is often easier and necessary to pay with currency. If you buy postage stamps for the office or gas for a company delivery truck, for example, you may have to use currency. Because these payments are in small, or "petty," amounts, they are called **petty cash payments.**

A business usually keeps all its cash in a checking account. Thus, the currency needed for these petty cash payments is usually initially obtained by writing and cashing a check. The amount of the check is an estimate of how much money will be needed for a certain time period, such as a week or month. After cashing the check, the office places this currency in a container called a *petty cash box.*

Let's assume you work for Ms. Larson, and she puts you in charge of the petty cash fund. Ms. Larson starts the petty cash fund by cashing a check for $75. Here are the steps you, as the petty cash clerk, will follow in handling a typical transaction.

Al, your company's delivery person, comes to you and needs $5 to fix a flat tire on the delivery truck. You first fill out a *petty cash voucher*. This is a receipt that verifies that Al received $5 in cash. When Al returns with a receipt from the tire repair, you staple the petty cash voucher and the tire repair receipt together. At the end of the day, you count the currency and total the petty cash vouchers in the box. With Al's transaction, your petty cash balance will look like this:

| Total of vouchers in box | $ 5 |
|---|---|
| Plus cash in box | 70 |
| Equals original fund | $75 |

This example balances, but sometimes the petty cash fund doesn't. A *cash shortage* occurs when the actual currency in the petty cash box is less than the balance shown in the petty cash book. A petty cash book records receipts and disbursements. A *cash overage* occurs when the actual currency in the petty cash box is more than the balance shown in the petty cash book. The goal is to make petty cash balance. If it doesn't, then something is wrong because you either have too much or too little money accounted for. Any discrepancies are recorded in the petty cash book and the balance is corrected.

When the petty cash fund runs low, you remove all vouchers from the box, add them, and give them to Ms. Larson. She gives you enough money to replenish the fund back up to the regular amount of $75.

OFFICE TIP

If you are unable to locate errors while reconciling a bank statement, remember that banks provide a service that can help you. The bank may have made an error in entering amounts of money. It would appreciate being informed as soon as possible.

# R ecall Time

*Answer the following questions:*

1. What are the advantages to businesses that use banking services?
2. Why must checks be endorsed?
3. What is the purpose of reconciling a bank statement immediately upon receipt?
4. Why do businesses try to put one person in charge of a petty cash fund?

# ■ SUMMARY

Accounting involves recording, classifying, and summarizing financial information. An office worker assists in the preparation of accounting records. These records ultimately provide the data to prepare financial statements like balance sheets and income statements. Balance sheets are prepared according to the accounting equation Assets = Liabilities + Capital. Income statements are concerned with the bottom line or net profit, which results when total expenses are subtracted from total revenue.

Today's office worker will also perform certain record-keeping functions. These include banking tasks like depositing, endorsing, and writing checks. In addition, reconciling a bank statement and maintaining a petty cash fund are still important office functions.

When you perform accounting and record-keeping functions, remember the following points:

- The accounting cycle involves recording, classifying, and summarizing financial information.
- The series of procedures in the accounting cycle is repeated for each accounting period.
- Changes in financial information are reported for specific periods of time in the form of financial statements.
- A balance sheet shows the financial conditions of a business at a particular time.
- Balance sheets must satisfy the accounting equation:
  $$\text{Assets} = \text{Liabilities} + \text{Capital.}$$
- Assets are everything of value that a company owns.
- Liabilities are a business's financial obligations or debts.
- Capital, or owner's equity, is the claim that an owner has against a firm's assets.
- An income statement is a summary of all income and expenses for a certain period of time.
- Income statements must satisfy the accounting equation:
  $$\text{Net income} = \text{Revenue} - \text{Expenses.}$$
- Revenue or income is all funds an organization raises from the sale of its goods and services.
- Expenses are the costs a business incurs as it buys the resources it needs to produce and market its goods and services.
- Credit transactions are accounted for through the use of accounts receivable and accounts payable accounts.
- An inventory is an itemized listing showing the value of goods on hand in a business.
- Businesses monitor inventory by using the periodic and perpetual inventory methods.
- Order processing includes the procedures followed when merchandise is ordered, received, sold, or returned.
- A payroll is the total amount paid to all employees for a pay period.
- The most common methods for paying employees include yearly salary, hourly wages, and straight commission.
- Banking tasks often performed by office workers include preparing deposits, writing checks, and reconciling bank statements.
- A petty cash fund is used to make small payments with currency.

## In Conclusion . . .

*When you have completed this chapter, use an electronic typewriter or a microcomputer to answer the following questions:*

1. *What types of accounting and record-keeping tasks do office workers perform?*
2. *Why are these accounting and record-keeping tasks important to a business?*

# Review and Application

## REVIEW YOUR VOCABULARY

Match the following by writing the letter of the vocabulary word that is described below.

_____ 1. the claim an owner has against a firm's assets

_____ 2. a summary of all income and expenses for a certain time period

_____ 3. involves recording, classifying, and summarizing financial information for owners, managers, and other interested parties

_____ 4. refers to money a company owes to its creditors when it buys supplies or materials on credit, rather than paying cash

_____ 5. an itemized list showing the value of goods on hand in a business

_____ 6. a statement that shows the financial condition of a business at a particular time

_____ 7. everything of value that a company owns

_____ 8. the procedure of comparing the check stubs or the check register entries against the bank's summary of all checking account transactions

_____ 9. cash payments for small amounts made from an office fund

_____ 10. the costs a business incurs as it buys the resources it needs to produce and market its goods and services

_____ 11. the amount of money that remains after expenses are subtracted from revenues

_____ 12. represents an accounting of money that credit customers owe to a business

_____ 13. changes in financial information are reported for a specific period of time on these forms

_____ 14. a business's financial obligations or debts

_____ 15. all funds an organization raises from the sale of its goods and services

_____ 16. is the total amount paid to all employees for a pay period

a. accounting cycle
b. accounts payable
c. accounts receivables
d. assets
e. balance sheet
f. capital
g. expenses
h. financial statements
i. income statement
j. inventory
k. liabilities
l. net income
m. payroll
n. petty cash payments
o. reconciliation
p. revenues

## DISCUSS AND ANALYZE AN OFFICE SITUATION

1. Mary has been working for two months at the Pen Shop, an office supply wholesaler in town. She had not realized that pens came in so many different colors, sizes, and shapes. It is her job to take orders for pens over the phone from office supply stores and to take inventory periodically.

   Rodriguez has worked in the stockroom of the Pen Shop for over a year. When his work is caught up, he often helps with inventory.

   Mary and Rodriguez take turns writing and counting. When it is Rodriguez's turn to count, Mary is sure he is not reporting an accurate count. Instead, she fears he is just guessing.

   If you were Mary, what would you do? Would you confront Rodriguez? Would you tell the owner of your suspicions? Or would you just redo the whole inventory when Rodriguez went home? Role-play your best solution to the problem with another class member.

## PRACTICE BASIC SKILLS

### Math

1. Complete the bank reconciliation form on the next page. (Follow the instructions listed on page 306 and note figure 8–10.)

Cookies by Blanche
Bank Reconciliation Form
May 31, 19—

| | |
|---|---|
| Checkbook balance | $592.25 |
| Less: service charge | 5.60 |
| Adjusted chkbk balance | ? |
| | |
| Bank balance | $674.25 |
| Add: o/s deposit | 105.00 |
| Less: o/s checks | |
| #152   $ 90.00 | |
| #155   $102.60 | |
| Total o/s checks | ? |
| Adjusted bank balance | ? |

2. Calculate weekly gross pay for the following employees:

   a. Gary Valentine, who worked 47 ½ hours at $7.00 per hour
   b. Philip Grant, who worked 35 hours at $5.15 per hour

3. Calculate monthly gross pay for the following employees:

   a. Maureen Ogden, who sold $30,000 at 8.5 percent commission
   b. Benny Bishop, who earns a salary of $35,625 per year
   c. Del Blue, who earns a base salary of $18,000 per year and sold $21,350 at 5 percent commission

4. Calculate the amount for each item and determine the total amount due. (Follow the sales slip example shown in figure 8–5 on page 298.)

SALES SLIP
LEE'S UNIQUE FASHIONS
1018 9th Avenue
Beach City, CA 90266

SOLD TO: Modern Fashions
4050 N Arrow Way
Tucson, AZ 88706

Date: 12/12/—

Number: 8314

Sold by: rls   Cash: X   Charge: _

| QUANTITY | DESCRIPTION | UNIT AMOUNT | TOTAL AMOUNT |
|---|---|---|---|
| 6 ea | Dress; Style 222/M | $50.00 | |
| 3 ea | Dress; Style 222/S | $50.00 | |
| 9 ea | Skirt; Style 343/L | $25.00 | |
| 6 ea | Skirt; Style 343/M | $25.00 | |
| 3 ea | Skirt; Style 343/S | $25.00 | |
| | | Total Due | |

### English

1. Purchase orders that contain shipping instructions and quantities often use abbreviations to save space on forms. On a separate sheet of paper, write the meanings of the following abbreviations. Refer to an office reference book if you aren't sure of a meaning.

   a. c/o   _____
   b. COD   _____
   c. dept   _____
   d. doz   _____
   e. gal   _____
   f. pkg   _____
   g. ea   _____
   h. @   _____
   i. min   _____
   j. max   _____
   k. qty   _____

### Proofreading

1. Rewrite or retype the following paragraph, correcting all errors.

   When enterring data and manetaining acounting and recordkeeping reacords, it is importantt to proof read very acurately. Data entry errors cost companys millions of dolars each year. These additional costs ulltimately effect salaries and product pricing.

## APPLY YOUR KNOWLEDGE

1. Below are examples of balance sheet items. On a separate sheet of paper, write the letter *A* if it is an asset account and the letter *L* if it is a liability account.
   \_\_\_\_ a. office supplies
   \_\_\_\_ b. cash
   \_\_\_\_ c. notes payable (City Bank)
   \_\_\_\_ d. accounts payable (Smith's Furniture)
   \_\_\_\_ e. merchandise
   \_\_\_\_ f. office equipment
   \_\_\_\_ g. accounts receivable (May Johnson)
   \_\_\_\_ h. accounts receivable (Della Fry)
   \_\_\_\_ i. accounts payable (Surface Supply Company)
   \_\_\_\_ j. FICA tax payable

2. Below are examples of income statement items. On a separate sheet of paper, write the letter *R* if it is a revenue account and the letter *E* if it is an expense account.
   \_\_\_\_ a. advertising expense
   \_\_\_\_ b. secretarial fees collected
   \_\_\_\_ c. sales of office supplies
   \_\_\_\_ d. salary expense
   \_\_\_\_ e. sales of caps
   \_\_\_\_ f. postage expense
   \_\_\_\_ g. miscellaneous expenses
   \_\_\_\_ h. selling expenses
   \_\_\_\_ i. attorney fees collected

# QUIZ

*Write a **T** if the statement is true or an **F** if the statement is false.*

_____ 1. Performing the accounting cycle in a consistent, timely, and accurate manner is an important business activity.

_____ 2. A balance sheet reflects the assets and expenses of a business.

_____ 3. Assets are everything of value that a company owns.

_____ 4. Liabilities are a business's financial obligations or debts.

_____ 5. An income statement reflects the revenue, expenses, and net income of a business.

_____ 6. Expenses are the costs a business incurs as it buys the resources it needs to produce and market its goods and services.

_____ 7. Examples of net income are salaries, rent, and supplies.

_____ 8. Accounts receivable and accounts payable transactions involve credit purchases.

_____ 9. The phrase, "our inventory is low," means that the shelves are low relative to the floor.

_____ 10. The key to solving inventory problems is a good record-keeping system that provides accurate and timely information.

_____ 11. The two methods used to monitor inventory in businesses are periodic and perpetual.

_____ 12. Inventory systems kept by hand have just as many advantages as those kept by computer.

_____ 13. Documents that authorize changes to be made in a computer system are called source documents.

_____ 14. There is only one acceptable endorsement to use when preparing checks for deposit.

_____ 15. Petty cash funds use checks when making purchases.

## Financial Statements

After reading and studying the financial statement section in the text, prepare a Balance Sheet (Part I) and an Income Statement (Part II) for Global West Travel Agency as of December 31, 1994, in the spaces provided. Use the accounts and amounts listed below. Follow the correct format for each as shown in the text.

Part I

Balance Sheet Accounts:

| | |
|---|---|
| Cash | $10,000 |
| Ticket Suppliers | 5,375 |
| Building | 80,000 |
| Mortgage on Property | 63,000 |
| Capital | (calculate) |

Global West Travel Agency

Balance Sheet, December 31, 1994

Assets

Liabilities

Capital

(continued on next page)

Part II

Income Statement Accounts:

| | |
|---|---|
| Salaries | $110,000 |
| Commissions | 215,500 |
| Supplies | 10,000 |
| Utilities | 1,285 |
| Advertising | 2,250 |
| Net Income | (calculate) |

Global West Travel Agency
Income Statement
For Year Ended December 31, 1994

Revenue

Expenses

Net Income

## Word Processing

Keyboard the following paragraphs accurately according to the proofreaders marks. Save and print a copy of the document.

### Financial Statements

Financial statements permit owners, managers, and accountants to analyze business activities and their effectiveness. All businesses should prepare financial statements on a regular basis so that any changes *or trends* can be noted immediately.

### Balance sheet

A balance sheet shows the financial condition of a business at a particular time. Only an accurate, up-to-date balance sheet can provide a view of a business's finances that shows assets, liabilities, and net worth.

### Income statement

An income statement is a summary of all income and expenses for a certain period of time, such as a month or a year. This statement reflects a business's profitability over a given time period.

## ACTIVITY 8-3

### Word Processing

1. Keyboard the November 15 income statement on page 293 for the Cap Company. Note, in particular, to align the decimal points in all figures and to stay within the format shown.

2. Save and print a copy.

3. Edit the income statement in the following ways and print a second copy.

   A. Use boldface to enhance these words: Revenue, Expenses, and Net Income

   B. Change from double-spacing to single-spacing.

## ACTIVITY 8-4

### Word Processing

1. Keyboard the November 16 balance sheet on page 291 for the Cap Company. Prepare according to the format shown.

2. Save and print a copy.

3. Edit the balance sheet in the following ways and print a second copy.

   A. Change from italics to boldface for these words—Total Assets and Total Liabilities and Capital.

   B. Use single-spacing for the two-line heading.

## Advantages and Disadvantages of Credit

With reference to credit sales, react to the following statements on the lines following each statement. If you agree with the meaning or intent of the statement, state why; if you disagree, explain your reasons.

1. Buying on credit is bad because you are only spending money you haven't made yet.

   Agree or Disagree? _____

   _____

   _____

   _____

   _____

2. To get ahead in business, you have to buy and sell on credit. It is just a risk of doing business that people must take in order to become successful.

   Agree or Disagree? _____

   _____

   _____

   _____

   _____

3. Accounts receivable is like cash because it is converted to cash over a period of time. Accounts payable, on the other hand, is like a debt because it must be paid (using cash) at some time in the future.

   Agree or Disagree? _____

   _____

   _____

   _____

   _____

## Inventory

As an office worker for Global West Travel Agency, you are responsible for maintaining the inventory of necessary travel documents that agents fill out for clients each day. Using the Stock Record Card on page 296 in the text as a guide, follow these instructions as you complete the three blank record cards for airline tickets, invoices, and prepaid ticket advice forms.

1. All maximum amounts must be 100.
2. All minimum amounts must be 25.
3. Calculate a new balance for each received or issued entry you make.
4. Below are the entries for March for you to complete.

| | Airline Tickets | Invoices | Prepaid Ticket Advice Forms |
|---|---|---|---|
| Mar 1 | | | |
| Balance | 100 | 75 | 50 |
| | | | |
| Mar 8 | | | |
| Received | — | 25 | 50 |
| Issued | 80 | 35 | 66 |
| | | | |
| Mar 15 | | | |
| Received | 80 | 35 | 66 |
| Issued | 49 | 51 | 81 |
| | | | |
| Mar 22 | | | |
| Received | 49 | 51 | 81 |
| Issued | 38 | 45 | 72 |
| | | | |
| Mar 29 | | | |
| Received | 38 | 45 | 72 |
| Issued | 57 | 63 | 52 |

(continued on next page)

ITEM  Airline Ticket Forms

MAX _____

MIN _____

| Date | Quantity Received | Quantity Issued | Balance |
|------|-------------------|-----------------|---------|
| _____ | _____ | _____ | _____ |
| _____ | _____ | _____ | _____ |
| _____ | _____ | _____ | _____ |
| _____ | _____ | _____ | _____ |
| _____ | _____ | _____ | _____ |


ITEM  Invoice Forms

MAX _____

MIN _____

| Date | Quantity Received | Quantity Issued | Balance |
|------|-------------------|-----------------|---------|
| _____ | _____ | _____ | _____ |
| _____ | _____ | _____ | _____ |
| _____ | _____ | _____ | _____ |
| _____ | _____ | _____ | _____ |
| _____ | _____ | _____ | _____ |


ITEM  Prepaid Ticket Advice Forms

MAX _____

MIN _____

| Date | Quantity Received | Quantity Issued | Balance |
|------|-------------------|-----------------|---------|
| _____ | _____ | _____ | _____ |
| _____ | _____ | _____ | _____ |
| _____ | _____ | _____ | _____ |
| _____ | _____ | _____ | _____ |
| _____ | _____ | _____ | _____ |

## Record-keeping Activities

Write an appropriate response on the blank lines following each statement. Refer to pages 302–307 in the text, as needed.

1. Using your own name to endorse a check, show on the lines below: a) a restrictive endorsement and b) a blank endorsement.

   a. _____

   _____

   b. _____

2. When you prepare to reconcile a bank statement, what are some of the items you should have in your work area in order to do the task? List all equipment, supplies, and forms.

   _____

   _____

   _____

   _____

   _____

3. If you were in charge of the office petty cash fund, describe two safety precautions you would take to safeguard the money left in your trust.

   _____

   _____

   _____

   _____

   _____

## Word Processing

1. Survey three businesses in town and ask them these questions about a) the types of accounting and record-keeping activities they perform and b) which activities are computerized and which are still performed manually.

2. Use as a guide the following checksheet in gathering your information. Use C for computers or M for manual to indicate how work is performed under each business's column. Leave blank if that activity is not performed.

|  | Business #1 | Business #2 | Business #3 |
|---|---|---|---|
| Do you perform these accounting activities in your office? |  |  |  |
| Prepare Balance Sheets? |  |  |  |
| Prepare Income Statements? |  |  |  |
| Prepare Accounts Receivable? |  |  |  |
| Prepare Accounts Payable? |  |  |  |
| Maintain Inventory Control? |  |  |  |
| Calculate Payroll? |  |  |  |
| Do you perform these record-keeping activities in your office? |  |  |  |
| Prepare Banking Activities? |  |  |  |
| Maintain Petty Cash Fund? |  |  |  |

3. You may report the above information in paragraph form or in table form with explanations. Keyboard whichever format you choose, save, and print a copy.

# Sending and Receiving Mail

# Objectives

After completing this chapter, you will be able to do the following:

1. List and explain four procedures for sorting mail in an office.
2. List and explain the way to arrange mail before presenting it to an employer.
3. List and explain the major classifications of outgoing mail.
4. List and describe postal equipment used in an office.
5. Use a zip code directory to locate zip codes.

# New Office Terms

annotating mail
bar code sorter (BCS)
centralized mail department
confidential mail

priority mail
routing mail
sorting mail

## Before You Begin . . .

*Using an electronic typewriter or a microcomputer, answer the following to the best of your ability:*

1. *What are at least three classifications of mailing? Explain why each one may be used.*
2. *In what order should an address be typed on an envelope? Create a sample.*

---

At 9 a.m. in a city on the East Coast, Vivian starts her day by sorting the mail in the mail-processing department of a large corporation. At the same time in a town in the South, Maynard begins to sort the mail for his three bosses in the accounting department of a small firm. Vivian is a mail clerk, and Maynard is an administrative assistant. Both know the procedures for processing mail. When you begin to work in a business office, you also must know the procedures for processing incoming and outgoing mail.

In a large company, mail may be processed in a **centralized mail department.** The employees in this department will be responsible for all the mail that comes in or goes out of the company. At various times during the day, they will distribute incoming mail to all the company personnel and pick up mail that is to be sent out. They will also distribute interoffice correspondence (mail sent to and from offices within the company).

A small company may not have a centralized mail department. In this case, an office employee receives the mail as it is delivered each day by a postal carrier. Once the mail is received, certain procedures are to be followed for processing it.

*This is what the mail room for a large company might look like. Notice the wooden mail slots where the mail is put for each department or person.*

# INCOMING MAIL

The procedures for processing incoming mail include the following:

- sorting the mail
- opening the mail
- date and time stamping the mail
- reading and annotating the mail, if your boss prefers
- other helpful procedures
- arranging the mail for your boss

## Sorting the Mail

In office terms, **sorting mail** means arranging or separating mail according to the kind it is and who is to receive it. For example, it means separating the letters from the magazines. It also means separating the manager's mail from the supervisor's mail.

Before you begin the process of sorting the mail, clear a work area on your desk. You do not want to have the mail lost or mixed up with other papers. Push all clutter aside and concentrate on this one project.

You may handle the mail for more than one boss or for more than one department. If so, first sort the mail for each person or for each department. It is easy to do this by sorting into individually marked folders or trays. Once this is done, the mail is sorted within the individual trays by grouping into piles of correspondence, advertisements and circulars (papers intended for wide distribution), and magazines and newspapers.

As you are sorting, you may notice mail that has been delivered to your company in error. First check with your boss to see if the mail belongs to anyone within the company. If not, cross out the incorrect address, write "Not at this address" on the envelope, and put it back in the mail. Only first-class mail will be forwarded without adding extra postage. *First-class mail* is mail that will generally be delivered overnight to locally designated cities and in two days to locally designated states. These areas are selected by the post office and usually have distances of up to 600 miles. Beyond 600 miles, standard service is three days.

## Opening the Mail

Many office workers are asked to open the mail for their bosses. This does not necessarily mean they are to read the mail. At some companies, an office worker uses a letter opener to open the mail and then places the mail on the boss's desk. At other companies, an office worker is required to remove the contents from the envelope. It is always best to check company policy on this matter.

Stop! Don't open anything yet. Before beginning to open the mail, separate all letters that say Confidential or Personal. These letters are **confidential mail** and should be opened only by the person to whom they are addressed. It is also a good idea to assume that a letter written in longhand is personal and should be opened only by the person to

*It is helpful to have a clear work area and all the necessary supplies before you begin to open the mail for the day.*

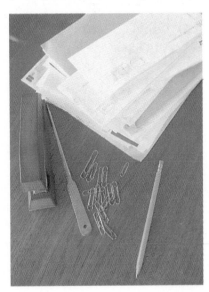

whom it is addressed. If you open a personal letter in error, be certain to write on the envelope "Sorry, opened by mistake." Sign your name or initials and tape the letter closed.

It is helpful to have all necessary supplies ready for opening the mail. You will need a letter opener, a stapler, a pencil, and some paper clips.

Once you have opened the mail, your boss may want you to remove the contents from the envelopes. If so, do the following:

- If the address of the sender is not on a letter, staple or paper clip the envelope to the letter.
- Check the bottom of each letter for the words *enclosure* or *attached*. If you see one of these words, check to see that the material is enclosed or attached. If not, make a pencil notation on the letter that the enclosures were not in the envelope when it was opened.
- Use a paper clip to attach enclosed material.
- Put all the envelopes aside until you have finished sorting the mail. You may have to check for overlooked contents or addresses.
- If a letter is undated, write the postmarked date from the envelope onto the letter.
- Attach enclosures to the back of the letters.

## Date and Time Stamping the Mail

Have you ever received an announcement of an event after the day had already gone by? This may have happened because the letter was temporarily lost during shipment or because the announcement sat unopened in your house for a few days.

Mail is sometimes received late in a business office. For this reason, companies have the person who processes the mail put a date and time on the letters to show when they were received. This is usually done with a rubber stamp but can also be done with a pen.

Why are companies concerned with the exact date the mail is received? One reason is to prove if a payment is late or a person has not met a payment deadline. A time difference may exist between the date a letter was received and the date the letter was typed.

Another reason is to prove if a person has met the application deadline for a job. Many civil service jobs have deadlines when applications must be received. If a person does not meet the deadline, she or he will not be considered for the job.

## Reading and Annotating the Mail

Chiara Briganti is a busy executive for a management consulting firm. To save time, she has her secretary read and annotate the mail each day. **Annotating mail** means underlining important facts and making comments or special notations in the margin of a letter. Examples of facts to underline are model numbers, prices, and meeting dates. An example of a notation you may write in the margin is that you verified that your boss has no other meetings on the date in question.

FIGURE 9–1
*Sample Annotated letter*

# STONEHILL
# CHAMBER OF COMMERCE

345 Alpine Terrace
Stonehill, NH 03062

May 15, 19—

Chiara Briganti
HiTech Associates
45 Tower Place
Stonehill, NH 03062

*Date OK
no conflict*

Dear Ms. Briganti:

Congratulations! You have been selected to receive our annual
Woman Of the Year Award for your dedication to the business
community. All our members agree that you deserve this award.

The award will be presented to you at our annual luncheon
awards meeting Thursday, June 30, 12 Noon at the Pines
Conference Center. Please confirm that you will attend by
contacting Rose Perez.

Sincerely,

*Rosylin Thomas*

Rosylin Thomas
Awards Committee

cb

---

See figure 9–1 for a sample of an annotated letter. Note how Ms.
Briganti's secretary underlined the date, time, and place of the luncheon
meeting. She also made a notation in the margin that no conflicting
appointments were scheduled on this date. Can you see how valuable
this process could be for a busy executive?

# Recall Time

*Answer the following questions:*

1. What are three duties of the employees in a centralized mail department?
2. What are the procedures for processing incoming mail?
3. Alexandra is an office support person for a small firm. One of her duties is opening her bosses' mail. She opens a letter that is marked Confidential. What should she do?
4. If you were sorting the mail into piles, what three groupings might you use?
5. You open a business letter for your boss. The letter does not have a return address on it. What should you do?

## Other Helpful Procedures

Office workers use many other procedures to help their bosses process the daily mail. A few examples are attaching related materials, using action-requested slips, saving advertisements and circulars, keeping an outgoing mail record, routing mail, and accepting special mail.

**Attaching Related Material** Frequently, before your boss can respond to or take action on a particular piece of correspondence, he or she will need to see other documents. In these cases, you will be helping your boss a great deal if you attach any related material to the letters. You may attach previous correspondence or the file folder that correlates with a letter.

For example, Ken is an insurance clerk for an automobile insurance company. A client writes to his boss concerning an accident. After opening the letter and before giving it to his boss, Ken will attach the client's file folder to the letter.

**Using Action-requested Slips** If you process and forward lots of mail for your boss, it is helpful to use action-requested slips. You can either purchase these from a stationery store or create them yourself. A sample is shown in figure 9–2. You simply check the action you wish to be taken.

**Saving Advertisements and Circulars** It may be of advantage to save some of that so-called junk mail. This is a good way for you and your boss to notice trends in new products. These circulars may be particularly helpful to the advertising department, which is always looking for new ideas and also wants to see what the competition has to offer.

If you or your company is concerned about helping save the environment, you may also put this junk mail in a special box. When the box is full, you can deposit it at a recycling center. You can recycle other items in addition to the advertisements. Call your local recycling center for more information.

- ☐ For your approval
- ☐ For your comments
- ☐ Please forward
- ☐ Please return
- ☐ Note and file
- ☐ ____________________

■ FIGURE 9–2
*Sample Action-requested Slip*

**Keeping an Outgoing Mail Record** Many companies have found it helpful to keep a daily record of all the mail they send out that requires another person outside the company to take action. The secretary can refer to this record on a regular basis and do any necessary follow-up when action is supposed to occur.

See figure 9–3 for a sample of an outgoing mail register. In the Description column, you will record the name of the company each letter is going to, the subject of the letter, and the actual date of the letter. The date column is for the date of the entry, usually the date mailed.

**Routing Mail** It may be necessary for certain magazines, reports, and special documents to be seen by more than one person in the company. The most efficient way to handle this situation is by routing the mail. **Routing mail** means attaching a routing slip to correspondence and

MAIL REGISTER

| DATE | DESCRIPTION | TO WHOM | ACTION TO TAKE | FOLLOW UP |
|---|---|---|---|---|
| 6/13 | Perry Winkler Brothers | Perry Winkler | Confirm | |
| | | | | |
| | | | | |
| | | | | |
| | | | | |
| | | | | |
| | | | | |

■ FIGURE 9–3
*Sample Mail Register*

Esteban and Nathan have been word processing operators in the same department for two years. They work well together, are close friends, and take breaks and lunch together. The department has ten operators and two lead operators. Everyone gets along well.

One lead operator leaves, and this creates a promotional opening for one operator. Esteban and

Nathan both apply for the job, and Esteban is chosen for the promotion. Esteban is now in charge of five operators including Nathan.

1. Should the relationship between Esteban and Nathan change now that Esteban is a supervisor?
2. Should Esteban and Nathan continue to take breaks and lunch together? Why or why not?

then having each person initial the routing slip after she or he has read the correspondence.

A routing slip is usually a preprinted form that is commonly used by businesses. See the sample in figure 9–4.

**Accepting Special Mail**  Mail is sometimes delivered by special delivery, by a messenger, or by a private delivery service. If the mail is delivered to you and it is your job to sign the required receipt for it, be certain the addressee (person to whom the mail is addressed) works for your company, you sign the required mail receipt, and you bring the mail immediately to the addressee. This type of mail delivery denotes important information.

## Arranging the Mail for Your Boss

Before putting the mail on your boss's desk, arrange it according to importance. Check with your boss's preference, but the following arrangement is acceptable for most executives. The first item listed is on the top of the stack, and the last item listed is on the bottom of the stack.

- confidential and personal letters
- correspondence from outside the company
- interoffice correspondence
- advertisements
- newspapers and magazines

The mail is usually placed in the boss's in–basket, and any parcels are put in a separate pile on the desk.

## ■ OUTGOING MAIL

Office workers use many helpful procedures for processing outgoing mail. A few examples are assembling the mail, selecting classifications for the mail, using the U.S. Postal Service, using private delivery services, using postal equipment, following mailing guidelines, and packing for mailing.

FIGURE 9–4
*Sample Routing Slip*

```
                    ROUTING SLIP

                 (initial after reading)

   Foster, J.                              ——

   Morales, E.                             ——

   Prentice, B.                            ——

   Shapiro, W.                             ——

   Bala, M. (last)                         ——
```

## Assembling the Mail

No letter should be mailed from a business without the proper signature. Therefore, it may be necessary for you to prepare mail for your boss to sign. This is usually done just before a letter is ready for mailing, so also have the envelope ready.

The usual way to have a letter signed is to place the flap of the envelope over the front of the letter and attach a paper clip to the flap. Most employers want their mail to get out as quickly as possible, so place any letter needing a signature on your boss's desk in an area where it will easily be seen. Check back on a regular basis to see if the letter has been signed so that you can proceed with the next step.

Once a letter has been signed, bring it back to your desk and prepare it for mailing. However, before you prepare it for mailing, check the following:

- Has the letter been signed?
- Are enclosures included with the letter?
- Are the address on the letter and the address on the envelope the same?
- One last check—Did you miss any errors or did your boss make any further changes?

Once all this has been checked, it is time for you to fold the letter and insert it into the envelope. Figure 9–5 shows how to fold a full-size (8½ × 11-inch) letterhead into a legal-size (long) envelope.

If you have enclosures or attachments to go with a letter, do the following: If the enclosures are the same size as the letter, fold and insert them with the letter itself. If they are smaller than the letter, staple them to the top left of the letter. If they are larger than the letter, mail them

Step 1
Lay the
letter flat

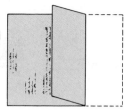
Step 2
Fold one-third
of the sheet,
from the
bottom up

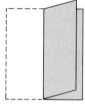
Step 3
Fold the top
down to within
one-half inch
of the fold

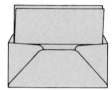
Step 4
Insert the letter
into the envelope,
with the folded
end in first

in a large manila envelope with the letter unfolded and inserted as the first page on top of the enclosures.

## Selecting Classifications for the Mail

When Melanie becomes employed as a mail clerk for a large law firm, she is quite confused about which classification to use for all the outgoing mail. Her supervisor explains that the final decision is based upon the most efficient way. This decision should be made for each particular piece of mail by asking yourself, Should this item be delivered to the destination as quickly as possible, or can money be saved by using a slower, but less expensive, means of delivery? Melanie's supervisor also tells her that she can better understand mailing classifications by reading the U.S. Postal Service's *A Consumer's Directory of Postal Services and Products*. In this directory, any office worker will be able to review information on the various classifications of mail: first class, priority, second class, third class, fourth class, and express.

**First Class** Use first-class mail for letters, postcards, and postal cards. First-class mail must weigh twelve ounces or less. If first-class mail is not letter size, make sure it is marked First Class.

First-class mail will generally be delivered overnight to locally designated cities and in two days to locally designated states, usually up to six hundred miles away. Beyond six hundred miles, standard service is three days. Money can be saved on first-class mail if the mail is sorted according to destination with a minimum of five hundred pieces or if zip + 4 (the regular zip code plus an additional four-digit code) is used.

**Priority** Priority mail is first-class mail weighing more than twelve ounces. The maximum weight for priority mail is seventy pounds. Free priority mail stickers are available from your local post office.

**Second Class** Only publishers and registered news agents who have been approved for second-class mailing privileges may mail at the second-class bulk rate. Second-class mail allows them to do large mailings at a reduced rate.

**Third Class** Third-class mail is also referred to as bulk business mail or advertising mail. It may be sent by anyone, but it is used most often by large mailers. Nonprofit agencies such as a chamber of commerce or a church group may use it. This class includes printed material and merchandise weighing less than sixteen ounces.

**Fourth Class** Fourth-class mail is also called parcel post. Use this service for packages weighing one pound or more. This service may take up to eight days for coast-to-coast delivery, depending upon the availability of transportation.

**Express** Express mail is the fastest mail service. It is also the most expensive service. Express mail guarantees delivery the next day, or in some cases the same day. To use it, take the item to be mailed to the post office by 5 p.m. or deposit it in an express mail collection box. The item will be delivered to the addressee by 3 p.m. the next day (even if it is a Saturday, Sunday, or holiday), or it can be picked up at the destination post office as early as 10 a.m. the next day.

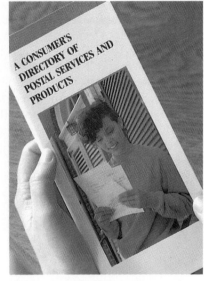

*The U.S. Postal Service has lots of free literature available for the public. It can be most helpful to save time and money.*

## Recall Time

*Answer the following questions:*

1. What are two ways to save money on first-class mail?
2. What is another name for third-class mail?
3. What is fourth-class mail?
4. What is the name for the fastest mail service? Explain how it works.
5. How do you fold a sheet of letter-size paper to be inserted into an envelope?

## Using the U.S. Postal Service

In *A Consumer's Directory of Postal Services and Products*, Melanie is able to read about the other options available through the postal service. These include special delivery, certificates of mailing, certified mail, collect on delivery, return receipts, insurance, registered mail, international mail, the Postal Answer Line, and other services.

**Special Delivery** Special delivery provides for delivery, even on Sundays and holidays, during hours that extend beyond those for ordinary mail. You can buy this service on all classes of mail except bulk third class. Make sure the mailing is endorsed Special Delivery.

Mike is working as a secretary to the vice president of the legal department of a large corporation. In his department are five other clerical workers—a word processor, a researcher, and three general office clerks. Mike's status as a secretary is much higher than the status of the other office workers. He has more responsibility and gets paid more money.

It is late Thursday afternoon, and Mike has his usual work to get done. He has no urgent work, but enough to keep busy.

A general office clerk is stuffing and sealing envelopes for a large mailing that must be in tonight's mail. The general office clerk is complaining that the mail may not get done in time.

1. Should Mike help with the envelopes, or should he continue with his own work? Explain your answer.

**Certificates of Mailing** A certificate of mailing proves an item was mailed. It does not provide insurance coverage for loss or damage.

**Certified Mail** Certified mail provides a mailing receipt, and a record of delivery is maintained at the recipient's post office. For an additional fee, the sender can also buy a return receipt to provide proof of delivery.

**Collect on Delivery** Use collect-on-delivery (COD) service if you are sending merchandise and you want to collect the money owed for its purchase when it is delivered.

**Return Receipts** A return receipt is a sender's proof of delivery. It shows who signed for an item and the date of delivery.

**Insurance** Insurance can be purchased on registered mail up to a maximum replacement value of twenty-five thousand dollars. It is also available up to five hundred dollars for third- and fourth-class mail.

**Registered Mail** Registered mail is the most secure option offered by the postal service. It is designed to provide added protection for valuable and important mail. Registered articles are controlled from the point of mailing to delivery. First-class postage is required on registered mail.

**International Mail** Airmail and surface mail can be sent to virtually all foreign countries. Four types of international mail are provided: letters and cards, other articles, parcel post, and express. Limited registry service and insurance are available. Information on international mail regulations can be found in *The International Mail Manual*, a manual sold by the U.S. Government Printing Office.

**Postal Answer Line** Automation has also come to the postal service with its Postal Answer Line. Now you do not have to stand in information lines at the post office—or make unnecessary trips for your boss. Postal Answer Line, the post office's automated telephone service, puts information at your fingertips.

Postal Answer Line is quite simple to use. First, you must get a pamphlet called *Postal Answer Line* listing the information available and the message number to dial. Information is provided on all the services listed earlier in this chapter, plus post office hours, box rentals, zip-coding, and problem with fraud or security.

Once you have the pamphlet, you will do the following using a touch-tone telephone:

1. Look up the message number for the information you want.
2. Key in the number for your local Postal Answer Line.
3. Let the recorded instructions tell you when to push the buttons on your telephone that correspond to the desired message number.
4. Wait a few moments for your message to begin.
5. For information on another service or to have the message repeated, wait for the tone, then press the appropriate message number.

**Other Services** Other services available through the U.S. Postal Service include passport applications, money orders, postage meters, and stamps by mail.

## Using Delivery Services

Many office workers have found that sometimes it is more convenient or cost-effective to use a private delivery service. These companies deliver parcels by truck within a city or by airplane to other cities or countries. Firms that specialize in delivery services usually offer the convenience of pickup and delivery. You can locate these firms by looking in the Yellow Pages of your telephone book. Examples of companies that you might find in this section are United Parcel Service (UPS), Federal Express, and Emery Worldwide.

In large cities, private messenger services are even used to go short distances—a few buildings or a few blocks. These are often bicycle messengers. Messenger service is expensive, but the end result of fast delivery is worth the expense to the company. Names of these messenger services can also be located in the Yellow Pages.

A secretary or administrative assistant will keep a file of frequently used private delivery services. The file should be updated regularly. The telephone numbers for the most frequently used service can be coded into a company's system for speed dialing (see chapter 5 in this text).

It may be an advantage to open a company charge account with the frequently used delivery services. After doing this, when you have a letter or item to send, you will only need to telephone the service and request pickup. The delivery service will ask you for an account number and will bill your company at a later date. This allows you to save time by not having to repeat company information every time you call and by making payments less frequently, which saves on check writing and processing.

*Private delivery services such as these companies are frequently used by businesses. The services provided by Federal Express and UPS include convenient pickup and delivery.*

# Recall Time

*Answer the following questions:*

1. What is the maximum amount of insurance available on registered mail?
2. What is the maximum amount of insurance available on third- and fourth-class mail?
3. Are the following statements true or false?

   a. Passports are available through the U.S. Postal Service.
   b. Federal Express delivers overnight for the U.S. Postal Service.
   c. If you call the Postal Answer Line, an operator will answer and give you information about services available.
   d. Money orders can be purchased at a local post office.

## Using Postal Equipment

Special postal equipment used by office workers helps to efficiently process the mail. Examples of this equipment are a scale and a meter, as well as other items.

*This office worker is using a postage meter and scale to process his boss's mail before leaving the office at the end of the day.*

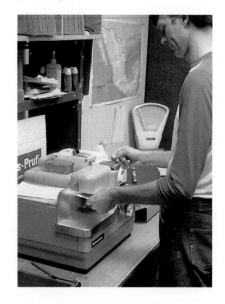

**Scale and Meter** Whether you work for a large or small company, you will find that a postage scale and a postage meter are the two pieces of equipment needed to process outgoing mail. The scale can be purchased at any office supply store. The postage meter must be obtained from a manufacturer that has a product approved by the U.S. Postal Service. It is possible for the scale and meter to be one piece of equipment.

The scale shows the weight of an item to be mailed. An electronic postage scale will also show the postage required. However, to get this amount, you must first key in such information as zip code and class of mail.

The meter imprints the amount of postage as well as the cancellation mark for the U.S. Postal Service. This imprint appears on a strip of paper that comes out of the meter and is sealed in place on the envelope. You pay the post office in advance for large sums of postage. Usually, you must take the meter to the post office to be reset for new postage. However, if your company purchases a special computerized system, you can reset your own meter from your office.

An added feature of the postage meter is that it will wet and seal the envelopes so they do not have to be licked. In addition, many companies do not keep loose stamps in the office; they do all the mailing through the meter. This saves on loss or waste of stamps.

**Other Items** Companies that process large volumes of mail may use automatic folding and inserting machines as well as collators. Collators automatically assemble items in proper order. Office workers also find it helpful to have sorting trays or racks, mailbags, and mailbag holders.

## Mail

If you did a survey in your area, you would find that large offices have their own mail rooms where all the processing of the mail takes place. You would also find that the duties of the mail room employees are involved solely in the processing of incoming and outgoing mail and the distribution of interoffice mail. Since many pieces of mail must be handled daily in these large offices, you would find automatic letter openers and sorting equipment in addition to the standard postage meters and scales.

A survey of small offices would give you a slightly different view of the role of office workers in the handling of mail. In a small office, the mail processing is done by a variety of office support staff, who handle the mail in addition to their other clerical duties. Your survey would show the receptionist, typist, secretary, and other clerical employees processing the mail for themselves and for their bosses. It would also show that the postal equipment in a small office is usually limited to a postage meter and scale.

*Would you like to begin your office career as a mail room clerk for a large company? Why or why not? Do you like the idea of having someone else handle your mail for you, or would you prefer making occasional trips to the mail room to process your own mail?*

Other helpful items are rubber stamps or stickers for special classifications such as Special Delivery or Priority Mail.

## Following Mailing Guidelines

Part of Melanie's mail room training includes a workshop sponsored by her local post office. At this workshop, she learns that postal sorting centers use special equipment to rapidly process the mail. The main two parts of this equipment are the optical character recognition scanner and bar code sorter. The optical character recognition (OCR) scanner reads an address until it locates the zip code. It then converts the zip code digits into a bar code. The **bar code sorter (BCS)** then sorts or separates the mail into geographic areas. This continues until the mail is sorted into the final delivery area.

For this equipment to work properly, the postal service recommends using the following sequence when addressing mail:

1. recipient's name
2. recipient's street address, post office box number, or rural route number and box number, with any room or apartment number to the right of this line
3. recipient's city, state, and zip code

For even better service, the U.S. Postal Service recommends that you do the following:

- Capitalize everything in the address.
- Use common abbreviations found in the *National Zip Code Directory*.
- Eliminate all punctuation.
- Use the two-letter state abbreviations.
- Use zip codes.

When both a post office box number and a street address are used, make sure the place where you want the mail delivered appears on the line immediately above the city, state, and zip code line. For example:

GRAND PRODUCTS INC
475 HOLIDAY PLAZA SW
PO BOX 320   [will be delivered here]
WASHINGTON DC 20260-6320

Your local post office can supply you with free brochures on addressing requirements. Following these requirements will ensure faster processing of the mail.

Office workers use both electronic typewriters and microcomputers to type and print envelopes. With an electronic typewriter, the envelope is put into the typewriter and the address is typed directly onto the envelope. With a computer, the address is typed into a file and the output comes through the computer printer. When printing, you may put a single envelope onto the printer or your company may use continuous-feed envelopes to do many addresses at one time. For the continuous-feed method, envelopes are attached to each other as they go through the printer. This is the same process as with continuous-feed printer paper.

## Packing for Mailing

When Melanie first begins working in the mail room, she is quite surprised that at least once a week she has to prepare and wrap packages for mailing. She has binders to mail to attorneys. She has broken merchandise to return to suppliers. She even has personal packages to wrap for the top executives.

Melanie again relies on a brochure from the U.S. Postal Service to give her information on preparing and wrapping packages. It tells her how to select the proper container, cushion the contents, wrap and close the package, and address and mark the package.

**Select the Proper Container** Fiberboard containers are generally strong enough to ship material of average weight and size. These are common boxes that are readily available at stationery stores. A container should be large enough to hold the contents, but not so large as to permit shifting or joggling of the contents. It also should contain adequate cushioning to prevent damage.

**Cushion the Contents**  Cushioning distributes and absorbs shocks and vibrations while preventing contents from shifting. Even single items packed alone should be cushioned for safety. Many types of suitable cushioning materials are available, including polystyrene, shredded or rolled newspaper, or bubble plastic. You will want to cushion items that may break, bend, or otherwise be damaged. A glass item is one example.

**Wrap and Close the Package**  Do not use wrapping paper if the box itself is an adequate shipping container. However, you may use wrapping paper equivalent to the strength of an average large grocery bag if needed. Use filament-reinforced tape for the closure and reinforcement of parcels whenever possible. Do not use twine and cords.

**Address and Mark the Package**  The same mailing guidelines for addressing letters apply to packages. A parcel should be clearly marked with the address, including the zip code of both sender and receiver. Any special marking should be placed on the outside of the parcel to alert postal service employees to the nature of the contents. Examples are Fragile, Perishable, and Do Not Bend. Your post office window clerk has a set of rubber stamps indicating these special markings and will apply them to your parcel on request.

## ■ REFERENCE MATERIALS

While working in the mail room of the law firm, Melanie finds it is necessary to refer to a zip code directory. These directories are available for national and state listings. They can be purchased, or the national listing can be found in post office lobbies. Figure 9–6 is a sample page from the *National Five-Digit Zip Code and Post Office Directory.*

The states, cities, towns, and streets within a zip code directory are all listed in alphabetic order. To use the directory, you will first locate the state and city or town at the top of the page. You will then look down the columns until you find the street and the number. The zip code is located to the right. Refer to figure 9–6, which is a page for the state of Texas and the city of Dallas. Find Hamburg Street and notice that the zip code is 75215. Now locate Green Terrace Drive and notice that the zip code is 75220.

Will you know how to locate the zip code for a numbered house on a street with more than one zip code? Locate Gilbert Avenue and notice that is has two zip codes. If you live at 3620 Gilbert Avenue, your zip code is 75219. If you live at 5175 Gilbert Avenue, your zip code is 75209. Refer to the listing for 600 Haskell Avenue North and notice that the zip code is 75246.

No, all these numbers are not a waste of time to use. The zip codes are necessary for efficient use of optical character recognition scanners. The scanners will read the numbers and sort the mail into the right piles by the number locations. Using the 75246 zip code as an example, the first three digits, 752, represent a major geographic area, either a section

## FIGURE 9–6 *Sample Page from the* National Five-Digit Zip Code and Post Office Directory

**DALLAS** — **TEXAS**

| | |
|---|---|
| Gay St | 75210 |
| Gayglen Dr | 75217 |
| Gaylord Dr | |
| 1300-2099 | 75217 |
| 2100-2299 | 75227 |
| Gaywood Rd | 75229 |
| Gemini Ln | 75229 |
| Genetta Dr | 75228 |
| Genoa Ave | 75216 |
| Genstar Ln | 75252 |
| Gentle Knoll Ln | 75248 |
| Gentle River Dr | 75241 |
| Gentle Wind Ln | 75248 |
| Gentry Dr | 75212 |
| George Haddaway St | 75248 |
| Georgetown Pl | 75214 |
| Georgia Ave | |
| 400-1599 | 75216 |
| 1600-1699 | 75203 |
| Georgian Ct | 75240 |
| Geraldine Dr | 75220 |
| Gertrude Ave | 75210 |
| Ghent St | 75215 |
| Gibbons Dr | 75252 |
| Gibbs William Cir | 75224 |
| Gibbs William Rd | 75233 |
| Gibsondell Ave | 75211 |
| Giddings Cir | 75238 |
| Gifford St | 75223 |
| Gilbert Ave | |
| 3600-4699 | 75219 |
| 5100-5199 | 75209 |
| Gilford St | 75235 |
| Gill St | 75227 |
| Gillespie St | 75219 |
| Gillette Cir & St | 75217 |
| Gillis Rd | 75244 |
| Gillon Ave | 75205 |
| Gilmer St | 75212 |
| Gilpin Ave, N & S | 75211 |
| Ginger Ave | 75211 |
| Givendale Rd | 75241 |
| Glade St | 75232 |
| Gladeside Ct | 75248 |
| Gladewater Rd | 75216 |
| Giadiolus Ln | 75233 |
| Gladstone Dr | |
| 2100-2399 | 75208 |
| 2400-2899 | 75211 |
| Gladwood Ln | 75243 |
| Glasgow Dr, N | 75214 |
| Glasgow Dr, S | |
| 100-399 | 75214 |
| 400-1199 | 75223 |
| Glass St | 75207 |
| Gleason St | 75223 |
| Glen Ave | 75216 |
| Glen Albens Cir | 75225 |
| Glen Arbor Ct & Dr | 75241 |
| Glen Canyon Dr | 75243 |
| Glen Creek Ct | 75243 |
| Glen Cross Dr | 75228 |
| Glen Curtis Dr | 75248 |
| Glen Echo Ct | 75238 |
| Glen Falls Ln | 75209 |
| Glen Forest Ln | 75241 |
| Glen Heather Dr | 75252 |
| Glen Lakes Dr | 75231 |
| Glen Oaks Blvd & Cir | 75232 |
| Glen Oaks Shopping Vlg | 75232 |
| Glen Park Dr | 75241 |
| Glen Regal Dr | 75243 |
| Glen Springs Dr | 75243 |
| Glenacre St | 75243 |
| Glenaire Dr | 75229 |
| Glenburnie Dr | 75225 |
| Glencairn Dr | 75232 |
| Glenchester Ct | 75225 |
| Glencliff Cir, Ct & Dr | 75217 |
| Glencoe St | 75206 |
| Glencrest Ln | 75209 |
| Glenda Ln | 75229 |
| Glendale St | |
| 700-1099 | 75214 |
| 1200-1399 | 75206 |
| Glendora Ave | 75230 |
| Gleneagle Dr | 75248 |
| Glenfield Ave | |
| 1300-2399 | 75224 |
| 2400-3299 | 75233 |
| Glenfinnin Ln | 75232 |
| Glengariff Dr | 75228 |
| Glengold Dr | 75234 |
| Glengreen Dr | 75217 |
| Glenhaven Blvd | 75211 |
| Glenhollow Ct | 75248 |
| Glenhurst Dr | 75240 |
| Glenkirk Ct | 75225 |
| Glenleigh Dr | 75220 |
| Glenmeadow & Ct | 75225 |
| Glenmont Ln | 75228 |
| Glennox Ln | 75214 |
| Glenridge Rd | 75220 |
| Glenrio Ln | |
| 9990-9999 | 75220 |
| 10000-10099 | 75229 |
| Glenrose Ct | 75214 |
| Glenshannon Cir & Dr | 75225 |
| Glenside Cir & Dr | 75234 |
| Glenstone Ln | 75232 |
| Glenview St | 75217 |
| Glenwick Ln | |
| 3900-4599 | 75205 |
| 5300-5599 | 75209 |
| Glenwood Ave | 75205 |
| Glesman St | 75232 |
| Glidden St | 75203 |
| Globe Ave | 75228 |
| Glorietta Ln | 75241 |
| Gloster Rd | 75220 |
| Glover Pass | 75227 |
| Gloyd St | 75203 |
| Goat Hill Rd | 75201 |
| Godfrey Ave | 75217 |
| Goforth Cir & Rd | 75238 |
| Gold Rd | 75237 |
| Gold Dust Trl | 75252 |
| Golden Creek Rd | 75248 |
| Golden Gate Cir & Dr | 75241 |
| Golden Hills Dr | 75241 |
| Golden Oak St | 75234 |
| Golden Triangle Sc | 75224 |
| Golden Trophy Dr | 75232 |
| Goldendale Dr | 75234 |
| Goldfield Dr | 75217 |
| Goldie Ave | 75211 |
| Goldman Rd | 75212 |
| Goldmark Dr | 75240 |
| Goldspier Dr | 75215 |
| Goldwaite Dr | 75230 |
| Goldwood Dr | 75232 |
| Golf Dr | 75205 |
| Golf Hills Dr | 75232 |
| Golf Lakes Trl | 75231 |
| Golfing Green Cir, Ct, Dr & Pl | 75234 |
| Goliad Ave | |
| 5700-6099 | 75206 |
| 6100-6499 | 75214 |
| Gonzales Dr | 75227 |
| Gooch Ave | 75241 |
| Good Latimer Expy, N | |
| 100-299 | 75226 |
| 300-999 | 75204 |
| Good Latimer Expy, S | |
| 400-2299 | 75226 |
| 2300-2699 | 75215 |
| Goodfellow Dr | 75229 |
| Gooding Dr | |
| 9800-9999 | 75220 |
| 10000-10599 | 75229 |
| Goodland Pl & St | 75234 |
| Goodman St | 75211 |
| Goodnight Ln | |
| 10500-10799 | 75220 |
| 11000-11699 | 75229 |
| Goodshire Ave | 75231 |
| Goodwater St | 75234 |
| Goodwill Ave | 75210 |
| Goodwin Ave | 75206 |
| Goodyear Dr | 75229 |
| Gordon Pl | 75246 |
| Gordon St | 75204 |
| Gorman St | 75223 |
| Gould St | 75215 |
| Governors Row | 75247 |
| Gracefield Ln | 75248 |
| Graceland St | 75216 |
| Gracey St | 75216 |
| Grader St | 75238 |
| Grady Ln | 75217 |
| Grady Niblo Rd | 75236 |
| Grafton Ave | 75211 |
| Graham Ave | 75223 |
| Gramercy Pl | 75230 |
| Granada Ave | 75205 |
| Grand Ave | |
| 1200-3199 | 75215 |
| 3200-3399 | 75210 |
| Grand Ave, E | |
| 4200-7199 | 75223 |
| 7200-7899 | 75214 |
| Grand Plz | 75215 |
| Grand Oaks Rd | 75230 |
| Grandview Ave | 75223 |
| Granger St | 75224 |
| Granis St | 75243 |
| Granite Hill Dr | 75241 |
| Grant St | 75203 |
| Grantbrook Ln | 75228 |
| Grantwood Dr | 75229 |
| Grassmere Ln | 75205 |
| Grassy Ridge Trl | 75241 |
| Gray Rock St | 75243 |
| Graycliff Dr | 75228 |
| Grayport Dr | 75248 |
| Grayson Dr | 75224 |
| Graystone Dr | 75248 |
| Graywood Dr | 75243 |
| Great Lakes Dr | 75235 |
| Great Oak Dr | 75253 |
| Green St | 75208 |
| Green Acres Ter | 75234 |
| Green Ash Dr | 75243 |
| Green Castle Dr | 75232 |
| Green Hill Dr | 75232 |
| Green Meadow Dr | 75228 |
| Green Oaks Cir | 75243 |
| Green Oaks Dr | 75238 |
| Green Terrace Dr | 75220 |
| Greenbay St | 75210 |
| Greenbriar Ln, E | 75203 |
| Greenbriar Ln, W | 75208 |
| Greenbrier Dr | |
| 3000-4499 | 75225 |
| 5400-5799 | 75209 |
| 7400-7599 | 75225 |
| Greenbrook Ln | 75214 |
| Greencove Ln | 75232 |
| Greencrest Dr | 75241 |
| Greendale Dr | 75217 |
| Greenfield Dr | 75238 |
| Greengrove Ln | 75253 |
| Greenhaven Dr | 75217 |
| Greenhollow Ln | 75240 |
| Greenhurst Dr | 75234 |
| Greenland Dr | 75228 |
| Greenlawn Dr | 75253 |
| Greenleaf St | 75212 |
| Greenmere Pl | 75227 |
| Greenmound Ave | 75227 |
| Greenport Dr | 75228 |
| Greenspan Dr | 75232 |
| Greensprint Dr | 75238 |
| Greenstone Dr | 75243 |
| Greentree Ln | 75214 |
| Greenview Dr | 75244 |
| Greenville Ave | |
| 1300-6699 | 75206 |
| 6700-8499 | 75231 |
| 8500-12999 | 75243 |
| Greenway Blvd | 75209 |
| Greenway Blvd, E & W | 75209 |
| Greenwich Ln | 75230 |
| Greenwood St | 75204 |
| Greer St | 75215 |
| Gregg St | 75235 |
| Gregory Dr | 75232 |
| Grenadier Ct & Dr | 75238 |
| Grenore Dr | 75218 |
| Gretchen Ln | 75252 |
| Gretna St | 75207 |
| Greyfriars Ln | 75238 |
| Griffin Pl | 75202 |
| Griffin St E & W | 75215 |
| Griffin St, N & S | 75202 |
| Griffith Ave | 75208 |
| Grigsby Ave | 75204 |
| Grinnell St | |
| 100-499 | 75224 |
| 900-1699 | 75216 |
| Grissom Ln | 75229 |
| Grogan St | 75253 |
| Groom Ln | 75227 |
| Gross Rd | 75228 |
| Groton Ln | 75217 |
| Grove Hill Rd | |
| 2400-2499 | 75228 |
| 2700-2799 | 75227 |
| Grove Oaks Blvd | 75217 |
| Grovecrest Dr | 75217 |
| Grovedale Dr | 75230 |
| Groveland Dr | 75218 |
| Groveridge Dr | 75227 |
| Grovetree Ln | 75253 |
| Groveview Dr | 75233 |
| Groveway Dr | 75232 |
| Grovewood St | 75210 |
| Grumman Dr | 75228 |
| Guadalupe Ave | 75233 |
| Guam St | 75212 |
| Guaranty St | 75215 |
| Guard Dr | 75217 |
| Guernsey Ln | 75220 |
| Guest St | 75208 |
| Guildhall Dr | 75238 |
| Guillot Ct | 75201 |
| Guillot St | |
| 2600-2899 | 75204 |
| Gulden Ln | 75212 |
| Gulf Palms Dr | 75227 |
| Gulfstream Dr | 75244 |
| Gulledge Ln | 75217 |
| Gunnison Dr | 75231 |
| Gunter Ave | 75210 |
| Gurley Ave | 75223 |
| Gus Thomasson Rd | 75228 |
| Guthrie St | 75224 |
| Guymon St | 75212 |
| Haas Dr | |
| 4600-4899 | 75216 |
| 5000-5199 | 75241 |
| Habersham Ln | 75248 |
| Hacienda Dr | 75233 |
| Hackney Ln | 75238 |
| Hadley Dr | 75217 |
| Haggar Way | |
| 3300-3599 | 75235 |
| 3600-3899 | 75209 |
| Hague Dr | 75234 |
| Haines Ave | 75208 |
| Hale St | 75211 |
| Hale St | 75216 |
| Half Crown Dr | 75237 |
| Halifax St | 75247 |
| Hall St, N | |
| 100-499 | 75226 |
| 500-599 | 75246 |
| 600-699 | 75226 |
| 700-899 | 75246 |
| 900-3299 | 75204 |
| 3400-4599 | 75219 |
| 4900-5199 | 75235 |
| Hall St, S | 75226 |
| Hallett Ave | 75237 |
| Hallmark Dr | 75229 |
| Hallshire Ct | 75225 |
| Hallsville St | 75204 |
| Hallum St | 75243 |
| Halprin Ct & St | 75252 |
| Halsey St | 75224 |
| Halsley Rd | 75217 |
| Halwin Cir | 75243 |
| Hambrick Rd | 75218 |
| Hamburg St | 75215 |
| Hamilton Ave | |
| 3200-4599 | 75210 |
| 4600-4899 | 75223 |
| Hamilton Dr | 75203 |
| Hamilton Park Sc | 75243 |
| Hamlet Ave | 75203 |
| Hamlin Dr | 75217 |
| Hamlin Rd | 75212 |
| Hammerking Rd | 75232 |
| Hammerly Dr | 75212 |
| Hammond Ave | 75223 |
| Hampshire Rd | 75241 |
| Hampstead Ln | 75230 |
| Hampton Rd, N | |
| 100-2499 | 75208 |
| 2600-4199 | 75212 |
| Hampton Rd, S | |
| 100-1899 | 75208 |
| 2200-4299 | 75224 |
| 4300-8899 | 75232 |
| Hancock St | 75210 |
| Handicap Cir | 75211 |
| Handley Dr | 75208 |
| Handlin Rd | 75253 |
| Hanford Dr | 75243 |
| Hanging Cliff Cir & Dr | 75224 |
| Hanover Ave | |
| 2700-4499 | 75225 |
| 7800-7999 | 75225 |
| Hanover Ave, W | 75209 |
| Hansboro Ave | |
| 1100-1899 | 75224 |
| 2800-3399 | 75233 |
| Hanszen St | 75203 |
| Happy Ln | 75230 |
| Happy Canyon Cir, Ct & Dr | 75241 |
| Happy Hollow Ln | 75217 |
| Haraby Ct | 75248 |
| Harbin St | 75208 |
| Harbinger Ln | 75252 |
| Harbor Rd | 75216 |
| Harbor Town Dr | 75252 |
| Harden St | 75203 |
| Harding St | 75215 |
| Hardwick St | 75208 |
| Hardwood Trl | 75249 |
| Hargrove Dr | 75220 |
| Harkness Dr | 75243 |
| Harlandale Ave | |
| 600-899 | 75203 |
| 900-3399 | 75216 |
| Harlee Dr | 75234 |
| Harlem Ct | 75204 |
| Harlingen St | 75212 |
| Harmon St | |
| 3100-3199 | 75215 |
| 3300-3499 | 75210 |
| Harmony Ln | 75241 |
| Harold Walker Dr | 75241 |
| Harrell Ave | 75203 |
| Harriet Cir & Dr | 75244 |
| Harris Ct | 75223 |
| Harrisburg Cir | 75234 |
| Harrison Ave | 75215 |
| Harry Hines Blvd | |
| 2400-3399 | 75201 |
| 3600-4599 | 75219 |
| 4600-9399 | 75235 |
| 9400-10999 | 75220 |
| 11000-11699 | 75229 |
| 11700-14199 | 75234 |
| Harrys Ln | 75229 |
| Harston St | 75212 |
| Hart St | 75203 |
| Harter Rd | 75218 |
| Hartford St | 75219 |
| Hartline Dr | 75228 |
| Hartsdale Ave | 75211 |
| Harvard Ave | 75205 |
| Harvest Rd | 75217 |
| Harvest Glen Dr | 75248 |
| Harvest Hill Rd | |
| 3900-5199 | 75244 |
| 5200-5999 | 75230 |
| Harvester St | 75207 |
| Harwell Dr | 75220 |
| Harwich Dr | |
| 9900-9999 | 75220 |
| 10000-10199 | 75229 |
| Harwood St, N | 75201 |
| Harwood St, S | |
| 100-1299 | 75201 |
| 1500-4999 | 75215 |
| Haselwood Ln | 75238 |
| Haskell Ave, N | |
| 100-199 | 75226 |
| 200-899 | 75246 |
| 900-3499 | 75204 |
| Haskell Ave, S | |
| 100-499 | 75226 |
| 500-3399 | 75223 |
| Haslett St | 75208 |
| Hastings St | 75215 |
| Hasty St | 75228 |
| Hatcher St | |
| 1600-3499 | 75215 |
| 3500-6099 | 75210 |
| Hathaway St | 75220 |
| Hatton St | 75203 |
| Havana St | 75215 |
| Haven St | 75215 |
| Havencove Dr | 75227 |
| Havendon Cir | 75203 |
| Havenglen Dr | 75248 |
| Havenhurst Ave | 75234 |
| Havenlake Cir, Dr & Pl | 75238 |
| Havenrock Cir | 75248 |
| Havenside Dr | 75244 |
| Havenwood Dr | 75232 |
| Haverford Rd | 75214 |
| Haverhill Ln | 75217 |
| Haverty St | 75223 |
| Haverwood Ln | 75252 |
| Hawes Ave & Ct | 75235 |
| Hawick Ln | 75220 |
| Hawkins St, N | |
| 100-299 | 75226 |
| 300-799 | 75204 |
| 900-1099 | 75201 |
| Hawkins St, S | 75226 |
| Hawley Ln | 75217 |
| Hawthorne Ave | 75219 |
| Hay St | 75223 |
| Haydale Dr | 75244 |
| Hayfield Dr | 75238 |
| Haymarket Rd | |
| 500-1299 | 75217 |
| 1300-2799 | 75253 |
| Haymeadow Cir & Dr | 75240 |
| Haynie Ave | 75205 |
| Haywood Pky | 75232 |
| Hazel Rd | 75217 |
| Hazelcrest Dr | 75253 |
| Hazelhurst Ln | 75227 |
| Healey Dr | 75228 |
| Hearne Ave | 75208 |
| Hearthstone Dr | 75234 |
| Heartside Dr | 75234 |
| Heartsill Dr | 75235 |
| Heather Ln | 75229 |
| Heatherbrook Dr | 75244 |
| Heathercrest Rd | 75249 |
| Heatherdale Dr | 75243 |
| Heatherglen Dr | 75232 |
| Heatherknoll Dr | 75248 |
| Heathermore Dr | 75248 |
| Heatherwood Dr | 75228 |
| Hebron St | 75226 |
| Hector St | 75210 |
| Hedgdon Dr | 75216 |
| Hedge Dr | 75249 |
| Hedgeapple Dr | 75243 |
| Hedgerow Dr | 75235 |
| Hedgeway Dr | 75229 |
| Heinen Dr | 75227 |
| Helen St | 75223 |
| Helena St | 75217 |
| Helsem Bnd & Way | 75230 |
| Hemlock Ave | 75231 |
| Hemphill Dr | 75216 |
| Henderson Ave, N | |
| 100-699 | 75214 |
| 1500-3099 | 75206 |
| Henderson Ave, S | |
| 100-399 | 75214 |
| 400-1799 | 75223 |
| Hendricks Ave | 75216 |
| Henry St | 75226 |
| Hensley Ct | 75211 |
| Herald St | 75215 |
| Herbert St | 75212 |
| Heritage Cir | 75234 |
| Heritage Pl | 75217 |
| Hermitage St | 75234 |
| Hermosa Dr | 75218 |
| Herndon St | 75223 |
| Herrling St | 75210 |
| Herschel Ave | 75219 |
| Hervey Trl | 75207 |
| Hester Ave | 75205 |
| Heyser Dr | 75224 |
| Heyworth Ave | 75211 |
| Hi Line Dr | 75207 |
| Hialeah St | 75214 |
| Hiawatha St | 75212 |
| Hibernia St | 75204 |
| Hibiscus Dr | 75228 |
| Hickman St | 75215 |
| Hickory St | |
| 1400-2499 | 75215 |
| 2300-3599 | 75226 |
| Hickory Xing | 75243 |
| Hickory Hill Dr | 75248 |
| Hidalgo Dr | 75220 |
| Hidden Cove Dr | 75248 |
| Hidden Creek Dr | 75252 |
| Hidden Glen Dr | 75248 |
| Hidden Springs Ct | 75240 |
| Hidden Trail Dr | 75241 |
| Hidden Valley Dr | 75241 |
| Hideaway St | 75214 |
| Higgins Ave | 75211 |
| High St | 75203 |
| High Bluff Dr | 75234 |
| High Brook Dr | 75234 |
| High Court Pl | 75240 |
| High Forest Dr | 75230 |
| High Hill Blvd | 75203 |
| High Hill Pl, N & S | 75203 |
| High Hollows Dr | 75230 |
| High Lark Dr | 75234 |
| High Meadow Cir, Ct & Pl | 75234 |
| High Meadow Dr | |
| 11800-12399 | 75234 |
| 12400-12799 | 75244 |
| High Meadow Mews | 75244 |
| High Mesa Dr | 75234 |
| High Oaks Cir | 75231 |
| High Plain Ln | 75249 |
| High Point Cir | 75243 |
| High School Ave | 75205 |
| High Star Ln | 75252 |
| High Summit Dr | 75244 |
| High Valley Dr | 75234 |
| High Vista Dr | |
| 3200-3699 | 75234 |
| 3700-3799 | 75244 |
| Highcrest Dr | 75232 |
| Highdale Dr | 75234 |
| Highedge Dr | 75238 |
| Highfall Dr | 75232 |
| Highfield Dr | 75227 |
| Highgate Ln | 75214 |
| Highgrove Dr | 75220 |
| Highland Dr | 75205 |
| Highland Rd | |
| 1300-1799 | 75218 |
| 1800-3499 | 75228 |
| Highland Glen Trl | 75248 |
| Highland Heather Ln | 75248 |
| Highland Hill Sc | 75241 |
| Highland Hills Dr | 75241 |
| Highland Meadow Dr | 75234 |
| Highland Oaks Dr | 75232 |
| Highland Park Vlg | 75205 |
| Highland Place Dr | 75236 |
| Highland View Dr | 75238 |
| Highland Village Dr | 75241 |
| Highland Woods Cir & Dr | 75241 |
| Highmark Sq | 75240 |
| Highmont St | 75230 |
| Highplace Cir | 75240 |
| Highridge Dr | 75238 |
| Highspire Dr | 75217 |
| Hightower Pl | 75244 |
| Highview St | 75211 |
| Highwood Dr | 75228 |
| Hilandale St | 75216 |
| Hilda Cir | 75241 |
| Hildebrand St | 75211 |
| Hill Ave, N | |
| 100-199 | 75226 |
| 200-899 | 75246 |
| Hill Ave, S | |
| 100-499 | 75226 |
| 500-699 | 75223 |
| Hill Fawn Cir | 75248 |
| Hill Haven Dr | 75230 |
| Hill View Dr | 75231 |
| Hillard Dr | 75217 |
| Hillbriar Dr | 75248 |
| Hillbrook St | 75214 |
| Hillburn Dr | |
| 100-2099 | 75217 |
| 2100-2699 | 75227 |
| Hillcrest Ave | |
| 5000-7099 | 75205 |
| 7100-9699 | 75225 |
| Hillcrest Rd | |
| 9700-12999 | 75230 |
| 13000-14799 | 75240 |
| 14800-17299 | 75248 |
| Hillcrest Plaza Dr | 75230 |
| Hillcroft St | 75227 |
| Hilldale Dr | 75231 |
| Hillglenn Rd | 75228 |
| Hillgreen Cir & Dr | 75214 |
| Hillguard Rd | 75243 |
| Hillhouse Ln | 75227 |
| Hillmont Dr | 75217 |
| Hilloak Dr | 75232 |
| Hillpark Dr | 75230 |
| Hillpoint Dr | 75238 |
| Hillsboro Ave | 75228 |
| Hillside Dr & Vlg | 75214 |
| Hillstar Cir | 75217 |
| Hilltop Dr | 75227 |
| Hillvale Dr | 75241 |
| Hillview Dr | 75231 |
| Hillwood Cir & Ln | 75248 |
| Hilton Ct & Dr | 75204 |
| Hilton Head Dr | 75252 |
| Hines Pl | 75235 |
| Hinton St | 75235 |
| Hobart St | 75218 |
| Hobbs St | 75223 |
| Hoblitzelle Dr | 75243 |
| Hobson Ave, E | 75216 |
| Hobson Ave, W | 75224 |
| Hockaday Dr | 75229 |
| Hodde St | 75217 |
| Hodge St | 75215 |
| Hoel Dr | 75224 |

center (for example, a block with many buildings) or a large city. The last two digits, 46, represent the local post office in that area.

The postal service encourages businesses to use zip + 4 for their mailings. This system adds four extra digits at the end of a zip code. An example is 94114-0929. The number 09 represents a group of streets or several blocks, and the number 29 represents a building or a floor or department within a building.

## ■ UNAUTHORIZED USE OF POSTAGE AND SUPPLIES

Businesses do not allow their employees to use postage or postage supplies for personal business. This includes using the postage meter for personal mail. It also includes taking company envelopes, stationery, labels, or stamps.

Over a period of time, a business can lose lots of money if employees misuse postage meters or use company postage supplies. Some companies consider this stealing by an employee.

## R ecall Time

*Answer the following questions:*

1. What information can you get from an electronic postage scale?
2. What does a collator do?
3. Where can you get an up-to-date brochure on requirements for addressing mail?
4. What are three types of materials used for cushioning items before wrapping?

## ■ SUMMARY

An office worker has to know a lot of information to efficiently process incoming and outgoing mail. When you begin working in an office, it is important that you remember this information in order to follow proper procedures for processing mail.

Use the following list to see if you are prepared to handle the processing of mail in an office environment:

- Once the mail is received in my office, I know the procedures to follow for processing it.
- Before putting the mail on my boss's desk, I know how to arrange the mail according to importance.
- Before the outgoing mail is sealed, I know the procedures for getting signatures, checking for enclosures, and addressing envelopes.
- Before putting postage on the outgoing mail, I know how to determine which class of mail to use.

- After determining which class of mail to use, I know how to use postal equipment that will determine the cost.
- If items need to be packed and wrapped for mailing, I know the most efficient way to do this.
- If addresses need zip codes, I know how to use reference materials to locate the proper zip codes.

## In Conclusion . . .

*When you have completed this chapter, use an electronic typewriter or a microcomputer to answer the following questions:*

1. *What are at least three classifications of mailing? Explain why each one may be used.*
2. *In what order should an address be typed on an envelope? Create a sample.*

# Review and Application

## REVIEW YOUR VOCABULARY

Supply the missing words by choosing from the new office terms listed below.

1. In a large company, the processing of mail may be done in a _____ _____ department.
2. An office worker may _____ _____ into individual trays for more than one supervisor.
3. _____ _____ is first-class mail weighing more than twelve ounces.
4. The secretary was underlining important facts in the letter; she was _____ the letter.
5. BCS stands for _____ _____ _____.
6. A secretary should not open _____ _____.
7. A routing slip is used for _____ _____ to more than one person in a company.

| | |
|---|---|
| a. annotating | d. confidential mail |
| b. bar code sorter | e. priority mail |
| c. centralized mail | f. routing mail |
| | g. sort mail |

## DISCUSS AND ANALYZE AN OFFICE SITUATION

1. Henrico is an office worker for a construction company. He also is local chairperson of a fund-raiser for his church. Henrico has fifty letters to mail for the church. He is trying to decide if he should put them through the company postage meter and not tell anyone. This way he would save money for the church.

   What would you advise Henrico? Explain your answer.

## PRACTICE BASIC SKILLS

### Math

1. You go to the post office for your boss. It costs $13.90 to send the mail. How much change do you receive from a twenty-dollar bill?

2. At Lucas Advertising, the employees must record mail charges for each client. What is the total monthly charge for Levis on the following mail expense register?

#### MAIL EXPENSE REGISTER FOR APRIL

| Charge To | Amount | Charge To | Amount |
|---|---|---|---|
| Levis | $14.89 | Chevron | $8.90 |
| HewPac | 7.13 | Levis | 2.90 |
| Levis | 43.90 | Cal Milk | 0.75 |
| Levis | 0.56 | Chevron | 3.78 |
| PacTel | 8.90 | Levis | 0.55 |
| Levis | 0.45 | Chevron | 8.90 |
| Admin | 6.60 | Levis | 2.67 |

3. You need to reimburse petty cash up to $40. You have used $8.90, $3.45, $15.78, and $0.35 for postage. How much is needed to reimburse back up to the $40?

4. At the post office, you mail a package costing $13.50 and a letter costing $0.65, and you purchase a sheet of stamps costing $12.50. How much change do you receive if you give the postal clerk $30?

### English

1. *Rule:* For the possessive form of a noun that does not end in *s*, add *'s*.
   *Examples:* cat's paw, men's hats, clerk's pay, children's lunch
   *Practice Exercises:* Rewrite the following sentences placing apostrophes to form the possessive where needed.
   a. One customers last name was omitted from the mailing list.
   b. Ms. Chins secretary attended the workshop on data bases for mailing labels.
   c. Why is the receptionists letter opener sitting on that managers desk?
   d. The mail operators position was eliminated because of all the new PCs.
   e. Invitations were mailed to each members supervisor in order to gain new members.

### Proofreading

1. Retype or rewrite the following memo, correcting all errors.

April 5,

TO: Office Staff
FROM: Orin Martin
SUBJECT: EXPRESS MAIL

Teh following informtion was recieved from the US Postal Service concerning Espress Mail.

Express mail has always been a great value. Now that we've introduced our new overnight letter rate, you can fly with the Eagle for less than ever before.

For a low rate, you can send up to eight ounses throughout the US overnight. Thanks to our ovrnight reliabelity, your get guaranteed before-noon delivery between all major markets.

And the conveniences of 13,5000 Express Mail boxes, 2,6000 Express Mail post offices and 265,000 letter cariers. More drop-off points than all our competitors combined. So whether you've got an overnight letter or package, why not soar with the Eagle.

## APPLY YOUR KNOWLEDGE

1. Arrange the following words into alphabetic order. Using a microcomputer or an electronic typewriter, tabulate the words in three columns.

| | |
|---|---|
| centralized | annotate |
| clutter | personal |
| opened | addressee |
| sender | envelope |
| label | meter |
| scale | stamp |
| magazine | enclosure |
| inserted | registered |
| international | postage |
| coding | delivery |
| cancellation | recipient |
| directory | reference |

2. Type the following handwritten names and addresses as they would appear for mailing. Use uppercase and no punctuation.

a. kate roper
tristate
115 montebello rd
jamaica plain ma 02130

b. judy wan
aaa hauling
85 whipper lane
stratford, ct 06497

c. doro gutierrez
gunn hotel
350 rockingstone ave
larchmont ny 10538

d. karl wolfe
us air
1313 gardner blvd
norton oh 44203

e. oscar rosa
calistoga water
3607 - 4th avenue
minneapolis mn 55409

f. bette waller
san lorenzo high school
1719 grange circle
longwood fl 32750

g. daryl lee
lee catering
115 upper terrace
vicksburg ms 39180

h. roger fine
fine word processing
2246 flossmoor rd
flossmoor il 60422

i. harriet gandi
calstate
4515 dromedary rd
phoenix az 85018

j. mariliee fong
amador appliance
543 sonoma ave
livermore ca 94525

# QUIZ

*Write a **T** if the statement is true or an **F** if the statement is false.*

_____ 1. In office terms, sorting the mail means preparing it for the post office.

_____ 2. First-, second-, and third-class mail will all be forwarded without adding any extra postage.

_____ 3. Confidential and personal mail may be opened by the executive's secretary.

_____ 4. Annotating mail means underlining important facts and making comments or special notations in the margin of a letter.

_____ 5. Routing mail means attaching a routing slip to correspondence and then having each person initial the routing slip after she or he has read the correspondence.

_____ 6. When arranging mail for your boss, always place advertisements on the top of the pile.

_____ 7. First-class mail must weigh twelve ounces or less.

_____ 8. Any business can get a permit to mail second class.

_____ 9. The Postal Answer Line can only be used by businesses that pay a fee for the service.

_____ 10. Private delivery firms such as UPS or Federal Express deliver in a hurry, but they never pick up items for delivery.

_____ 11. OCR stands for optical character recognition.

_____ 12. When a post office box number and a street address are used, the post office will deliver to the address that appears on the line immediately above the city, state, and zip code line.

_____ 13. The U.S. Postal Service recommends that you capitalize everything in the address.

(continued on next page)

_____ 14. Twine and cords are no longer allowed by the U.S. Postal Service for wrapping packages.

_____ 15. The U.S. Postal Service encourages businesses to use zip + 4 for their mailings.

## Word Processing

1. Use proofreaders marks to correct any errors you find in the paragraph that follows.

   In office terms, sorting the mail means arranging ort separating mail according to the kind it is and whom is to recieve it. BEfore you begin the process of sortting mail, clear a work area on your desk. Push all clutter aside and concentrat on this one project. Before beginning to open mail, seperate all letters that say Confidential or personal. These letters should be opened only by the person to who they are addressed.

2. Keyboard the paragraph accurately, save, and print a copy.

### Word Processing

Type, save, and print the following memo.

To: Ronald James

From: Grace Fong

Subject: Articles of Incorporation

As you requested, I have itemized the charges for preparing the Articles:

| | |
|---|---|
| Recording Fees | $ 75.00 |
| Notary Fee | 25.00 |
| Preparation Time | 150.00 |
| Long Distance Charges | 59.83 |
| Photocopying | 42.00 |

You may either remit the balance or make monthly payments. Thank you.

## Word Processing

1. Retrieve the document DURPOWER from Activity 5–6 and make the following changes.

2. Insert the following as number 4.

   4. <u>Limitations on Power, Principal's Desires</u>

   In exercising the authority under this durable power of attorney, my attorney-in-fact shall be subject to the limitations set forth below, and shall act in a manner consistent with my desires, as set forth below:

   This power of attorney shall be exercised consistent with my directive to physicians executed this date.

3. Insert the following as number 6.

   6. <u>Documents, Waivers, Releases</u>

   My attorney-in-fact shall have authority to execute, on my behalf, any and all documents necessary to implement health care decisions made in accordance with this durable power of attorney. Said documents include (but are not limited to) refusals and consents to permit treatment, discharge papers, and waiver of hospital or physician liability.

4. Save under DURPOWER.2. Print a copy.

5. Prepare the fax sheet on the following page. Send to Roberta Acman at 755-8251. This is from Grace Fong.

(continued on next page)

## FONG & FAMILY ATTORNEYS-AT-LAW

### FAX COVER

DATE: _____    TRANSMITTED BY: _____

TIME: _____

TO:        _____

FROM:      _____

NO OF PAGES (INCLUDING THIS COVER): _____

BILL TO:

_____

If you do not receive all pages, call 815.055.8225

ADDITIONAL MESSAGES:

_____

_____

_____

_____

_____

## Word Processing

```
WORD PROCESSING ORDER

RUSH _____

DATE  today                          DEADLINE  none

TO  temp                             FROM  YF

CLIENT _____      JOB # _____

COPIES TO _____
_____
_____

FAX TO _____ AT _____

OVERNIGHT _____ NEXT DAY _____

PRINT:    DISK # _____ DOC # _____ PAPER _____

SPECIAL INSTRUCTIONS _____
    Please type these names and addresses
    onto the label paper attached. Use
    all caps.
_____
```

ERNST & YOUNG LEGAL
CONSULTING
277 PARK AVENUE
17TH FLOOR
NEW YORK, NY 10172

LAW OFFICE CONSULTING GROUP
1707 L STREET NW
SUITE 360
WASHINGTON, DC 20036

(continued on next page)

LEGAL SUPPORT SERVICES
110 BROAD STREET
BOSTON, MA 02110

PRICE WATERHOUSE LAW FIRM &
LAW DEPARTMENT SERVICES
6500 ROCK SPRING DRIVE
BETHESDA, MD 20817

PRENTICE HALL ONLINE
500 CENTRAL AVENUE
ALBANY, NY 12206

AMERICAN LEGAL SYSTEMS
475 PARK AVENUE SOUTH
NEW YORK, NY 10016

ATLIS LEGAL INFORMATION
SERVICES
6011 EXECUTIVE BOULEVARD
ROCKVILLE, MD 20852

COMPEX LITIGATION SERVICES
14735 CALIFORNIA
VAN NUYS, CA 91411

COMPULIT, INCORPORATED
200 ALTA DALE, S.E.
ADA, MI 49301

COOPERS & LYBRAND
1100 LOUISIANA
SUITE 4100
HOUSTON, TX 77002

LEGAL RESEARCH ASSOCIATES
8383 WILSHIRE BOULEVARD, #516
BEVERLY HILLS, CA 90211

LITIGATION COMMUNICATIONS
1209 PRINCE STREET
ALEXANDRIA, VA 22314

LITIGATION RESOURCES
111 EIGHTH AVENUE
NEW YORK, NY 10011

TECHLAW SYSTEMS, INC.
14500 AVION PARKWAY
CHANTILLY, VA 22021

ATTORNEYS' COMPUTER
NETWORK
333 EAST 43RD STREET
SUITE 803
NEW YORK, NY 10017

BARRISTER INFORMATION
SYSTEMS
45 OAK STREET
BUFFALO, NY 14203

COMPULAW, LTD.
3520 WESLEY STREET
P.O. BOX 232
CULVER CITY, CA 90232

COMPUTER LAW SYSTEM, INC.
11000 WEST 78TH STREET
EDEN PRAIRIE, MN 55344

JURIS, INC.
151 ATHENS WAY
NASHVILLE, TN 37228

LAWTRAC DEVELOPMENT
CORPORATION
57 EAST 11TH STREET
NEW YORK, NY 10003

LAWYERS SOFTWARE PUBLISHING
1095 KLISH WAY
P.O. BOX 2765
DEL MAR, CA 92014

LEGAL EASE AUTO SYSTEMS
6424 CENTRAL AVENUE
ST. PETERSBURG, FL 33707

LEGALWARE
2445 M STREET NW
SUITE 275
WASHINGTON, DC 20037

LIBRA LEGAL SYSTEMS, INC.
2209 ROUTE 9 NORTH
HOWELL, NY 07731

|  |  |  |
|---|---|---|
|  |  |  |
|  |  |  |
|  |  |  |
|  |  |  |
|  |  |  |
|  |  |  |
|  |  |  |

|  |  |  |
|  |  |  |
|  |  |  |
|  |  |  |
|  |  |  |
|  |  |  |
|  |  |  |
|  |  |  |

## Zip Codes

In chapter 9 you read all about Melanie being employed in a large law firm as a mail clerk. Occasionally this law firm also had need for temporary employees due to employee absences or due to an overload of work.

The following is an example of how a temporary employee might be used at the law firm. See how fast and accurate you could be if you were hired to do the tasks.

You are to type a list of the zip codes and their locations in <u>numeric</u> order using the state and the first two zip numbers as the column heading. The state listings are **Massachusetts 02, New York 10, Florida 33, Illinois 61, Texas 76, California 94.**

For example:

MASSACHUSETTS 02                    NEW YORK 10

02159 Boston                        10004 Governors Island
02358 Plymouth                      10024 New York City
02542 Otis AFB                      10310 Staten Island
etc.                                etc.

Following are the locations to be grouped.

| Arlington | 76004 | Berkeley | 94710 |
|---|---|---|---|
| Boca Raton | 33434 | Boston | 02159 |
| Boynton Beach | 33436 | Bradenton | 33506 |
| Bronx | 10467 | Brooksville | 33512 |
| Champaign | 61820 | Clearwater | 33518 |
| Concord | 94518 | Daly City | 94015 |
| Euless | 76040 | Fall River | 02726 |
| Fort Lauderdale | 33313 | Fremont | 94536 |
| Fort Worth | 76117 | Fort Pierce | 33452 |
| Fort Myers | 33904 | Governors Island | 10004 |
| Hayward | 94541 | Homestead | 33032 |
| Irvington | 10533 | Lakeland | 33802 |
| Larchmont | 10538 | Mountain View | 94040 |
| Napa | 94559 | New York City | 10024 |
| New Bedford | 02747 | Newton | 02649 |
| North Attleboro | 02763 | Oakland | 94602 |
| Otis AFB | 02542 | Peoria | 61650 |
| Plymouth | 02358 | Pound Ridge | 10576 |
| Richmond | 94806 | Rockford | 61102 |
| San Mateo | 94404 | San Angelo | 76903 |
| San Francisco | 94112 | Staten Island | 10310 |
| Taunton | 02780 | Truro | 02666 |
| Waco | 76703 | Walnut Creek | 94598 |
| Wichita Falls | 76305 | Yonkers | 10710 |

## Word Processing

1. Keyboard a definition in your own words to each of the following classifications of mail. Maintain the order as they are presented. Use a spell check disk to check your errors. Save and print a copy single-spaced.

   First Class

   Priority

   Second Class

   Third Class

   Fourth Class

   Express

2. Edit the definitions by:

   A. underlining each of the six classifications,

   B. putting the definitions in alphabetical order according to the first word, and

   C. numbering each definition 1 through 6.

3. Print a second copy double-spaced.

# *Managing Office Activities*

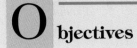

# Objectives

After completing this chapter, you will be able to do the following:

1. Organize your desk and work area so you can work efficiently.
2. Use a calendar and tickler file to arrange appointments and plan upcoming events.
3. Plan business meetings and conferences.
4. Plan business trips for executives and other travelers.

# New Office Terms

priorities
time management

## Before You Begin . . .

*Using an electronic typewriter or a microcomputer, answer the following questions to the best of your ability:*

1. *How would you organize your pens and pencils?*
2. *What type of work activity would you plan for the first project in the morning?*
3. *How would you handle interruptions?*
4. *What are five steps you would cover in planning a business meeting?*
5. *What are the first several steps in planning a business trip?*
6. *What would you schedule for an executive on the first day after he or she returns from a business trip?*

Someone said that great minds love chaos, that they love to set about organizing and straightening things to make them work better. This may be true for a few people, but most of us need order and organization in our lives to be efficient and effective.

Organization is essential in an office environment because you will be receiving, sorting, rearranging, and communicating vast amounts of information. This environment can be overwhelming unless you have systems of sorting and storing details so nothing gets lost or forgotten.

Many helpful systems exist that can make your job easier and less chaotic. This chapter details many current ideas about how to organize your space, time, and duties in ways that can help you do your job efficiently.

 ## ORGANIZING YOURSELF

### Your Desk

You will be spending much of your work time at your desk or work area. You will accomplish more in less time if you have all your work within easy reach. An efficient way to organize your work is to use a desk organizer.

Two types of desk organizers are available. One has horizontal slots in which you can place documents upright so tabs can easily be read. The other type is made up of several stacked trays. Trays can be of different colors, making it easier to identify their contents. Label each section or tray with what it will contain. For example, labels that say In Mail, Out Mail, In Work, Out Work, Mr. Jones, Ms. Wong will reflect what you are doing.

Keep tools that you use often on your desk top. These tools usually include pens and pencils (in an upright container), cellophane tape, paper clips, a stapler, and a pad for phone messages and notes. If you use a computer and store magnetic diskettes on your desk, do not use magnetic paper clip holders, as they may damage data stored on your diskettes. You will want your calendar or plan sheet within easy view. Some people also like a few reference items on their desk top, such as a

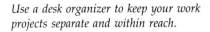

dictionary, an index containing frequently used telephone numbers and addresses, or a user's manual for the computer or other office machines that they use on a regular basis.

You will probably have a telephone. Place it close enough that you can reach it easily and jot notes while you talk. If you're right-handed, your telephone might be to the upper left, so you can answer it with your left hand, freeing your right hand to write. The opposite would apply if you're left-handed.

Different tasks will require different tools. Before you begin a task, decide which tools you will need and place them on the top of your desk. You can store some of these tools in your desk drawers until you need them. A desk drawer organizer will keep many of these items separated so they are easy to locate when you need them.

You will also keep stationery, envelopes, typing paper, and other supplies in your drawers. Keep them neat and tidy so you can easily access the items you need.

If you use a microcomputer, you can save a lot of your desktop space by placing it on end beside your desk. Several types of supports will allow you to do this. Some microcomputers are housed in *tower cabinets* (which are vertical rather than horizontal) and have built-in floor supports. You can place your microcomputer monitor on a swing-away arm that will allow you to push it out of the way when you need your desk space for other work.

## Your Materials

Besides providing small quantities of supplies that you keep on your desk and in the drawers, most offices have a central storage area for large quantities of supplies, such as computer diskettes, oversized envelopes, large quantities of paper, stationery, file folders, labels, ribbons, and pens and pencils.

If you work in a small office, you will probably be expected to keep supplies stocked by reordering them from an office supply store as they run low. This can be tricky with company stationery because it requires printing time. So keep track of the materials on hand and reorder early enough that new stock can be delivered when needed. Put newly received supplies behind or under older supplies so the older ones are used first.

## Your Responsibilities

To be well organized and efficient, you will need to understand thoroughly what is expected of you and what your duties entail, not only for a day at a time but for the week, subsequent weeks, and coming months. It will help if you acquire an understanding of the overall picture of what is being accomplished by your office.

Someone will probably provide some on-the-job training to get you started. This may be the person you're replacing, an office manager, an administrative assistant, or your new boss. You will receive either a verbal or written outline of what is expected of you. You may be given a desk manual outlining many of your duties in detail. If so, refer to it often—and if not, start one of your own, as it will help anyone relieving you when you are on vacation.

Take notes as you are receiving your training so you can refer to them in the future. Your boss may have some definite ideas about how certain things should be done. Listen carefully and learn your boss's ideas and preferences about how to perform your work. If you stay in your job but your boss is replaced, ask your new boss for her or his preferences. Become aware of your boss's duties, too, so you can coordinate your work activities with your boss's activities.

Study carefully any materials made available to you. These might include an office procedures manual and notes from the person who previously held your job. If you are given instructions for specific jobs, make certain you understand those instructions. Examine the files, and determine the status of the jobs that are currently being worked on. Become familiar with the different types of stationery and notepads, learning which items are customarily used for which tasks.

It will be helpful to learn the names of co-workers and of the executives in your office. You will be needing their assistance in the first few weeks, and they will appreciate it if you call them by name.

You may have no one to train you when you arrive at your new job. In that case, you may only receive a procedures manual to guide you. Be resourceful but careful as you sort out what is expected of you and how and when to seek answers. When in doubt, ask your supervisor or a co-worker who is willing to help. It may all seem overwhelming at first, but you will catch on; and in a few weeks, you will create a comfortable routine.

# MANAGING YOUR TIME

In a busy office, some eight-hour workdays seem to be only about three hours long. When you're deeply involved in a complicated project, you may ask yourself, "Where did the time go?" It feels as if you have accomplished only part of what you set out to do during the day. A remedy for this apparent disappearance of time is efficient time management.

**Time management** means the art of knowing what you need to do in a given time frame, setting priorities for projects, and completing projects in the time allotted.

## Set Priorities

**Priorities** are preferences in the order of work activities, usually decided according to levels of importance or deadlines. Setting priorities is the first task in time management, and it is also the most difficult. First, determine exactly what you have to accomplish in a given time frame, then order the tasks in sequence of their importance. Your supervisor will establish some of your day's priorities. If he or she comes to you and says, "This is very important, and I need it before noon," then you have no decision to make about where to begin your work.

After you set your priorities, establish a time during which you will complete each task. You can learn to do this by keeping a log detailing how much time it takes to complete different tasks. After a while, you will know how long it will take to complete specific tasks. For example, after you open and sort the mail for a couple weeks, you can estimate the average time required to open and sort the mail. After you type several ten-page reports, you will know how long it takes to type ten-page reports—and you can put a time value on such reports in the future.

You will find that setting priorities for your tasks is not just convenient but essential. Your boss's effectiveness will depend upon whether you complete your tasks in a timely manner. If you do your job well, your boss will be able to do her or his job well, too. Helping the boss often helps the whole company become more productive, and this benefits all employees—and your boss will probably be especially appreciative of your efforts.

## Plan Your Work

Plan your work, then follow your plan. Learn how to create a "things to do" list by noting the tasks you need to accomplish, placing them in order of priority, then allotting them a time for completion. This will help you dispatch your duties efficiently, but it may not always be as easy as it sounds. Although it is important to establish priorities for your workday, you must be flexible enough to comfortably shift your plan if your supervisor's needs require that you do so.

One of your major responsibilities is to save time for your supervisor by being aware of her or his schedule and doing as much of her or his

work as you're capable of doing. This necessitates being flexible with your own time.

When making up your plan for the day, leave some fifteen-minute time spaces between scheduled events. You can use these intervals to finish projects that take longer than you expect or for unexpected things that come up and displace your priorities.

Once you begin to address one task, think it through and plan how you will accomplish it from beginning to end, step by step. Visualize how it will look when completed so you will have a clear understanding of the desired outcome. If you are unclear about the desired outcome, don't guess. Find out who does know what the end product should look like and ask questions. Do the appropriate research before you begin and have all the necessary tools at hand. The point is, you want to do the task correctly the first time. Repeating tasks squanders valuable time; spending time at the beginning of each project to properly plan saves time in the end.

Many people find it is helpful to make the first task of the day a difficult one. Some workers take the first half hour after arriving at work to calm down, get centered, and get ready to work. Do all that before you come to the office. It's a waste of valuable time and will invariably put unwanted pressure on you during the day because you will spend all day trying to catch up. You might be unable to accomplish all the tasks you need to complete.

People differ in what time of the day they are most energetic, creative, and efficient. You might hear people say they are "morning persons" or "night persons." Regardless of when you feel you do your best work, try starting your day with a difficult, creative task. Then you can feel early in the day that you have already accomplished something, setting the pace for the rest of the day.

## Manage Details

The endless barrage of details in an office environment is often perplexing. Details about meetings, purchases, scheduling, staffing, marketing, phone messages, and hundreds of miscellaneous items must be dealt with and stored away in the proper place. All these bits of information have a way of sliding away from you if you're not well prepared.

Not only must you devise a way of recording details immediately, but you must devise methods of storing them so you can access them easily when you need to. This requires a system that you use consistently.

One helpful way to manage details is to create forms for different types of information. For example, information collected from people walking into the office could be on one form and telephone information on another. However, don't get carried away and design more forms than you need or collect and keep unnecessary information.

You can store the bits of information you have collected in several ways. One method is to place them in the task file to which they are related. Another method is to store them according to accounts; for example, any information coming from Computers Unlimited through the mail would be on your mail form, stored in the Computers Unlimited file. Often, information and details will simply be passed on to the next person and can be stored, temporarily, in that person's mailbox or file.

Devise a system of initials, check marks, or other codes that indicate to you the status of information that comes across your desk. Then the next time you see it, you will know where it has been and where it is supposed to be going.

## Work On One Task at a Time

When you're planning your day and assigning times and tasks on your "to do" list, allocate blocks of time for individual tasks. You will be more likely to gain a sense of accomplishment when you are able to complete something. On some jobs, your time is not your own and you find yourself jumping from task to task, never feeling as though you have accomplished anything. However, with careful planning, you can usually complete a few tasks each day.

Longer, more complicated tasks take even more planning. For example, if you have a task that will be time-consuming but is not due immediately, set apart a reasonable block of time to work on it and find a reasonable place to stop your work. Make clear notes to yourself about what part has been left undone and exactly where you ceased working.

Whenever possible, work on one task at a time until you have completed it. This way, you are less likely to omit an important part of the task, and your job will be less confusing and more gratifying.

## Cope with Interruptions

The glitch in your planning will come with interruptions. The first thing to realize about interruptions is that these are part of your job. The attitude you have in dealing with them will determine how successful you are in returning to the work and the train of thought you pursued before the telephone rang or your co-worker asked you a question. So don't become annoyed by interruptions. If you do, your distress will slow you down much more than the interruption does.

For a few days, keep track of how many times you answer the telephone, you assist a co-worker, or your supervisor asks to speak to you. Then you will know how much time to allow for interruptions in your planning. Knowing this, you need not be frustrated by not being able to accomplish all you set out to do. You can plan to do only what you will be able to accomplish, allowing for interruptions.

## Schedule Time to Relax

Your company, by law, will allow a lunch break and two fifteen-minute rest breaks—one in midmorning, one in midafternoon. It is assumed that your relaxation needs will be met during these breaks.

However, relaxation periods can be planned in other ways. You will soon discover that some tasks in the office are more difficult, more intense, and more energy consuming than others. For example, sorting mail requires less energy than setting up a data base on your computer.

You will also recognize your own stamina levels. That is, you may find that after two hours of intense concentration, you need a break.

With these two bits of information, you can plan your schedule with built-in relaxation periods by surrounding a difficult, lengthy task with easier, shorter tasks. In this way, you can plan your day so you are not exhausted before the day is over.

## Plan Tomorrow's Work

Before it's time to quit for the day, review the projects you worked on, making notes on what was completed and what was not completed. Begin to prepare your "to do" list for the next day by estimating how much time each carryover item will require and placing those items into time slots. With this kind of preparation, you can leave the office confident that your work for the next day is well organized.

## R ecall Time

*Answer the following questions:*

1. Why is getting organized in a busy office essential?
2. What are several items you will want to place on your desk top? How would you place these items for greatest convenience?
3. How would you order and store materials and supplies?
4. To organize your work efficiently, you will first need to know your job well. What are some ways you can help yourself become better acquainted with a new job?
5. Managing time may seem difficult at first. What are some ways to ensure that your time is managed well?

## ■ KEEPING A CALENDAR

A busy office requires that someone arrange the order of events for the day. It may be part of your job to schedule appointments for one or several people, as well as for yourself. The best way to keep track of and to schedule appointments, meetings, and events is to use an appointment calendar.

Appointment calendars come in many different formats with different features. If you won't be scheduling many appointments, you can use a simple desk calendar with some space for writing. If your office is especially busy, with many appointments each day, you will need a calendar with the workday separated into fifteen-minute intervals. These calendars come in many sizes. Determine your needs, go to an office supply store, and purchase the one that best suits your needs.

Some offices use special computer programs for keeping their calendars electronically. Electronic calendars have some advantages, including neatness and readability. If you use an electronic calendar, you will probably access it by keying in a special code that ensures the calendar will remain confidential. Several software programs can satisfy the appointment calendar needs in most offices. In addition, some appointment calendar programs are designed specifically for certain types of offices. If you are responsible for purchasing such a program, check the *Data Sources Guide to Computer Software* (available at most local computer program vendors). If your type of office has special requirements, check with vendors of software designed specifically for that type.

Joann is an excellent office worker. She worked for her previous employer for several months, and she knew her job well. Because of the good work she did, she was transferred to a new job in a different section.

In her new position, Joann works more closely with her boss than she did in her previous position. She is responsible for making decisions about scheduling appointments and ensuring that her boss's time is well managed. This is all new to her. She has no prior experience with time management.

Joann is enthusiastic about doing her job well, but she worries that she will be inadequate in her new position.

1. Which of the following should Joann do?
   a. Quit her job and look for something she feels more comfortable doing.
   b. Continue in her position, trying to do the best she can on her own.
   c. Discuss her problem with her supervisor.
2. Would most supervisors understand and appreciate an employee being open about her or his shortcomings?
3. If Joann decides to discuss the problem with her supervisor, should she offer to attend a Saturday seminar on time management or ask for time off during the week to attend the seminar?

## Making Appointments

Scheduling is crucial to the efficient running of your office. Furthermore, people who come in will think highly or poorly of your business based to some extent on how scheduling is conducted.

If you're careful, setting appointments will not be difficult, but you must follow some guidelines:

- Don't schedule two people at once. This sounds obvious, but it does occasionally happen.
- Don't schedule appointments too close together, so they're in danger of overlapping. That is, schedule enough time for each appointment. People expect their appointments to be on time. They consider their time to be of value, so they won't be happy sitting around waiting while your boss finishes with someone else.
- If you know the nature of appointments or meetings, don't schedule two intense ones back to back. Give your boss some breathing room.
- Write neatly and clearly on the calendar. It's of no value if what is scheduled can't be read.
- On the calendar, write the name of the individual your boss is meeting, that person's telephone number, and the type of appointment. This saves time if it becomes necessary to reschedule the appointment.
- Acknowledge that an appointment was kept by making a check mark on the calendar.
- Keep appointment calendars from year to year for reference.

You will devise your own system of how to keep your calendar. These guidelines can help you fill appointments efficiently.

# Handling Appointment Requests

Before you take over responsibility for setting appointments, establish guidelines with your managers so you fully understand to what extent you have authority to set appointments. The guidelines should answer the following questions: Which kinds of appointments will require an OK from your supervisors? Are there certain times of the day they would prefer not to have appointments? Are there certain people they will always see? Is there anyone they will absolutely not see?

Some executives set their own appointments, others leave this task to their assistants in the office, and still others share this responsibility with their assistants. These differences usually depend on the type of office. If, for example, you work in a doctor's office, you will probably set patient appointments without conferring with the doctor.

Some people will make their appointment requests in person, others will call on the telephone. You will receive some requests in the mail and still others by electronic message. Regardless of how you receive a request, you will need to gather the following information:

- the name and telephone number of the individual making the request and the company she or he represents
- the date and time when the individual desires to have the appointment and the approximate length of time necessary to complete her or his business
- the location where the meeting will take place if different from your supervisor's office
- the purpose of the meeting request, if your supervisor wants you to find this out

Most appointment requests will come by telephone. Remember, when you answer the telephone, you are the frontline representative of your business. So always be courteous while dealing with appointment requests. An example of the type of request you might receive and how you should handle it follows.

Kim [Answering the telephone]: Good afternoon, Moon Beam Publications. Kim speaking. May I help you?

Mr. Marquez [Speaking on the other end of the line]: Hello, this is Sergio Marquez. I'd like to drop by tomorrow to discuss my contract with Ms. Bradshaw.

Kim: Thank you. One moment please. It looks as if Ms. Bradshaw has some free time at three o'clock tomorrow afternoon. Would that be a good time for you? And, by the way, how long do you think you'll need with Ms. Bradshaw?

Mr. Marquez: No more than a half hour, I wouldn't think. That'll be fine, thank you.

Kim: Good, may I have your telephone number? I'll confirm this with Ms. Bradshaw and call you right back.

Mr. Marquez: Thank you. My number is 963-4295. Good-bye.

Kim: Good-bye.

This phone call was efficient and courteous. Kim will OK this meeting with Ms. Bradshaw according to previously established guidelines. Then Kim will call Mr. Marquez to confirm the appointment and enter the appointment into the appointment calendar, blocking off the allotted one-half hour.

## Entering Recurring Commitments

Some events and meetings in the office will be recurring. For example, many offices have a regular weekly staff meeting. Block off this special time on the calendar so unwanted appointments are not inadvertently set—even though everyone already knows this meeting is a regular occurrence.

Perhaps your supervisor or the office manager has a regular Wednesday afternoon manicure or a Thursday afternoon tennis game. In some offices, a special client may have a regular, weekly appointment. All these events that preclude setting outside appointments should have time blocked off the calendar—in effect, reserving this time.

## Handling Cancellations

Invariably, emergencies arise, people become ill, other activities take precedence, and plans change. Occasionally, you will have to cancel some appointments. If an individual calls to cancel an appointment, cross her or his name off the calendar and, if the person still wants an appointment, suggest another time.

If your supervisor directs you to cancel an appointment, call the individual to offer other time options, and be as courteous as possible, apologizing for your supervisor. If someone arrives for a canceled appointment because you were unable to contact him or her, apologize and explain that your boss had an emergency. If possible, suggest another person in the office who might be of service, and offer to set another appointment if that is what the individual requests.

## Coordinating Calendars

Some managers share the responsibility of keeping the calendar with their assistants. In this case, at least once each day the manager and the assistant must meet to check the calendar. This is when you will make adjustments in time allotments, record newly set appointments, delete cancellations, and record rescheduled appointments. It is imperative that this kind of coordination take place each day to avoid confusion and scheduling problems.

Keeping the calendar for a busy office can be challenging, but with a good system, you may find it fun and interesting.

# Using a Tickler File

A **tickler file** is a follow-up file that uses dates to help you remember work that is pending for a week, a month, or longer. You can devise a tickler file in many different ways. The most common is to use a three-by-five-inch card file with dividers or guides showing months (January through December) and dates (1 through 31). The divider for the current month is the first divider in the file, and it is followed by the numbered dividers for the dates. (See figure 7–9 in chapter 7.)

The purpose of this file is to remind you of future action that you must take. Suppose you call your office supply house to order a particular product. The person on the line tells you the item is not in stock but to check with the supply house next week, when it expects a new shipment. You make a note to yourself to call the supply house and place it in your tickler file behind the number that corresponds with the date one week in the future.

You can also use your tickler file when your boss tells you she or he is expecting out-of-town guests next week and asks you to call to make dinner reservations for next Thursday. Again, you write a note to yourself, this time to make a call to the restaurant, and file it behind the card for a date early in the week.

Your tickler file will only be useful to you if you make a practice of using it every day. Whenever you plan your day, either the night before or first thing in the morning, take out the notes from your tickler file for that day. Make it a part of your planning process, assigning time for each task you find in the file for that day.

As you complete each task, either throw the note to yourself away or describe on it the outcome of the task and place it in the appropriate business job or account file.

Between your tickler file and your calendar, you should be able to handle future events effectively.

# Recall Time

*Answer the following questions:*

1. How and why would you keep a calendar of events and meetings?
2. Managing your boss's or several people's appointments can be complicated. What are four tips that will help you keep everything in order?
3. If you have the responsibility of handling appointment requests, what information will you need from a person wishing to make an appointment?
4. Suppose you are answering the telephone and the person on the line requests an appointment with your boss. How does the conversation go?
5. What is a tickler file, and how will you use it?

## ■ PLANNING AND SCHEDULING BUSINESS ─ MEETINGS

Meetings play an important role in the communication of information in every kind of business. They are held to conduct business, to follow up on a previously discussed activity, or simply to communicate information to an individual or to a group.

The content and style of meetings vary greatly. A worker may meet with his or her supervisor for direction or evaluation. An executive may meet with the board of directors to communicate information and decide on the future course of the business. Salespeople meet with outside businesspeople to strike a deal. People in similar positions from different businesses meet to learn how to become more efficient in their jobs.

The list is endless. The one thing common in all kinds of meetings is that they must be run efficiently and effectively so as to avoid wasting valuable time. Careful planning and preparation are the keys to efficiently run, worthwhile meetings.

### Informal Meetings

Much of the business associated with operating any company is conducted in small, informal meetings. These require little preparation and take place either in someone's office or in a small conference room. In spite of the informal nature of many meetings, everyone who is expected to be in attendance must be notified that they are taking place.

Very informal meetings can happen at a moment's notice and take place all day long in a busy office. Your supervisor may say "Lee, will

*Small, informal meetings are often used to plan projects and activities in a business office.*

you come into my office? I need to talk to you about something," and thus a meeting is set.

More formal but still considered informal are staff meetings, committee meetings, and client meetings. These require only that a time and place be set and that everyone who is supposed to be in attendance be notified. Whoever calls the meeting will oversee and conduct the meeting.

Staff meetings are the most common type of meeting and are usually held in a supervisor's office. Everyone who reports to that supervisor will be in attendance. The purpose of staff meetings is to discuss and plan new projects and directions, solve problems, assess progress, make decisions, and give assignments. Some staff meetings are used to settle disputes and problems between different staff members. You may be asked to make some arrangements for such meetings, and you will likely be asked to attend them.

Committees are small groups of people assigned to work on a particular project or task together. These people will meet to plan their approach and make assignments. They may meet once or several times. They will probably set their own meeting times and places, by mutual agreement, and notify anyone who should be in attendance.

Client meetings are very important even though they are often conducted in a casual atmosphere such as at a restaurant during lunch or dinner. These meetings are set according to the convenience of the individuals involved.

## Formal Meetings

Formal meetings have more structure and require more complicated preparation and planning than do informal meetings. They usually have a predetermined set of business items to cover and thus follow a preset agenda.

An **agenda** is a list of topics to be covered during a meeting. These topics are usually agreed upon and distributed before the meeting convenes, allowing participants time to prepare for the discussion of them. Sometimes approximate times are listed next to each topic to indicate when the discussion of each topic is scheduled. A sample agenda appears in figure 10–1.

You may have responsibilities before, during, and after formal meetings. Your supervisor may ask you to arrange for a meeting room, order food, and prepare materials. You may also be asked to prepare and distribute the documents that describe the meeting to potential participants. Another task might be to make arrangements for travel or accommodations for out-of-town participants.

**Preparation** Because meetings are so important and because businesspeople's time is so valuable, preparation for formal meetings must be carefully thought through and executed. For example, if participants must make flight arrangements to arrive in time for a meeting, you will need to begin planning earlier than if all the participants live in the same city. The following processes will help you organize and plan these meetings.

AGENDA

Board of Directors
Sunbeam Corporation

7 p.m., June 8, 19—

1. Call to order: Ms. Dunlop, chief executive officer
2. Roll call and introductions: Mr. Olson, secretary
3. Minutes of the last meeting: Mr. Olson, secretary
4. Treasurer's report: Ms. Smith, chief financial officer
5. Committee reports
6. Old business
7. New business
8. Date of next meeting
9. Adjournment

*Record Information on the Meeting*  As information about an upcoming meeting comes to your desk, record details in your tickler file according to the dates when action must be taken. Also record on your calendar the dates when you will be doing tasks concerned with the planning—such as meeting with the hotel manager to make room arrangements.

*Set Up a Meeting Folder*  As soon as the meeting is scheduled, create a folder labeled for it. Place in this folder all the bits of information concerning the meeting as they are created. Include such information as names, telephone numbers, and addresses of participants; agenda items; and planning notes.

*Reserve a Meeting Room and Equipment*  Your supervisor may give you the responsibility of arranging for a meeting place. As soon as you can determine the number of people expected to attend and the time and date of the meeting, begin looking for a room.

Large conferences will often be held in hotels, which usually have meeting rooms for rent. Check the prices before making reservations, as they may be prohibitive. Make arrangements for this type of conference well in advance of the conference date.

Some companies have conference rooms, but you must reserve them so that two meetings are not scheduled in a room at the same time. Many restaurants have meeting rooms where groups hold luncheon and dinner meetings. Some banks and churches have rooms you may use for community meetings.

You may also be responsible for arranging for equipment for a meeting. Whoever is organizing the meeting can tell you what equipment is required, such as a public-address system, videotape machine, overhead projector, chalkboard, chairs, and tables. Large hotels have many of these items available for use in their conference rooms. Some companies have equipment for use in meetings.

Make arrangements for rooms and equipment as far in advance as possible so you do not get caught in a crunch as the meeting date nears.

*Notify Participants* You can let participants know of a forthcoming meeting in several ways. The time to notify participants and the type of notification depend on the type of meeting. Some groups and organizations have bylaws that describe procedures for notifying participants of upcoming meetings. You must follow these guidelines to ensure that the meeting is official.

In the written notice of the meeting, give the date, time, and place of the meeting. Describe the purpose of the meeting and request that participants let you know whether they plan to attend.

For a formal meeting, prepare written notices and send them at least three weeks before the meeting. For a less formal meeting with fewer participants, telephoning is fine. If you use an electronic calendar, you may be able to send electronic messages to all the people involved.

Your notices will require follow-up. If the meeting is mandatory, those invited will contact you with valid reasons if they are unable to attend.

If the meeting is voluntary and some people have not let you know whether they will be attending, make follow-up calls to learn how many people to plan for. Keep a careful roster of who will attend and who will not. It is handy to keep your roster close to the telephone so when participants call, you can easily locate them on your list and jot down pertinent notes.

You may wish to make a final follow-up call the day before the meeting to further ensure good attendance.

*Prepare the Agenda* Usually, the person who will conduct the meeting, the chairperson, or the secretary will prepare the meeting agenda. The agenda will have a format similar to the sample on page 378, and the same format will be followed for subsequent meetings. Those who will participate in the meeting will submit items that make up the agenda. The chairperson or secretary may also place items on the agenda. It may be your job to keep track of these items, type the agenda, and make copies and distribute them either by mail or at the meeting.

*Set Up the Meeting Room* If it is your job to set up the meeting room, arrive early on the day of the meeting to ensure that you have everything needed. For example, make certain you have enough tables and chairs for everyone to sit comfortably.

Be sure the room is a comfortable temperature. Also make sure the lighting is adequate for people to take notes and see each other clearly. A room that is too dark or too bright can be uncomfortable.

Check to see that the equipment you reserved previously is in place and functions properly. Don't wait until the participants are arriving before checking the public-address system or other equipment. The squeaks and squawks of an errant loudspeaker system can be embarrassing.

If food is being provided, check to be certain those arrangements are proceeding smoothly. Even if refreshments are not provided, you will probably want to serve coffee, tea, and ice water. Your meeting will go much smoother if the participants are comfortable and feel you are concerned about their comfort.

*Organize Materials and Handouts* In the days before the meeting, prepare materials that will be part of the meeting. Design the materials to help communicate information and ensure that the meeting is efficiently run.

These materials might include folders with copies of special information developed by those planning the meeting. You may distribute pens or pencils and pads for the participants' convenience. In a large meeting where people are not familiar with one another, you will want to provide name tags. These make communication much easier and help participants past the difficulty of having so many names to remember.

You may place these materials on the tables where individuals will be seated or you may hand them to participants when they arrive, as part of signing in. Other pieces of literature and handouts may be displayed on the table for the participants to examine so they may take what they wish.

**Participation** Your role in the meeting should be clearly defined beforehand by your supervisor. As the person who made the arrangements, it may be your responsibility to continue monitoring the meeting to ensure that all goes smoothly. Perhaps you will greet people at the door. If so, greet them with a smile and a pleasant attitude so they will feel welcome and comfortable. Keep the water and coffee supplies replenished and attend to participants' other needs, such as requests for photocopies of specified documents.

*Discuss Ideas* Apart from the role you play as assistant and organizer, your supervisor may ask you to share your own ideas or to state your opinion about what others have to say. If so, then participate in that way. However, if your supervisor limits your participation to planning the meeting and taking minutes, then do not attempt to participate in the discussion of ideas.

*Take the Minutes* A role often delegated to secretaries and assistants is recording the events and actions of the meeting by taking minutes. The minutes are the official record of the meeting and concisely document facts about the meeting, though statements and events are not recorded verbatim (word for word). The minutes should provide a clear, accurate accounting of what transpires at the meeting.

Various formats for minutes are acceptable, but minutes will always contain the following:

- the date, time, and place of the meeting
- the name of the organization or group sponsoring the meeting
- the name of the person conducting the meeting
- a listing of the people present—and if others were expected to attend, a listing of absentees

In general, if the meeting is conducted according to the agenda, the minutes will take that general form—call to order, roll call and introductions, minutes of the last meeting, treasurer's report, and so on.

Your minutes might begin like the following:

On June 8, 1995, the meeting of the Sunbeam Corporation Board of Directors was convened at 7 p.m. at the Red Lion Inn. Ms. Dunlop, the chief executive officer, called the meeting to order. . . .

As you are recording the minutes, recognize that the actions are more important than what the participants say. Write the minutes clearly, ensuring that you don't lose any crucial information about business conducted at the meeting.

*Correct the Minutes* Part of the agenda for the meeting will be reading and correcting the minutes of the previous meeting. Someone may disagree with what has been recorded as having taken place. If the correction or addition is small, you may cross out the error and write in the correction. If the correction requires more writing, cross out the mistake and attach another page to record the correct information. Index the correction by placing a reference number next to the crossed-out section, directing the reader to the new page and new information.

After the minutes have been approved by the attending participants, don't add anything to them.

**Follow-up** Several tasks will require completion after the meeting. If these tasks are assigned to you, do them as soon as possible, demonstrating efficiency to all the parties involved. These tasks may include

> OFFICE TIP
>
> Locate files according to activity. Locate files used daily in a deskfile drawer or a small cabinet next to your desk. Locate other often-used files in a larger cabinet near by. Place inactive files in a storeroom.

paying bills, preparing correspondence, or completing reports determined by the business conducted at the meeting. The sooner you do these, the better—so the events of the meeting remain fresh in your mind.

*Prepare and Distribute the Minutes* Sometimes the person who takes the minutes at the meeting is not the person who prepares and distributes them. Therefore, you may have to prepare minutes that someone else has written. This means neatly typing them according to the format the group has agreed upon. If you are not sure about a word or phrase because of difficult handwriting, question the person who took the minutes to avoid any misunderstandings.

Distribute the minutes according to the group's wishes, either mailing them immediately or mailing them along with the next meeting notice.

*Prepare Related Correspondence* Your supervisor may ask you to prepare correspondence directly related to the meeting. This might include requests for more information, thank-you notes to participants or speakers, and follow-up information about ideas discussed at the meeting. These, again, should be completed as soon as possible after the meeting is held.

## R ecall Time

*Answer the following questions:*

1. What are the main differences between formal and informal meetings?
2. What is an agenda? How is it prepared and how is it used?
3. Several tasks are required when making arrangements for a meeting. What are four of them?
4. How are minutes taken? What information must be in them, and what format is used?
5. A meeting is not over when it's over. You may be responsible for many activities after a meeting. What are some of them?

## ▮ HANDLING TRAVEL ARRANGEMENTS

You may be asked to make arrangements for your managers to travel to a meeting or for participants to come to a meeting. Your company will give you guidelines to follow about company policy regarding travel. As soon as you learn that it will be your responsibility to make these arrangements, begin to prepare a travel folder.

Consider the following questions when planning travel for someone else:

1. What are the exact destinations and dates when the traveler wants to leave and return?
2. How does the traveler wish to get from one place to another? Some people are uncomfortable flying and would prefer to go by train.
3. Does the traveler have special requests, such as a specific time of day she or he wishes to leave and return or, if traveling by plane, a preferred seating assignment? Some people insist on an aisle seat, whereas others want to look out the window. Is a certain airline preferred? Does the traveler have any special food requirements?
4. Will someone at the destination be driving, or will a car rental be required?
5. Does the traveler have a favorite hotel in the destination city or a favorite hotel chain that he or she feels provides good service in most cities? Does the traveler require a specific type of accommodation? Will the traveler require a meeting room at the hotel?
6. Does your manager want you to arrange any other detail of preference or special request?

When you know the answers to these questions, you can plan and complete the travel arrangements.

## Planning

Travel can be complicated and exhausting if not properly planned and orchestrated. You will discover that in any business activity, proper planning in the beginning saves valuable time in the end.

**Early Preparations** Begin your trip folder as early as possible so you don't have loose papers lying about that might contain helpful information. Your trip folder will be a file folder that contains all the information relevant to a particular trip. Prepare separate travel folders for different trips.

When you first learn the approximate dates of a trip, make some notes about the time frame for planning. That is, how long do you have to make all the arrangements, and when must you accomplish each task? Make notes about the various aspects of planning the trip and about the tasks and responsibilities assigned to you.

Outline the trip, including the meetings to be attended during it. If possible, do this initial outlining and planning while meeting with the person who will be traveling. The outline will keep you focused on what you need to accomplish and the status of things as your plans proceed.

**Final Preparations** Prepare a checklist to use as the final preparations are being made. After your outline is complete and the designated tasks are accomplished, prepare your traveler's final itinerary. If you use the services of a travel agent, you should receive a final itinerary of the travel arrangements from her or him.

*Confirm Appointments* Call each person your supervisor plans to meet and confirm the appointments. Recheck the times, date, and places of all meetings.

Louise is an administrative assistant in the home office of a large manufacturing company. Louise understands quite well most of the computer programs used in the office. Word processing, spreadsheet, and data base programs all seem simple to her. So simple, in fact, that she cannot understand why many of the new workers frequently have difficulty understanding how to use these programs.

Arnold is a new person in the office. He spent four hours one morning reading manuals and trying to understand how to use a data base program, but he couldn't figure it out. He was feeling frustrated, a little bit stupid, and angry when he walked into the staff meeting. Although using computer programs was not on the agenda for the day, Arnold announced that he wanted this item added to the agenda. Louise, who was chairing the meeting, agreed, and added it as the first item for discussion.

Arnold, still frustrated and angry, began by saying, "This company must use the worst programs on the market—the one for data base management is terrible!"

Louise, who not only understood the programs well but had personally selected the data base management program, was not sympathetic. She replied, "We have the best programs on the market. The data base management program is simple and easy to learn for anyone of average intelligence."

Feeling he had just been insulted, Arnold said, "Excuse me," stood, and walked out of the meeting.

For the past two days neither Arnold nor Louise has spoken to the other.

1. What would have been a more effective way for Arnold to share his frustration with the computer program?
2. What could Louise have said that would have promoted more effective human relations?
3. What should Arnold and Louise say to one another now?

*Make Reservations* Make any reservations that have not previously been made. A travel agent may have made most reservations—but with the final setting of the itinerary, some of these might have to be changed.

*Prepare an Itinerary* When you have your outline, your reservations are made, and your meetings are confirmed, you can prepare the final itinerary for your traveler. The itinerary contains a calendar of meetings and hotel and travel reservations with addresses and telephone numbers. Include any instructions about special considerations.

Ask the traveler, who will probably be your boss or supervisor, who else should receive a copy of the itinerary. She or he may need several copies—one to carry, one to stash away in the baggage, and one for her or his family.

*Assemble Related Items* Place with your boss's itinerary the tickets, travel money, hotel confirmations, and forms for recording expenses.

Early in the planning, your supervisor began to think about the materials she or he wished to take along. Gather those materials and prepare them in the appropriate manner.

By carefully planning early on, following your checklist, and preparing a detailed itinerary, you can create an easy, well-organized, successful trip. Your boss will be able to accomplish much more on the trip because of your careful work, since it will allow her or him to spend energy on conducting business instead of tending to other details.

## Using Travel Agents

Your company may not expect you to personally arrange travel plans. You may be dealing with a travel agency that can make all the arrangements from booking the flights and hotel reservations to reserving a car rental at the destination.

Travel agencies are paid a commission for booking hotels and airlines, and they have access, through computers, to arrival times, departure times, and ticket prices for most airlines. Therefore, they can efficiently take care of these details for you. Even if you do work with a travel agency, though, you will need the information listed above to ensure a comfortable, enjoyable trip.

Before you begin searching for a travel agent, ask your supervisor if the company ordinarily uses a particular agency that has provided satisfactory service in the past. If not, you may ask other people for references to a good agency. Using one that specializes in business travel will probably be your best bet.

Before you contact an agency, determine company policy regarding paying for the trip. Is the travel agency to bill the company for expenses, or will you be given a credit card number to give to the agency? When you call the agency, have your trip folder in front of you with the information you will need to give the agent. This information consists of specific details, and you will need to give the agent, as nearly as possible, specific instructions about setting up the trip.

As soon as the agency completes the arrangements, it will send you the tickets along with a computer printout of the itinerary it has arranged and an invoice listing charges. The **itinerary** is an outline that includes flight numbers, departure and arrival times and places, hotel accommodation information, and car rental information. Check this information carefully, then ask your supervisor or the traveler to check it, too. Make needed corrections with the travel agent without delay to ensure a convenient and pleasant trip.

## Arranging Trips Yourself

Sometimes you may be required to make travel arrangements yourself. For example, if a rush trip comes up suddenly, you may not have time to enlist the aid of a travel agent. Though this will be less convenient for you, you should be able to handle the plans adequately.

**Scheduling Air Travel** You will need to do a bit of research when booking airline tickets yourself. If you will be doing a lot of scheduling, subscribe to one of the many periodicals that help people make travel arrangements. You can find these and other books about travel in your local library.

If you live in a large city, you will have several airlines from which to choose. Perhaps your supervisor has a preference for one airline.

Most airlines provide updated timetables with the following information:

- arrival and departure times
- days each flight is available
- flight numbers
- special services and features of each flight
- toll-free number where more information can be gathered and reservations can be made

Attempt to secure the best price for tickets as well as the most convenient departure and arrival times. All this will require that you call airlines and ask questions. Use the airlines' toll-free numbers so you can make the calls without paying long-distance fees. Be sure to consider any special programs for frequent flyers or business travelers.

As soon as you make your decision about which airline to use, book the flight. Before you get on the telephone, place your trip folder in front of you so you can make the special arrangements requested by your traveler. You will need to know how you will be paying for the tickets. The airline may prefer a credit card number. You may make arrangements to pick up the tickets and pay for them in person, or you may request that the airline bill your company for the tickets.

You will probably not have time to have the tickets mailed. So, unless you plan to pick the tickets up ahead of time, arrange for your traveler to pick them up at the airport on the day of departure.

**Car Rental**   Whether your traveler needs a car at her or his destination or will be making the entire trip by automobile, arrangements have to be made in advance when renting a car. If you're using a travel agency, it will take care of car rental details as part of its service to you.

If you will be making the arrangements, do some research to secure the best rates. The rates will depend on the size and model of car, the destination, and the length of time the car is needed. The costs will include a daily rate plus an additional cost for miles over a certain daily allotment. Most of these items are negotiable and vary from agency to agency.

You can look in the Yellow Pages of your telephone directory and begin to call the rental agencies in your area. Several are usually located at major airports, and most medium-sized towns also have several from which to choose.

**Hotel and Motel Accommodations**   Your traveler may have to spend the night or several nights at her or his destination. A travel agency will be able to make accommodations for you.

Your traveler may have hotel or motel preferences if she or he is acquainted with the town to be visited. Ask before you begin your search. The chamber of commerce in the community being visited can help you with finding and arranging accommodations. Most large hotels have toll-free numbers for bookings.

## Continuing Your Work When the Executive Is Away

You may feel that everything will come apart while the boss is out of town, but this is unlikely. For the most part, you can continue your work as usual. Sometimes, without your boss's interruptions, you will accomplish more with her or him out of the office.

Keep careful track of events in the office, visitors, incoming mail, and phone calls, so you can fill your boss in upon her or his return. Don't set any appointments on the day your boss is due to return to the office. You both will have a lot of catching up to do.

## Following Up When the Executive Returns

When your boss returns, a lot of follow-up work will need to be done. You will need to write thank-you letters to people who provided services or assistance. You will also need to prepare other correspondence associated with the business conducted during the trip.

You may need to prepare detailed reports showing what was accomplished on the trip. You and your boss will have your hands full for several days after she or he returns.

Managing activities and duties in a busy office can appear complex and sometimes nearly impossible. But you can learn some systems that make it easier for you. After you have been working in the office for a while, you may be surprised at how routine all this will become.

## R ecall Time

*Answer the following questions:*

1. Whether you make your supervisor's travel arrangements or leave the details to a travel agency, you need to consider several things before you begin. What are these considerations?
2. Usually, people use travel agencies for their travel needs. How do travel agencies work and what can they do for you?
3. If it is up to you to schedule your supervisor's air travel, you will have to do some research. What kinds of information will you seek?
4. How do you rent an automobile?
5. How do you arrange hotel or motel accommodations?

## SUMMARY

You may have heard the phrase, "Time is money." This is especially true in business. In a busy office, you may quickly become overwhelmed and waste valuable time if you do not get organized. Think through every item from how you will organize the tools on your desk top to setting up conferences and planning trips.

The first step in getting organized is to understand your new job. Someone may train you for a few days, or you may be given a procedures manual to show you the way. After you understand clearly your responsibilities, you can begin to organize things so that you can handle them.

Managing your time will be crucial to your success. This will require planning your day carefully. Set priorities, assign each task a time for completion, and follow your plans as nearly as possible while continuing to be flexible.

Design ways of managing details. These will include using files and folders and notes to yourself. Details have a way of disappearing if they are not managed correctly and systematically.

You can often work on just one task at a time until it is completed. However, be prepared for interruptions. They are part of the job, so schedule time for them in your daily work plan, too. Adjust your schedule so that the intensity of your work does not last all day. Schedule easier tasks between more difficult ones.

Part of organizing a busy office is keeping a calendar. List all upcoming meetings, events, and appointments. You may be asked to schedule your supervisor's appointments. If so, you will be the "keeper of the calendar." You will block out time for recurring events, handle cancellations, and coordinate your calendar with others in the office.

A tickler file is a follow-up file that alerts you to tasks you need to do. Using a tickler file in conjunction with your calendar, you should be able to deal with all the events of a busy office.

Much of the business of a company is conducted in formal or informal meetings. You may be responsible for making arrangements for formal meetings. These will include reserving a room, organizing equipment and refreshments, and preparing materials. Begin your planning by setting up a folder in which to keep details, recording all information that passes your desk about the meeting, notifying participants, and preparing an agenda.

An agenda is an announcement and listing of what will be discussed at a meeting. Minutes are an accounting of the meeting. You may be asked to take minutes, then prepare and distribute them after the meeting is over. Other follow-up activities to the meeting will be preparing correspondence, such as thank-you notes, and perhaps conducting further research on a project or preparing follow-up reports.

Your boss may attend meetings out of town, and it may be your job to make travel arrangements. If so, make a listing of your boss's preferences and special needs before you make any arrangements. A travel agent can schedule flights, book hotel rooms, rent cars, and take care of other details for you. Most businesses today use travel agencies because of their access to information about arrivals, departures, cost, and so on. If it is up to you to make the travel arrangements, with a little research you can do the same things the travel agent does.

While the boss is away, take care of business as usual. When the boss returns, you will need a few days to catch up and you may have follow-up tasks that have been generated by the trip.

Modern Office Procedures

Plan, plan, plan. Managing office activities is about careful, thoughtful, systematic preparation and planning so time will be used profitably.

Managing office activities will include some or all of the following tasks:

- Organize your desk top and desk drawers.
- Organize the purchase and storage of materials and supplies.
- Clearly learn and understand your responsibilities in the office.
- Manage your time.
- Set priorities.
- Plan your work for the day before beginning.
- Create a system for managing details.
- Whenever possible, work on one task at a time.
- Learn to cope with interruptions, which are part of any busy office.
- Schedule time to relax.
- Keep a calendar, handling appointments and cancellations.
- Learn to keep a tickler file.
- Plan, schedule, and make arrangements for meetings.
- Take minutes, and prepare and distribute them.
- Make travel arrangements yourself, or with the assistance of a travel agent.

## In Conclusion . . .

*When you have completed this chapter, use an electronic typewriter or a microcomputer to answer the following questions:*

1. *How would you organize your pens and pencils?*
2. *What type of work activity would you plan for the first project in the morning?*
3. *How would you handle interruptions?*
4. *What are five steps you would cover in planning a business meeting?*
5. *What are the first several steps in planning a business trip?*
6. *What would you schedule for an executive on the first day after he or she returns from a business trip?*

# Review and Application

## REVIEW YOUR VOCABULARY

Match the following by writing the letter of the vocabulary word that is described below.

____ 1. preferences in the order of work activities, usually decided according to levels of importance

____ 2. a follow-up file that uses dates to help you remember work pending for a week, a month, or longer

____ 3. a list of topics to be covered during a meeting

____ 4. the art of knowing what you need to do in a given time frame, setting priorities for projects, and completing projects in the time allotted

____ 5. an outline that includes flight numbers, departure and arrival times and places, hotel accommodation information, and car rental information

a. agenda
b. itinerary
c. priorities

d. tickler file
e. time management

## DISCUSS AND ANALYZE AN OFFICE SITUATION

1. Fred has accepted a new job in a new company. The person he is replacing left the job in a hurry because of a health emergency. The boss has given him a little time, but she is busy and training Fred is not her main priority. Other people in the office have similar jobs and are helpful to some extent. Still, Fred is not sure what his duties are and does not clearly understand his responsibilities. If you were Fred, what would you do?

2. Gretchen was in the habit of scheduling her boss's appointments and carefully keeping a calendar of events. One day, Gretchen woke up with a terrible cold and felt she should not go to the office. She called her boss and explained. When she returned to the office, someone else had been doing the scheduling. That person had set some overlapping appointments and had not blocked out time for a special meeting. How can Gretchen fix the confusing calendar?

## PRACTICE BASIC SKILLS

### Math

1. It is your job to rent an automobile for your boss's trip. He will be driving to a city 300 miles away and back. He will need the car for three days and you estimate that he will drive it about 100 miles while in his destination city. He requested that you rent a four-door sedan. You research the matter carefully, asking people what company to use and calling companies in the Yellow Pages. You discover that different companies charge different rates:

- Company 1 charges $34.99 per day for the rental fee and allows 150 free miles per day. Each mile over 150 will cost $0.20.
- Company 2 charges $39.95 per day for the rental fee and allows 100 free miles per day. Each mile over 100 will cost $0.15.
- Company 3 charges $36.95 per day for the rental fee and allows 120 free miles per day. Each mile over 120 will cost $0.25.

Calculate which company offers the best price for renting a car.

### English

1. You may be called upon to welcome meeting participants as they arrive. In the following greeting, remembering that you are representing your company, underline words and phrases that are inappropriate because they are rude or simply not standard English.

Hey there, how ya doin'? Where would you like to set it down? This will be a pretty cool meeting, don't ya think? If you want coffee ya gotta get it yourself. Over there on the table below that ugly picture. You'll find it. Hope you dig on the meeting, and have some laughs.

## Proofreading

1. If it is your responsibility to record and prepare the minutes to a meeting, you will want to proofread them carefully so they contain no spelling or punctuation errors. Check the following minutes and correct any errors.

The metting was called to orden at 7:00 pm by the Presidant, Mrs. Brown. Then Mrs. Brwon led the fleg slute. The secretary red the minites from the last metting and thee wear approvd as red.

The tresurer gave her reprot and a discussion follwoed. Old buesness include discusion about the water problum.

There was no newer business.

The meetin was ajourned at 8:00 PM

---

### APPLY YOUR KNOWLEDGE

---

1. Carefully plan your day (tomorrow). Set priorities for events and activities, and assign times to each item on your list.
2. Prepare a calendar for yourself, detailing all the activities you have planned for the month. Give everything a time value. See if this kind of planning keeps your activities organized for you.
3. Plan a business trip. Select a city, an airline, a hotel, and a car rental company—and determine the cost of each service you will require. Refer to maps, airline schedules, American Automobile Association (AAA) books, and any other references you can locate. For guidance, you may discuss your trip with a travel agent, if you wish.

# QUIZ

*Write a **T** if the statement is true or an **F** if the statement is false.*

____ 1. A desk organizer is a consultant who advises workers on office efficiency.

____ 2. Most offices have a central storage area where supplies such as envelopes, computer disks, and pens and pencils are kept.

____ 3. Once you have set your priorities for the day's work, nothing should persuade you to change them.

____ 4. It's a good idea to start the day with an easy task, so that you will be relaxed when it's time to start the more difficult ones.

____ 5. If you are interrupted during your workday by phone calls or people asking you to do extra tasks, the best policy is to ask the people to return at the end of the day, when you will deal with them.

____ 6. You are entitled by law to two fifteen-minute breaks in addition to your lunch period during an eight hour workday.

____ 7. Schedule appointments as close together as possible to avoid wasting time between them.

____ 8. Getting the name, phone number, and address of people who call you for appointments with your boss is your responsibility, not the caller's.

____ 9. A tickler file helps you keep a record of what went on in the office in the past.

____ 10. If your boss asks you to call and cancel an appointment he had scheduled, you should emphasize in your call that it isn't your fault the appointment has been canceled.

____ 11. In business, informal meetings happen much more often than formal meetings.

(continued on next page)

_____ 12. The agenda for a business meeting includes a list of who was present, what action was taken, and what time the meeting began and ended.

_____ 13. A travel agent can help with airline tickets, but you will have to make hotel reservations yourself for any trips you plan for your boss.

_____ 14. Preparing an itinerary for a trip is an important part of trip planning.

_____ 15. While your boss is away on a business trip, there is normally much less work to do in the office.

## ACTIVITY 10–1

### Word Processing

1. Interview at least two instructors or administrators in your school and ask them the following questions:

   A. To work effectively, do you organize your desk in any special way? If so, describe in what way.

   B. To work effectively, do you use any special techniques to manage your time so you'll be able to:

      — know what you need to do in a given time frame?
      — set priorities for projects?
      — complete projects in the allotted time?

   C. If you keep a calendar, what type of calendar do you keep and do you always carry it with you to enter appointments, etc.?

2. Keyboard the responses in paragraph form at the computer. Use a spelling disk to check for errors. Save and print.

## ACTIVITY 10-2

### Word Processing

1. Using the information from this chapter about managing your time, prepare some advice you might give to a fellow student or friend on this topic. From a student perspective, what would you say about these topics and being successful in school?

   A. Setting priorities

   B. Planning your work

   C. Managing details

   D. Working on one task at a time

   E. Coping with interruptions

   F. Scheduling time to relax

   G. Planning tomorrow's work

2. Compose what you would say in two or three paragraphs. In your last paragraph, respond to the following question: "Do time-management behaviors for students transfer over to the way workers manage their time?"

3. Save and print.

## Keeping an Appointment Calendar

Proper scheduling of appointments requires that you meet the needs of both your employer and the clients. Assume you are a receptionist for Dr. Martinez, a pediatrician at the Channel City Medical Clinic. Read the directions Dr. Martinez has given you for scheduling appointments. Then read the summaries of phone conversations from people requesting appointments. Using this information as well as the information from pages 000–000 of the text, complete the sample appointment page included with this activity.

Office hours are from 8:00 a.m. to 5:30 p.m. The last appointment is at 5:15 p.m. The time between 12:00 noon and 1:30 p.m. is blocked out for lunch and hospital visits to newborn babies. All well-baby checkups or routine physicals are to be scheduled from 8:00 a.m. to 9:00 a.m. or from 1:30 p.m. to 2:30 p.m. All appointments should generally be allotted 15 minutes unless special circumstances require more time. Patients who are sick or injured should be scheduled from 9:00 a.m. to 12:00 noon and from 2:30 to 5:30. Emergency cases of course need to be seen as quickly as possible. Dr. Martinez has requested that you schedule appointments to allow a fifteen-minute break midmorning as well as midafternoon. On the calendar, you are to include the name of the patient as well as the parent, the age of the patient, a phone number, and a brief description of the reason for the appointment. A sample appointment has been scheduled on the calendar at 8:30.

Read the following summaries of phone requests for appointments and schedule the appointments appropriately on the calendar. If you are unable to schedule an appointment for the time requested, use the line following the summary to make a brief comment on how you would handle the request.

---

1. Mrs. Harris calls to inquire about the symptoms of chicken pox. She says her three-year-old son Josh has a fever and rash. She requests to see the doctor as early as possible because her son is very fussy. Her home phone is 967-3052.

---

2. Mrs. Ruiz calls for a well-baby checkup for her two-week-old daughter Elena. She would like the appointment in the middle of the day so her husband can come with her during his lunchtime. Her home phone is 685-3489.

---

3. Mr. Green calls for a physical for his fourteen-year-old son Todd so he can play on the school football team. He would like an appointment as late as possible in the afternoon so that Todd will not have to miss school. His work phone is 533-4020, home phone is 685-3395.

---

4. Mrs. Andrews calls and demands to see the doctor immediately. Her five-month-old son has been crying since early in the morning. Her home phone is 567-8812.

---

5. Mrs. Bowman calls and requests annual physicals for her three children—Tom, age five, and Joy and Debra, both age three. She would prefer afternoon appointments so her children will not miss

(continued on next page)

preschool and she will not need to take time off from her morning job. Her home phone is 965-4388, work phone 533-5972.

6. Ms. Robles calls to cancel her 8:30 appointment.

7. Mr. Cantwell calls to schedule a consultation for himself and his wife. They are expecting their first baby and are shopping for a pediatrician. His work phone is 685-4437, home phone 964-3309.

8. Mrs. Finlay calls at 10:20 because her seven-year-old daughter Renee has just fallen and she is concerned about a broken arm. She also has a cut that may require stitches. She lives about fifteen minutes from the clinic. Her home phone is 685-4473.

9. At 11:30 the hospital calls to inform Dr. Martinez that his patient Grace Hanlon just delivered a baby that is experiencing complications. They would like him available for consultation as soon as possible.

10. Mrs. Daly calls to say her nine-year-old daughter Laura has been sent home from school because the school nurse suspects she has pinkeye. Mrs. Daly must rely on the bus for transportation and so requests an appointment that will allow her time to catch the last bus home, which leaves the clinic at 4:30. She does not have a home phone. Her neighbor's phone number is 687-3351. The neighbor's name is Georgia Layton.

11. At 1:30 Mr. Duarte calls. His four-year-old son Jessie, who has a history of asthma, is having difficulty breathing. He requests an appointment as soon as possible. His home phone is 685-4728.

12. Anita Jones calls to schedule an appointment for a routine physical for her eleven-year-old daughter Sandra. Her home phone is 685-3456, work phone 967-1127.

13. Mrs. Winters calls to schedule an appointment for her thirteen-year-old daughter who has a sore throat and fever. She requests a late afternoon appointment so she will not have to leave work before 4:00 p.m. Her work phone is 964-3856, home phone 687-9945.

14. At 3:30 the hospital calls to request that Dr. Martinez come over as soon as possible for another consultation on the condition of the Hanlon baby.

What suggestions would you make to help you schedule the types of appointments at the times Dr. Martinez requested?

_____

_____

_____

_____

_____

_____

_____

_____

_____

_____

_____

_____

_____

_____

(continued on next page)

June 24

| Time | | | |
|------|------|------|------|
| 8:00 | | | |
| 8:15 | | | |
| 8:30 | Sandra Jones / Anita | 685-3456 967-1127 | physical |
| 8:45 | | | |
| 9:00 | | | |
| 9:15 | | | |
| 9:30 | | | |
| 9:45 | | | |
| 10:00 | | | |
| 10:15 | | | |
| 10:30 | | | |
| 10:45 | | | |
| 11:00 | | | |
| 11:15 | | | |
| 11:30 | | | |
| 11:45 | | | |
| Lunch | | | |
| 1:30 | | | |
| 1:45 | | | |
| 2:00 | | | |
| 2:15 | | | |
| 2:30 | | | |
| 2:45 | | | |
| 3:00 | | | |
| 3:15 | | | |
| 3:30 | | | |
| 3:45 | | | |
| 4:00 | | | |
| 4:15 | | | |
| 4:30 | | | |
| 4:45 | | | |
| 5:00 | | | |
| 5:15 | | | |

## Word Processing

1. Keyboard three personalized meeting notices to the following department heads using an acceptable memorandum style:

Send to:
Elsie Eperjesi, Personnel
Horst Brown, Accounting
Cherie Small, Marketing

MEMORANDUM

TO:

FROM:       Woody Francis

DATE:       January 18, 19___

SUBJECT:    Review of Activities for Previous Fiscal Year

Please plan to attend an important meeting in my office at 8:00 a.m. on January 25. As you know, the auditors will be here during the month of February and this would be a good time to review our records prior to their visit.

Bring any summary reports with you to this meeting. See you then.

2. Save and print three individual memos.

## Word Processing

1. Keyboard the following minutes, save, and print a copy.

MINUTES—CITIZENS FOR A COMMUNITY COLLEGE IN ALABASTER COUNTY
June 20, 19__ MEETING HELD IN COUNTY ADMINISTRATIVE OFFICES

PRESENT: John Kavanagh, Sue Curd, Patty Rodgers, Eugene Balzer, Mary Kuzell-Babbitt, Dan Baertlein, Clara Baertlein, Merle Wackerbarth, Roger L. Short, Trudy Jura and Leon Berger.

The meeting was called to order at 7:08 by John Kavanagh. Those in attendance introduced themselves. The minutes from the last meeting were approved as written. Under correspondence, a letter dated June 16 from Roger Short, Superintendent of Antelope School District, stated he would be actively involved in this committee's work.

Under old business, the following items were discussed:
1) Sue Curd presented a report from the petition and ballot committee in Bruce Hudgens' absence. The petition and ballot requirements are now better understood; however, the time frames will need more clarification by Mary Nackard as they are not clearly spelled out in the laws. This information should be available by the next meeting.

Under new business, the following items were discussed:
1) Sue Curd reviewed committees formation and how each would function. Names from last meeting's committee sign-up sheet were discussed. Additional names were added.
2) A listing of Fact Sheet questions prepared by Bob Kerwood was discussed. It was the aim of this committee to add to these questions any concerns or issues community members might have that could be answered via this Fact Sheet. Extensive discussion took place and additional ideas were developed.

The next meeting will be held on Tuesday, July 11, at 7:00 p.m. in the County Administrative Building. The meeting adjourned at 8:30 p.m.

Respectfully submitted,
Patty Rodgers, Secretary

## Getting Organized

Organization is essential in an office environment because of the large amount of information that must be handled. Assume you are an office supervisor at the Channel City Medical Clinic. One of your tasks is to revise the current employee handbook. Write a one-page entry describing suggested methods of organization for your office employees. Address the topics of desk organization, accessibility of supplies and materials, and knowledge of job responsibilities. You may use ideas presented in this text as well as ideas from other sources. Employee handbooks or your own work experience might be sources of information. Write a title for this handbook page, and subtitles for each topic. Write this handbook entry in your own words, giving clear and specific suggestions. Write an outline or first draft on this page. Use a typewriter or microcomputer to write the completed entry.

## Managing Time

Setting priorities for projects and completing projects in the time allotted are essential skills for success in an office job. Assume that you are the office manager for the Channel City Medical Clinic. Write a two-page entry for the employee handbook detailing a time-management plan. Include the topics of setting priorities, planning work, managing details, working on one task at a time, coping with interruptions, scheduling time to relax, and planning the next day's work. You may use this chapter as a reference, but be sure to write the manual in your own words. You may also wish to refer to other employee manuals, articles from magazines, or draw on personal experience. Write a title for this two-page entry. Also include subtitles for each section. Use this page to write an outline or first draft. Write your completed entry using a typewriter or microcomputer.

## Word Processing

1. Using the proofreaders marks section of the Reference Manual (page 428), proofread and correct the following paragraph. (Mark on this sheet.)

Meetings play an important role in the communication of informatin in every kind of business. They are held to conduct business, to followw up on a Previously discussed activity, or simply to communicate information to an individual or to a group. Careful planing and prepration are the kees to eficiently run, worthwhile meeting.

2. Keyboard the paragraph as you've marked it, save, and print a copy.

# *Reference Manual*

This section will expose you to different letter styles. All the rules given here are up-to-date with current business standards. However, when beginning a new office job, always check first with your boss to see if the company has its own rules and preferences.

## Major Parts of a Letter

**Date**—The date is typed 2 to 3 lines below the bottom of the letterhead. If you are not using letterhead paper, begin 12 to 14 lines from the top of the paper.

**Inside Address**—The inside address is typed 4 to 8 lines below the date. This placement is determined by the size of the letter. Long letters require fewer blank lines. Short letters require a greater number of blank lines between the date and inside address.

**Greeting**—The greeting is typed a double-space after the inside address.

**Body**—The body of the letter begins a double-space after the greeting.

**Closing**—The closing is typed a double-space after the ending of the body of the letter.

**Signee's Name**—The name of the person who signs the letter is typed 4 lines below the closing.

**Typist's Initials**—Your initials as typist are typed in small letters a double-space after the signee's name.

**Enclosure Notation**—The enclosure notation is typed a double-space after the typist's initials.

**Copies Notation**—The copies notation is typed a double-space after the typist's initials.

## Form

Letter styles will vary from company to company; however, the following are the three most common styles used by business today.

**Block Style**—The entire letter is typed even with the left margin (see figure A–1).

■ FIGURE A–1
*Block-Style Letter*

February 2, 19—
(4-8 line returns)

Mr. Jessie Johnson
44 Warren Avenue
San Antonio, TX 76435

Dear Mr. Johnson:

The next meeting of the Southwestern Association of CPAs will be held at the Newport Hyatt in San Antonio on April 8 at 7 p.m. This meeting will be a joint venture of the SACPA and the Future Accountants Association. The topic of the meeting will be, "Automating the Accounting Office."

The main speaker of the evening will be Katherine Cornell, president of the National Association of CPAs. Ms. Cornell has just completed designing and installing fully automated facilities for her firm's new location in Atlanta. The office of the future has arrived for this company.

I know you will not want to miss the meeting. Enclosed is your registration form, which must be returned to me by March 1.

Sincerely,


Harriet Yatamoto
Meeting Coordinator

ak

enclosure

**Modified Block, or Semiblock, Style**—The date and closing begin at the center (see figure A–2).

**AMS (NOMA) Simplified Style**—The simplified style of letter is recommended by the Administrative Management Society. The letter has no greeting or closing, has a subject line, uses the block arrangement (see figure A–3).

## Punctuation

Two different rules dominate letter punctuation for the greeting and closing. These rules are as follows:

**Mixed Punctuation**—For the mixed punctuation rule, a colon goes after the greeting, and a comma goes after the closing (see figure A–1).

**Open Punctuation**—For the open punctuation rule, no punctuation is used after the greeting, and no punctuation after the closing.

FIGURE A–2
*Modified-Block-Style Letter*

January 4, 19—

(4-8 line returns)

Robert Alvarez
46 Market Avenue
Plymouth, MA 02360

Dear Mr. Alvarez:

Because styles and popular tastes do change, we make it a point to see that our magazine stays ahead of the times. Apparently we have succeeded. The American Society of Styles recently presented our magazine with a national award.

Because the readers of such a magazine are also ahead of the times, we invite you to extend your subscription now before it expires. We have made it easy for you to do so with the postpaid reply envelope enclosed.

Thank you for your continued support. I look forward to your imminent reply.

Sincerely,

Diane Eastbrook

mk

enclosure

December 12, 19—

(4-8 line returns)

Mrs. Julia Chung
CRANCO
P.O. Box 139
Lowell, MA 02660

(3 line returns)

AMS SIMPLIFIED LETTER STYLE

(3 line returns)

This letter is written in the time-saving simplified style recommended by the Administrative Management Society (formerly called NOMA). To type this style, follow these steps:

1. Use the extreme block format with blocked paragraphs.

2. Type the address three or more blank line spaces below the date.

3. Always omit the formal salutation and complimentary close.

4. Use a subject heading and type it in all-capital letters a triple-space below the address: triple-space from the subject line to the first line of the letter body.

5. Type enumerated items flush at the left margin; indent unnumbered listed items five spaces.

6. Type the writer's name and title in all-capital letters at least three blank line spaces below the letter body.

7. Type reference initials, which consist of the typist's initials only, a double-space below the writer's name.

Correspondents in your company will like the AMS simplified letter style not only for the distinctive "eye appeal" it gives letters but also because it reduces letter-writing costs.


F. JAMES LUCEY - PRESIDENT

kc

c: Sue Rodeo

# Letter Placement

Before beginning to type a letter, decide where to set your margins. For some typists, this depends on the size of the letter. If you are not sure where to set your margins, use this as a guide:

| Size of Letter (Estimated) | Margin Setting |
|---|---|
| Short (fewer than 100 words in body) | 50 space line |
| Average (101–200 words in body) | 60 space line |
| Long (more than 200 words in body) | 70 space line |

Many progressive typists, especially those with word processing equipment, are leaving their margins at one setting for all work.

## ENVELOPE ADDRESSING

Many people blame the post office for lost or delayed mail. However, many times mail is lost or delayed because of errors in the address. This section will discuss good business practice for typing addresses on envelopes.

### Return Address

Most companies have their own envelopes with a printed return address. However, if these are not available, begin to type the return address 2 lines down and 3 spaces in.

### Main Address

An experienced typist puts the envelope in the machine and turns the roller to the correct place without counting. If you have not typed envelopes before, this can be a problem. Therefore, a good rule to remember is 15/55—go down 15 lines and in 55 spaces—for 12 pitch (15/50 for 10 pitch).

### Things To Remember

(1) Always single-space; (2) type all states with two capital letters and no periods; (3) current post office regulations state that the bottom of the envelope (about 6 lines up) must be free of all notations so that the envelope can go through the electronic scanning machines.

### Notations

1. Attention—in the address itself
2. Personal or Confidential—below the return address, about 3 lines

Listed below are some address samples. Table A–1 shows the post office abbreviations for the United States and Canada.

The Noodle Corporation
Attention: Ms. Shirley Gonzales
2399 Palm Avenue
Burlingame, CA 94060

Ms. Julia Singleton
Buy-Rite Company
9 Almond Way
Boston, MA 02368

Mr. Paul Wong
131 Battery Street
Portland, OR 93616

Miss Rose Marie Frazier
Personnel Department
Save Now Bank
34 Montgomery Street
San Francisco, CA 94115

Please note: The post office prefers all capital letters and no punctuation. This makes it easier for the scanning machines. Therefore, the preferred way to write the above addresses is as follows:

THE NOODLE CORPORATION
ATTN MS SHIRLEY GONZALES
2399 PALM AVE
BURLINGAME CA 94060

MS JULIA SINGLETON
BUY RITE COMPANY
9 ALMOND WAY
BOSTON MA 02368

MR PAUL WONG
131 BATTERY STREET
PORTLAND OR 93616

MISS ROSE MARIE FRAZIER
PERSONNEL DEPARTMENT
SAVE NOW BANK
34 MONTGOMERY STREET
SAN FRANCISCO CA 94115

## ■ INTEROFFICE MEMORANDUMS

Correspondence that stays within a company is typed using interoffice memorandum style. This style is set up in various ways, but always contains the headings: To, From, Date, and Subject. When typing memorandums, keep the following points in mind:

- Memorandums are informal and should never contain titles. This also holds true for the terms Mr., Mrs., Miss, Ms. Use no salutation or complimentary close.
- Use block style.
- Triple-space from the subject to the body of the memo.
- Type typist's initials, enclosure notation, and copies notation in the usual spots.

The following are samples of the styles you will find for memorandums:

1. TO:
   FROM:
   DATE:
   SUBJECT:

2.　　TO:
　　FROM:
　　DATE:
　　SUBJECT:

3. TO:　　　　　　　　　　　　DATE:

　　FROM:　　　　　　　　　　SUBJECT:

■ TABLE A–1
*Post Office Abbreviations*
These two-letter abbreviations have been authorized with the zip code system.

| U.S. STATE, DISTRICT POSSESSION, OR TERRITORY | TWO-LETTER ABBREVIATION | U.S. STATE, DISTRICT, POSSESSION, OR TERRITORY | TWO-LETTER ABBREVIATION |
|---|---|---|---|
| Alabama | AL | North Carolina | NC |
| Alaska | AK | North Dakota | ND |
| Arizona | AZ | Ohio | OH |
| Arkansas | AR | Oklahoma | OK |
| California | CA | Oregon | OR |
| Canal Zone | CZ | Pennsylvania | PA |
| Colorado | CO | Puerto Rico | PR |
| Connecticut | CT | Rhode Island | RI |
| Delaware | DE | South Carolina | SC |
| District of Columbia | DC | South Dakota | SD |
| Florida | FL | Tennessee | TN |
| Georgia | GA | Texas | TX |
| Guam | GU | Utah | UT |
| Hawaii | HI | Vermont | VT |
| Idaho | ID | Virgin Islands | VI |
| Illinois | IL | Virginia | VA |
| Indiana | IN | Washington | WA |
| Iowa | IA | West Virginia | WV |
| Kansas | KS | Wisconsin | WI |
| Kentucky | KY | Wyoming | WY |

| U.S. STATE, DISTRICT POSSESSION, OR TERRITORY | TWO-LETTER ABBREVIATION | CANADIAN PROVINCE, POSSESSION, OR TERRITORY | TWO-LETTER ABBREVIATION |
|---|---|---|---|
| Louisiana | LA | | |
| Maine | ME | | |
| Maryland | MD | | |
| Massachusetts | MA | Alberta | AB |
| Michigan | MI | British Columbia | BC |
| Minnesota | MN | Labrador | LB |
| Mississippi | MS | Manitoba | MB |
| Missouri | MO | New Brunswick | NB |
| Montana | MT | Newfoundland | NF |
| Nebraska | NE | Northwest Territories | NT |
| Nevada | NV | Nova Scotia | NS |
| New Hampshire | NH | Ontario | ON |
| New Jersey | NJ | Prince Edward Island | PE |
| New Mexico | NM | Quebec | PQ |
| New York | NY | Saskatchewan | SK |
| | | Yukon Territory | YT |

# ■ PUNCTUATION

Punctuation is a means of making written communication easier to read and comprehend. The following rules will provide you with an easy guide to the most common punctuation questions, but it should not be considered a final authority.

## Comma

An often-used form of punctuation, the comma, is also the source of much confusion and many errors. It should be used as follows:

*Rule:* Before conjunctions that join independent clauses.

*Examples:* The meeting is at three o'clock, and we will be on time.
The typist finished the project, but he did not get it mailed before the deadline.

*Rule:* To set off a subordinate clause preceding a main clause.

*Example:* If you finish your exam on time, you will be given an extra reward.

*Rule:* To separate words and phrases in series.

*Examples:* The company sold tires, batteries, plugs, and mirrors.
The secretaries in the office, the clerks in the plant, and the managers in the factory are all willing to change to flexible schedules.

*Rule:* To separate dependent clauses.

*Examples:* With your help, we will get the task completed by Wednesday.
As soon as the machines are repaired, we will return to work.

*Rule:* To set off nonrestrictive clauses.

*Examples:* Juanita, who is in the other room, unlocked the office this morning.
The Fifth Avenue bus, which is usually late, is the one for Clover City.

*Rule:* To set off introductory words or phrases.

*Examples:* Incidentally, I left the lights on.
By the way, I saw George yesterday.

*Rule:* To separate two or more adjectives when each modifies the same noun. Do not use a comma between the two adjectives if one modifies a combination of the noun and the other adjective.

| | |
|---|---|
| *Examples:* | The blue-eyed, blond young woman walked down the street. |
| | Mr. Jones was an important American diplomat. |
| *Rule:* | Before *Inc.* in a company name.* |
| *Example:* | Lewis & Wong, Inc. would like an answer to its letter. |
| *Rule:* | Before *Jr.* and *Sr.* in a person's name.* |
| *Example:* | Samuel Adams, Jr. was elected to the board of directors. |
| *Rule:* | To set off words in direct address. |
| *Examples:* | Thank you for the offer, Mr. Pate. |
| | Your services were most appreciated, Madam President. |
| *Rule:* | To separate the day of the month from the year, and the year when used with the month. |
| *Example:* | On July 20, 1991, Susan graduated from college. |
| *Rule:* | To set off unrelated numbers. |
| *Example:* | In the World Series of 1990, 45 runs were scored. |

*Trend is to leave out comma.

## Semicolon

Use the semicolon as follows:

| | |
|---|---|
| *Rule:* | To separate two independent clauses that are not joined by a conjunction. |
| *Examples:* | The plane flew low; it began to spray the plants. |
| | The new machine arrived; it was broken. |
| *Rule:* | To avoid confusion when two independent clauses contain other commas. |
| *Example:* | The word processing machine, which was broken, was purchased at Ames & Harris, Inc.; and they will replace it today. |
| *Rule:* | To avoid confusion when a sentence contains words in series. |
| *Example:* | We have offices in San Francisco, California; Portland, Oregon; Seattle, Washington; Reno, Nevada; and Ogden, Utah. |
| *Rule:* | To introduce an illustration composed of an independent clause. |
| *Examples:* | Be sure to ask good questions; for example, What is my future with the company? |
| | Manuel is the coordinator; that is, he schedules all the classes. |

## Colon

Use the colon as follows:

*Rule:*      To introduce a list or a quotation that follows.

*Examples:*    You may now purchase the following items: shoes, dresses, shirts, and ties.
Patrick Henry said: "Give me liberty or give me death."

*Rule:*      To separate hours and minutes.

*Example:*     It is now 10:15 p.m. in New York City.

*Rule:*      After the salutation in a formal business letter.

*Example:*     Dear Mr. Jones: I am writing in response . . .

## Hyphen

Use the hyphen as follows:

*Rule:*      To join compound numbers when they are spelled out.

*Examples:*    We have twenty-nine calculators in the office.
We began the employment office with forty-three job orders.

*Rule:*      To write fractions when they are used as words.

*Examples:*    Only one-half of the workers attended the party.
Exactly three-fourths of the work was done on time.

*Rule:*      To join compound adjectives modifying the same word.

*Examples:*    We decided to send the package by third-class mail.
She was the most hard-to-reach executive in the whole building.
He received an award for the best-kept plants within the complex.

*Rule:*      Sometimes to join *self, vice,* and *ex* to another word.

*Examples:*    He was known as a self-made man.
She was the first woman to become vice-president of a marketing firm.
His ex-boss was in the audience.

*Rule:*      To be certain your meaning is clear.

*Examples:*    The workers began to re-cover the office sofa.
He was quite mad because he was told to re-lay the carpet.

## Apostrophe

Use the apostrophe as follows:

| *Rule:* | To indicate the plural form of uncapitalized letters, symbols, and words. |
|---|---|
| *Examples:* | Your typing exercise had three *b*'s typed as *v*'s.<br>For line 3, use #'s and not #s.<br>Six misspelled *and*'s appear in the sentence. |
| *Rule:* | To indicate the omission of numbers and to indicate the omission of letters in contractions. |
| *Examples:* | She is from the class of '73.<br>I'll be at the office by 3 p.m. |

## Apostrophe in Possessive

| *Rule:* | For the possessive form of a noun that does not end in *s*, add "'s." |
|---|---|
| *Examples:* | cat's paw, clerk's pay, men's hats, children's milk |
| *Rule:* | For the possessive form of a noun that ends in *s*, if the word is singular, add "'s" unless the word is awkward to pronounce; if the word is plural, add the apostrophe only. |
| *Examples:* | singular—class's pet, press's ink, distress' signs, plaster of Paris' reputation;<br>plural—clerks' union, streets' lights, trucks' tires, houses' numbers |
| *Rule:* | For the possessive form of proper names; if the name is singular and has one syllable, add "'s"; if the name is singular and has more than one syllable, add the apostrophe only; if the name is plural and ends in *s*, add the apostrophe only. |
| *Examples:* | Ross's, Glenis', Hings', Charles's, Ulysis', Andersons' |
| *Rule:* | For the possessive form of compound nouns, add the apostrophe to the last word. (If the compound is plural, it may be best to reword the sentence and not use the possessive form.) |
| *Examples:* | mother-in-law's house<br>passerby's reaction<br>(Instead of saying my sisters-in-law's children, it would be wise to say the children of my sisters-in-law.) |

## Quotation Marks

Use quotation marks as follows:

| *Rule:* | To enclose direct quotations. |
|---|---|
| *Example:* | Mary asked, "Will you please repeat the assignment?" |

| *Rule:* | To set off titles of book chapters, short stories, articles, speeches, songs, poems, and movies. |
|---|---|
| *Example:* | The story was called, "The Boy and His Dog." |
| *Rule:* | To set off slang words, definitions, and words intended to show irony. |
| *Examples:* | The girl wore a "rad" outfit. |
| | Recessions cannot be gauged solely by the "gross national product." |
| | It's such a "beautiful" day here in the rain. |

## Quotation Marks with Other Forms of Punctuation

| *Rule:* | Periods and commas are always placed inside the closing quotation marks. |
|---|---|
| *Examples:* | Julia said, "I would like to go home now." |
| | "I would like to go home now," said Julia. |
| *Rule:* | Exclamation points and question marks go inside or outside a quotation mark depending on if they are part of the whole sentence or part of the quoted material. |
| *Examples:* | Mary asked, "Did I miss my dinner?" |
| | Did Mary say, "I must have missed my dinner"? |

## Parentheses

Use parentheses as follows:

| *Rule:* | To set off clauses, phrases, or words that clarify or explain part of a sentence but are not essential to the meaning of the sentence. |
|---|---|
| *Examples:* | The nicest car (the Lexus) was not chosen. |
| | The larger (20 × 20) rooms were much nicer. |
| | The merchandise was damaged (as were all the parcels in the lot), and we returned it unopened. |
| *Rule:* | To clarify dollar amounts. |
| *Example:* | The cost to you will be thirty dollars ($30). |

## ▮ GRAMMAR

## Abbreviations

| *Rule:* | Spell out titles of persons when they precede last names. Exceptions to this would be Mr., Mrs., Ms., Messrs. |
|---|---|

*Examples:*    Captain Poldark
Doctor Singh
Professor Rosario

*Rule:*    Abbreviate Jr., Sr., Esq. when they follow a name.

*Examples:*    Victor Worg, Jr.
Francis Borghi, Esq.

*Rule:*    Abbreviate academic titles when they follow a name.

*Example:*    Patricia Frazier, Ph.D.

*Rule:*    It is good business practice not to abbreviate days, months, addresses.

*Examples:*    The interview will be Thursday, June 11.
The company is located at 246 Corbett Avenue in San Ramon.

## Spacing in the Typing of Abbreviations

*Rule:*    Abbreviations that consist of all-capital letters usually do not have periods or spaces between the letters.

*Examples:*    YMCA
FBI

*Rule:*    The trend is for no periods and no spaces for academic degrees and geographic names.

*Examples:*    BS degree          USA
MD                CPA

*Rule:*    For time, use periods but no spaces.

*Examples:*    a.m.
p.m.

## Plurals

*Rule:*    The basic rule is to add *s* to form the plural of most words.

*Example:*    pencil, pencils

*Rule:*    If a noun ends in *y* and is preceded by a vowel, add *s* to form the plural.

*Example:*    key, keys

*Rule:*    If a noun ends in *y* and is preceded by a consonant, form the plural by changing the *y* to *i* and adding *es*.

*Example:*    deputy, deputies

| | |
|---|---|
| *Rule:* | If a noun ends in *o* and is preceded by a vowel, add *s* to form the plural. |
| *Example:* | trio, trios |
| *Rule:* | If a noun ends in *o* and is preceded by a consonant, add *es* to form the plural. |
| *Example:* | cargo, cargoes |
| *Rule:* | Some nouns form their plurals in irregular ways. |
| *Examples:* | child, children; mouse, mice; woman, women; ox, oxen |
| *Rule:* | If a compound noun is a solid word, form the plural by treating the last part of the word as if it were alone. |
| *Examples:* | doghouse, doghouses; guidebook, guidebooks |
| *Rule:* | If compound words are spaced or hyphenated, form the plural to the chief part of the word. |
| *Example:* | mother-in-law, mothers-in-law |

Please note: The English language has so many exceptions, it is best to consult a dictionary when in doubt.

## Numbers

| | |
|---|---|
| *Rule:* | Spell out numbers one through ten. Use figures for numbers above ten. |
| *Example:* | There will be five positions eliminated due to the contract loss. |
| *Rule:* | Spell out indefinite numbers. |
| *Example:* | There were thousands of people at the concert. |
| *Rule:* | Use both words and figures for large numbers. |
| *Examples:* | 23 billion, 9 million |
| *Rule:* | Spell out fractions. |
| *Example:* | Nearly one-half of the workers were absent. |
| *Rule:* | Spell out numbers that begin a sentence. |
| *Example:* | Eleven new restaurants opened in the area. |
| *Rule:* | Use both words and figures when two numbers come together. |
| *Example:* | Please order twelve 3-inch tapes. |

| | |
|---|---|
| *Rule:* | For measurements, use figures. |
| *Example:* | She gained 12 pounds last month. |
| *Rule:* | Use figures for clock time. |
| *Example:* | We begin work at 8:30 a.m. |
| *Rule:* | Use words for periods of time. |
| *Example:* | The project took thirty hours to complete. |
| *Rule:* | For numbers of street addresses, use the basic rule of spelling out numbers ten and under. |
| *Examples:* | We moved to Seventh Avenue.<br>The meeting will be held at 340 East 27th Street. |

## Capitalization

Capitalize words as follows:

| | |
|---|---|
| *Rule:* | To begin a sentence. |
| *Example:* | The secretarial position is advertised as that of an administrative assistant. |
| *Rule:* | When they are proper names of persons, places, and things. |
| *Examples:* | My uncle is Walter Gonzales.<br>We will be visiting Plymouth, Massachusetts.<br>They had a picnic on Angel Island in San Francisco. |
| *Rule:* | When the title of a person precedes his or her name. |
| *Example:* | Tell Uncle Harry to call Senator Wong. |
| *Rule:* | For names of organizations and companies. |
| *Examples:* | Girl Scouts, Chamber of Commerce, Elks, General Motors |
| *Rule:* | For periods of time—months, days, holidays. |
| *Examples:* | We will visit on the fourth Tuesday of July.<br>The parade will be on Memorial Day. |
| *Rule:* | When an adjective is derived from a proper name. |
| *Examples:* | Japanese art, Mexican food, Oriental rugs |
| *Rule:* | For titles of books, magazines, newspapers. |
| *Examples:* | A popular book in 1990 was *All I Really Need to Know I Learned in Kindergarten.*<br>Many people read the *New York Times.*<br>We have a subscription to *Sunset* magazine. |

| Rule: | For directions when they refer to specific sections of the country. |
|---|---|
| Examples: | The office will move to the South for cheaper labor.<br>The job is offered on the East Side of town. |
| Rule: | For personal titles when they refer to definite persons. |
| Example: | The President of General Motors will be at the meeting. |
| Rule: | For the first word of the salutation of a letter and the first word of the closing. |
| Examples: | Dear Ms. Jones<br>Yours truly |
| Rule: | For the first word of a direct quotation. |
| Example: | Mary Jane said, "Please wait for me." |
| Rule: | In hyphenated words, for the words you would ordinarily capitalize. |
| Example: | We plan to leave in mid-April. |

# ■ WORD DIVISION

The right-side margin is very important for the overall appearance of your typing work. Many times, you are at the right margin and must decide whether to divide a word—and if so, how to divide it. In current practice, typists are trying to avoid dividing words at the end of lines. However, if it is necessary to divide words, certain rules are to be used. You must remember that words can only be divided between syllables. Following are the preferred rules:

1. Never divide words of one syllable:
   curl, halves, raze
2. Divide compound words where the two words come together:
   hair/line, house/coat, land/lady, over/power
3. Divide hyphenated words at the point of hyphenation:
   self-esteem, one-half
4. Do not divide names, dates, addresses:
   Senator Alvin Wong, January 23, 1992, 239 Lincoln Avenue
5. Do not divide abbreviations or contractions:
   PT&T, PG&E, can't, didn't, wouldn't
6. Divide after a prefix and before a suffix:
   intra/state, post/script, regi/ment, wordi/ness
7. When a single-letter syllable comes within a word, divide between the letters:
   chari/oteer, concili/ation, evalu/ation, extenu/ation

Good business practice also states the following:

- When dividing a word, you must have more than 3 letters to bring to the second line.
- Never leave fewer than 3 letters in the first line.
- Never have more than one hyphenated line together. Appearance-wise, only one hyphen to a paragraph is a good rule to follow.
- Never divide the last word of a paragraph or of a page.

Remember, you, the typist, may be concerned about keeping the right margin even. However, it is much more difficult on the reader to encounter divided words. Think of your clients!

# RESUMES

Many times, the first step in landing a job is submitting a resume. An ad in the newspaper, a telephone call, or an inquiry may be the impetus to put yourself on paper. It is very important that your resume be neatly typed and provide the right information.

The information in the resume must fit the job for which you are applying; however, some basic rules are to be followed. All resumes should contain at least the following:

- identification
- education
- experience

Many resumes also contain these:

- personal data
- references

Resumes will vary according to the person and according to the position that is open. However, some good advice is this:

- Be brief in the description of the job duties. Explain in detail, but use brief phrases. Do not be repetitive.
- Use action words when describing past duties. Examples are *managed, produced, sold, trained, handled.*
- Include any special skills or knowledge you have, such as a foreign language.
- Be neat. Be sure the copy is free of errors. Place the information evenly on the paper.
- Try to keep the resume to one page and definitely no more than two.
- If you photocopy your resume, be sure the copy is top grade.

Figures A–4 and A–5 show samples of resumes.

# MANUSCRIPTS AND REPORTS

Many times, on your job, you will be asked to type a business report. Sometimes, you may have a manuscript to prepare. Following are in-

Elvira Lopez
115 Eastmont Drive
Eastmont, MA 02365
(213) 861-4352

EDUCATION

| | | |
|---|---|---|
| 1990 | Eastmont Business College<br>Eastmont, MA 02364 | AA in Secretarial Science |
| 1984 | Eastmont High School<br>Eastmont, MA 02363 | Graduated with a major<br>in business |

EXPERIENCE

| | | |
|---|---|---|
| 1986 to present | Boston Insurance<br>236 Coly Street<br>Boston, MA 02385 | Word Processor<br>Typed correspondence<br>from transcription<br>machines |
| 1984 to 1986 | Action Realty<br>One Plaza<br>Brookline, MA 02397 | General Office Clerk<br>Answered telephones,<br>typed letters, typed<br>forms, sorted mail, made<br>bank deposits |

REFERENCES

| | | |
|---|---|---|
| Joyce Wong<br>963 Eighth Avenue<br>Eastmont, MA 02365 | Walter Alverez<br>67 Warren Avenue<br>Eastmont, MA 02365 | Dr. Sheila Wakem<br>26 Second Avenue<br>Eastmont, MA 02365 |

structions for preparing these reports and manuscripts.

## Spacing and Margins

Manuscripts may be single-space, double-space, or space-and-a-half. Double-spacing is the easiest to read; however, many businesses presently tend to use the space-and-a-half.

Setting margins will depend on whether your report will be bound or unbound. For reports to be bound at the top, use the following guidelines:

- First page has 2½-inch top margin.
- All other pages have 1½-inch top margin.
- All pages have 1-inch bottom margin.
- Side margins are 1 inch.

For reports to be bound on the left side, use these guidelines:

- First page has 2-inch top margin.
- All other pages have 1-inch top margin.

```
                        Robert Mar
                      96 Ocean Avenue
                   Green Valley, CA 95261
                       (707) 952-2050

JOB OBJECTIVE          An entry-level typist position where I am able to
                       use my skills along with growth and advancement

SKILLS                 Typing—60 wpm          Electronic Typewriter
                       10 Key by Touch        Machine Transcription
                       Basic Filing           Photocopying

TRAINING               Regional Occupational Program
                       Office Occupations Class
                       212 - 90th Street
                       Green Valley, CA 95261

EDUCATION              Green Valley High School
                       Second and Downey
                       Green Valley, CA 95261

WORK EXPERIENCE        Federal Records Center
                       1000 Commodore Road
                       San Bruno, CA 94066
                       Duties: Filing and retrieving of Income Tax Forms
                       1990 to 1992

                       J. Gorman Warehouse
                       125 Field Street
                       Brisbane, CA 94005
                       Duties: Inventory, stock and labeling
                       1989 to 1990

PERSONAL STATEMENT     I am an industrious person who learns quickly and
                       can work well under pressure. I wish to have an
                       opportunity to prove myself and show that I would
                       be an excellent employee.

REFERENCES             To be furnished upon request
```

- All pages have 1-inch bottom margin.
- Left side margin is 1½ inch, right is 1 inch.

## Titles, Headings, Subheadings

Type the title centered and capitalized on page one (see "Spacing and Margins" section above for how far down).

Triple-space after the title.

Type subheadings at the left margin in all-capital letters. For spacing after the subheadings, (1) if you indent, use the same spacing as in a report, and (2) if you use block style, leave one extra line.

## Page Numbers

Page one can be typed at the bottom center ½ inch up. However, if the title is on the first page, many people are omitting the page number.

All other pages are numbered at the top right margin, 3 lines down.

Please note: Type the number only. Do not use the word *page* or the hyphen.

## Title Page

Depending on the size and formality of a report, you may want to prepare a title page. The title page will always contain the following:

- title of the report (centered)
- author of the report (centered)

The title may contain the following:

- name of the business
- date

## Bibliography

Credit is given at the end of a report to the sources of the information used in the report. This is usually the last page of the report. Use the following rules for the bibliography:

- Prepare it in alphabetic order.
- Include the names of the author, publication, and publishers and the date.
- Type the first line of each item at the left margin, all other lines indented.
- Single-space lines.
- Use the same margins as in a report.

## Table of Contents

Depending on the size and formality of a report, you may want to prepare a table of contents. If so, do the following:

- List the main divisions and page numbers.
- Use the same margins as in a report.
- Use leaders.

## Proofreading Marks

| MARK | MEANING | EXAMPLE |
|------|---------|---------|
| ℓ | Delete | We will ~~not~~ be on time. |
| ∿ | Transpose | She sent the fax. |
| ¶ | Start a new paragraph | . . . . at the office. After it . . . . |

| Symbol | Meaning | Example |
|---|---|---|
| ⌒ | Close up | She was al ready late. |
| # | Insert a space | She arrived;we started. |
| lc | Lowercase | Be there at 9 A.M. |
| uc | Uppercase | Call senator Kennedy. |
| ∼ | Boldface | The meeting is Monday. |
| STET | Leave words in | We will not attend. |
| · · · · · | Leave words in | We will not attend. |
| ⊙ | Insert a period | The meeting is 9 a m. |
| ∧ | Insert something | It will be the hall. |

# Glossary

## A

**Accounting cycle** The process of recording, classifying, and summarizing financial information for owners, managers, and other interested parties.

**Accounting software** Computer spreadsheet programs that perform accounting activities.

**Accounts payable** A record of money that a company owes to its creditors when it buys supplies or materials on credit, rather than by paying cash.

**Accounts receivables** Records of money credit customers owe to a business.

**Agenda** A listing of what is to take place during a meeting and the topics that are to be covered.

**Alphabetic filing system** The method of arranging files in order beginning with *A* and ending with *Z*. The most conventional and widely used filing method.

**Analytical business graphics** Computer-generated documents that view and analyze data and present this information as line, bar, and pie graphs and charts.

**Annotating mail** The process of underlining important facts and making comments or special notations in the margin of a letter.

**Appendix** A chart, graph, or table that contains supplementary information and usually follows the body of a business report.

**Application program** Computer software written to solve a particular problem for a computer user. Examples include word processing software and graphics software.

**Arithmetic/logic unit (ALU)** The part of a computer's central processing unit that performs all arithmetic computations on data—such as adding, subtracting, multiplying, and dividing—and also performs all logical operations involved in organizing data into information.

**Assets** Everything of value that a company owns.

**Attachment notation** A notation used in place of the enclosure notation when something is stapled or attached to a letter.

**Auxiliary storage** The procedure in which data and information are placed in another kind of computer storage that is separate from and outside of primary storage. The final step of the information processing cycle. Also called secondary storage.

## B

**Balance sheet** A financial statement that shows the assets, liabilities, and capital—or net worth—of a business at a particular time.

**Bar code sorter (BCS)** A special piece of equipment used by postal centers to sort or separate mail into geographic areas after the zip codes have been converted to bar codes.

**Bibliography** A listing that gives all the sources used to write a business report and usually appears at the end of the report.

**Block style** The format in which an entire letter is typed even with the left margin. The letter format most commonly used in industry.

**Body** In a business letter, the major part, consisting of paragraphs that tell the reason for the letter.

**Business letter** A written document that is sent to someone outside an organization and is usually formal in appearance, style, and tone.

**Business report** A written document of action that is more formal and usually longer than a letter and that generally focuses on problems.

## C

**Call screening** The process of finding out who is calling before putting that person on hold.

**Capital** The claim that an owner has against a firm's assets. Also called owner's equity.

**Centralized filing system** The method of keeping all a company's files in one central location.

**Centralized information processing approach** A word processing system in which like office tasks are specialized and combined.

**Centralized mail department** An area where all the mail in a large company is processed.

**Centralized reprographics** The process of reproducing or copying documents at one location that serves an entire company or office and may even serve branch offices in other buildings. Sometimes called a copy center.

**Central processing unit (CPU)** The part of a computer that contains the electronic circuits that cause the processing of data to occur. Also called the processor unit.

**Centrex** A telephone network with one general number for an incoming line directly to an operator and individual seven-digit numbers for incoming lines to each telephone in a company. Employees can place their outgoing calls direct, without going through the operator.

**Chronological filing system** The method of arranging files in order by date.

**Clones** Same as **Compatibles**.

**Closing** In a business letter, the part that follows the body. The two most common *closings* in a business letter are "Very truly yours" and "Sincerely."

**Command-driven software** Computer programs that perform an activity or action when given a command.

**Compatibles** Versions of the IBM Personal Computer that are produced by other microcomputer manufacturers but that use the same operating system instructions. Also called clones.

**Computer conference** A meeting in which participants work at a microcomputer and respond to questions or problems through entries on their keyboards.

**Computer system** A group of computer devices that are connected, coordinated, and linked together in such a way that they work as one to complete a task.

**Conference call** A telephone call that allows more than one party to participate from more than one location.

**Confidential mail** Letters that should be opened only by the person to whom they are addressed.

**Control unit** The part of a computer's central processing unit that maintains order and controls the activity that occurs in the central processing unit during processing.

## D

**Data** Unorganized facts that will be processed and converted into usable information.

**Data base management software** Computer programs that perform record-keeping and information tasks. Often called an electronic file cabinet.

**Decentralized information processing approach** A word processing system in which documents are prepared in different locations throughout a company, rather than in one centralized location.

**Decentralized reprographics** The process of reproducing or copying documents at various machines conveniently located throughout a company.

**Default margins** In a word processing program, margins that have been preset.

**Desktop publishing software** Computer programs that combine text and graphics in various sizes and styles to create an attractive, high-quality document.

**Disk drive** A mechanical storage device that rotates computer disks during data transmission.

**Diskette** A small circular, flexible, magnetically coated plastic disk that records and stores computer data. Also called a floppy disk.

**Display calculators** Machines that perform mathematical calculations automatically and display numbers as illuminated figures on a screen.

**Dot matrix printer** A device that can provide excellent, near-letter-quality (NLQ) office printing.

## E

**Electronic calculator** A ten-key machine with the capacity to solve math problems at an incredibly fast speed.

**Electronic calendaring** A telecommunications system that uses computer software to record appointments, meetings, and travel plans through entries on screens that resemble paper appointment calendars.

**Electronic mail** A telecommunications system that uses computers to send messages to and receive messages from other computers. Also called E-Mail.

**Electronic office** A work space that consists of several electronic and automated systems that increase productivity and efficiency.

**Electronic typewriters** Electric typewriters with additional automatic features that help an operator center and underline words and phrases, align decimal tabs, and use automatic carriage returns to align text within paragraphs. Most *electronic typewriters* also have internal memory capacity.

**Enclosure notation** The word *enclosure* typed on a letter to indicate that something is being enclosed or included with the letter.

**Ergonomics**  The study of the relationship between people and their work environment.

**Expenses**  The costs a business incurs as it buys the resources it needs to produce and market its goods and services.

# F

**Facsimile**  In telecommunications, a machine that translates copies of text or graphics documents into electronic signals, which are then transmitted over telephone lines or by satellite. Also called a fax.

**Field**  In a data base system, a unit of information.

**File**  In a data base management system, a collection of records that share the same format or have the same fields.

**Financial statements**  Reports that contain a business's financial information for a specific period of time.

**Fonts**  Same as **Type styles.**

**Forecasting**  The process of considering the implications of recommended solutions to a problem. Also called what-if games.

# G

**Geographic filing system**  The method of arranging, or grouping, files according to geographic location.

**GIGO**  Garbage in, garbage out. The idea that a computer will produce results that are as accurate, or inaccurate, as the data it receives from an operator.

**Graphics software**  Computer programs that present numerical data clearly and quickly in visual form.

**Greeting**  In a business letter, the part that follows the inside address and usually consists of the word *dear* followed by the name of the person receiving the letter.

# H

**Hard copy**  From a computer, output that is created at a printer and gives a permanent printed copy of processed information.

**Hard disk**  A metal storage device that is usually built right into a computer and can hold a large amount of data.

**Hardware**  The electronic computer devices that make up a computer system.

# I

**Income statement**  A summary of all income and expenses for a certain time period, such as a month or a year.

**Indexing**  The process of typing the name of a person or company in its proper order on a file folder or card.

**Information**  Raw data that has been turned into usable documents, charts, and tables.

**Input**  The procedure in which data is put into a computer's memory. The first step in the information processing cycle.

**Inside address**  In a business letter, the part that follows the date and includes the name, title, company, and address of the person receiving the letter.

**Integrated information system**  A method for sharing the same information with all departments in an organization by blending computer and automated functions with modern telecommunications technology and devices.

**Integrated software**  Computer programs that combine several independent software packages for coordinated use in one package.

**Intercom**  A telephone feature that allows a person to speak to another person in another office.

**Inventory**  An itemized list showing the value of goods on hand in a business.

**Itinerary**  An outline of travel plans that includes flight numbers, departure and arrival times and places, hotel accommodation information, and car rental information.

# K

**Keyboard**  The input device usually used in an office to enter data and instructions into a computer. Most *keyboards* consist of the typewriter keypad, the cursor movement–numeric keypad, and the function keypad. Also called a terminal.

# L

**Laser printers**  Devices that provide sharper, more appealing page results on paper documents than do dot matrix printers.

**Lateral files**  Collections of records in which file folders are arranged vertically, from side to side, inside drawers that rest sideways in metal cabinets.

**Leaders**  Periods used across the space between a topic name and its page number in a table of contents.

**Letter-quality printing** Top-quality printing that is usually associated with the consistent print of a typewriter.

**Liabilities** A business's financial obligations or debts.

**Local area networks (LANs)** Communication software and wire cables that physically link computers in the same general area.

# M

**Mainframe** A powerful, large computer that can handle many users at the same time, process large volumes of data at incredibly high speeds, and in many cases store millions of characters in primary memory.

**Memorandum** A written document that is less formal than a letter; stays within a company; and contains the headings To, From, Date, and Subject. Also called a memo.

**Menu-driven software** Easy-to-use computer programs that prompt users with a list of choices or options to select from in instructing a computer.

**Microcomputer** A computer system unit containing memory, a keyboard for entering data, a monitor for displaying what is entered through the keyboard, one or two disk drives for storing files on disks, and a printer for producing final copy. Also called a personal computer (PC).

**Minicenter** A small information processing operation that is geographically removed from a large information processing operation in a company. Also called a satellite center.

**Minicomputer** A computer system that can support a number of users performing different tasks at the same time and that has abilities similar to those of a mainframe but is smaller in size, is less expensive, and has less storage capacity.

**Minutes** A record of who attended a meeting and what actually took place.

**Mixed punctuation** The punctuation rule that in a letter, a colon goes after the greeting, and a comma goes after the closing. The most popular punctuation rule, preferred by the business world.

**Mobile files** Collections of records in which file folders are located in portable cabinets that may be moved from one location to another.

**Modem** A device that sends computer-generated data over telephone lines.

**Modified block style** The format in which the date and closing of a letter begin at the center of the page. Also called semiblock style.

**Modular design** A plan in which a structure is made of pieces that can easily be taken apart, rearranged, and put back together.

**Monitor** A computer device that resembles a television set in that it displays output on a screen.

# N

**Net income** The amount of money that remains after expenses are subtracted from revenues. Commonly called the "bottom line."

**Numeric filing system** The method of arranging files in numeric order according to numbers assigned to the files.

# O

**Office work flow** The activity that revolves around the processing of information in an office.

**Open files** Collections of records in which file folders are placed on open shelves resembling open bookshelves.

**Open punctuation** The punctuation rule that in a letter, no punctuation is used after the greeting, and no punctuation is used after the closing.

**Optical character recognition (OCR) scanner** A device that examines the shape of a character on a document, compares it with a predefined shape stored in its memory, converts the shape into a computer character, and then places the computer character into a computer's main memory.

**Output** The procedure in which a finished document is presented as hard copy or soft copy. The third step in the information processing cycle.

# P

**Partitions** Panels used to separate areas or divide a large area into smaller work spaces.

**Payroll** The total amount paid to all employees for a specified period of time.

**PBX** Private Branch Exchange. A telephone network with many incoming lines that are answered by an operator or receptionist, who transfers the calls to the appropriate individuals within a company. Employees can place their outgoing calls direct, without going through the operator or receptionist.

**Primary storage area** The part of a computer's central processing unit that electronically stores data and program instructions as they are being processed in the main memory.

**Printers** Devices that display computer output on paper documents. Examples are the dot matrix printer and the laser printer.

**Printing calculators** Machines that perform mathematical calculations automatically and print numbers on a paper tape.

**Printing-display calculator** A machine that performs mathematical calculations automatically and both prints numbers on a paper tape and displays numbers as illuminated figures on a screen.

**Priorities** Preferences in the order of work activities, usually decided according to levels of importance or deadlines.

**Priority mail** First-class mail weighing more than twelve ounces.

**Processing** The procedure in which data is manipulated by computer programs that perform mathematical calculations on numbers, or logically organize words or numbers for output. The second step of the information processing cycle.

**Program** Same as **Software.**

**Proofreader marks** Standard symbols that most office workers use on rough drafts of documents to denote changes that need to be made to those documents.

# R

**Random-access memory (RAM)** The portion of primary storage that serves as a temporary holding area for data entered into a computer.

**Read-only memory (ROM)** The portion of primary storage that performs specific but commonly used functions of a computer.

**Reconciliation** The procedure of comparing check stubs or check register entries against a bank's statement, or summary of all checking account transactions.

**Record** In a data base management system, a set of fields that describes one logical unit of information.

**Reference manuals** Texts that provide answers to questions. Office *reference manuals* that answer editing questions usually include a dictionary, a thesaurus, and a word usage book.

**Remuneration** Compensation, or pay, for doing a job. *Remuneration* may include benefits as well as a salary, a wage, or a payment for work accomplished.

**Reprographics** The process of reproducing or copying documents using copiers, duplicators, and electronic printers.

**Resolution** The clarity of an image or graph produced by computer graphics equipment.

**Revenues** All funds an organization raises from the sale of its goods and services. Also called income.

**Rotary files** Collections of records in which files are contained on a wheel that rotates in a circular motion. The wheel may be a small unit that sits on a desk or a large unit that operates on the floor.

**Routing mail** The process of attaching a routing slip to correspondence and then having each person identified on the routing slip initial the slip after reading the correspondence.

# S

**Safety hazard** A danger or a chance of being injured.

**Soft copy** From a computer, output that comes from a monitor and gives immediate but temporary access to processed information.

**Software** Sequenced instructions that direct computer hardware in performing assorted tasks. Also called a program.

**Sorting mail** The process of arranging or separating mail according to the kind it is and who is to receive it.

**Source document** A document from which data is taken.

**Spreadsheets** Financial planning tools that perform mathematical calculations.

**Stand-alone software** Computer programs that perform only one task at a time.

**Subject filing system** The method of arranging files by topics or subjects.

**Switchboard** An apparatus with many telephone lines in a business office.

**System** A term that implies organization and order.

**System program** Computer software that controls the operation of computer hardware and directly affects the way a computer works.

# T

**Telecommunications** The use of automated office equipment combined with telephone systems and communications technology.

**Telecommuting** The ability of individuals to work at home and communicate with their office by using personal computers and communication lines.

**Teleconferencing** The use of computers and telecommunications devices to conduct conferences and share information among people who are in remote locations.

**Telephone tag**   The ongoing annoyance where a series of telephone calls are made back and forth in an attempt to talk with someone.

**Tickler file**   A follow-up file that is set up by dates to remind a secretary of important deadlines and work that is pending for a week, a month, or longer.

**Time management**   The art of knowing what needs to be done in a given time frame, setting priorities for projects, and completing projects in the time allotted.

**Type styles**   Complete sets of letters, numbers, and symbols of a specific typeface. Some common examples used in business are Courier, Letter, Gothic, and Script. Also called fonts.

## U

**User friendly**   With regard to software packages, a term meaning they are easy to learn and to use.

## V

**Videoconference**   A meeting in which two or more sites are linked by video and audio systems.

**Voice mail**   An automated voice processing technology that is used to send and receive messages through the telephone system without installing additional equipment.

**Voice processing**   A system that conveys verbal messages in an office.

**Voice recognition systems**   Automated voice processing systems that use equipment that "understands" human speech.

## W

**WATS**   Wide-Area Telecommunications Service. A telephone feature that provides a volume discount for outbound calls from a given office.

**What-if games**   Same as **Forecasting.**

**Word processing**   The efficient processing of words or text. Also known as text processing.

**Word processing center**   A centrally located area where all typing activities are performed.

**Word processing cycle**   The way a document flows through an office from the time an idea begins through the final storage of the completed document.

**Word processing system**   An approach that requires the careful coordination of people, machines, procedures, and environment to produce written communication.

**Workstations**   Areas that are similar to desks except that they are larger and contain more electronic equipment.

**WYSIWYG**   "What you see is what you get." In desktop publishing, an acronym meaning that a printed page will be essentially the same as what is seen on the computer screen.

# *Index*

## A

Accounting,
  accounts payable, 99, 295
  accounts receivable, 99, 293–295
  cycle of, 288–289
  financial statements, 289–293
  inventory control, 295–296
  order processing, 296–299
  payroll, 299–302
  software for, 99
Accounts payable, 99, 295
Accounts receivable, 99, 293–295
Administrative assistant, 90
Agenda, 261, 262, 377, 378, 379
  filing system and, 209
Alphabetizing,
  filing system and, 209
  rules for filing, 219–220
Annotating mail, 330
Appendix, 256–257
Application programs, computer,
  42–43
Appointments, 372–374
Assets, 289
Association of Records Managers and
  Administrators (ARMA), 215
Attachment notation, 251
Attention line, of business letters, 251

Audio conference, 142
Auxiliary storage, computer, 52–54

## B

Balance sheet, 289–291
Banking tasks, 302–306
  checks, 305
  deposits, 303–305
  reconciling bank statements,
    305–306
Bar code sorter (BCS), 341
Bibliography, 257
Blind copy, 251
Block style, 252
Body, of business letter, 249
Business documents,
  envelopes, 254–255, 342
  letters, 248–252
  meeting documents, 261–263
  memorandums, 253
  processing of, 248–267
  reports, 256–257
  rough drafts and proofreaders
    marks, 262–264
  travel arrangement documents,
    258–261

Business letters,
  format for, 252
  major parts of, 248–252
  margins, 252
  punctuation, 252

## C

Calculators, electronic, 131–132
Calendar,
  appointment requests, 373–374
  cancellations, 374
  coordinating calendars, 374
  electronic, 140–141, 371
  keeping of, 371–375
  making appointments, 372
  recurring commitments, 374
  using a tickler file, 375
Call screening, 174–175
Capital, 290
Card files, 218
Career(s). *See also* specific job titles
  office, 89–91
  using word processing, 89–93
Centralized filing system, 222
Centralized information processing
  approach, 86
Centralized mail department, 328

Centralized reprographics, 136–137
Central processing unit (CPU), 48
Centrex telephone system, 184
Checks, 303–306
Chronological filing system, 211–212
Clark, Dwight W., 84
Clone, computer, 96
Closing, of business letter, 249
Command-driven software, 43
Commission, 300
Compatible computer, 96
Compensation, 300–302
Computer conference, 142
Computer program, 41–43
Computer system(s),
    classification of, 37–41
    defined, 37
    electronic mail with, 138–141
    hardware, 37–38
    information processing with,
        43–54, 78–107
    input for, 44–47
    output from, 50–52
    processing in, 48–50
    software for, 41–43, 94–107
    storage in, 52–54
Conference call, 141, 181
Confidential mail, 329
*Consumer's Directory of Postal Services
    and Products, A* (U.S. Postal
    Service), 336, 337
Copies notation, 251
Copy center, 136–137
Correspondence,
    envelopes, 254–255, 342
    letters, 248–252
    memorandums, 253
Cross-reference, 213–214
Cursor movement-numeric keypad,
    45

**D**

Data, 43
Data base management software, 42,
    43, 99–101
*Data Sources Guide to Computer
    Software*, 371
Decentralized information processing
    approach, 86–88
Decentralized reprographics, 137
Default margins, 252
Delivery services, 339

Deposits, 303–305
Desk, organization of, 364–365
Desktop publishing software, 42, 43,
    104–105
Dictation skills, 133–134
Disk drive, computer, 53
Diskette,
    defined, 53
    filing system on, 224–225
Dot matrix printer, 52

**E**

Electronic calculators, 131–132
Electronic calendaring, 140–141
Electronic filing systems, 224–227
    on disk, 224–225
    on mainframe tape, 225
    on microfiche, 226
    on microfilm, 225–226
Electronic funds transfer (EFT),
    302–303
Electronic mail (E-Mail), 11, 138–141
Electronic office, 130
Electronic typewriters, 131
Enclosure notation, 250
Envelopes, business,
    addressing, 254–255, 342
Equipment, office. *See* Office
    equipment
Ergonomics,
    defined, 7
    lighting and glare, 9–10
    posture and, 11
    time spent sitting and, 10–11
    workstations and, 7–8
Expense account form, 258–261
Expenses, 292

**F**

Facsimile (fax), 137–138
Field, data base, 100, 101
File, data base, 100, 101
Filing,
    alphabetizing rules for, 219–220
    centralized system, 222
    classification and retention of
        records and, 214–215
    electronic storage, 224–227
    equipment for, 217–218
    indexing files for, 218–219

locating folders, 223–224
    preparation of records for, 212–214
    procedures for, 221–223
    supplies for, 221–223
    systems for, 209–212
Financial statements, 289–293
    balance sheet, 289–291
    income statement, 291–293
Floppy disks, 53
Fonts, 104–105
Formal meetings, planning, 377–382
Function keypad, 46

**G**

Geographic filing system, 210–211
Gerard, William J., 187
Graphics software, 42, 43, 102–103
Greeting, for business letter, 249
Gross pay, 300

**H**

Hard copy, 51–52, 54, 208
Hard disk, 53
Hardware, computer, 37–38
Hillan, Nancy, 145

**I**

IBM Personal Computer (IBM PC), 96
Income statement, 291–293
Indexing, rules for, 218–219
Informal meetings, 376–377
Information overload, 78
Information processing, 78–107
    centralized approach to, 86
    decentralized approach to, 86–88
Information processing cycle, 11–12,
    43–54
    input, 44–47
    output, 50–52
    processing, 48–50
    storage, 52–54
Input, computer, 44–47
    keyboard and, 45–46
    optical character recognition (OCR)
        scanner, 46–47
    source documents and, 44–45
    in word processing cycle, 82–84

Inside address, for business letter, 249
Integrated information system, 130, 143–145
Integrated software, 42, 43, 106–107
Intercom, 173–174, 186–187
Internal Revenue Service (IRS), 39, 288
*International Mail Manual, The,* 338
Inventory control, 295–296
Itinerary, 258, 259, 384, 385

## K

Keyboard, computer, 45–46
    height of, 7–8

## L

Laser printer, 52
Lateral files, 217
Leaders, 257
Lead operator, 90
Lechnar, Richard L., 216
Legal documents, form for, 264–265
Legal-size envelopes, 254–255
Letters, business, 248–252
    form, 252
    margins, 252
    punctuation, 252
Liabilities, 289–290
Local area networks (LANs), 88

## M

Mail,
    annotating, 330
    classification of, 336–337
    delivery services for, 339
    guidelines for, 341–342
    incoming mail, 329–334
    opening, 329–330
    outgoing mail, 334–343
    packing of, 342–343
    personal, 345
    postal equipment for, 340–341
    references materials for, 343–345
    routing, 333–334, 335
    sorting, 329
    U.S. Postal Service for, 337–339
Mainframe computers, 39–40, 44
    cost of, 41
    memory capacity of, 41

Mainframe tape, filing system on, 225
Meetings,
    agenda, 261, 262
    formal, 377–382
    informal, 376–377
    minutes for, 261, 263, 381, 382
Memorandums, 253
Menu-driven software, 43
Microcomputers, 38–39, 44
    cost of, 41
    memory capacity, 41
Microfiche, filing system on, 226
Microfilm, filing system on, 225–226
Minicomputers, 40–41, 44
    cost of, 40–41
    memory capacity of, 41
Minutes, meeting, 261, 263, 381, 382
Mixed punctuation, 252
Mobile files, 218
Modem, computer, 139
Modified block style, 252
Modular design workstation, 6–7
Monitor, computer, 51
    height and angle of, 7–8

## N

*National Five-Digit Zip Code and Post Office Directory,* 343–345
National Office Products Association, 5
National Safety Council, 7, 8, 10
Net income, 292
Net pay, 300–302
Numeric filing system, 211

## O

Office,
    careers in, 89–91
    design of, 4
    environment of, 4–15
    integrated information system in, 130, 143–145
    management of, 364–387
    safety in, 14–15
    word processing in, 85–88
    work flow in, 11–12
Office equipment. *See also* Computer system(s)
    electronic calculators, 131–132
    electronic typewriters, 131

facsimile (fax), 137–138
    for filing, 217–218
    postal, 340–341
    reprographics, 135–137
    telephones, 184–187
    transcription and dictation, 133–134
Open files, 218
Open punctuation, 252
Optical character recognition (OCR) scanner, 46–47, 82
Order processing, 296–299
Organizational makeup, 12–13
Output, computer, 50–52, 85
    devices for, 51–52
    hard copy, 51–52
    soft copy, 51
    in word processing cycle, 84–85
Overtime, 300

## P

Packing slip, 297, 298
Partitions, 5
Payroll, 299–302
PBX (Private Branch Exchange) telephone system, 184
Personal computer (PC), 38–39
    cost of, 41
    memory capacity of, 41
Petty cash payments, 306–307
Photocopying, 136
Portable files, 218
Postal equipment, 340–341
Postal Service, U.S., 336, 340
    services of, 337–339
Primary storage area, computer, 49–50
Printer, computer, 51–52
Priority mail, 336
Processing, computer, 48–50
    in word processing cycle, 84–85
Program, computer, 42–43
Proofreader, 90
Proofreader marks, 262–264
Punctuation, for letters, 252
Purchase order, 297

## R

Random-access memory (RAM), 50
Read-only memory (ROM), 49–50

Reconciliation, of bank statements, 305–306
Record(s),
   classification and retention, 214–215
   data base, 100, 101
   permanent, 215–217
   preparation of, for filing, 212–214
Record-keeping, 302–307
   banking tasks, 302–306
   petty cash funds, 306–307
Reference material,
   for handling mail, 343–345
   for telephone procedures, 183
Reports, format and typing rules for, 256–257
Reprographics, 135–137
Responsibilities, organization of, 366
Return slip, 299
Revenues, 291–292
Rotary files, 218
Routing mail, 333–334, 335

S

Safety hazards, 14
Salary, 300
Sales slip, 298, 299
Schenck, Susan, 10
Secretarial service owner, 92–93
Skills,
   dictation, 133–134
Soft copy, 51
Software, 41–43
   accounting, 99
   application programs, 42–43
   command-driven, 43
   data base management, 42, 43, 99–101
   desktop publishing, 42, 43, 104–105
   graphics, 42, 43, 102–103
   integrated, 42, 43, 106–107
   menu-driven, 43
   spreadsheets, 42, 43, 97–99
   system programs, 42
   word processing, 42, 43, 94–97
Sorting mail, 329
Source documents, 44–45
Spreadsheet software, 42, 43, 97–99
Stand alone software, 107
Storage, computer, 52–54
Subject filing system, 209–210
Subject line, of business letters, 251

Supplies, organization of, 365–366
Switchboard, 173
System programs, computer, 42

T

Telecommunications, 137–143
Telecommuting, 91–92
Teleconference, 141–142
Telephone equipment, 184–187
   automatic callback, 184
   call forwarding-busy line-don't answer, 185
   call hold, 185
   call screening, 174–175
   call waiting, 185
   distinction ring, 185
   800 service, 186
   intercom, 173–174, 186–187
   main networks, 184
   night service, 184
   speed calling, 186
   wide-area telecommunications service (WATS), 186
Telephone procedures, 170–183
   coverage and, 180
   for disconnected calls, 180
   for hold or transfer calls, 174–175
   for incoming calls, 172–174
   for messages, 175–177
   for outgoing calls, 178–179
   for personal calls, 179–180
   proper voice and manners for, 171–172
   reference materials for, 183
   types of calls, 181–183
   using directory assistance, 182–183
   for wrong number calls, 180
Telephone tag, 139
Tickler files, 266
   using, 375
Time management, 367–370
   interruptions, 369–370
   managing details, 369
   planning work, 267–268
   priorities, 367
Time zone map, 181–182
Transcription skills, 133–134
Travel arrangements,
   documents for, 258–261
   planning for, 383–385
   scheduling of, 385–386
   travel agents and, 385

Typeface, 104–105
Typesetting terminology, 104–105
Typewriters, electronic, 131

V

Vertical files, 217
Video conference, 142
Voice mail, 142–143
Voice processing, 142
Voice recognition systems, 143

W

Wages, 300
WATS (wide-area telecommunications service), 186
Word processing,
   benefits of, 80
   careers using, 89–93
   cycle of, 82–85
   defined, 79
   in office settings, 85–88
   skills for, 88–89
   software for, 42, 43, 94–97
   system for, 80–81
Word processing center, 86, 91
Word processing specialist, 90
Word processing supervisor, 90
Work flow, 11–12
Workstations, 6–12
   adjustments to, 8
   ergonomics and, 7–8
   modular design, 6
WYSIWYG, 104

Y

Yellow pages, 183

# Photo Credits

**Page 2** John Coletti, Stock Boston; **4** Lawrence Migdale, Stock Boston; **5** Shelly Katz, Black Star; **9** Harry Wilks, Stock Boston; **34** Rob Fraserm, Black Star; **37** Tony Freeman, PhotoEdit; **38 (left)** Courtesy of IBM; **38 (right)** John Greenleigh, Courtesy of Apple Computer Inc.; **40** Courtesy of Digital Equipment Corporation; **46 (top)** Courtesy of IBM; **46 (bottom)** Courtesy of Oberon International; **50 (left)** Tony Freeman, PhotoEdit; **50 (right)** Smart Software Photos by permission of Innovative Software, Inc.; **51 (left)** Tony Freeman, PhotoEdit; **51 (right)** Tony Freeman, PhotoEdit; **52** Tony Freeman, PhotoEdit; **53** Phil Borden, PhotoEdit; **54** David Young-Wolff, PhotoEdit; **76** Courtesy of IBM; **79** Mary Kate Denny, PhotoEdit; **80** Phil Borden, PhotoEdit; **81** Courtesy of Apple Computer, Inc.; **87** Tony Freeman, PhotoEdit; **88** Courtesy of IBM; **92 (left)** Tony Freeman, PhotoEdit; **92 (right)** Courtesy of Apple Computer, Inc.; **95** Phil Borden, PhotoEdit; **97 (bottom)** Tony Freeman, PhotoEdit; **102** Courtesy of Microsoft Corporation; **103** Courtesy of Lotus Development Corporation; **128** Jon Feingersh, Stock Boston; **131** David Young-Wolff, PhotoEdit; **133** Lawrence Migdale, Stock Boston; **134** David Young-Wolff, PhotoEdit; **135 (left and right)** David Young-Wolff, PhotoEdit; **138 (top and bottom)** Courtesy of Xerox Corporation; **141** Courtesy of Compression Labs, Inc.; **168** Stacy Pick, Stock Boston; **170** David Young-Wolff, PhotoEdit; **173** David Young-Wolff, PhotoEdit; **175** Jon Feingersh, Stock Boston; **178** Stacy Pick, Stock Boston; **185** Courtesy of AT&T; **206** Liane Enkelis, Stock Boston; **208** Tony Freeman, PhotoEdit; **217 (bottom)** Werner Wolff, Black Star; **226** Lisa Schwaber-Barzilay; **246** Stephen Frisch, Stock Boston; **256** Robert Rathe, Stock Boston; **258** Richard G. Anderson; **286** Tony Freeman, PhotoEdit; **326** Tony Freeman, PhotoEdit; **328** Stacy Pick, Stock Boston; **337** Richard G. Anderson; **339 (top and bottom)** David Young-Wolff, PhotoEdit; **340** Richard Cash, PhotoEdit; **362** David Young-Wolff, PhotoEdit; **368** David Young-Wolff, PhotoEdit; **376** Frank Siteman, Stock Boston; **380** Bill Gallery, Stock Boston.

| DATE DUE | | | |
|---|---|---|---|
| | | | |
| | | | |
| | | | |
| | | | |
| | | | |
| | | | |
| | | | |
| | | | |
| | | | |
| | | | |
| | | | |
| | | | |
| | | | |
| | | | |
| | | | |
| | | | |
| | | | |
| GAYLORD | | | PRINTED IN U.S.A. |